3

GANGSTA:CURSED.
EP_MARCO ADRIANO

Story by KOHSKE   **Art by SYUHEI KAMO**

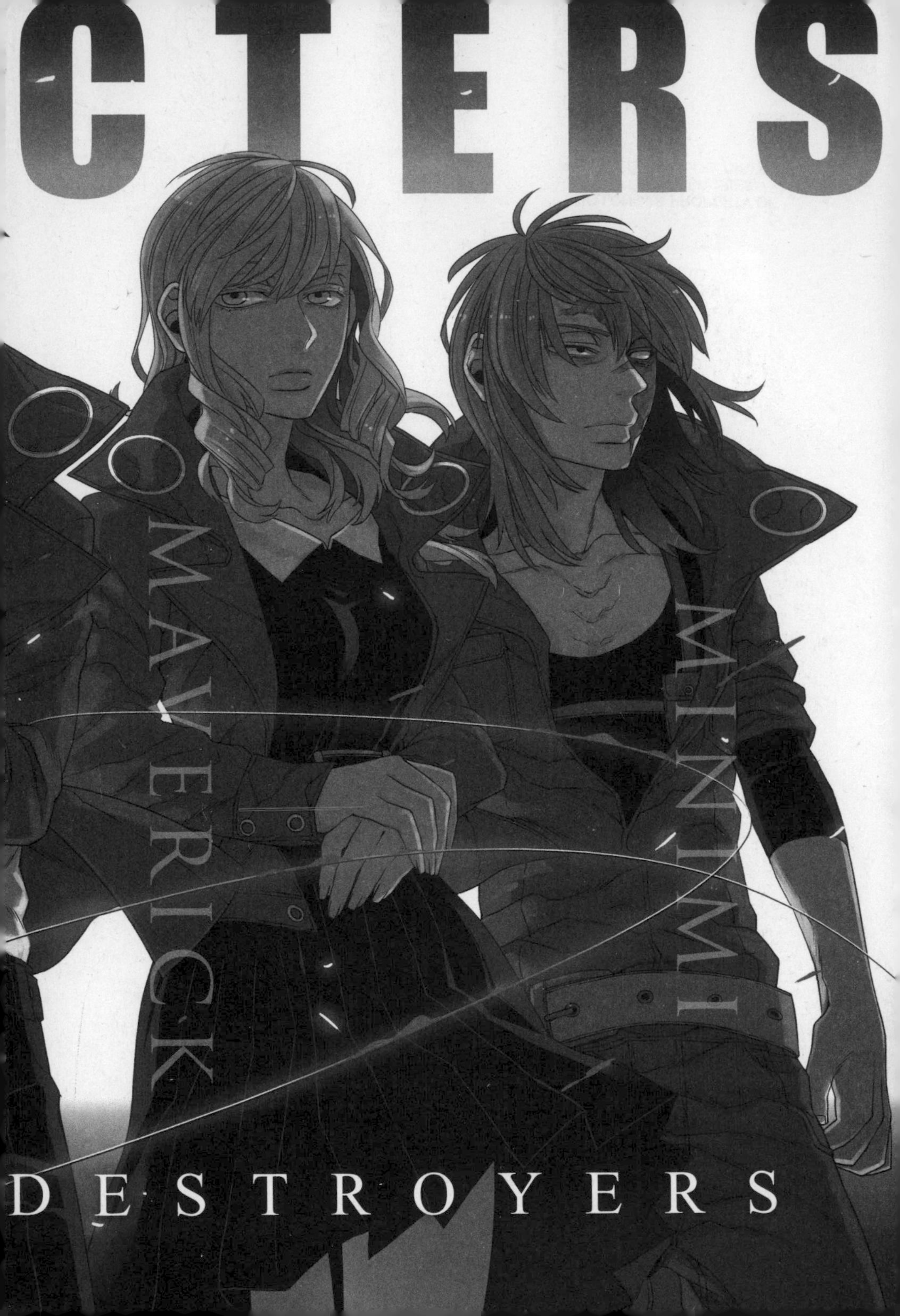
CTERS
MINMI
MAVERICK
DESTROYERS

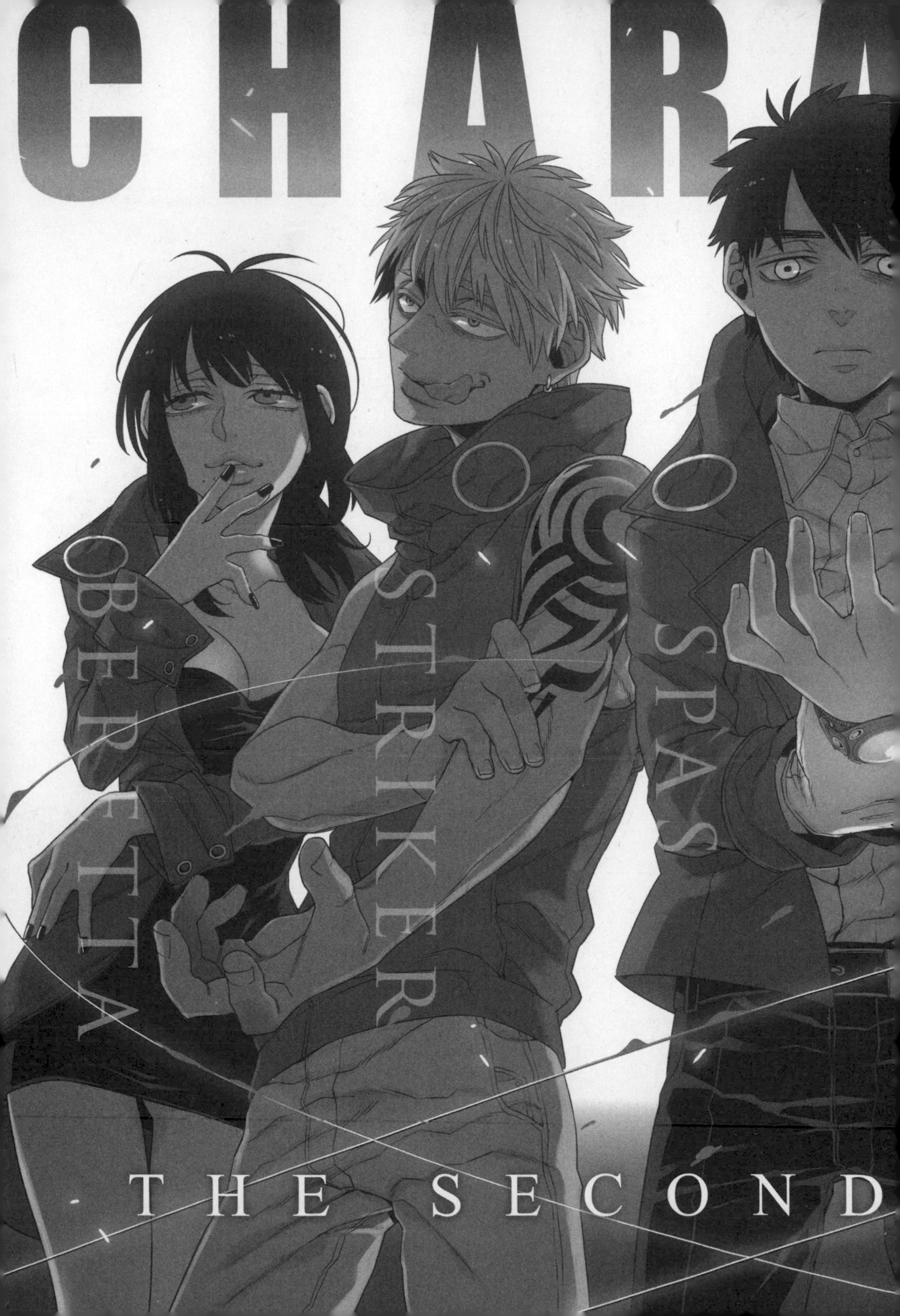
CHARA
SPAS
STRIKER
BERETTA
THE SECOND

CONTENTS

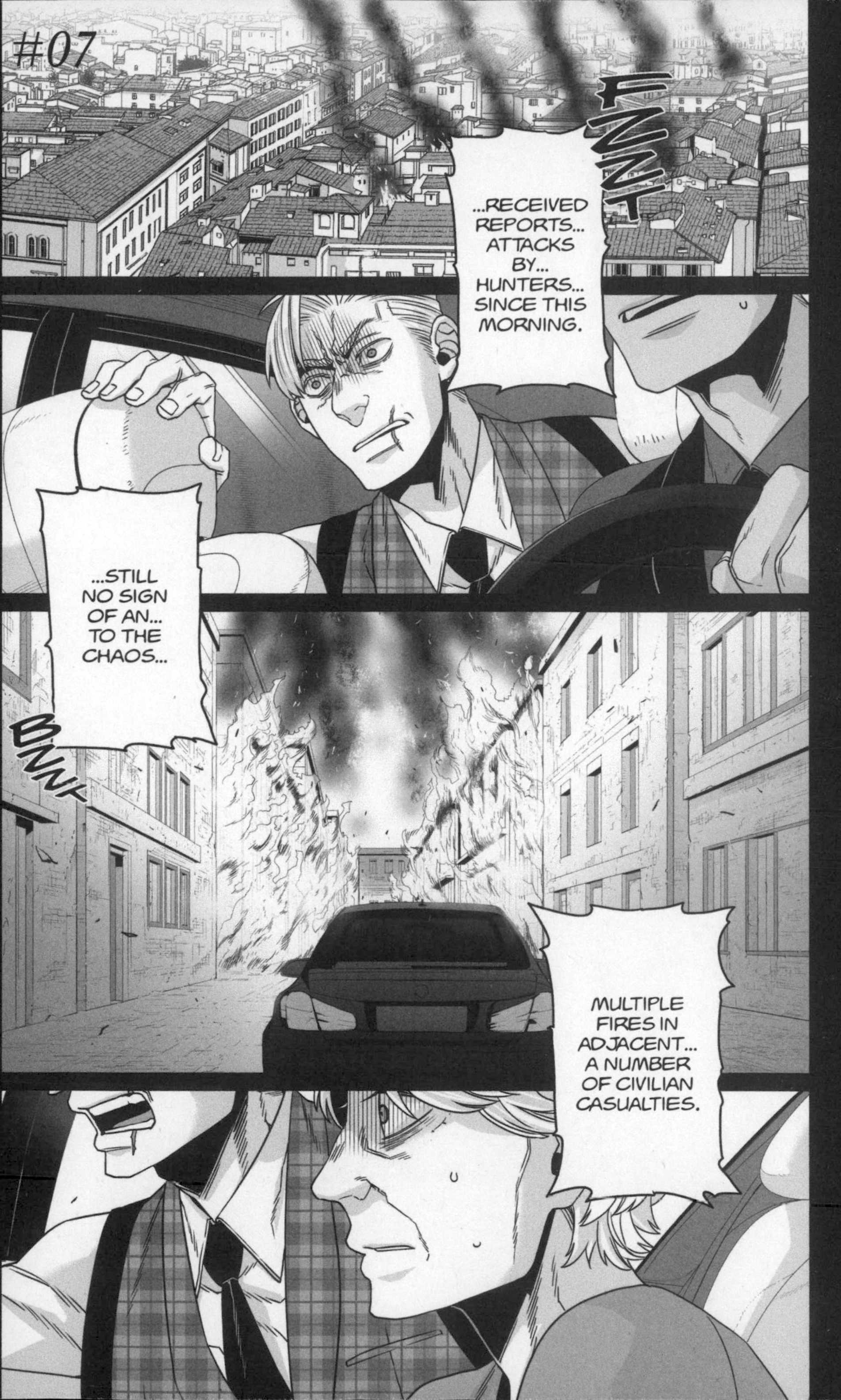
#07
FZZT
...RECEIVED REPORTS... ATTACKS BY... HUNTERS... SINCE THIS MORNING.
...STILL NO SIGN OF AN... TO THE CHAOS...
BZZK
MULTIPLE FIRES IN ADJACENT... A NUMBER OF CIVILIAN CASUALTIES.

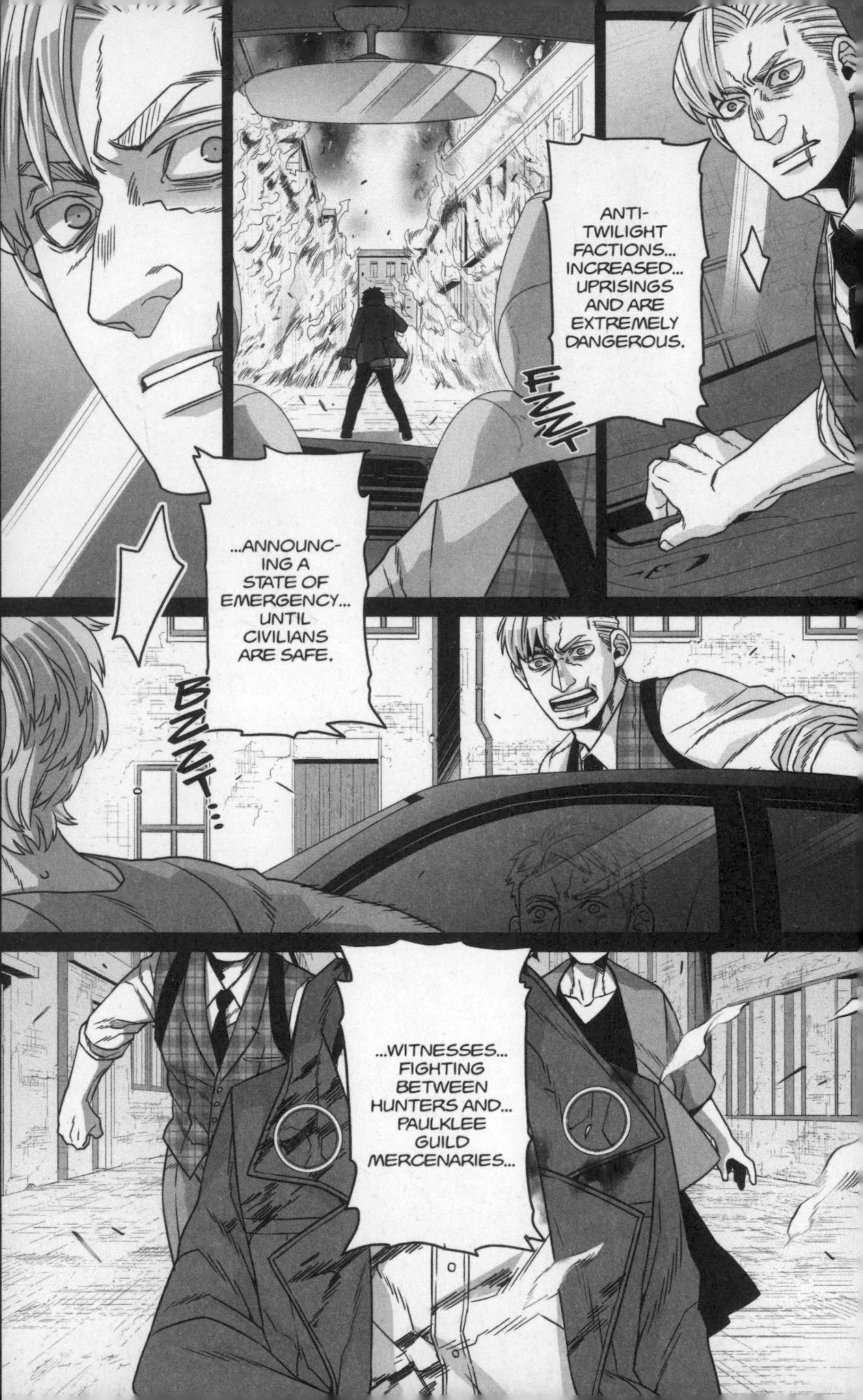
ANTI-TWILIGHT FACTIONS... INCREASED... UPRISINGS AND ARE EXTREMELY DANGEROUS.
FZZZT
...ANNOUNCING A STATE OF EMERGENCY... UNTIL CIVILIANS ARE SAFE.
BZZZT...
...WITNESSES... FIGHTING BETWEEN HUNTERS AND... PAULKLEE GUILD MERCENARIES...

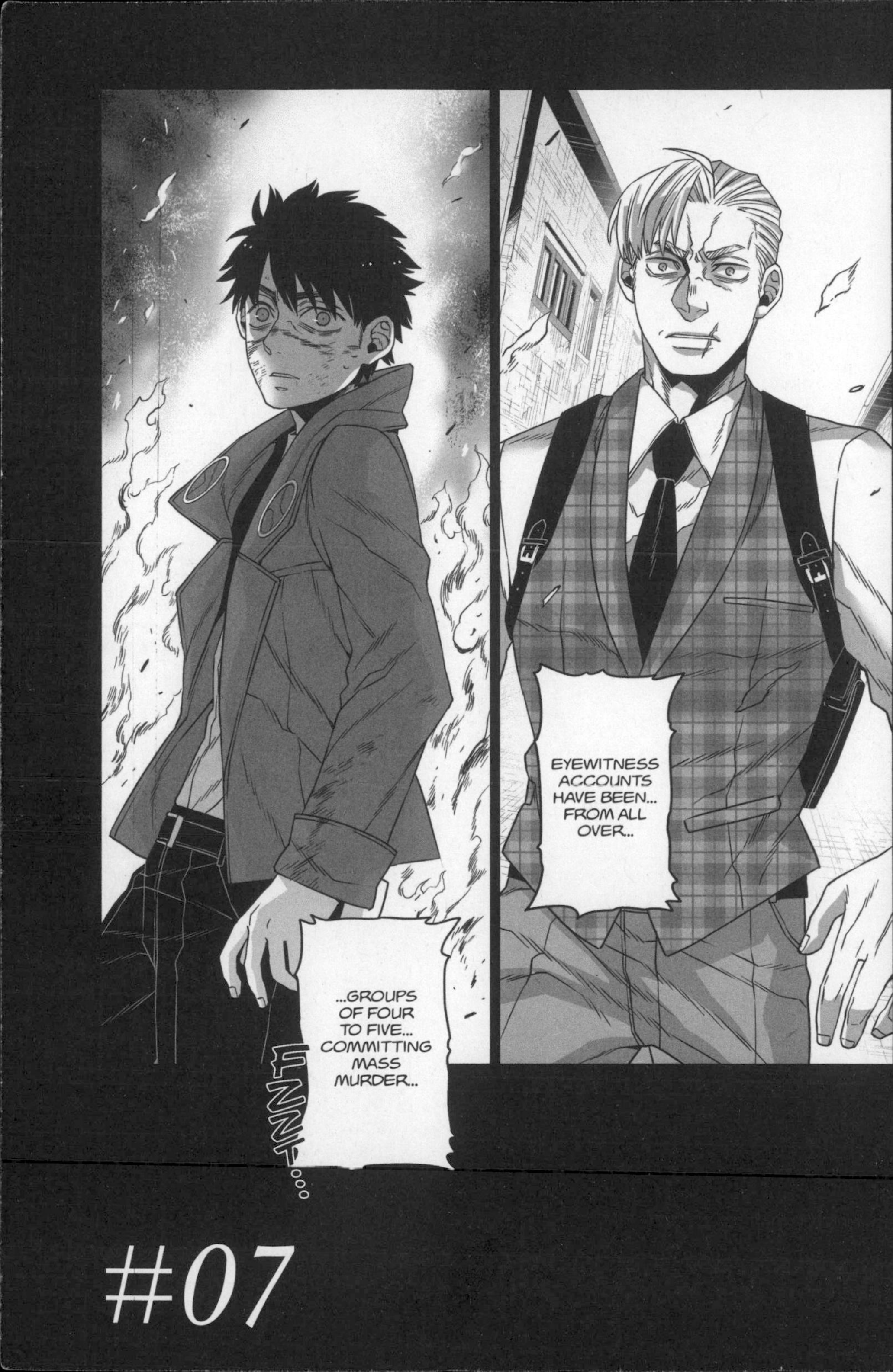
EYEWITNESS ACCOUNTS HAVE BEEN... FROM ALL OVER...
...GROUPS OF FOUR TO FIVE... COMMITTING MASS MURDER...
FZZZT...

#07

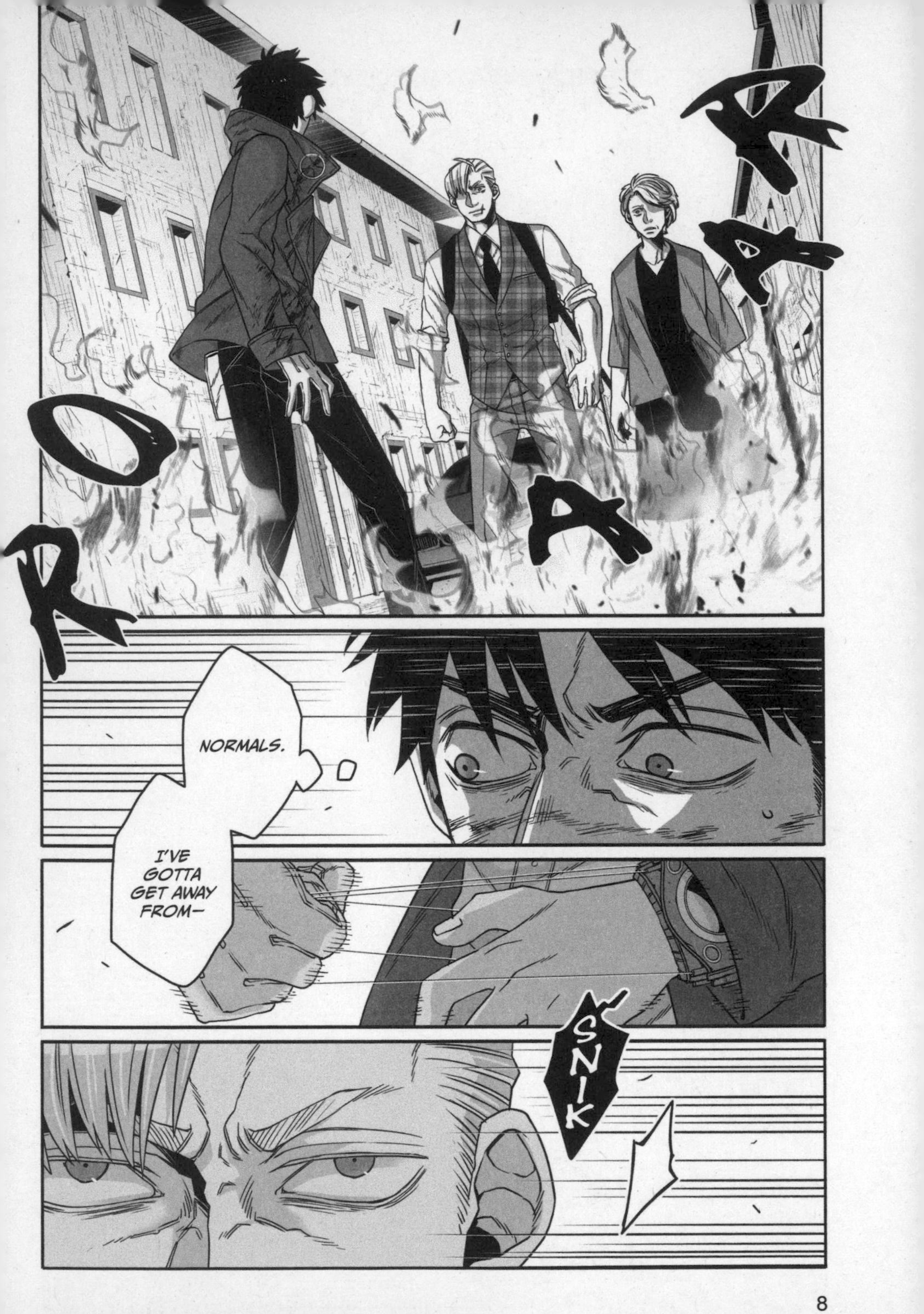
ROAR
NORMALS.
I'VE GOTTA GET AWAY FROM–
SNIK

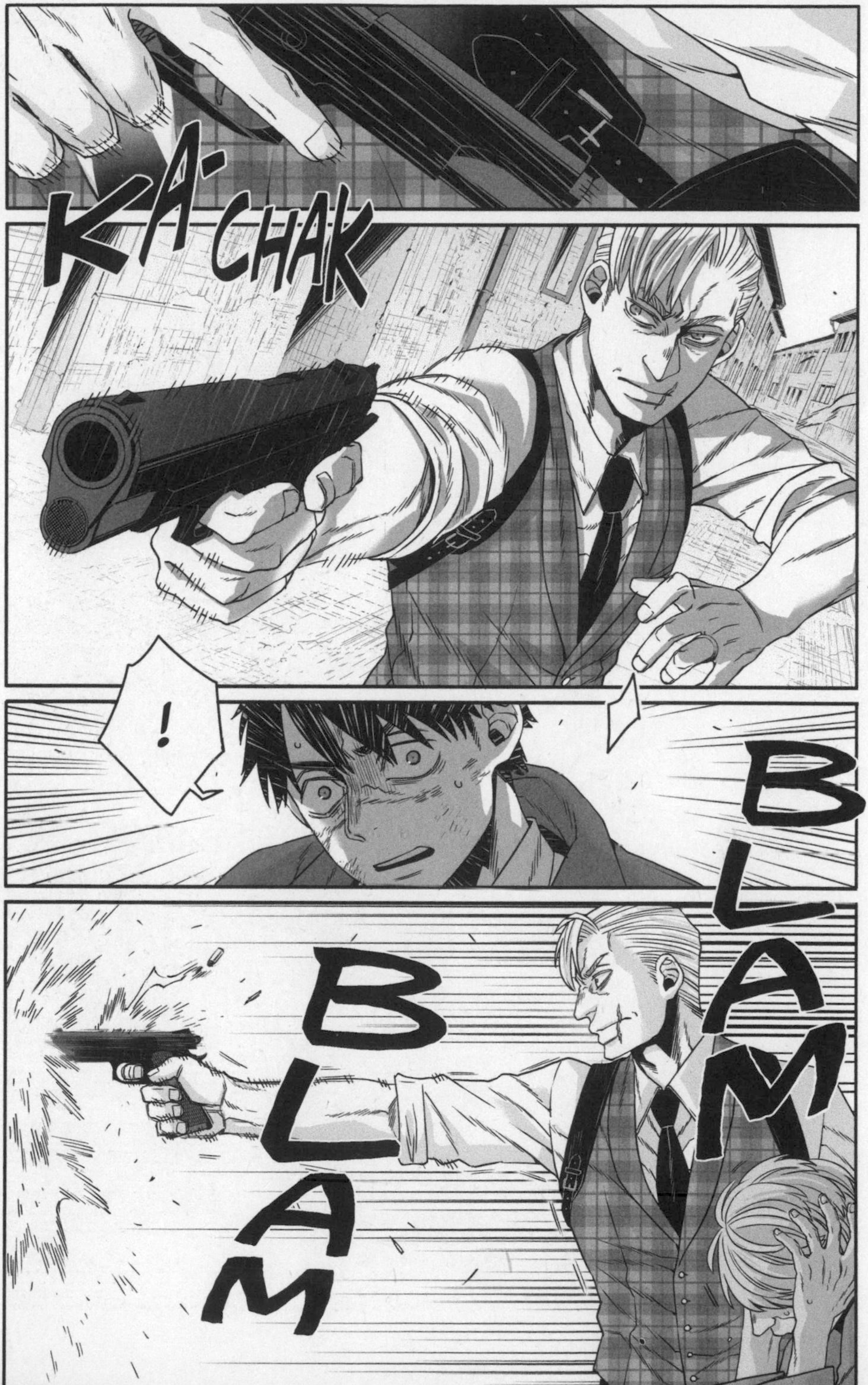
KA-CHAK
!
BLAM
BLAM

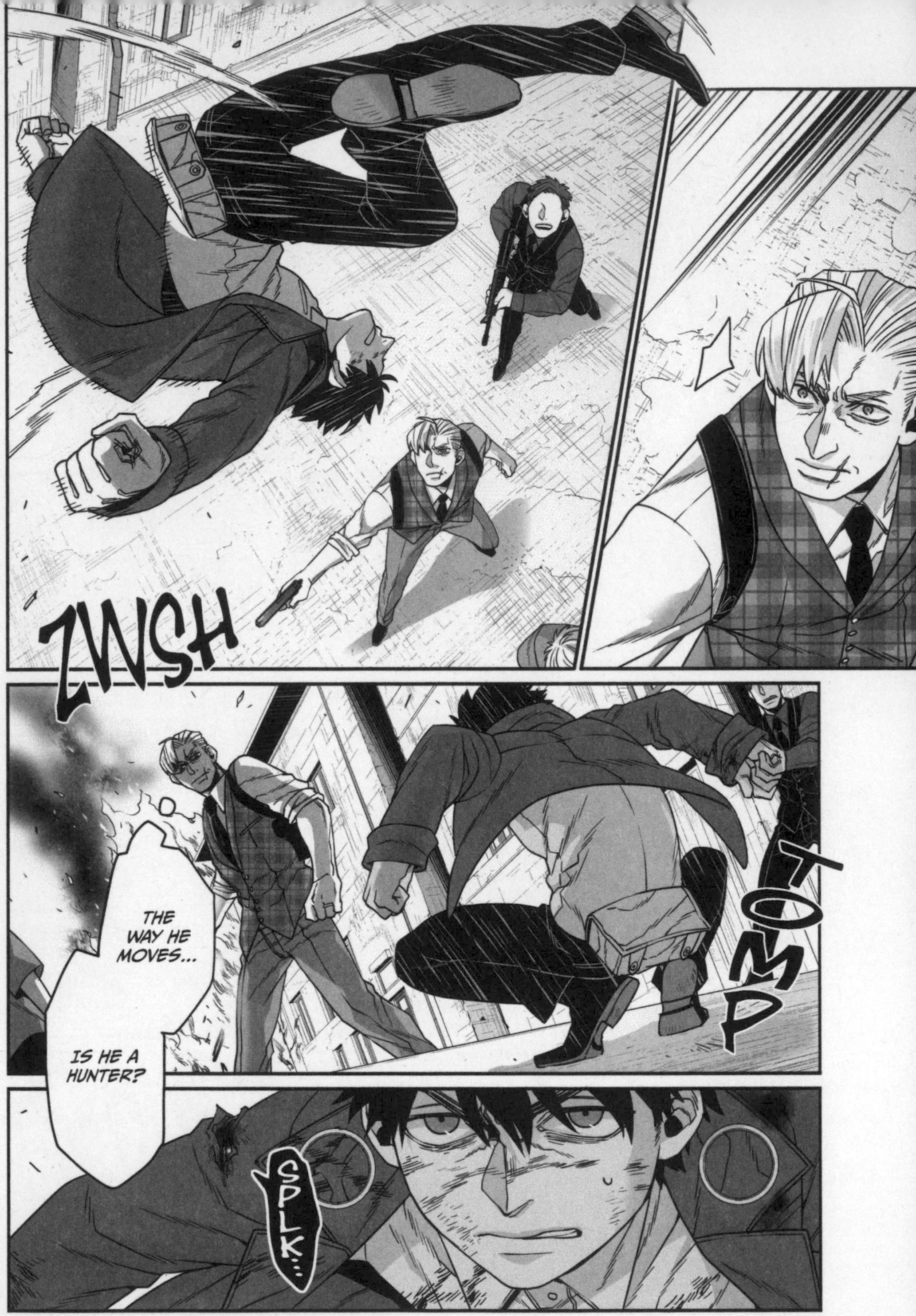
ZWSH
TOMP
THE WAY HE MOVES...
IS HE A HUNTER?
SPLK...

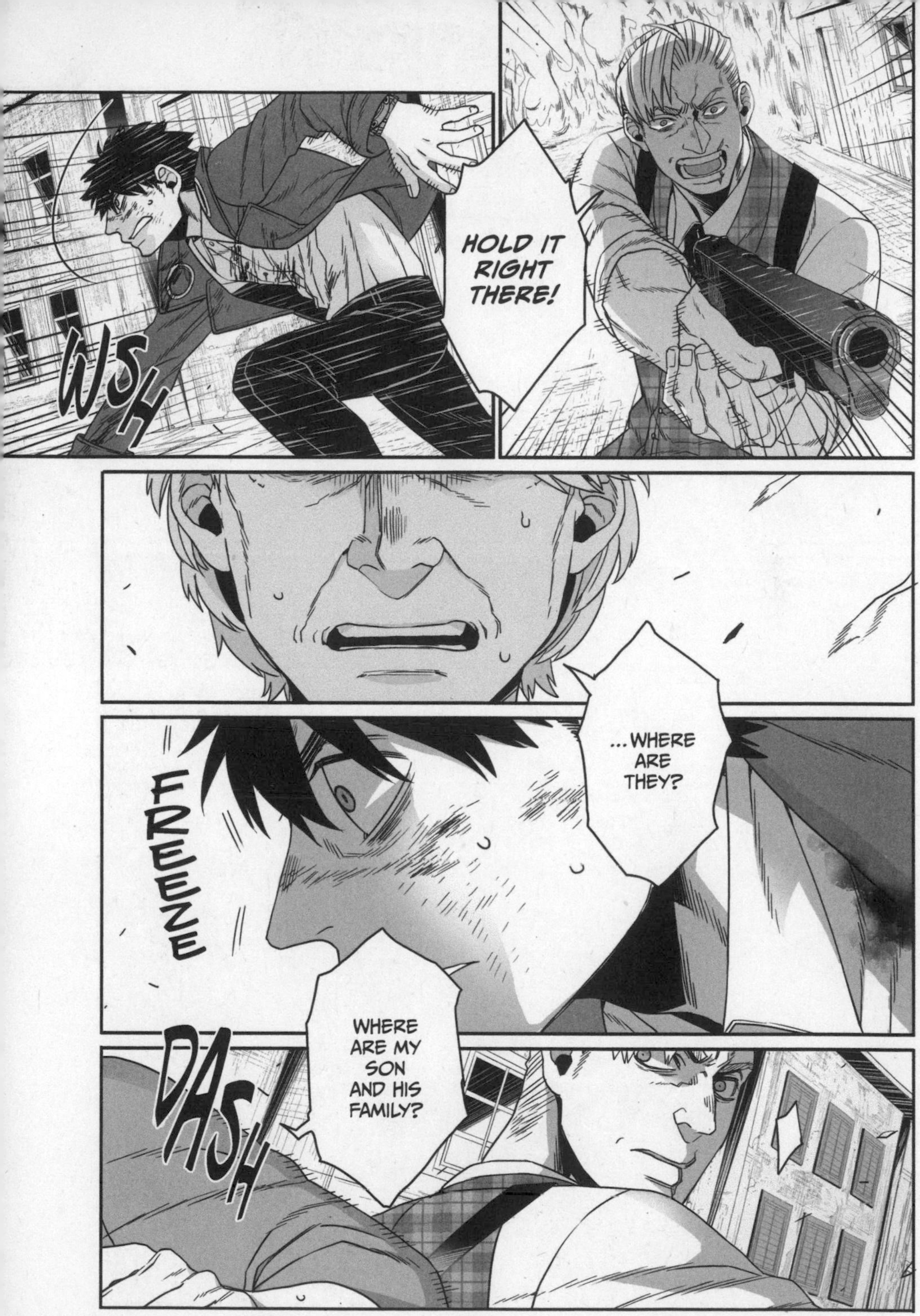
HOLD IT RIGHT THERE!
WSH
...WHERE ARE THEY?
FREEZE
WHERE ARE MY SON AND HIS FAMILY?
DASH

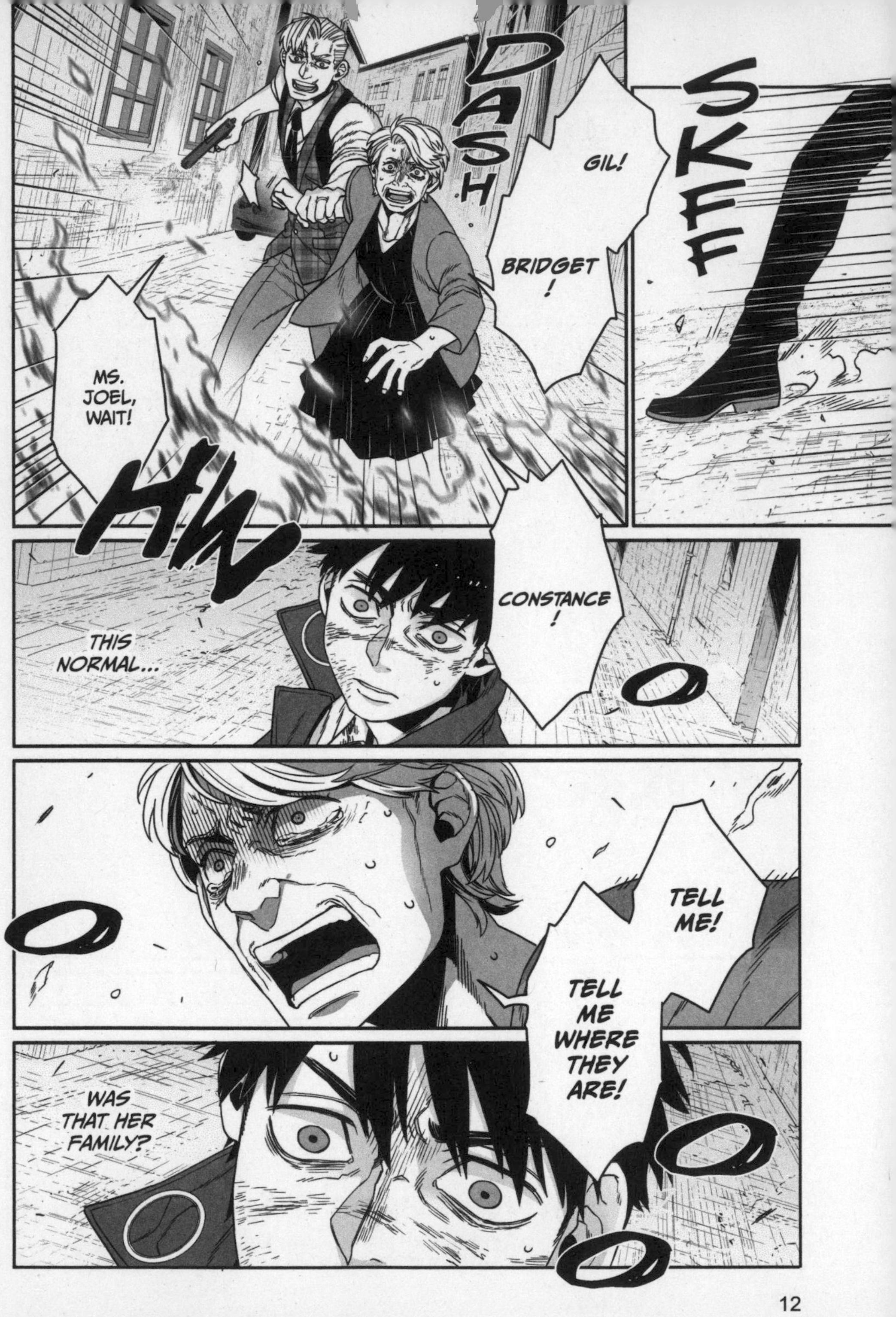
SKFF
DASH
GIL!
BRIDGET!
MS. JOEL, WAIT!
HW
CONSTANCE!
THIS NORMAL...
O
TELL ME!
TELL ME WHERE THEY ARE!
O
O
O
WAS THAT HER FAMILY?

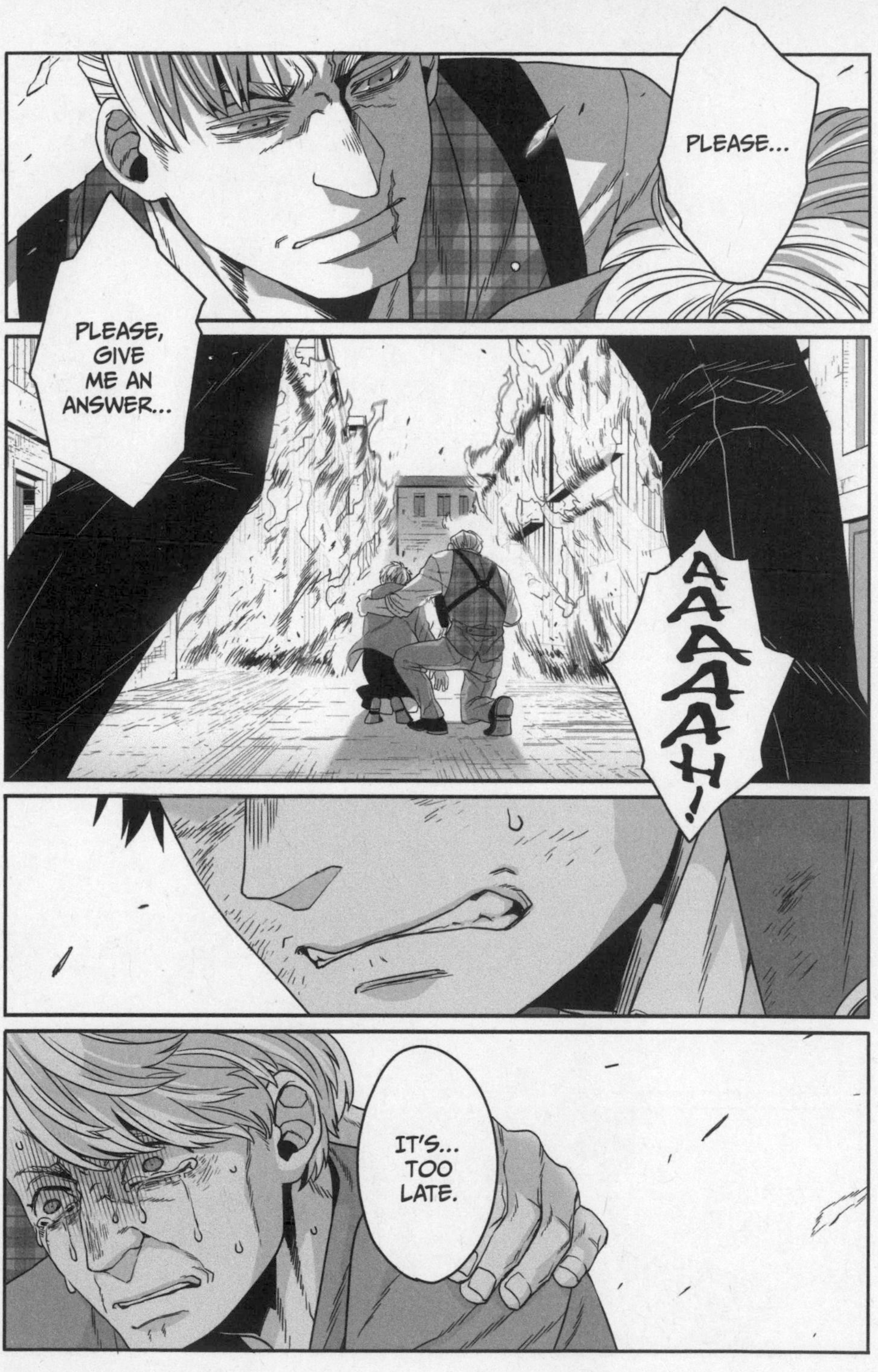
PLEASE...
PLEASE, GIVE ME AN ANSWER...
AAAAAH!
IT'S... TOO LATE.

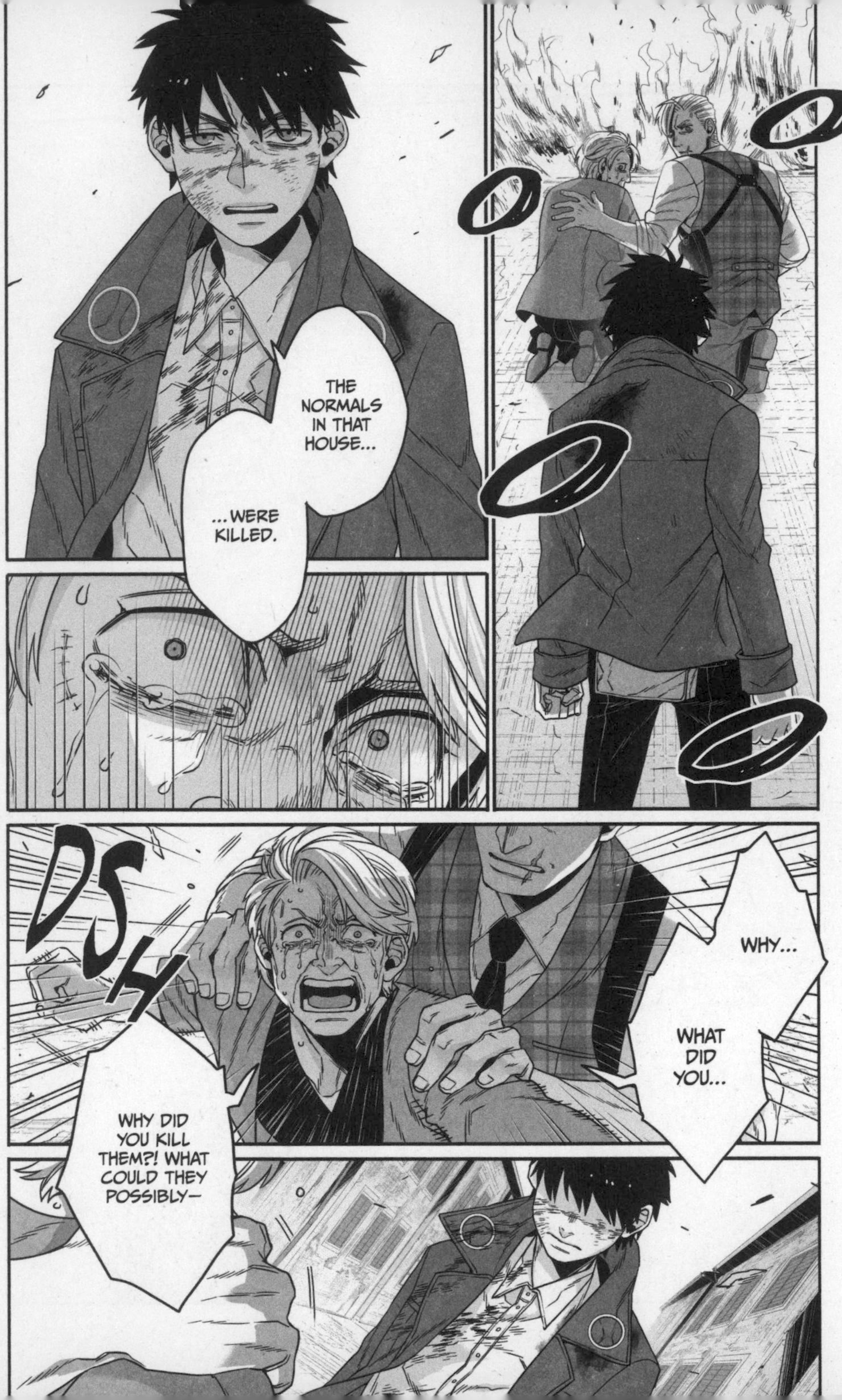
THE NORMALS IN THAT HOUSE...
...WERE KILLED.
WHY...
WHAT DID YOU...
DSH
WHY DID YOU KILL THEM?! WHAT COULD THEY POSSIBLY—

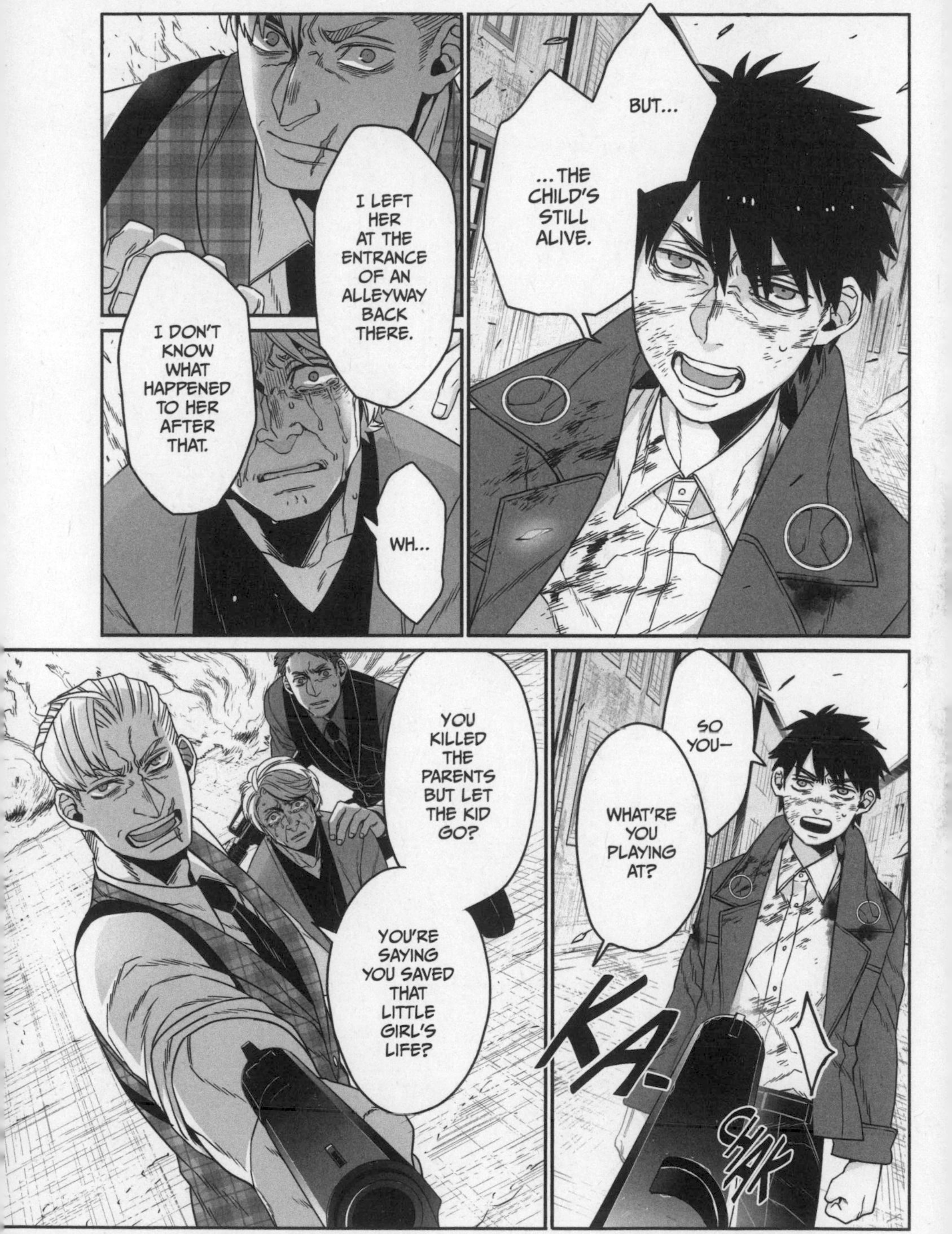
BUT...
...THE CHILD'S STILL ALIVE.
I LEFT HER AT THE ENTRANCE OF AN ALLEYWAY BACK THERE.
I DON'T KNOW WHAT HAPPENED TO HER AFTER THAT.
WH...
SO YOU—
WHAT'RE YOU PLAYING AT?
KA-
CHAK
YOU KILLED THE PARENTS BUT LET THE KID GO?
YOU'RE SAYING YOU SAVED THAT LITTLE GIRL'S LIFE?

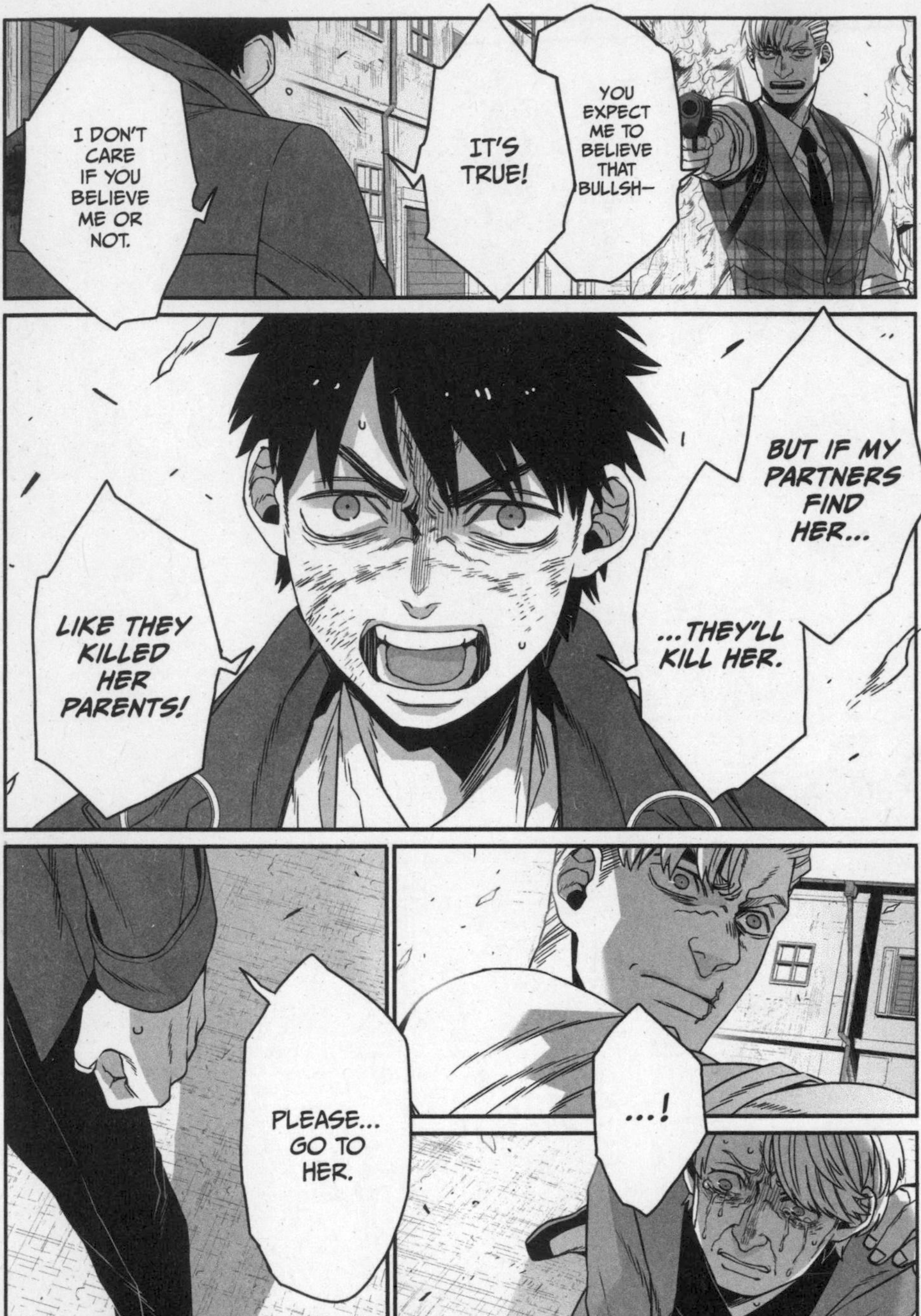
YOU EXPECT ME TO BELIEVE THAT BULLSH—
IT'S TRUE!
I DON'T CARE IF YOU BELIEVE ME OR NOT.
BUT IF MY PARTNERS FIND HER...
...THEY'LL KILL HER.
LIKE THEY KILLED HER PARENTS!
...!
PLEASE... GO TO HER.

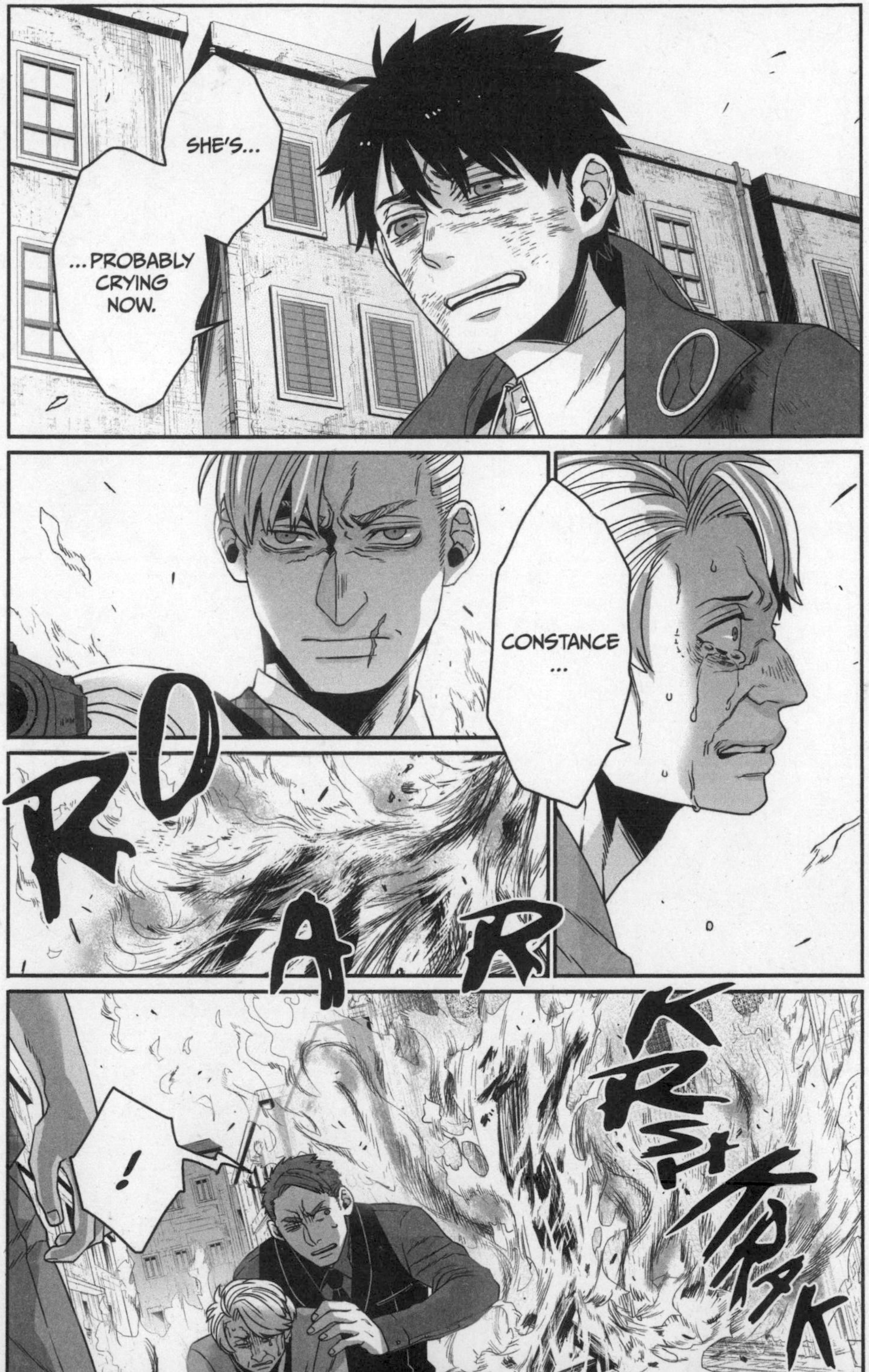
SHE'S...
...PROBABLY CRYING NOW.
CONSTANCE ...
ROAR
KRSHKRAK
!

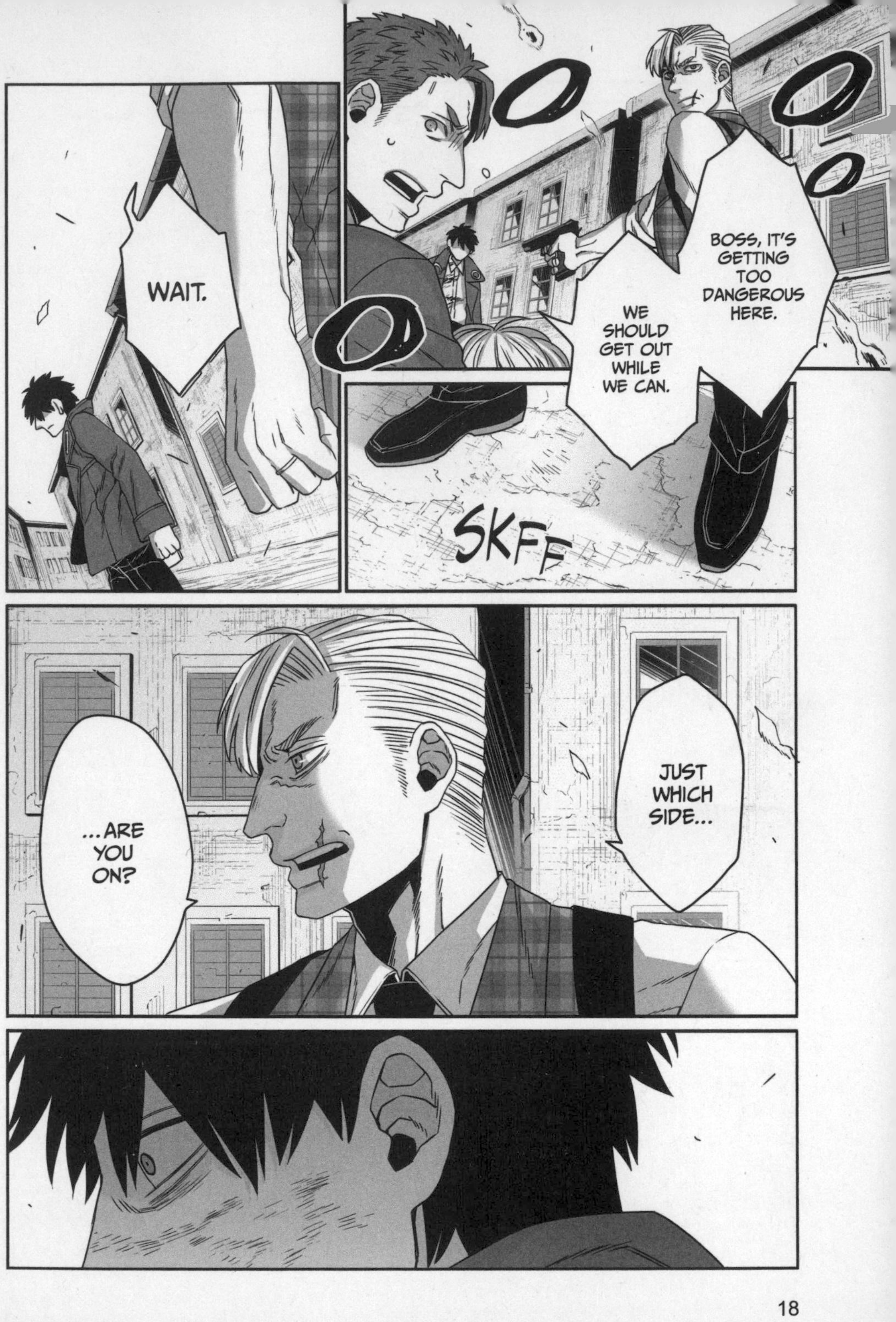
BOSS, IT'S GETTING TOO DANGEROUS HERE.
WE SHOULD GET OUT WHILE WE CAN.
SKFF
WAIT.
JUST WHICH SIDE...
...ARE YOU ON?

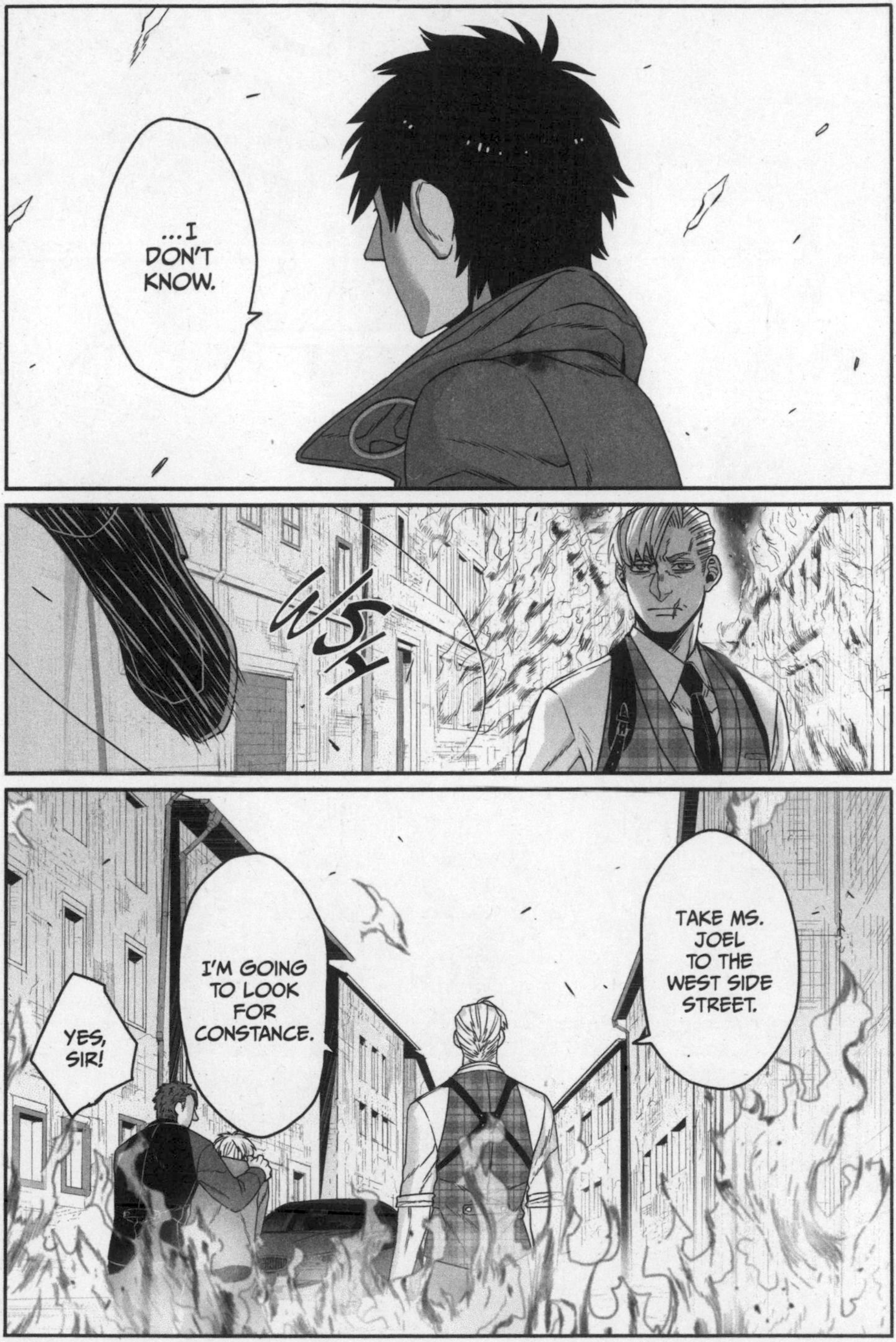
...I DON'T KNOW.
WSH
TAKE MS. JOEL TO THE WEST SIDE STREET.
I'M GOING TO LOOK FOR CONSTANCE.
YES, SIR!

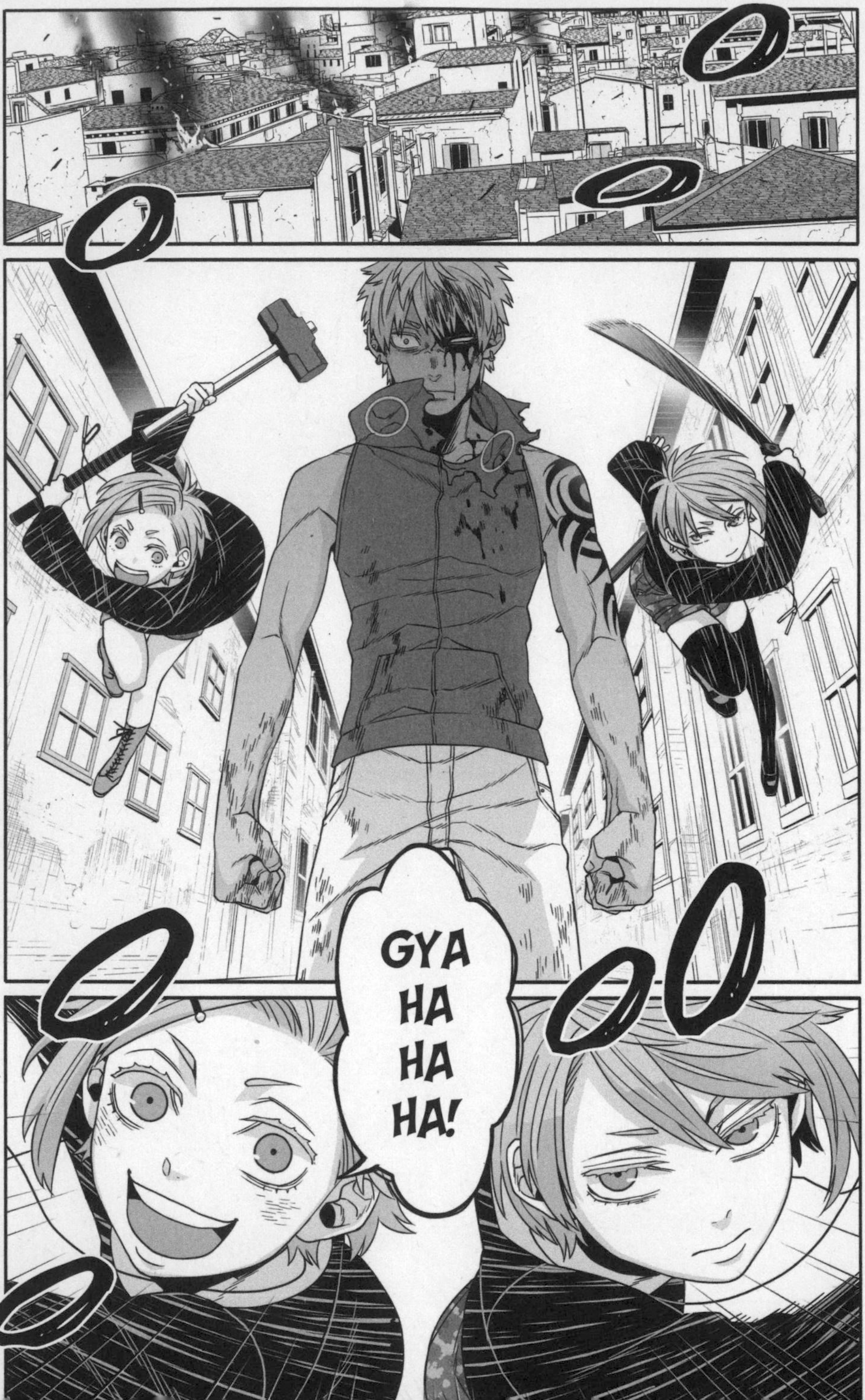
GYA HA HA HA!

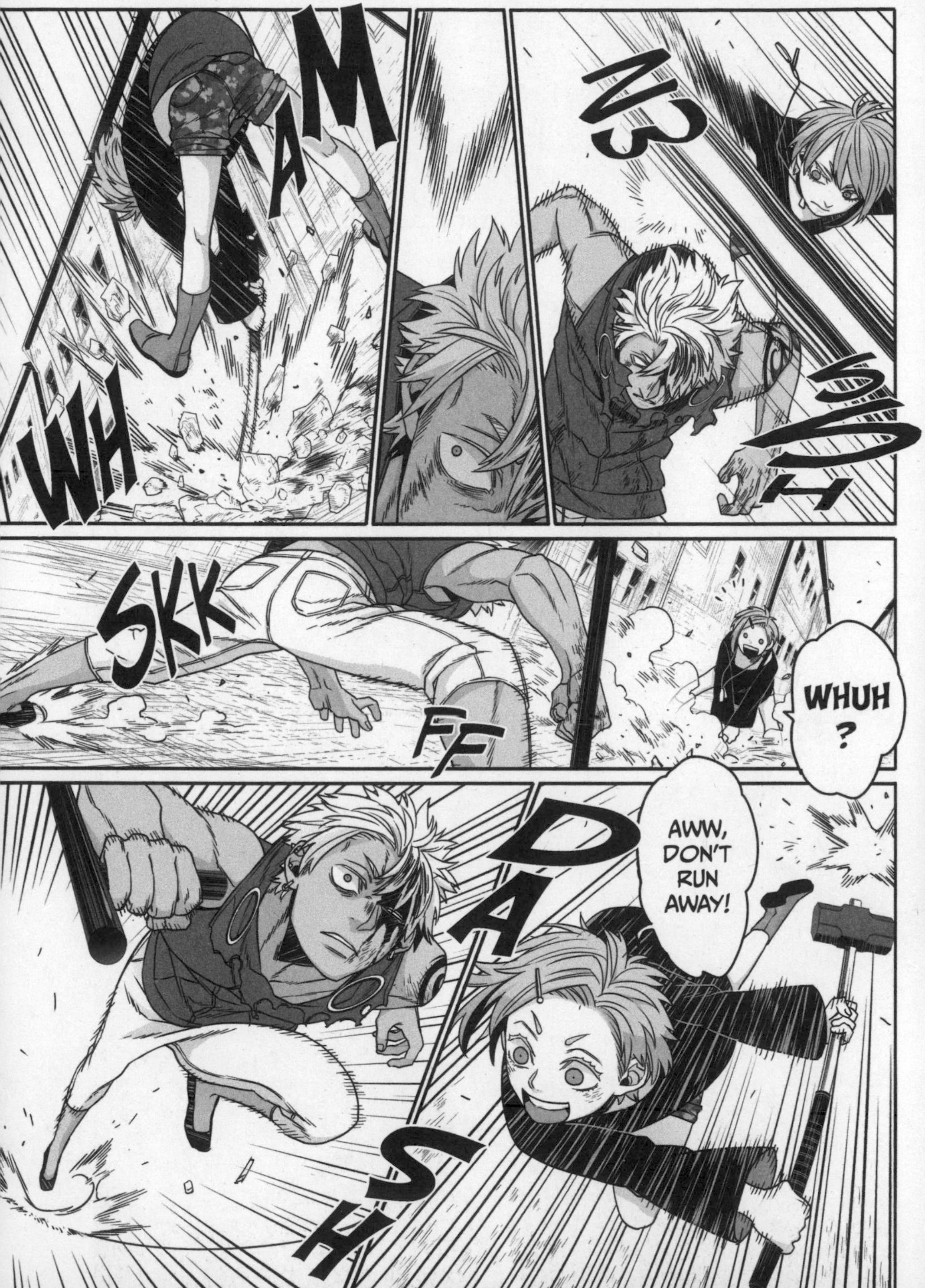
WHAM
WHUH?
SKK
FF
AWW, DON'T RUN AWAY!
DASH

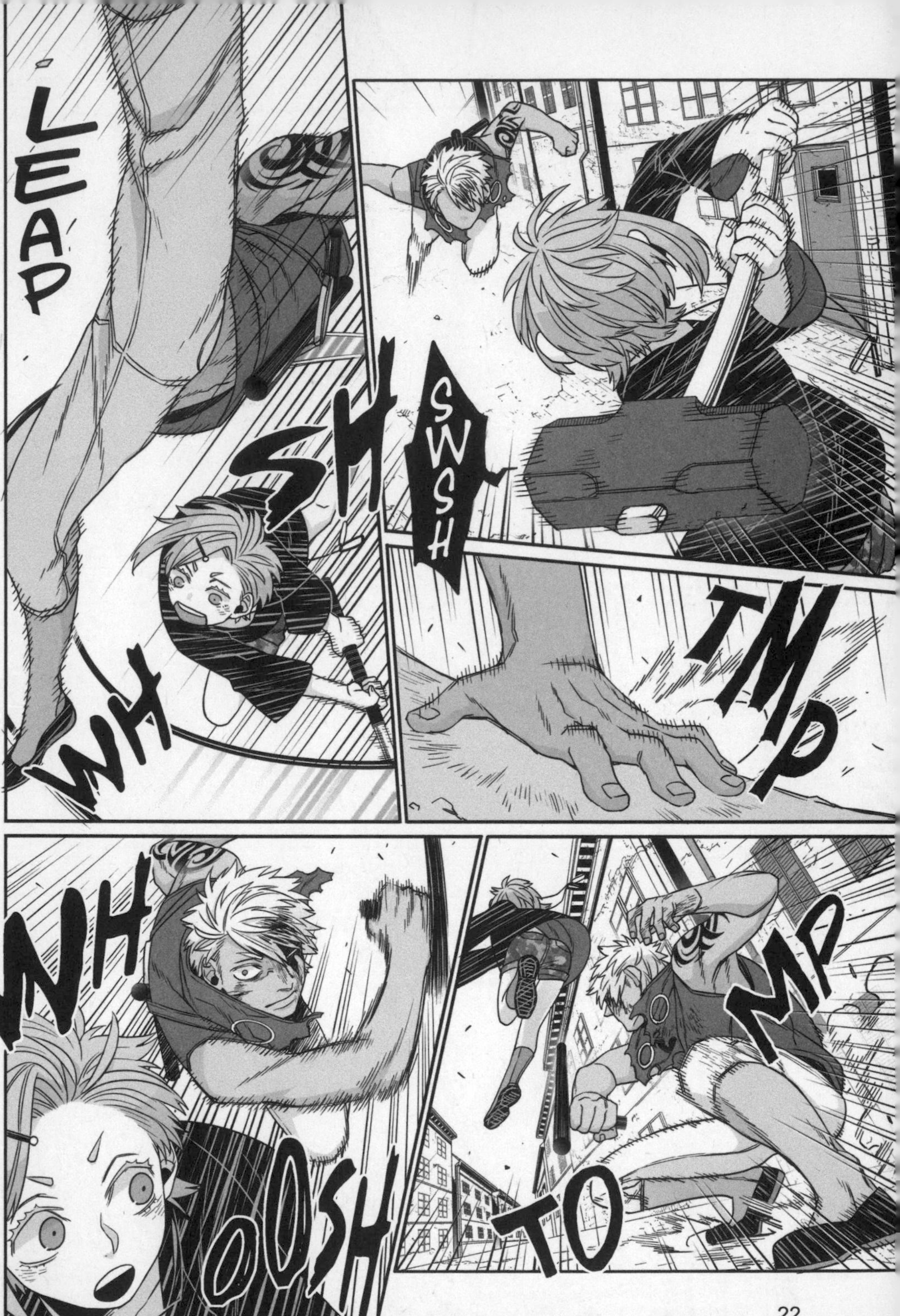

SWSH
TMP
LEAP
WH
SH
TOMP
WHOOSH

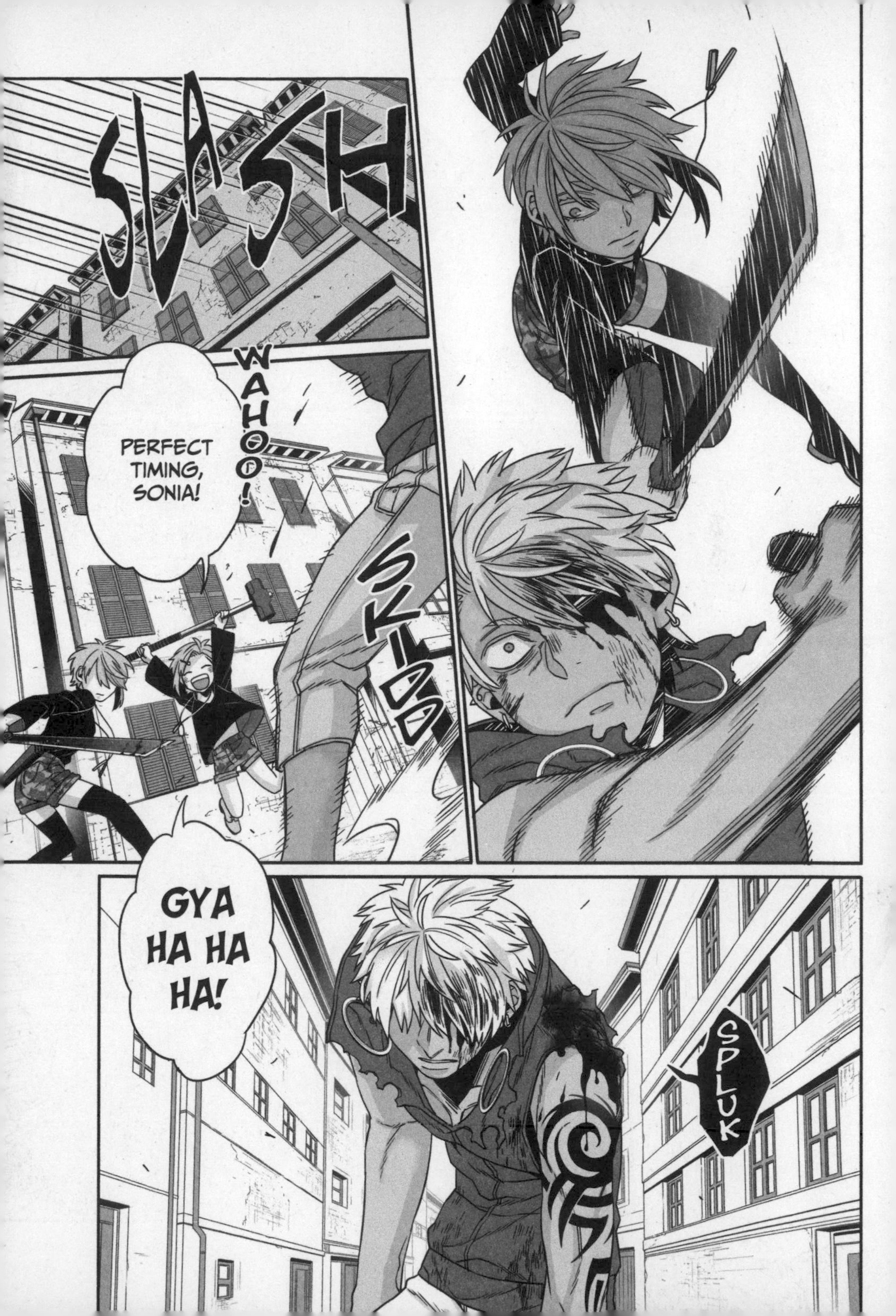
SLASH
WAHOOO!
PERFECT TIMING, SONIA!
SKIDD
GYA HA HA HA!
SPLUK

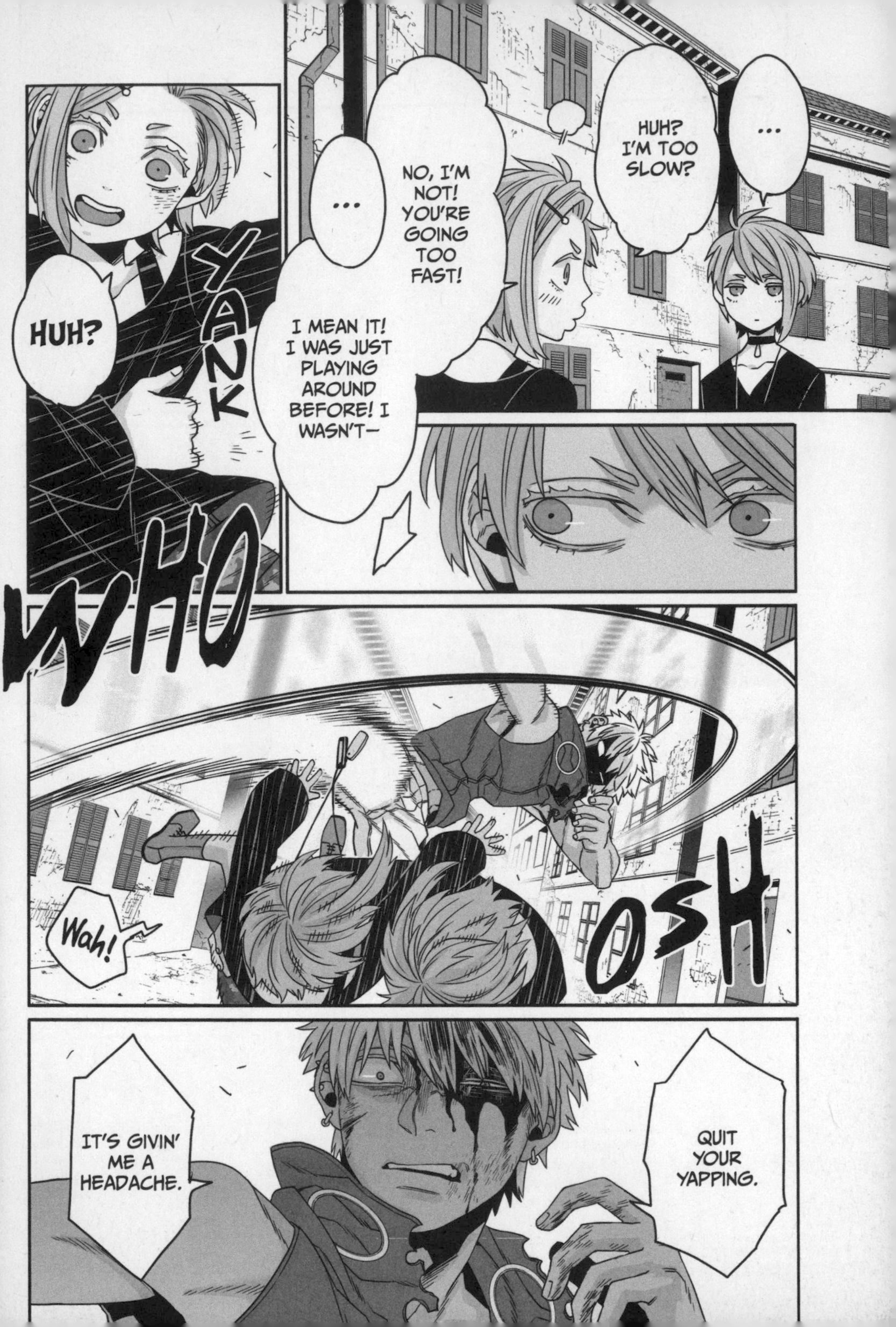
...
HUH? I'M TOO SLOW?
NO, I'M NOT! YOU'RE GOING TOO FAST!
...
I MEAN IT! I WAS JUST PLAYING AROUND BEFORE! I WASN'T—
YANK
HUH?
WHOOSH
Wah!
QUIT YOUR YAPPING.
IT'S GIVIN' ME A HEADACHE.

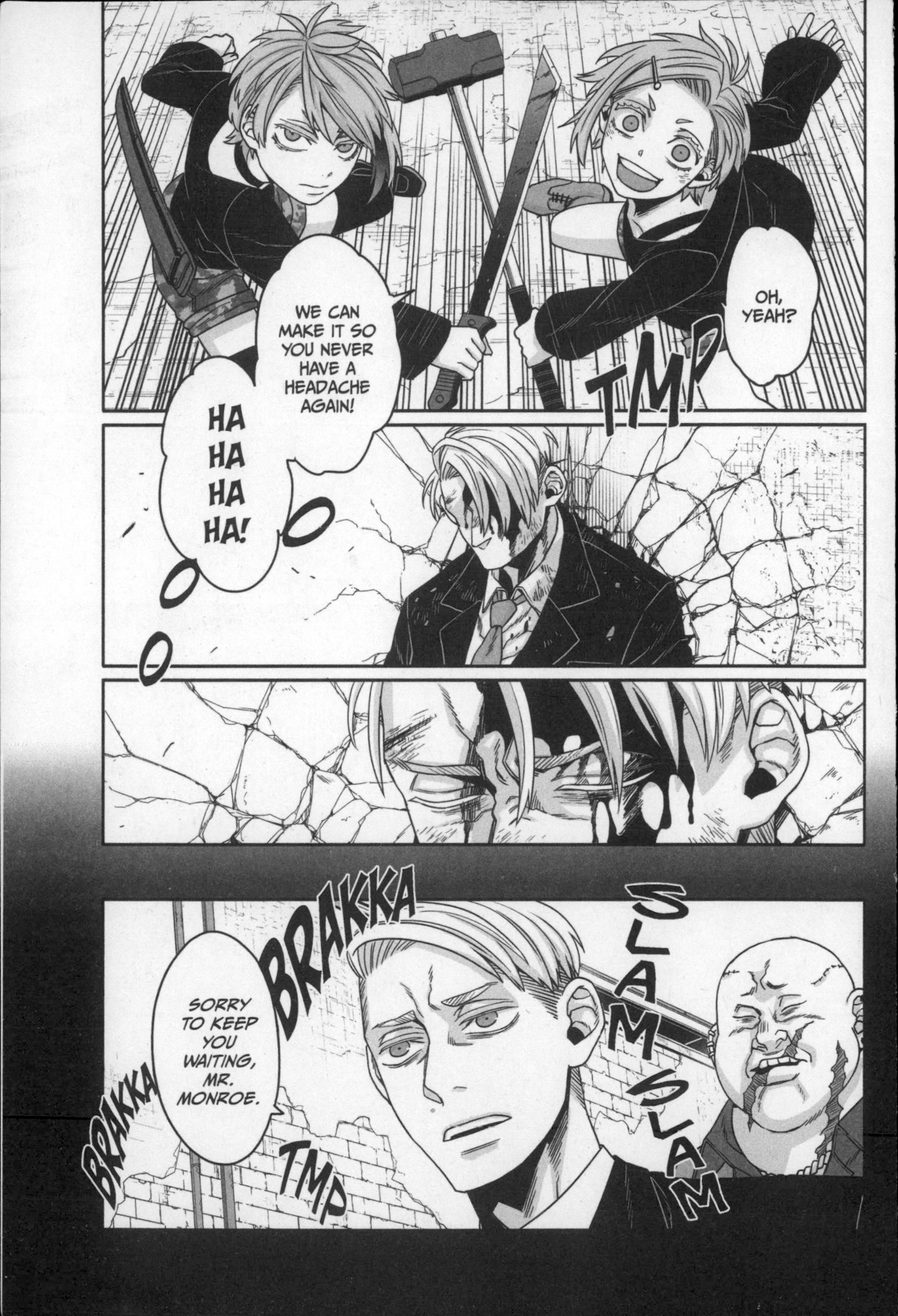
OH, YEAH?
TMP
WE CAN MAKE IT SO YOU NEVER HAVE A HEADACHE AGAIN!
HA HA HA HA!
SLAM SLAM
BRAKKA
SORRY TO KEEP YOU WAITING, MR. MONROE.
BRAKKA
TMP

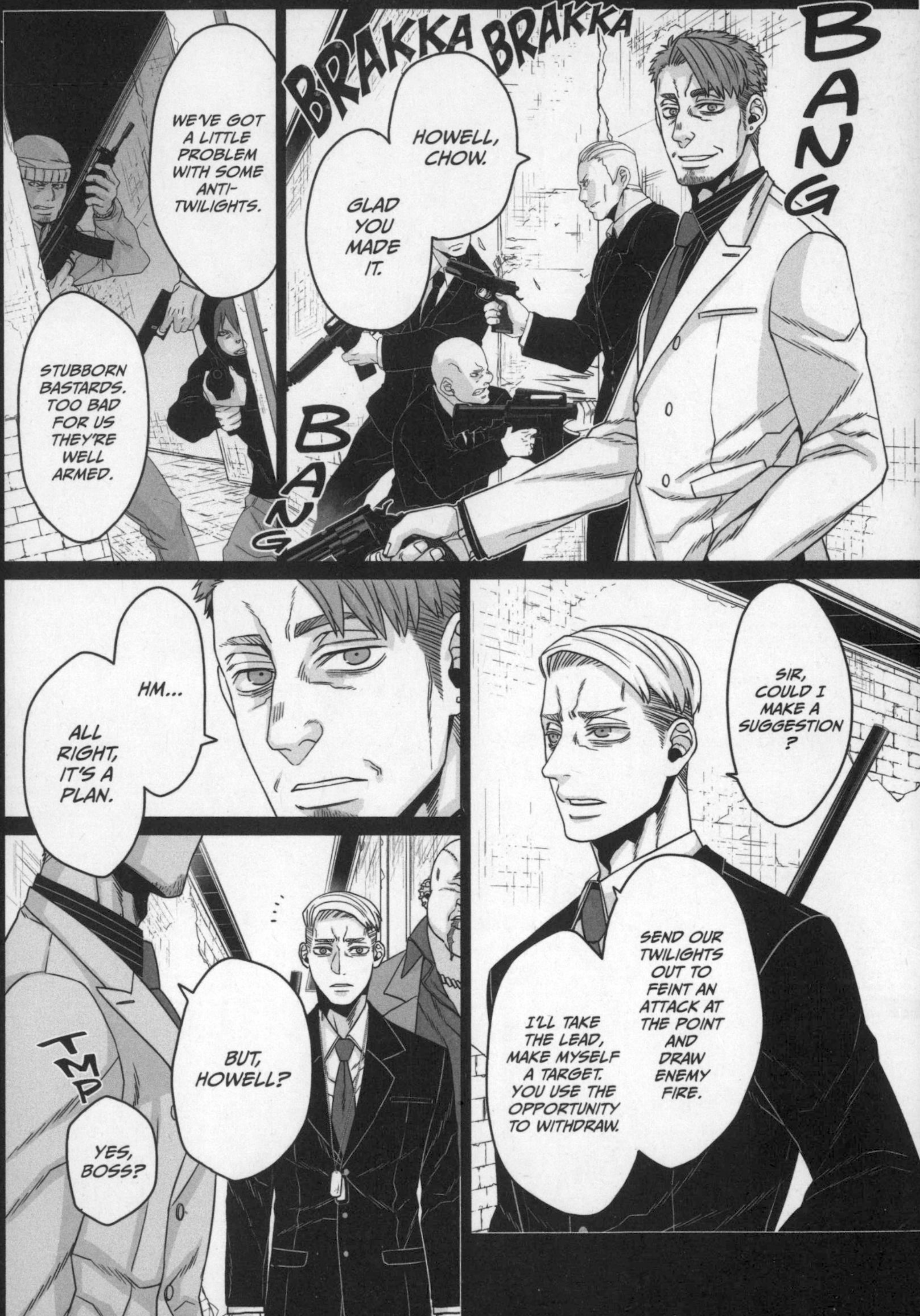
BANG
BRAKKA BRAKKA
HOWELL, CHOW.
GLAD YOU MADE IT.
BANG
WE'VE GOT A LITTLE PROBLEM WITH SOME ANTI-TWILIGHTS.
STUBBORN BASTARDS. TOO BAD FOR US THEY'RE WELL ARMED.
SIR, COULD I MAKE A SUGGESTION?
SEND OUR TWILIGHTS OUT TO FEINT AN ATTACK AT THE POINT AND DRAW ENEMY FIRE.
I'LL TAKE THE LEAD, MAKE MYSELF A TARGET. YOU USE THE OPPORTUNITY TO WITHDRAW.
HM...
ALL RIGHT, IT'S A PLAN.
BUT, HOWELL?
TMP
YES, BOSS?

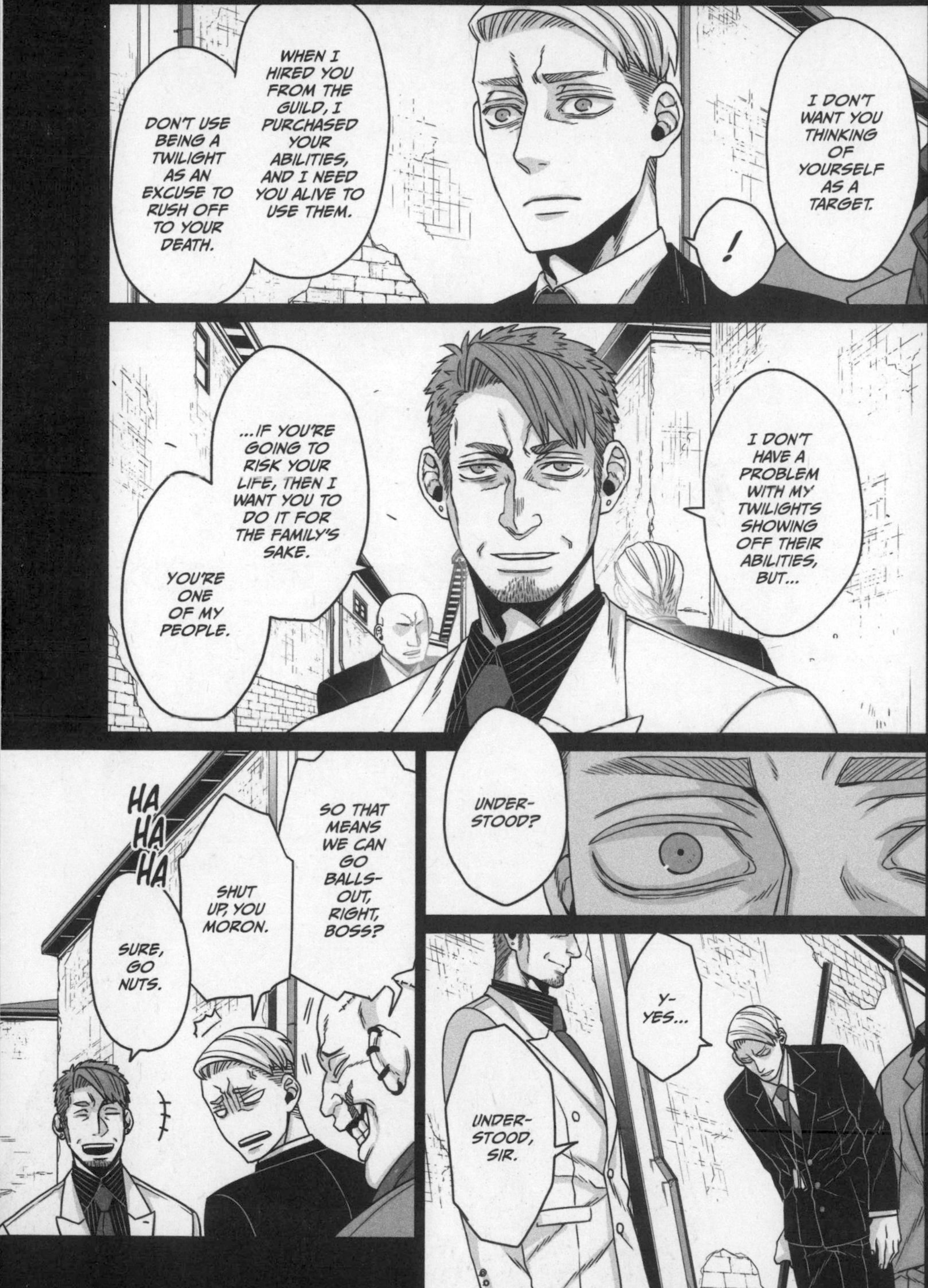
I DON'T WANT YOU THINKING OF YOURSELF AS A TARGET.
!
WHEN I HIRED YOU FROM THE GUILD, I PURCHASED YOUR ABILITIES, AND I NEED YOU ALIVE TO USE THEM.
DON'T USE BEING A TWILIGHT AS AN EXCUSE TO RUSH OFF TO YOUR DEATH.
I DON'T HAVE A PROBLEM WITH MY TWILIGHTS SHOWING OFF THEIR ABILITIES, BUT...
...IF YOU'RE GOING TO RISK YOUR LIFE, THEN I WANT YOU TO DO IT FOR THE FAMILY'S SAKE.
YOU'RE ONE OF MY PEOPLE.
UNDER-STOOD?
Y-YES...
UNDER-STOOD, SIR.
SO THAT MEANS WE CAN GO BALLS-OUT, RIGHT, BOSS?
SHUT UP, YOU MORON.
HA HA HA
SURE, GO NUTS.

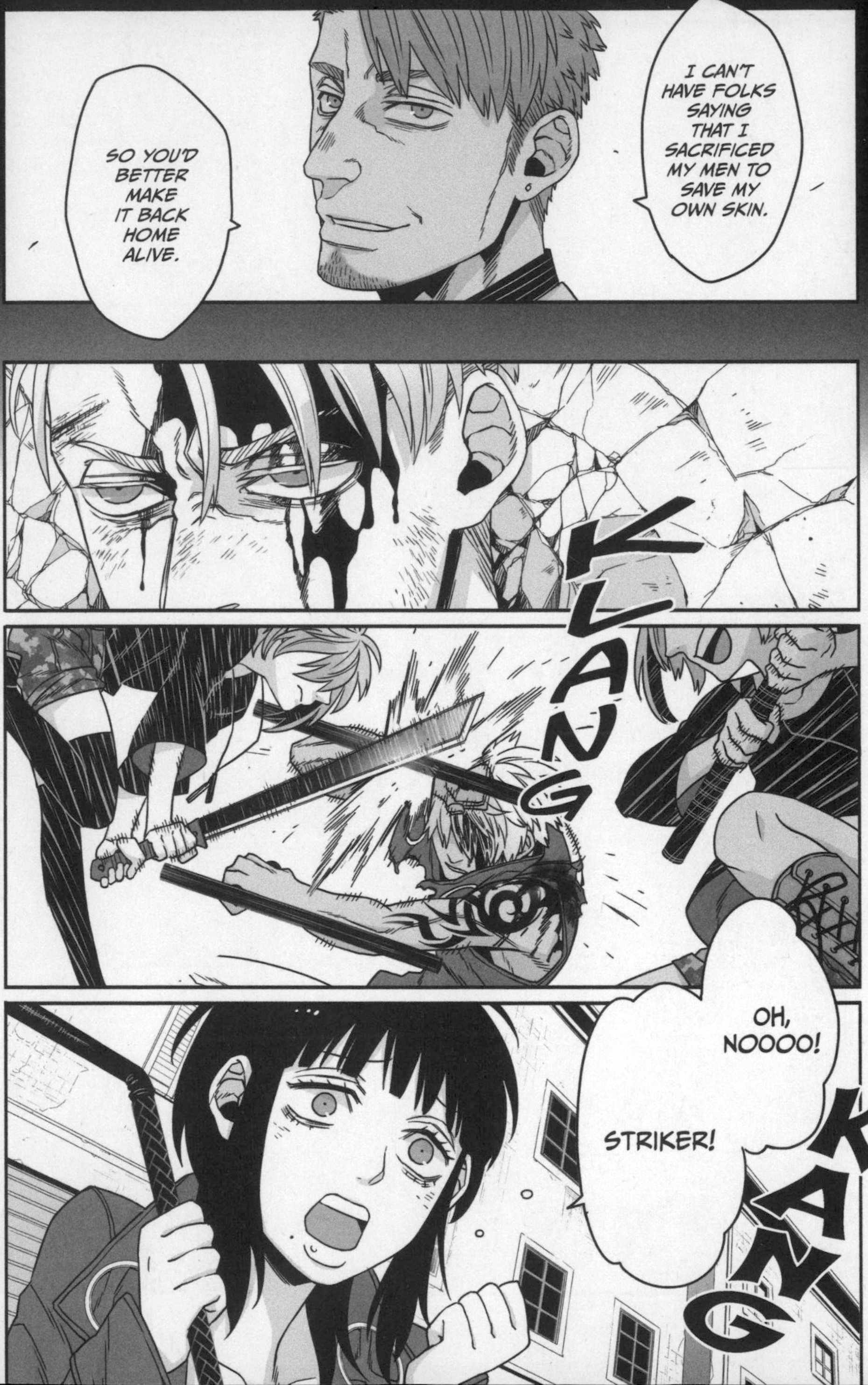

I CAN'T HAVE FOLKS SAYING THAT I SACRIFICED MY MEN TO SAVE MY OWN SKIN.
SO YOU'D BETTER MAKE IT BACK HOME ALIVE.
KLANG
...
OH, NOOOO!
STRIKER!
KANG

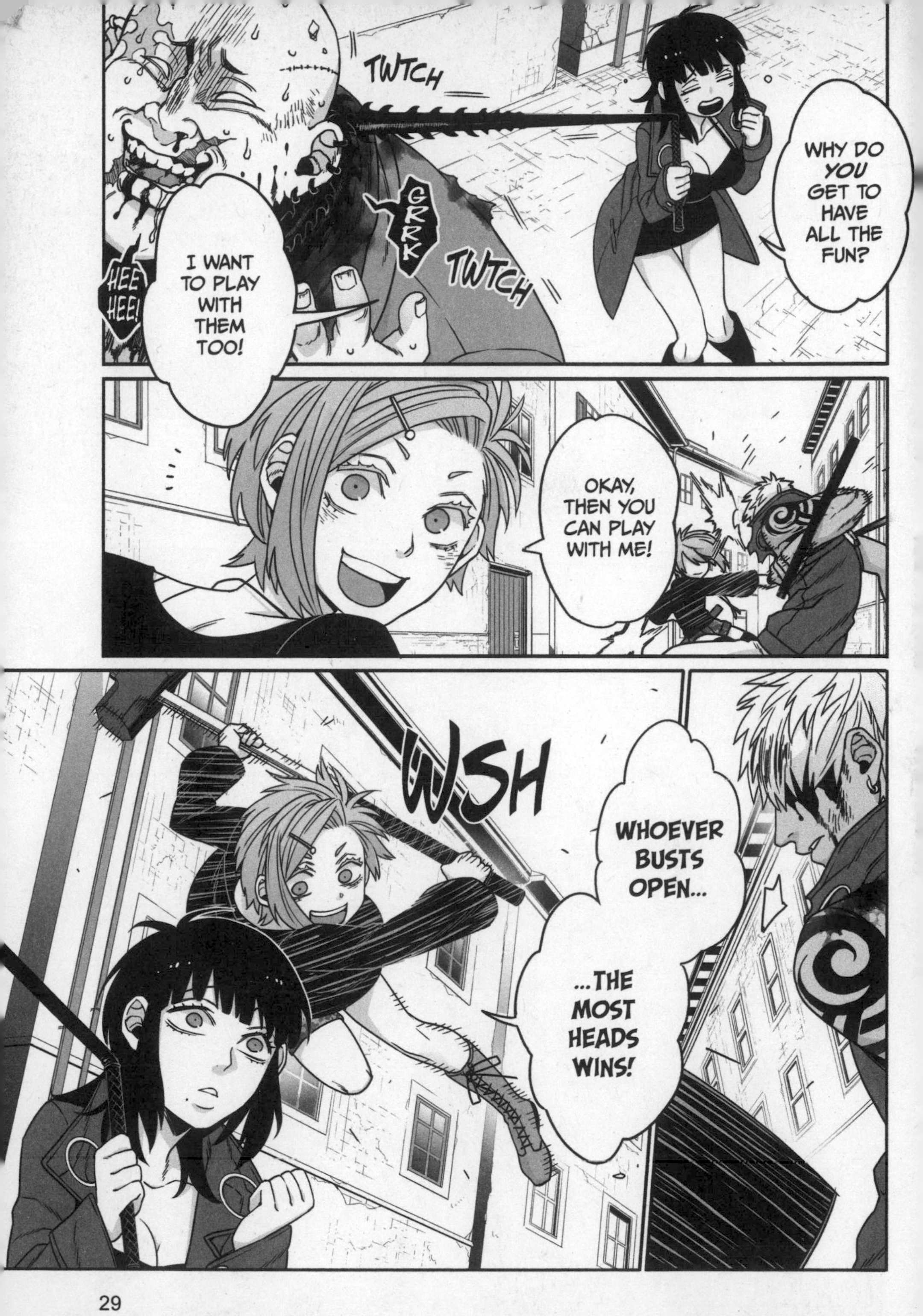
TWTCH
WHY DO YOU GET TO HAVE ALL THE FUN?
GRRK
TWTCH
I WANT TO PLAY WITH THEM TOO!
HEE HEE!
OKAY, THEN YOU CAN PLAY WITH ME!
WSH
WHOEVER BUSTS OPEN...
...THE MOST HEADS WINS!

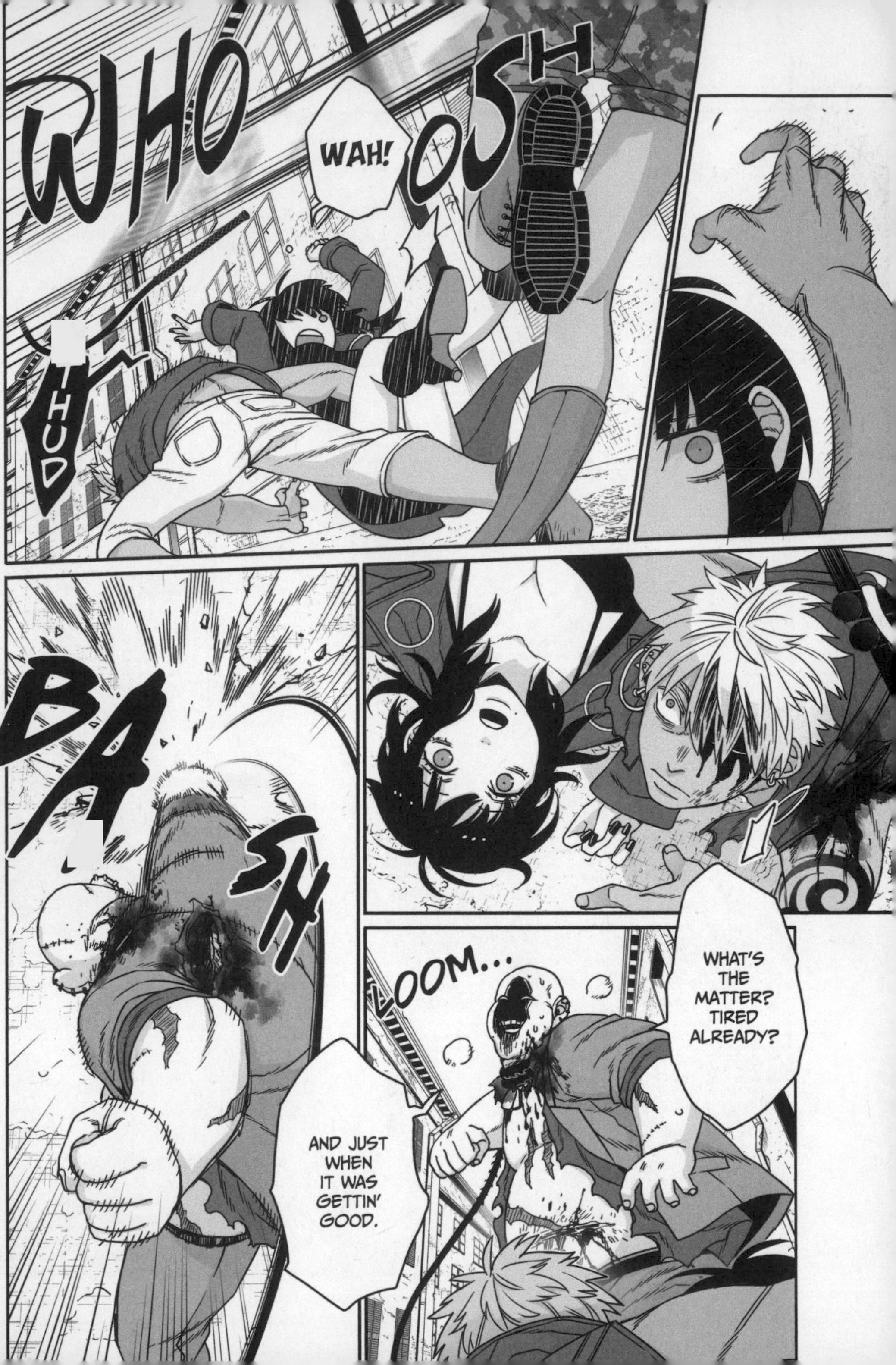
WHOOSH
WAH!
THUD
WHAT'S THE MATTER? TIRED ALREADY?
VOOM...
AND JUST WHEN IT WAS GETTIN' GOOD.
BASH

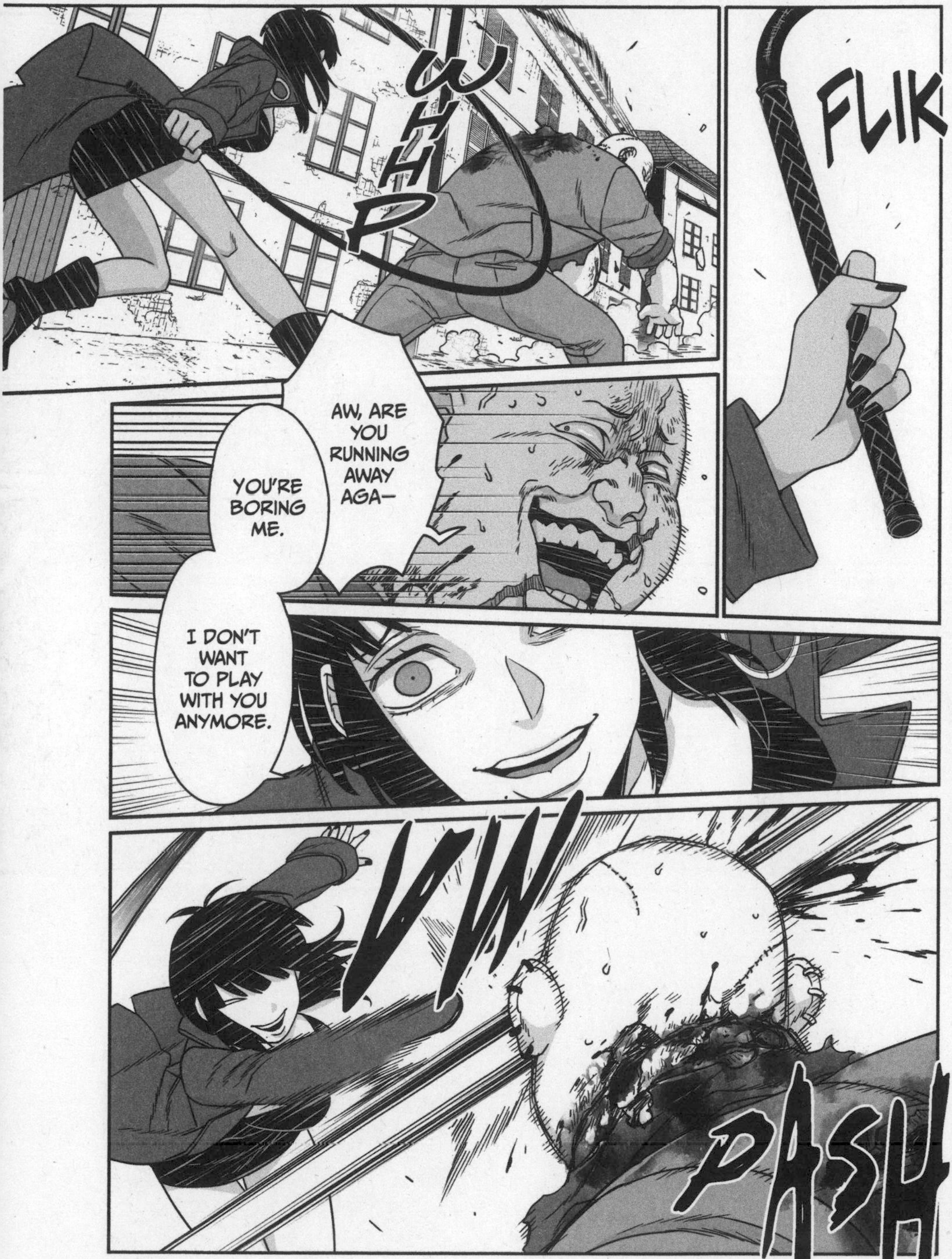
FLIK
WHHP
AW, ARE YOU RUNNING AWAY AGA—
YOU'RE BORING ME.
I DON'T WANT TO PLAY WITH YOU ANYMORE.
VW
PASH

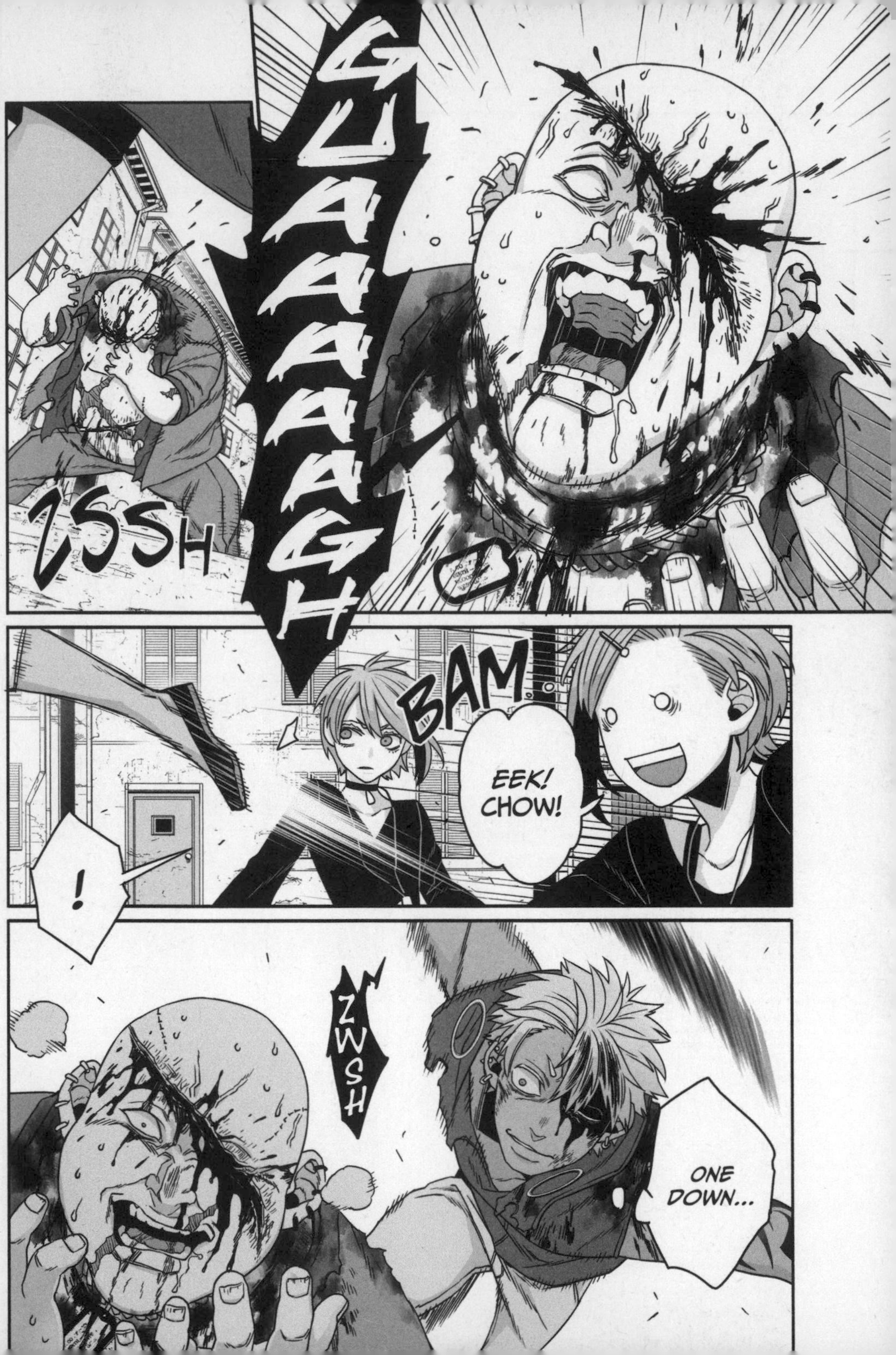
GUAAAAAGH
ZSSH
BAM
EEK! CHOW!
!
ZWSH
ONE DOWN...

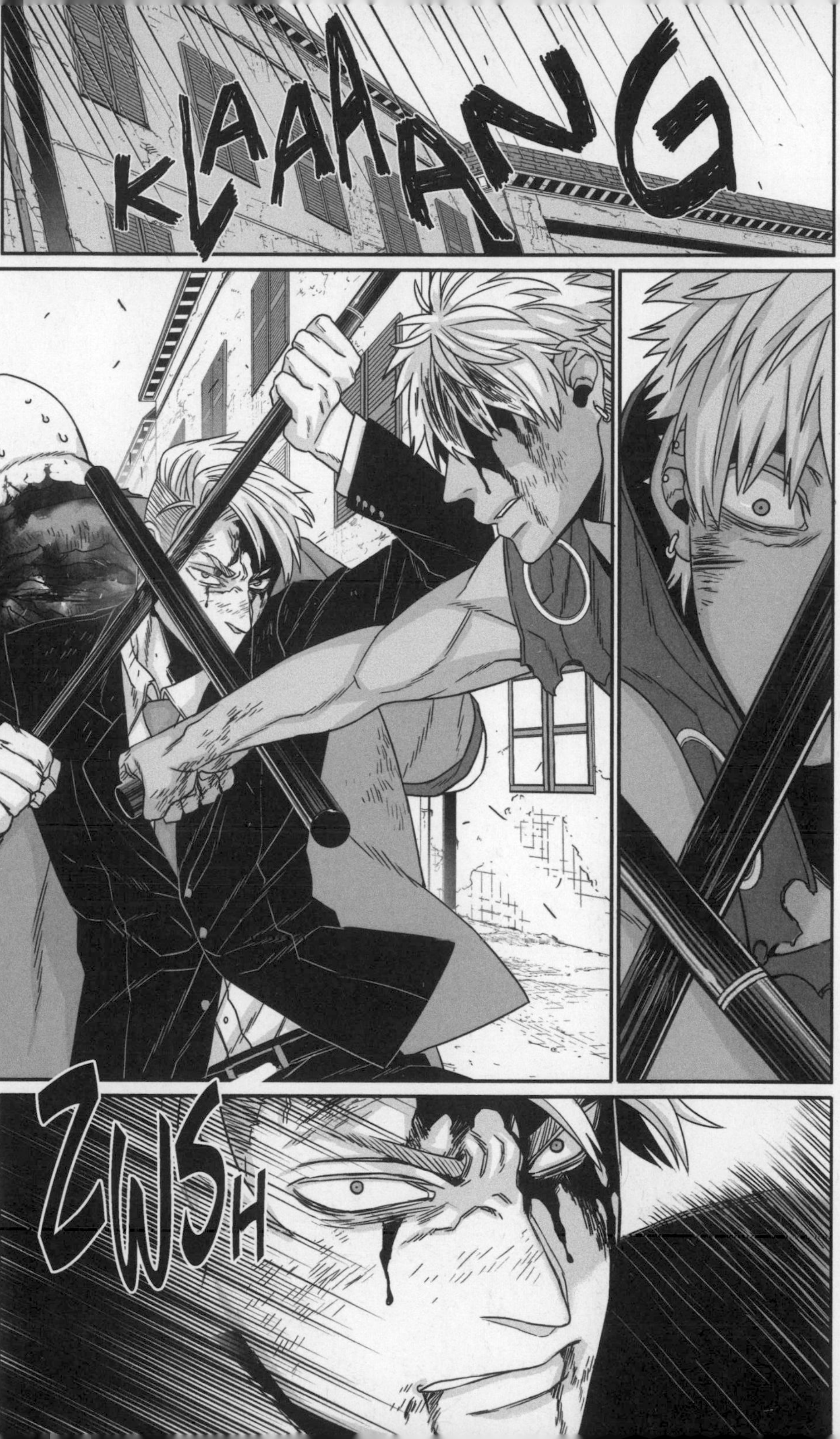
KLAAANG
ZWSH

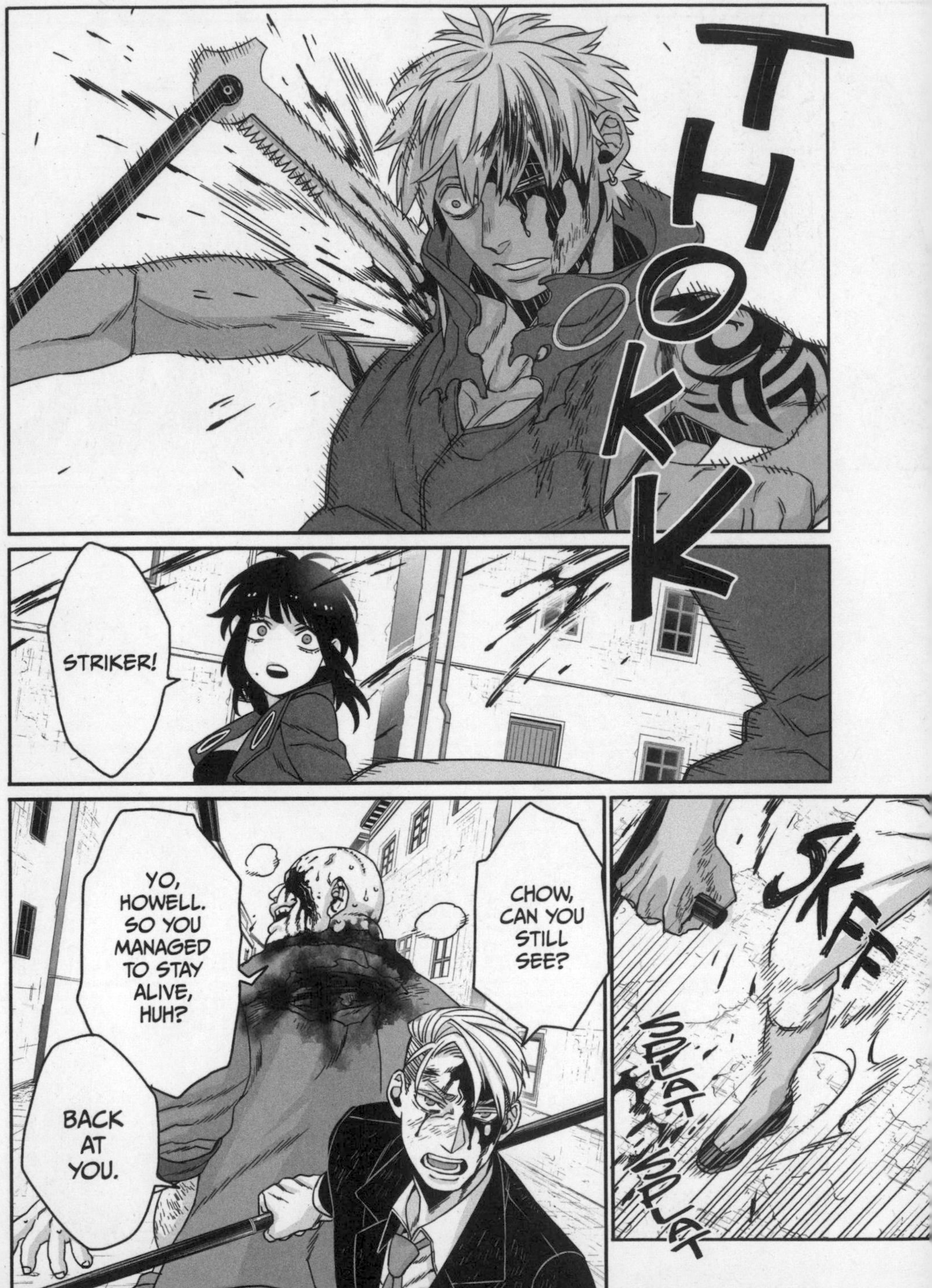
THOOKK
STRIKER!
SKFF
SPLAT SPLAT
CHOW, CAN YOU STILL SEE?
YO, HOWELL. SO YOU MANAGED TO STAY ALIVE, HUH?
BACK AT YOU.

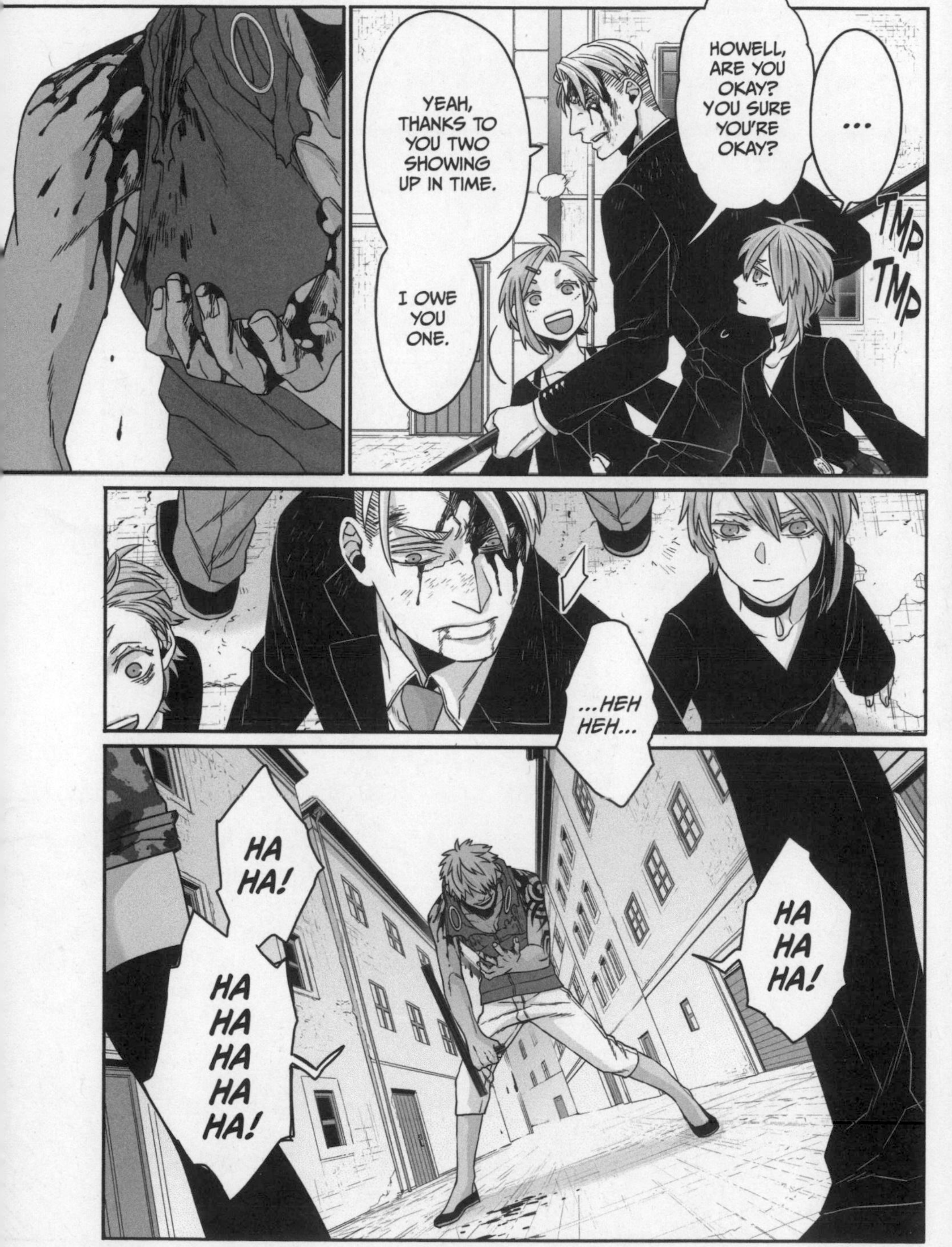
...
HOWELL, ARE YOU OKAY? YOU SURE YOU'RE OKAY?
TMP TMP
YEAH, THANKS TO YOU TWO SHOWING UP IN TIME.
I OWE YOU ONE.
...HEH HEH...
HA HA HA!
HA HA!
HA HA HA HA HA!

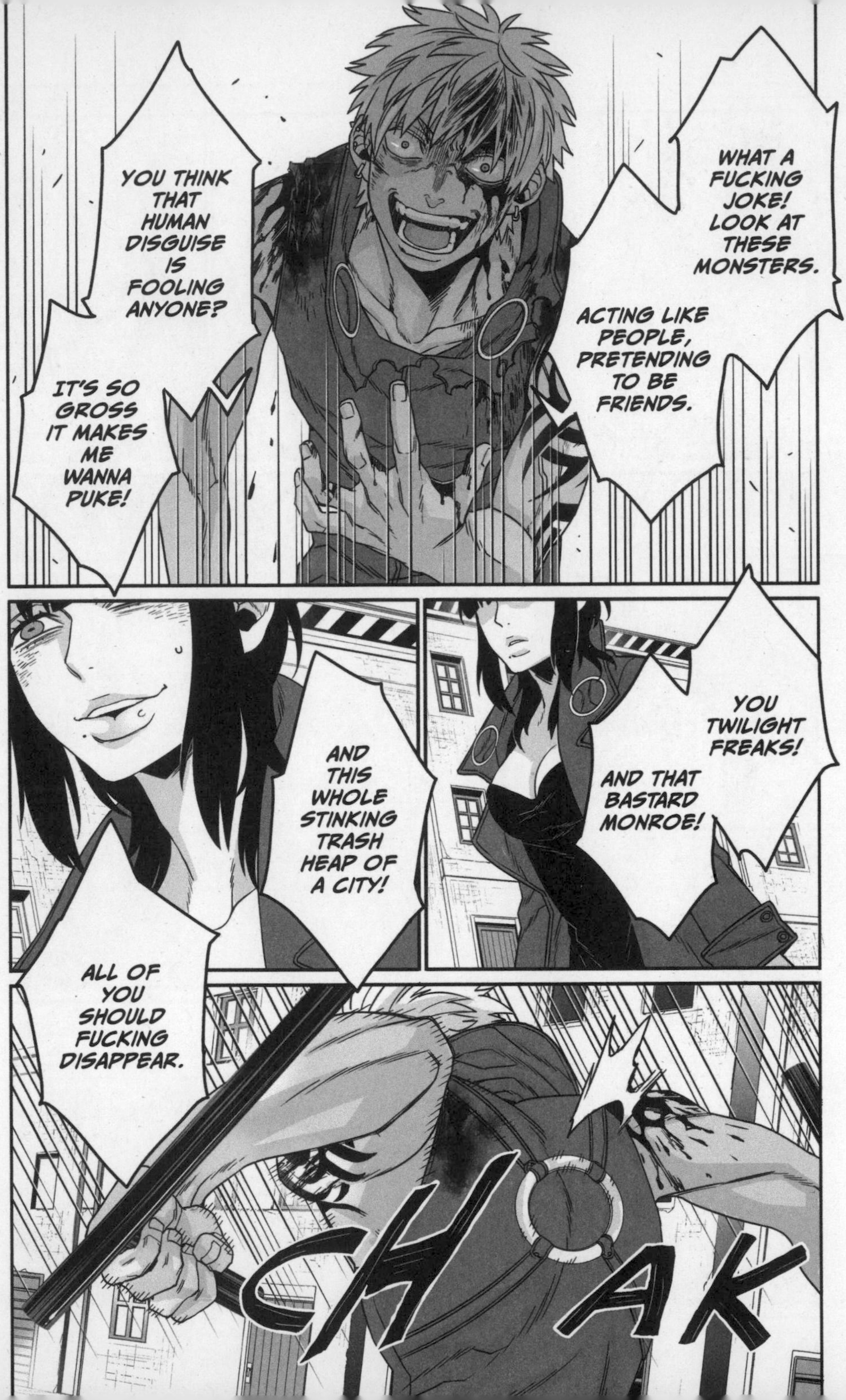
WHAT A FUCKING JOKE! LOOK AT THESE MONSTERS.
ACTING LIKE PEOPLE, PRETENDING TO BE FRIENDS.
YOU THINK THAT HUMAN DISGUISE IS FOOLING ANYONE?
IT'S SO GROSS IT MAKES ME WANNA PUKE!
YOU TWILIGHT FREAKS!
AND THAT BASTARD MONROE!
AND THIS WHOLE STINKING TRASH HEAP OF A CITY!
ALL OF YOU SHOULD FUCKING DISAPPEAR.
CHAK

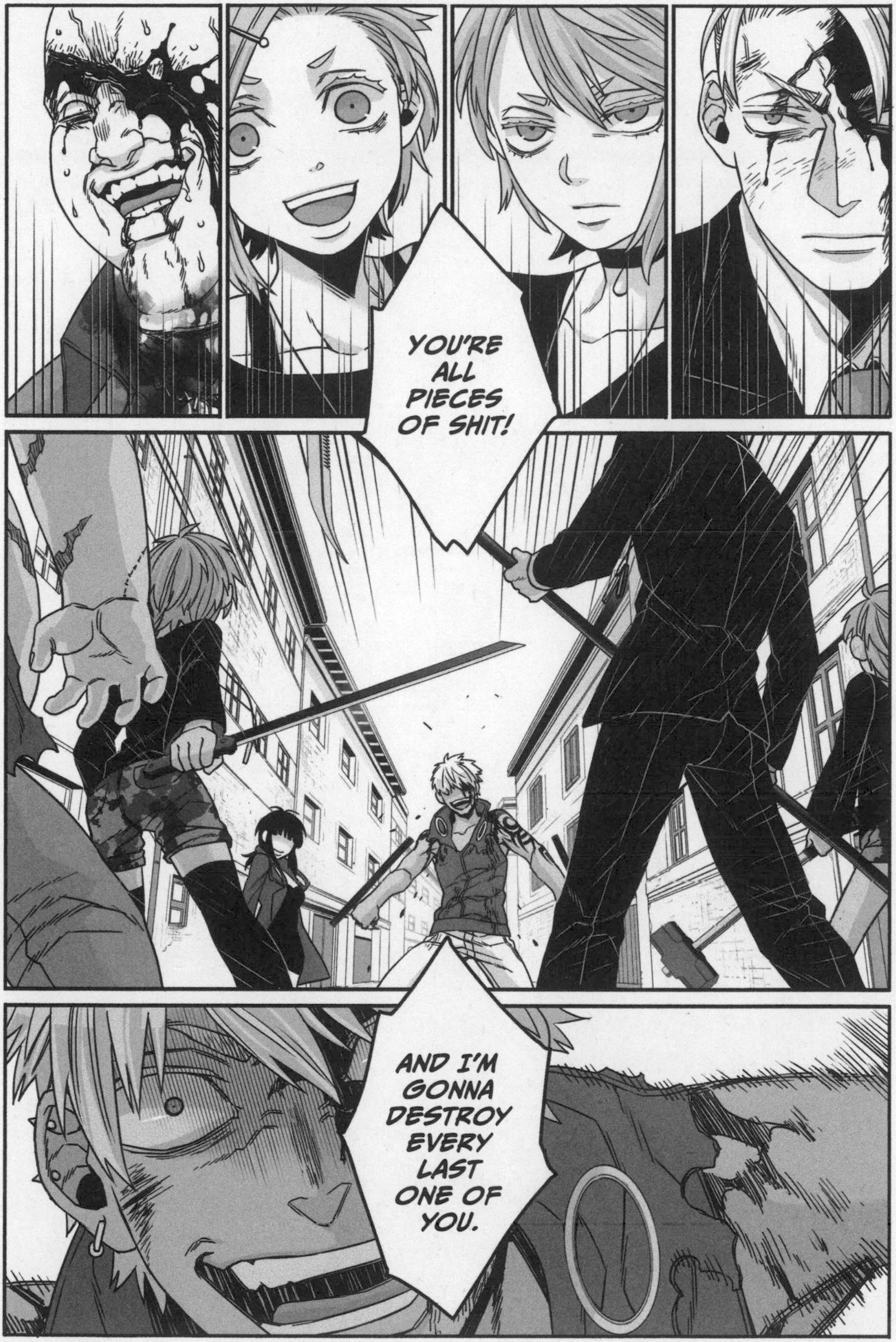
YOU'RE ALL PIECES OF SHIT!
AND I'M GONNA DESTROY EVERY LAST ONE OF YOU.

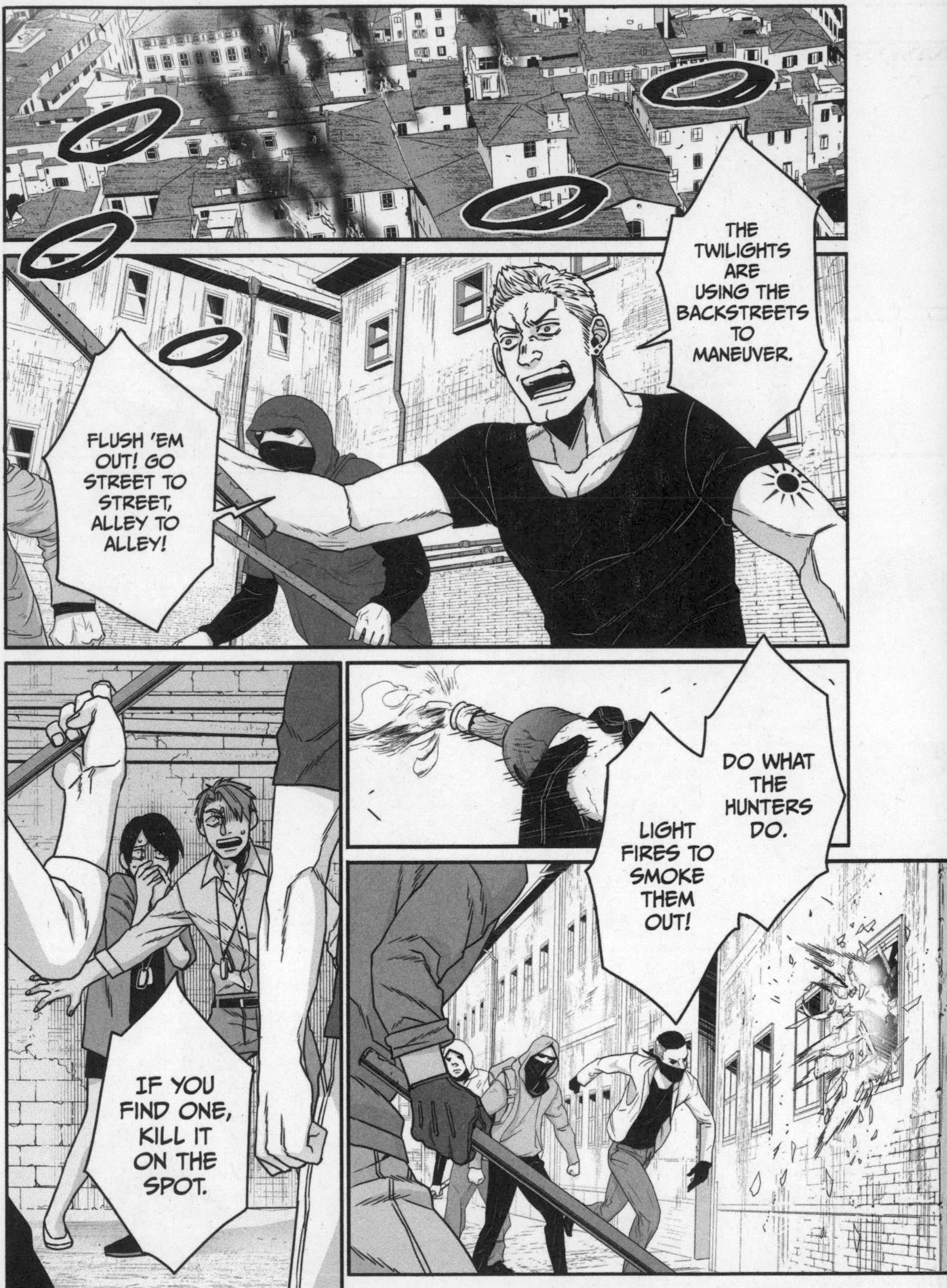
THE TWILIGHTS ARE USING THE BACKSTREETS TO MANEUVER.
FLUSH 'EM OUT! GO STREET TO STREET, ALLEY TO ALLEY!
DO WHAT THE HUNTERS DO.
LIGHT FIRES TO SMOKE THEM OUT!
IF YOU FIND ONE, KILL IT ON THE SPOT.

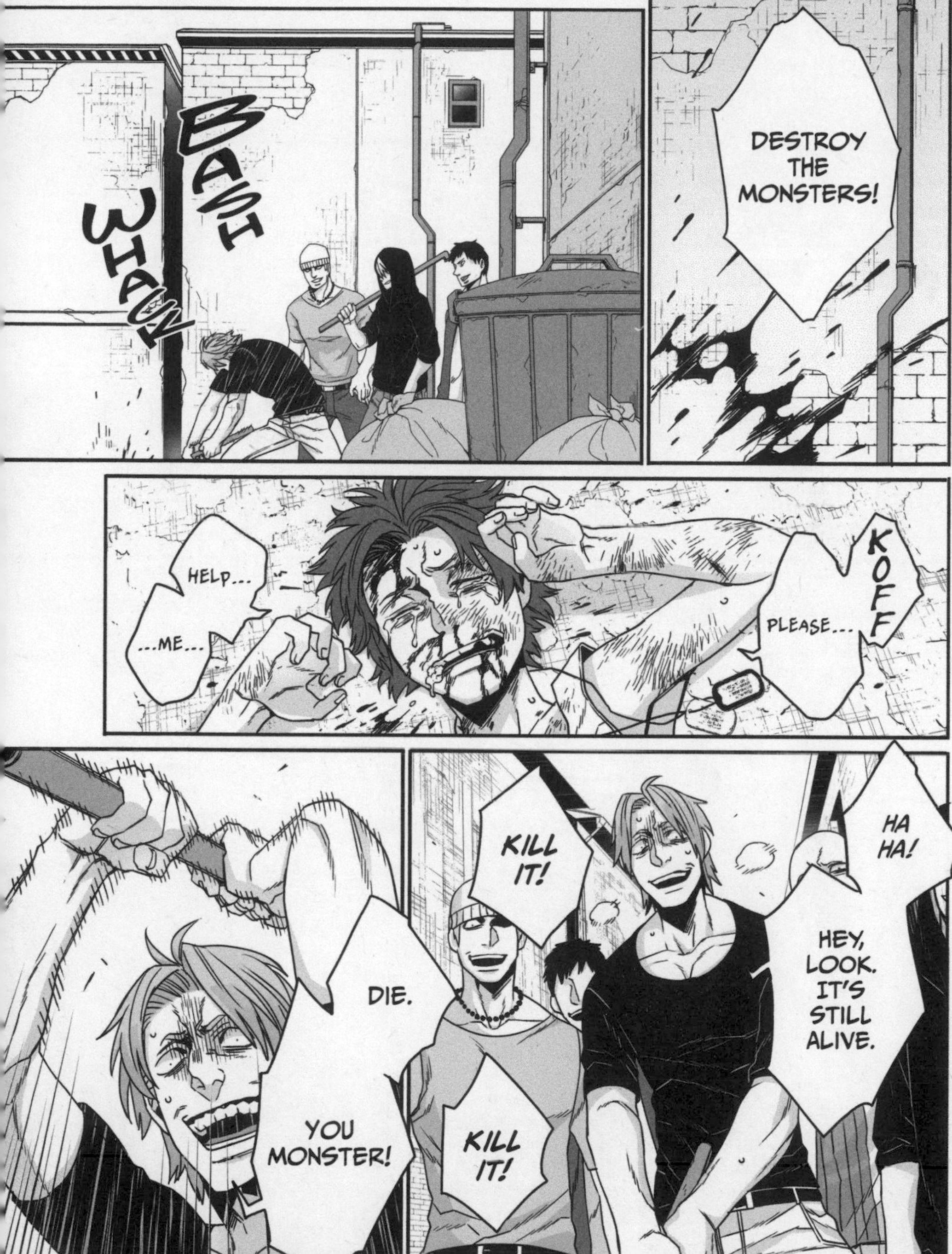
DESTROY THE MONSTERS!
BASH
WHACK
KOFF
PLEASE...
HELP...
...ME...
HA HA!
HEY, LOOK. IT'S STILL ALIVE.
KILL IT!
KILL IT!
DIE.
YOU MONSTER!

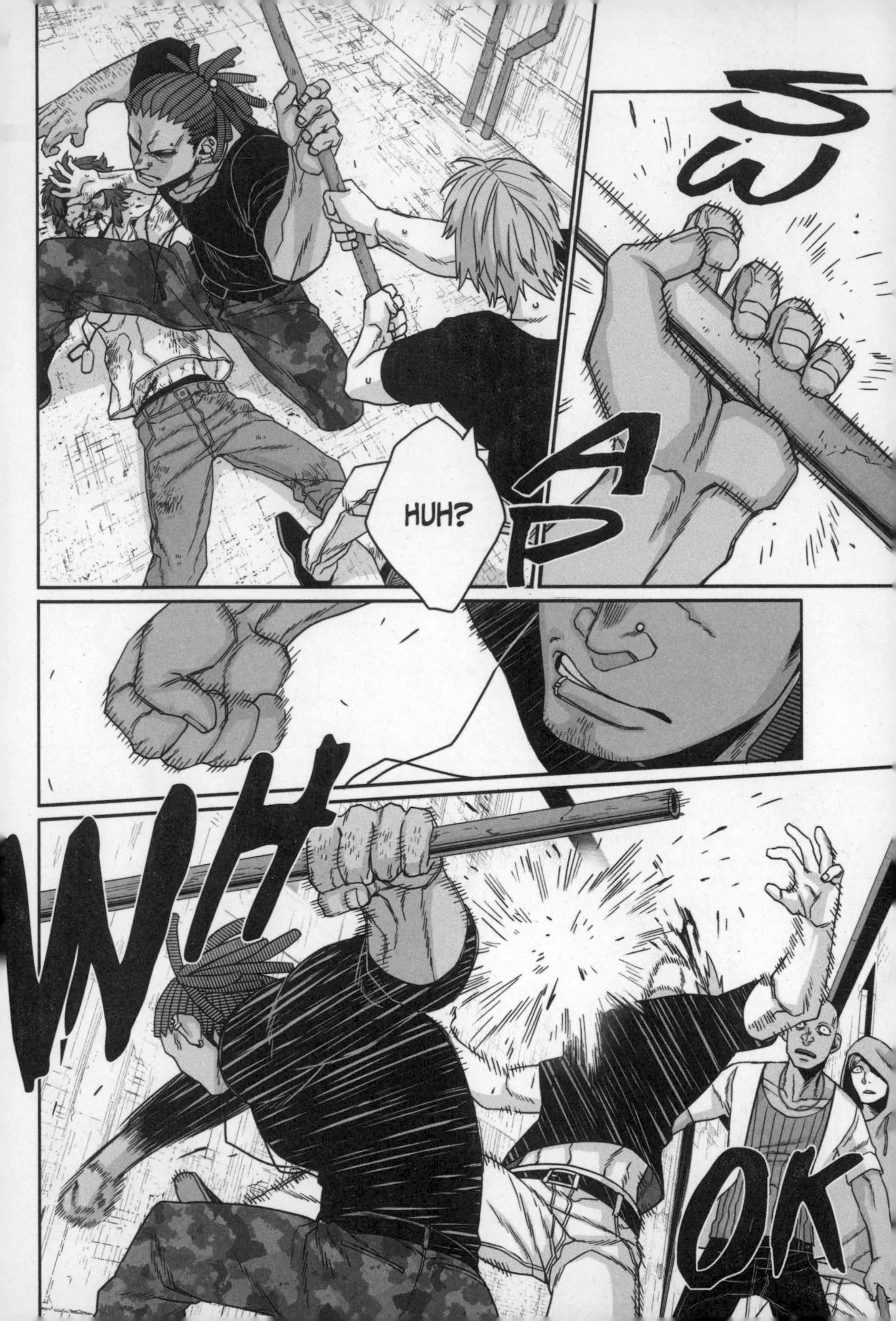
SWAP
HUH?
WH
OK

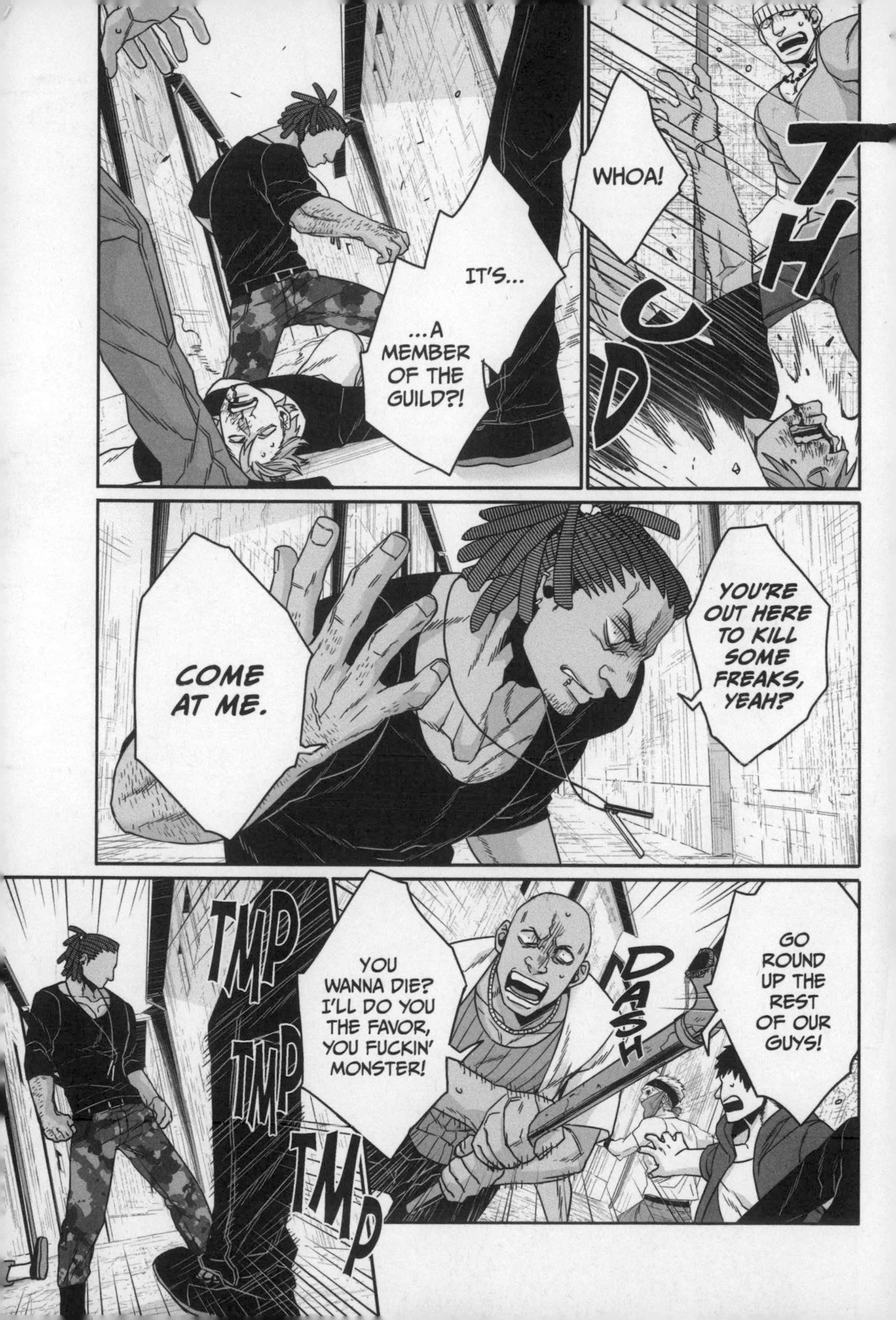
WHOA!
THUD
IT'S...
...A MEMBER OF THE GUILD?!
YOU'RE OUT HERE TO KILL SOME FREAKS, YEAH?
COME AT ME.
GO ROUND UP THE REST OF OUR GUYS!
DASH
YOU WANNA DIE? I'LL DO YOU THE FAVOR, YOU FUCKIN' MONSTER!
TMP
TMP
TMP

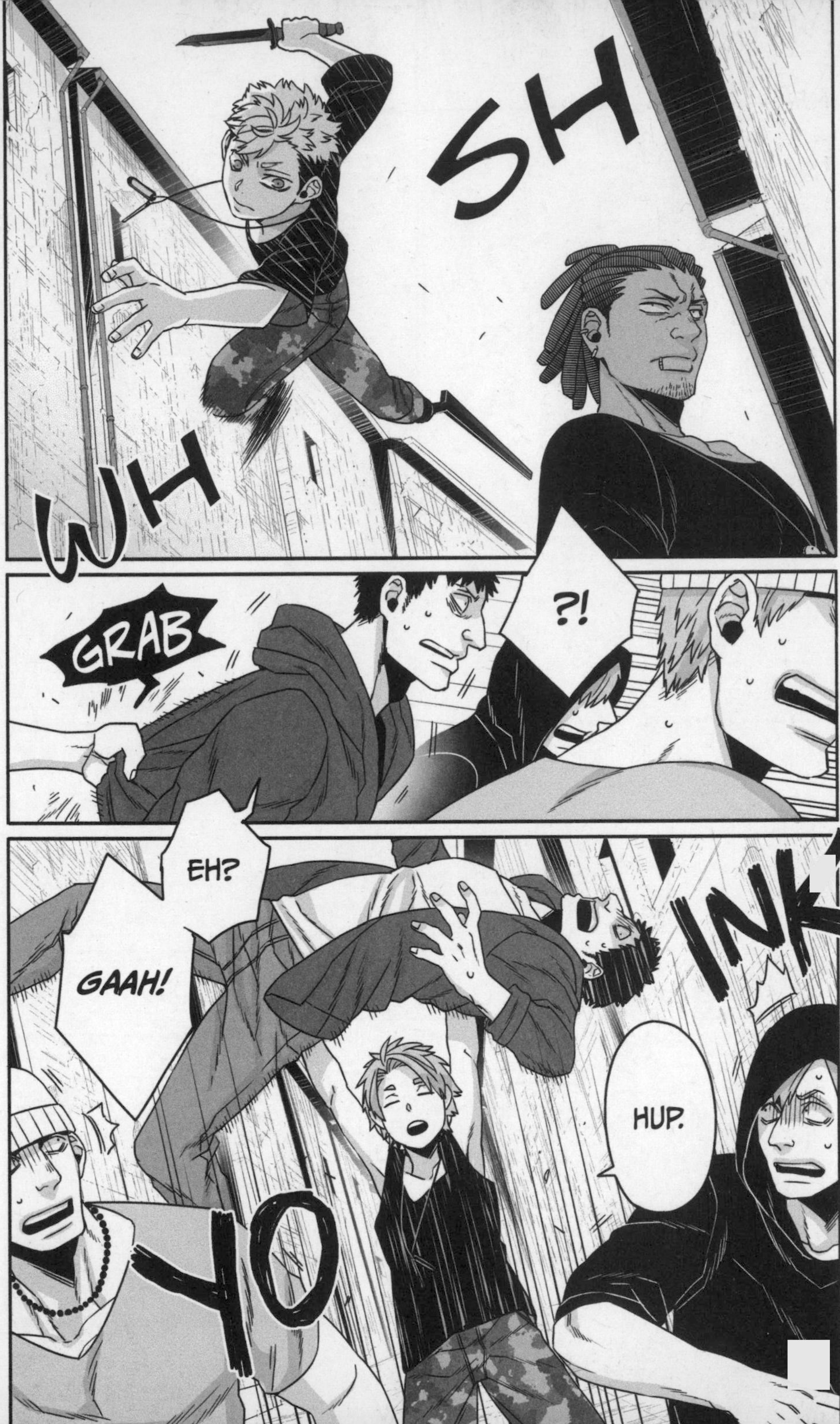
SH
WH
?!
GRAB
INK
HUP.
EH?
GAAH!
YO

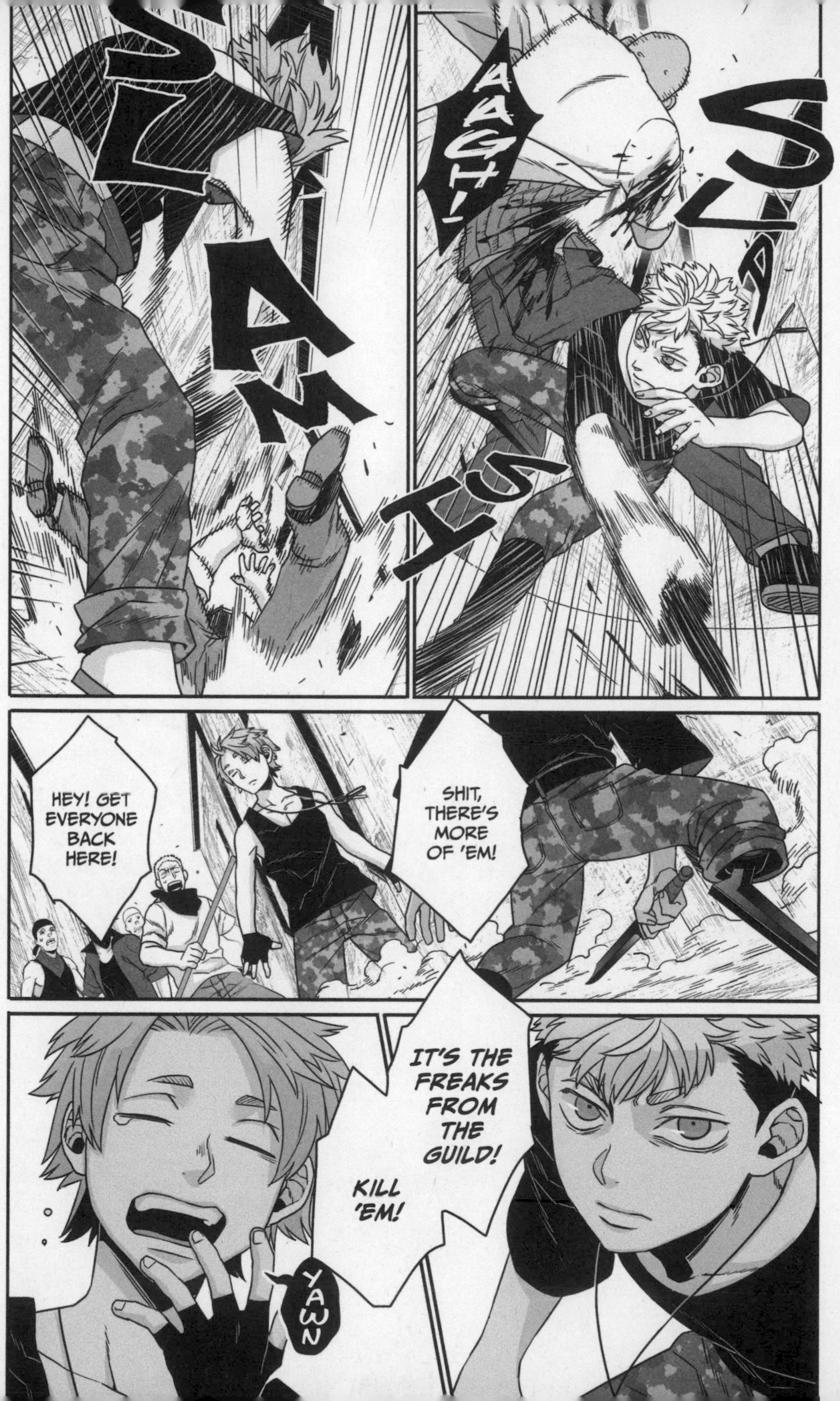
AAGH!
SLASH
SLAM
SHIT, THERE'S MORE OF 'EM!
HEY! GET EVERYONE BACK HERE!
IT'S THE FREAKS FROM THE GUILD!
KILL 'EM!
YAWN

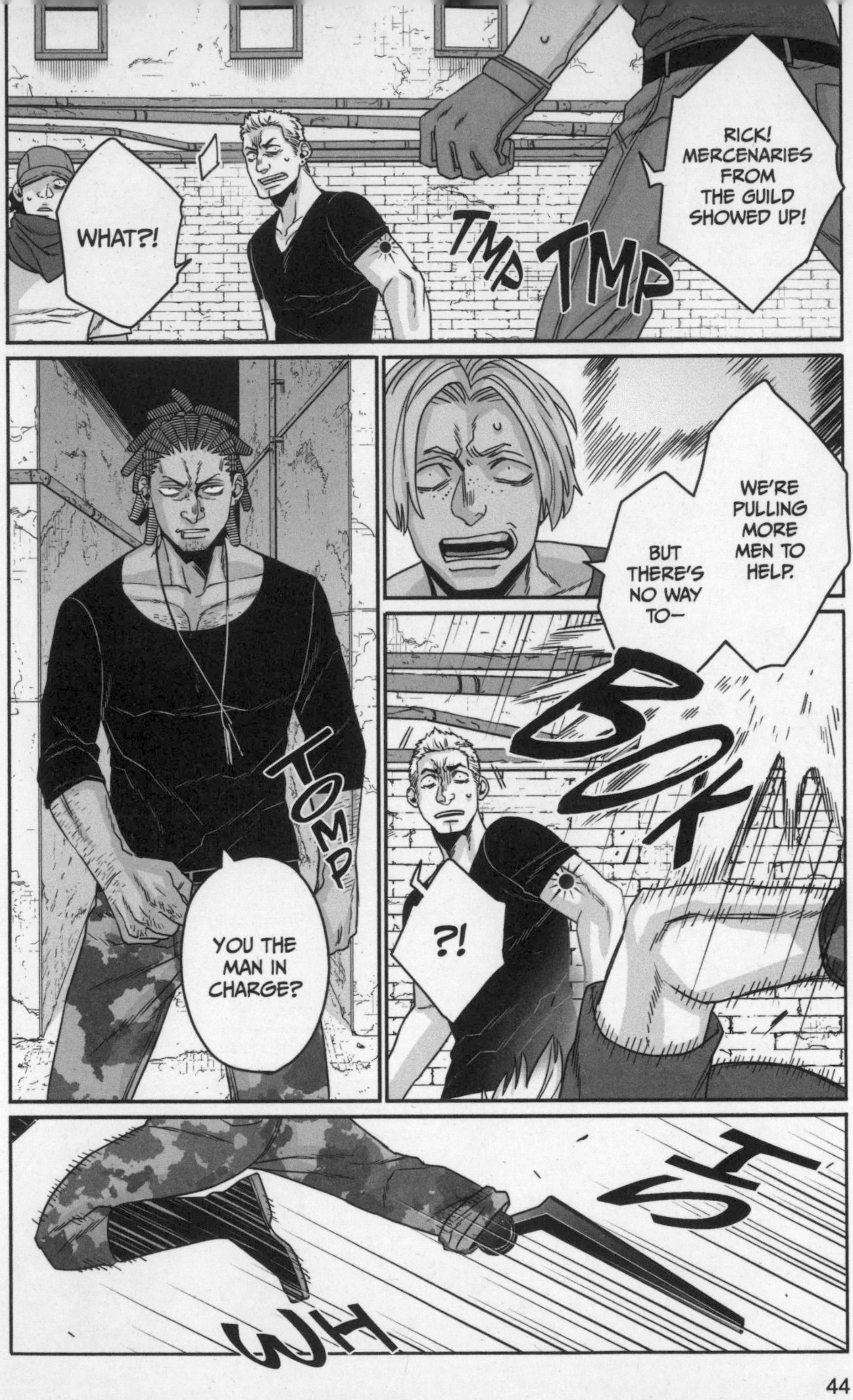
RICK! MERCENARIES FROM THE GUILD SHOWED UP!
TMP TMP
WHAT?!
WE'RE PULLING MORE MEN TO HELP.
BUT THERE'S NO WAY TO—
BOK
?!
TOMP
YOU THE MAN IN CHARGE?
SH
WH

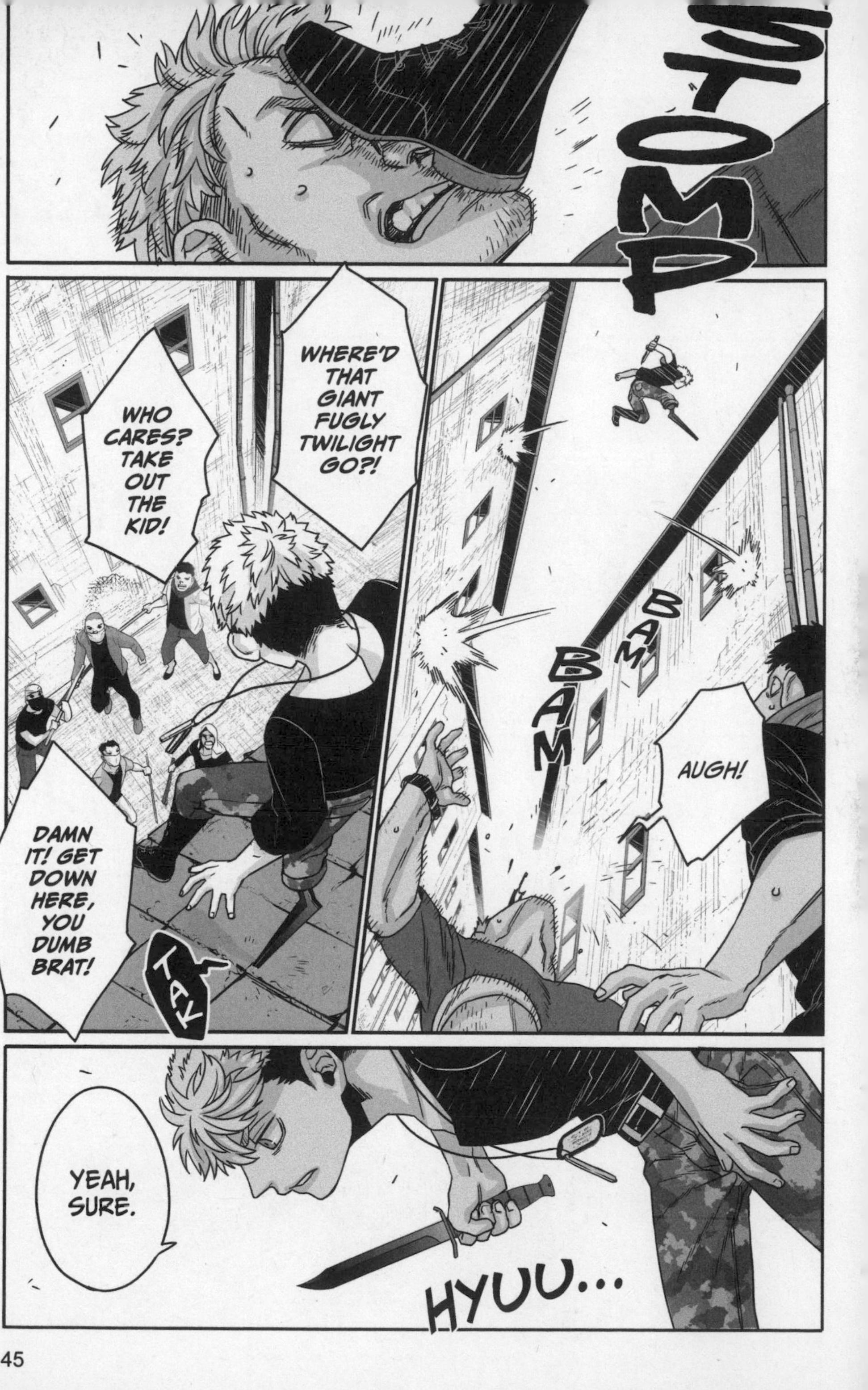
STOMP
BAM
BAM
AUGH!
WHERE'D THAT GIANT FUGLY TWILIGHT GO?!
WHO CARES? TAKE OUT THE KID!
DAMN IT! GET DOWN HERE, YOU DUMB BRAT!
TAK
HYUU...
YEAH, SURE.

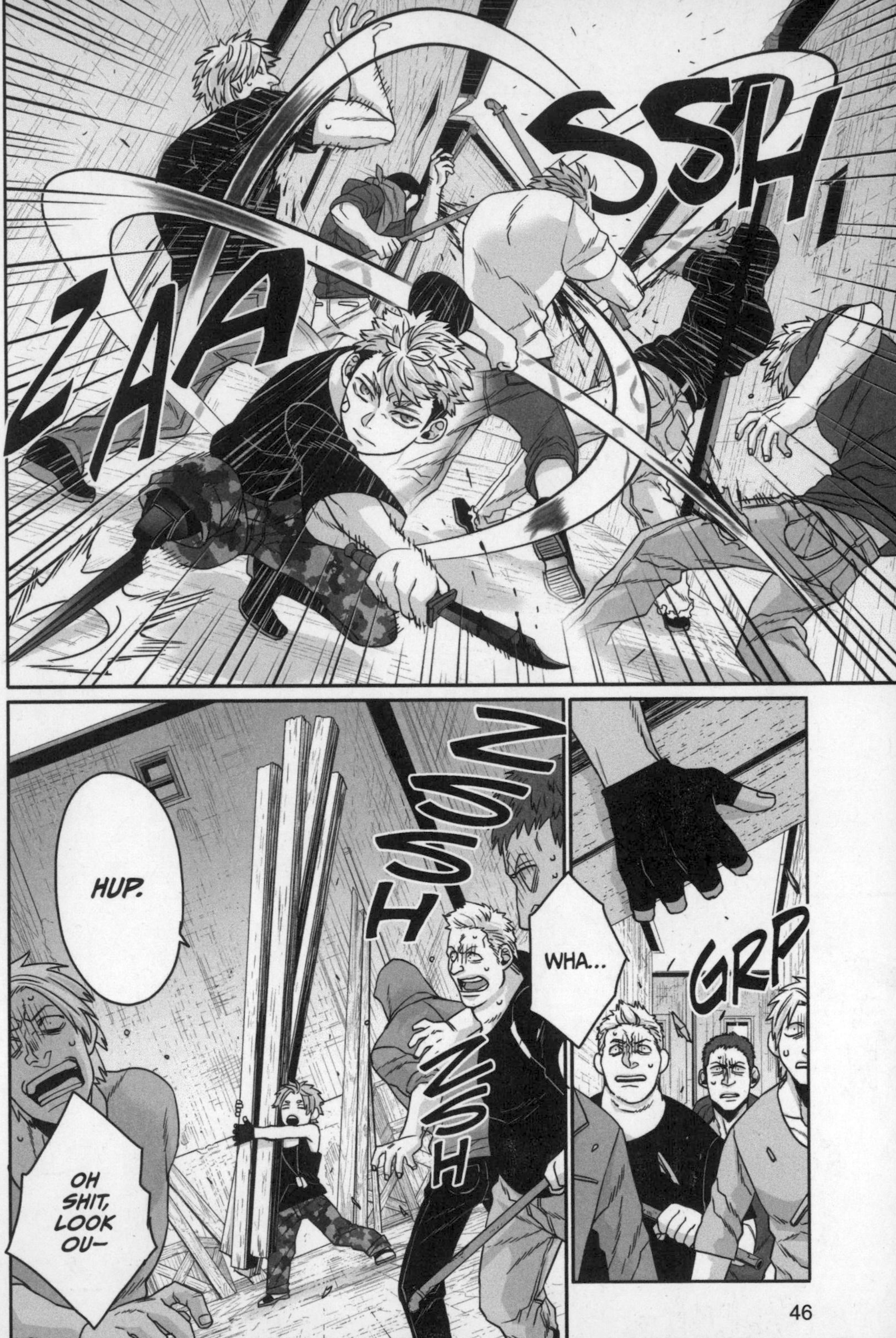
SSH
ZAA
GRP
WHA...
HUP.
WSSH
WSH
OH SHIT, LOOK OU—

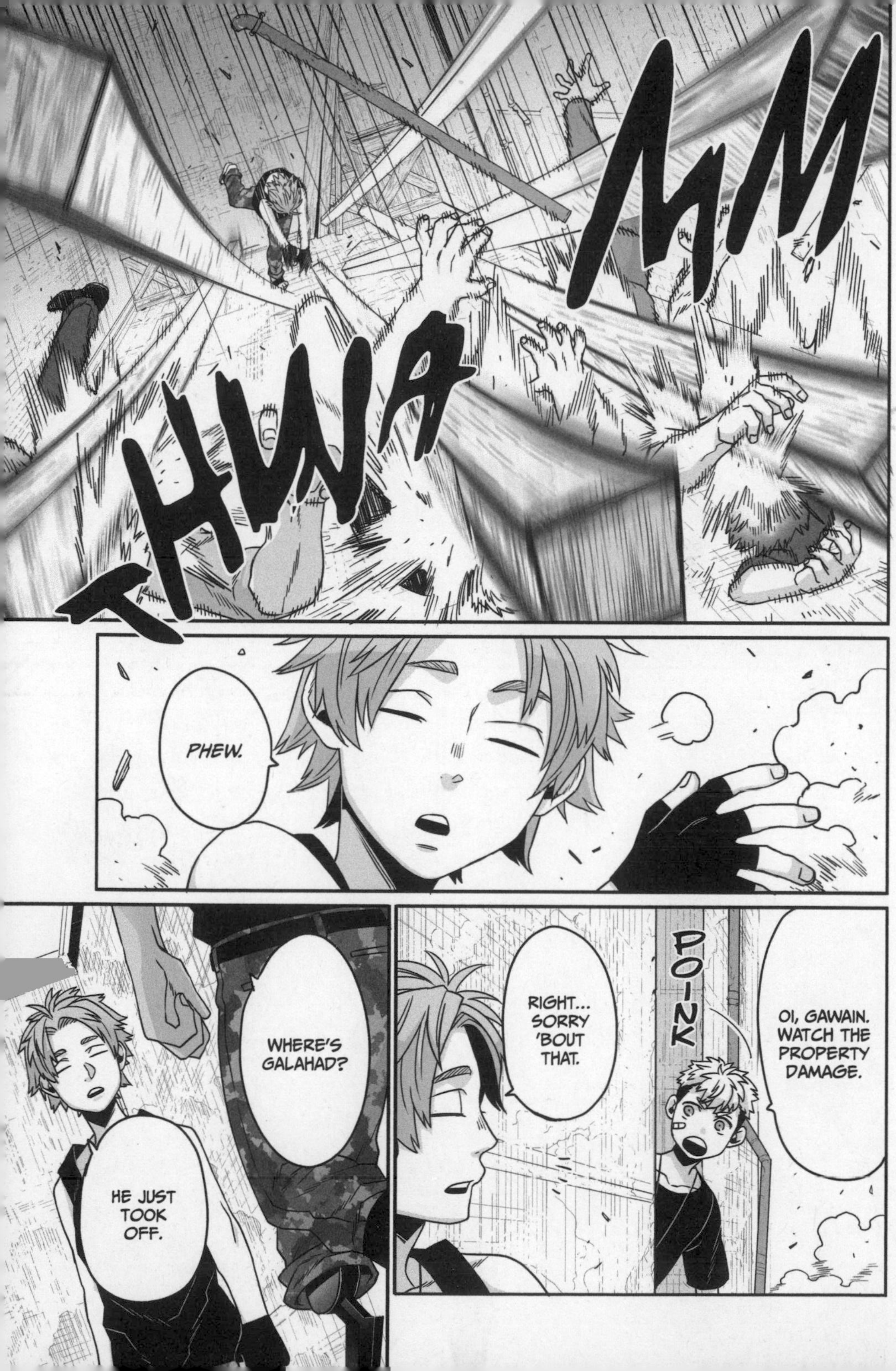
THWAMM
PHEW.
OI, GAWAIN. WATCH THE PROPERTY DAMAGE.
POINK
RIGHT... SORRY 'BOUT THAT.
WHERE'S GALAHAD?
HE JUST TOOK OFF.

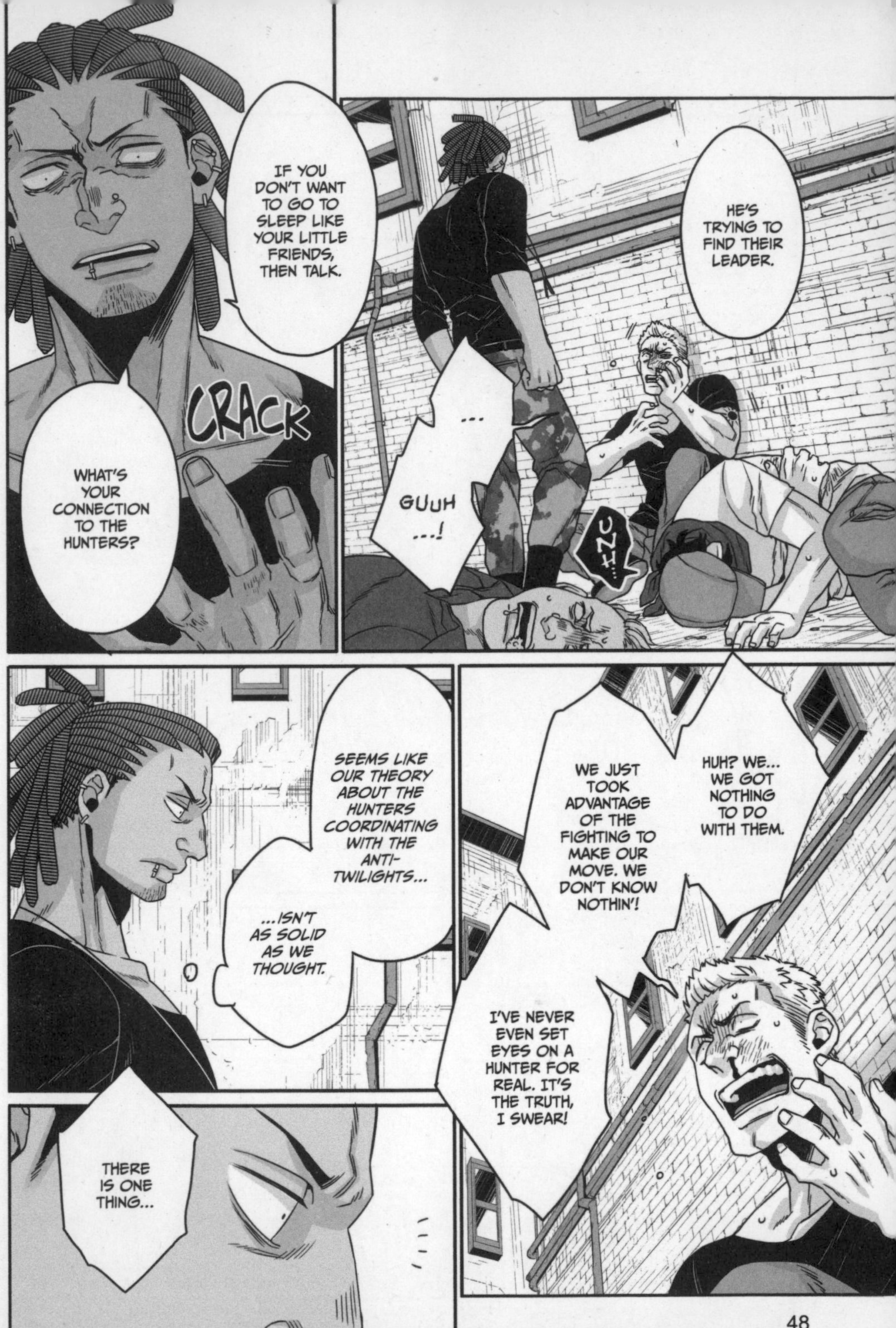
HE'S TRYING TO FIND THEIR LEADER.
...
GUUH ...!
UNH...
IF YOU DON'T WANT TO GO TO SLEEP LIKE YOUR LITTLE FRIENDS, THEN TALK.
CRACK
WHAT'S YOUR CONNECTION TO THE HUNTERS?
HUH? WE... WE GOT NOTHING TO DO WITH THEM.
WE JUST TOOK ADVANTAGE OF THE FIGHTING TO MAKE OUR MOVE. WE DON'T KNOW NOTHIN'!
I'VE NEVER EVEN SET EYES ON A HUNTER FOR REAL. IT'S THE TRUTH, I SWEAR!
SEEMS LIKE OUR THEORY ABOUT THE HUNTERS COORDINATING WITH THE ANTI-TWILIGHTS...
...ISN'T AS SOLID AS WE THOUGHT.
THERE IS ONE THING...

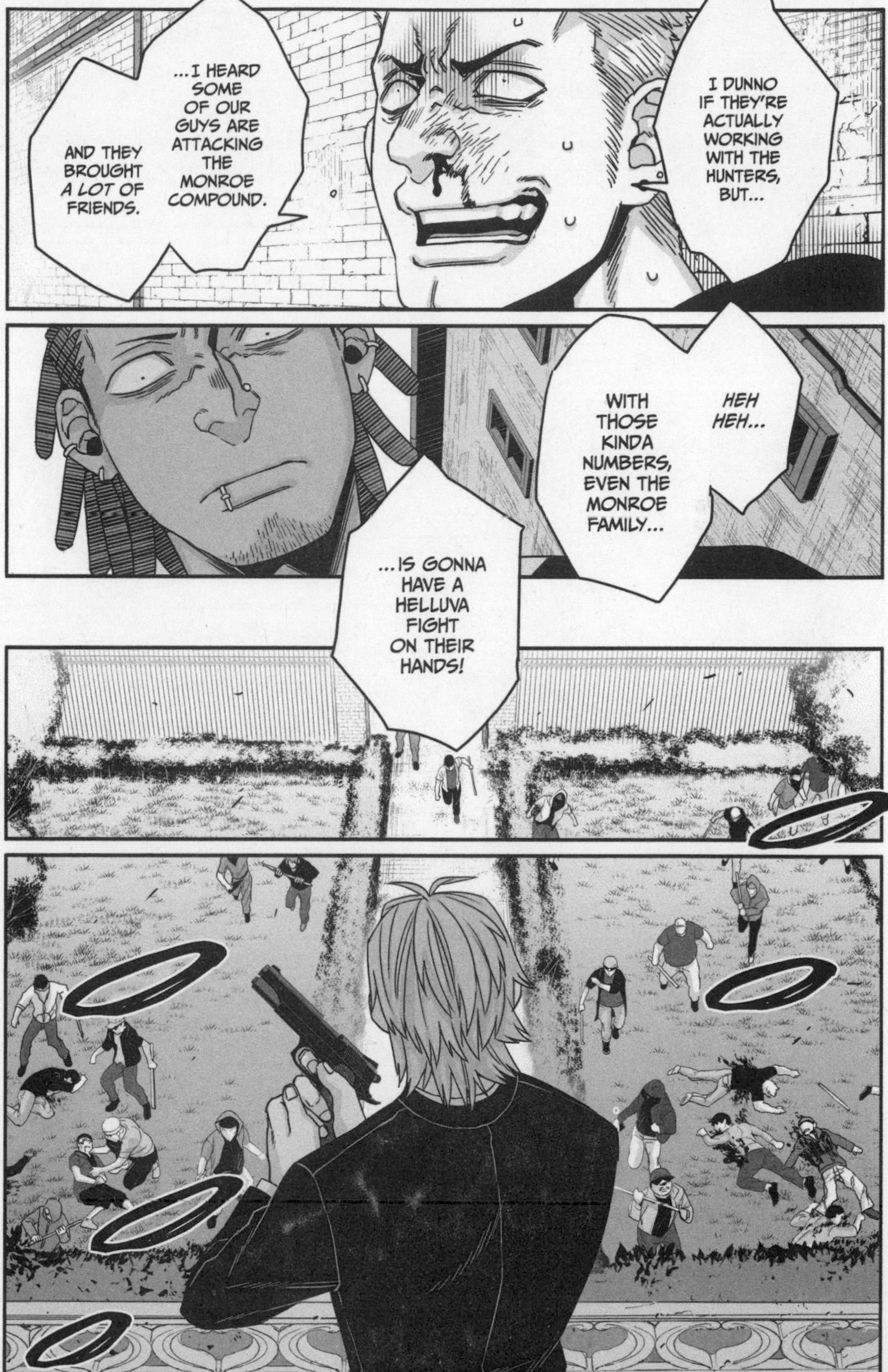
I DUNNO IF THEY'RE ACTUALLY WORKING WITH THE HUNTERS, BUT...
...I HEARD SOME OF OUR GUYS ARE ATTACKING THE MONROE COMPOUND.
AND THEY BROUGHT A LOT OF FRIENDS.
HEH HEH...
WITH THOSE KINDA NUMBERS, EVEN THE MONROE FAMILY...
...IS GONNA HAVE A HELLUVA FIGHT ON THEIR HANDS!

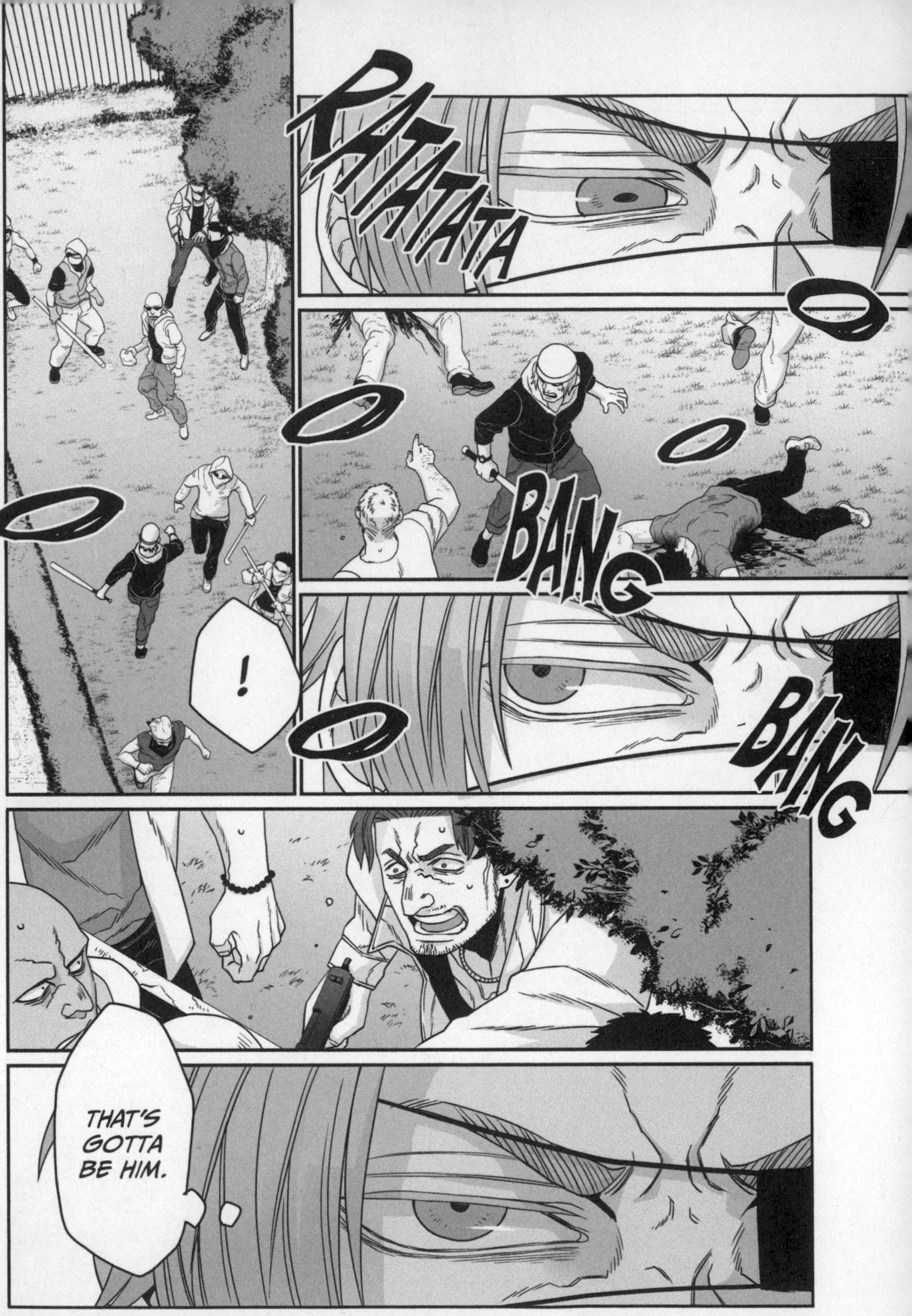
RATATATATA
BANG
BANG
!
THAT'S GOTTA BE HIM.

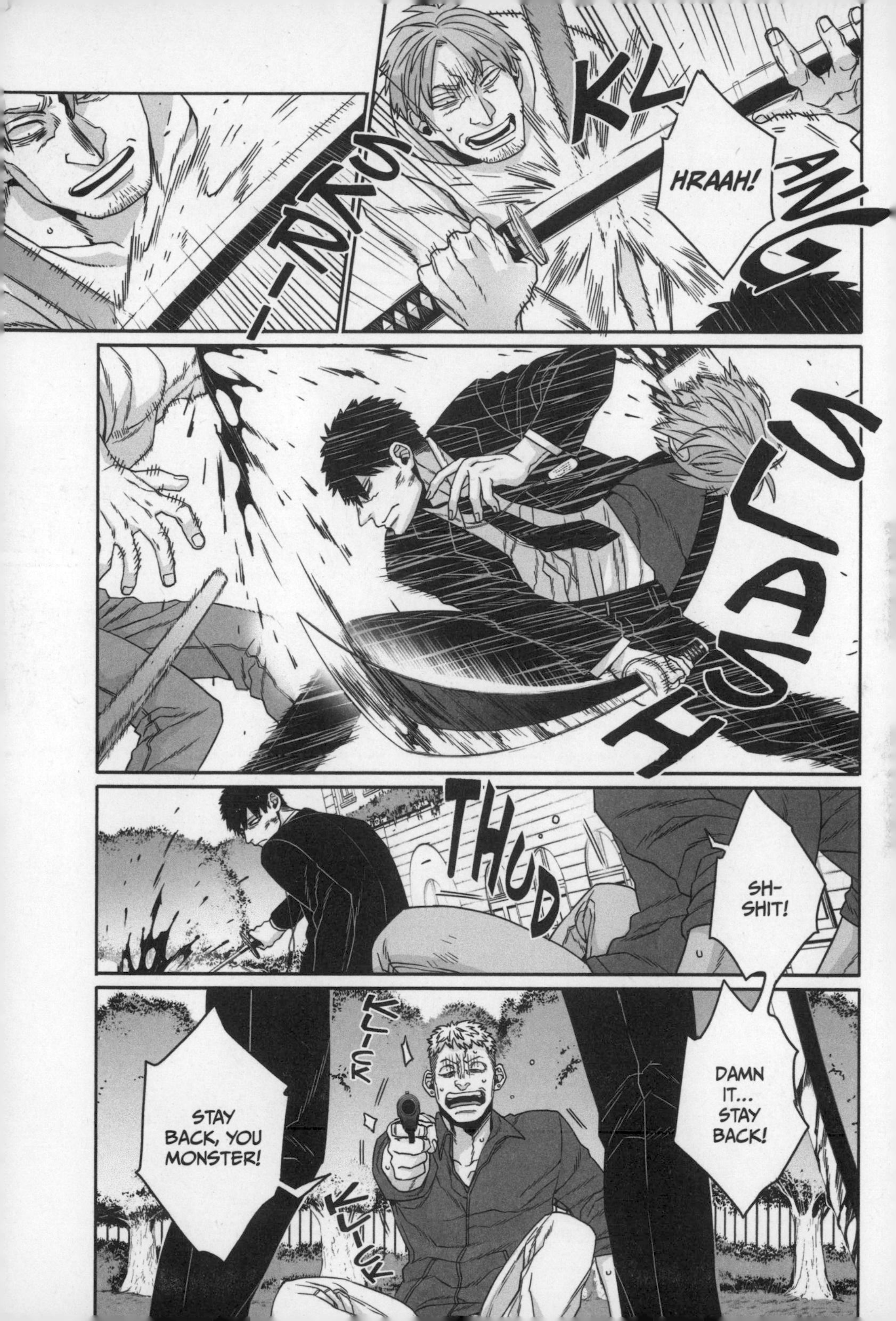
HRAAH!
KLANG
SLASH
THUD
SH-SHIT!
DAMN IT... STAY BACK!
KLICK
STAY BACK, YOU MONSTER!
KLICK

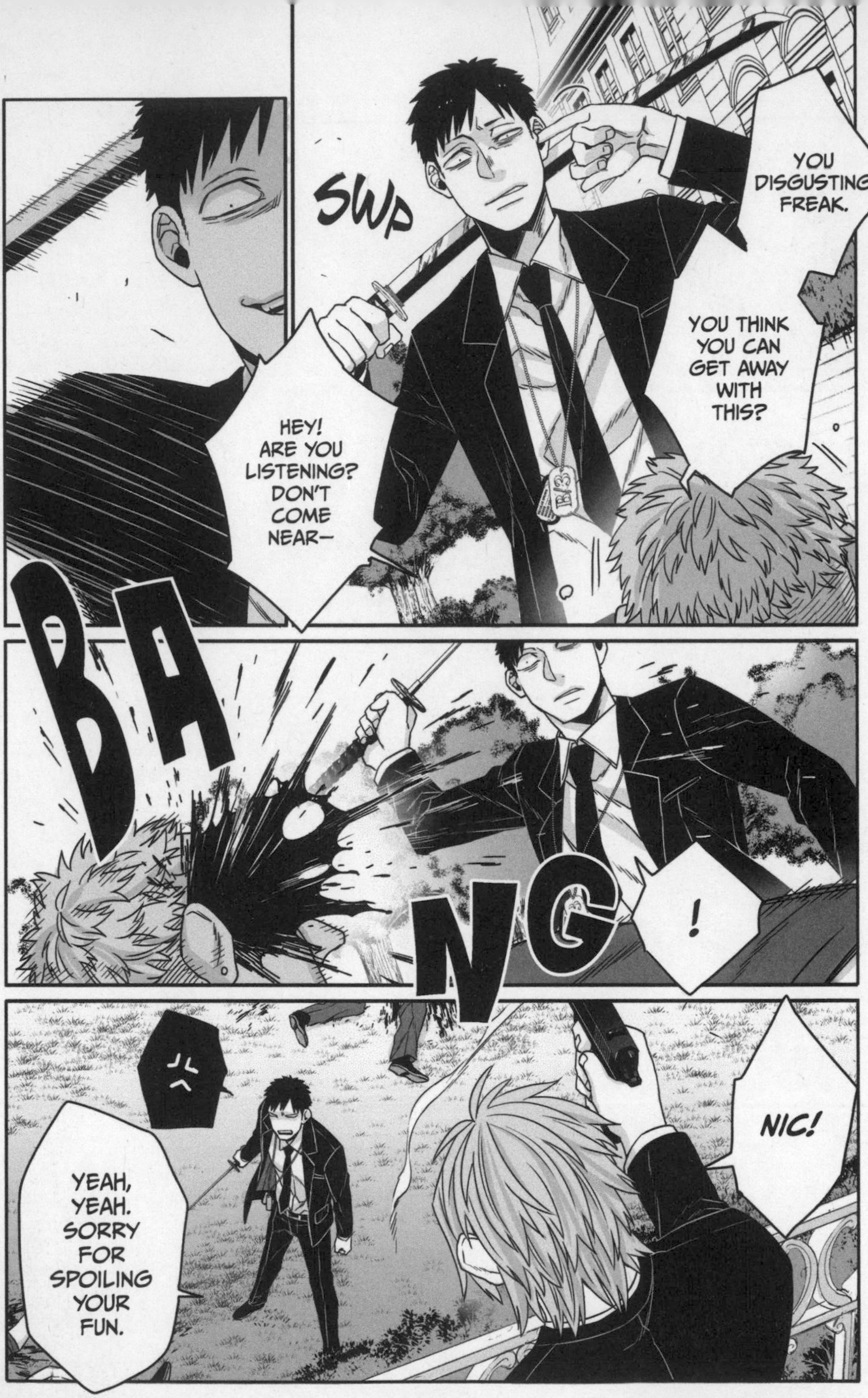
YOU DISGUSTING FREAK.
YOU THINK YOU CAN GET AWAY WITH THIS?
SWP
HEY! ARE YOU LISTENING? DON'T COME NEAR—
BANG
!
NIC!
YEAH, YEAH. SORRY FOR SPOILING YOUR FUN.

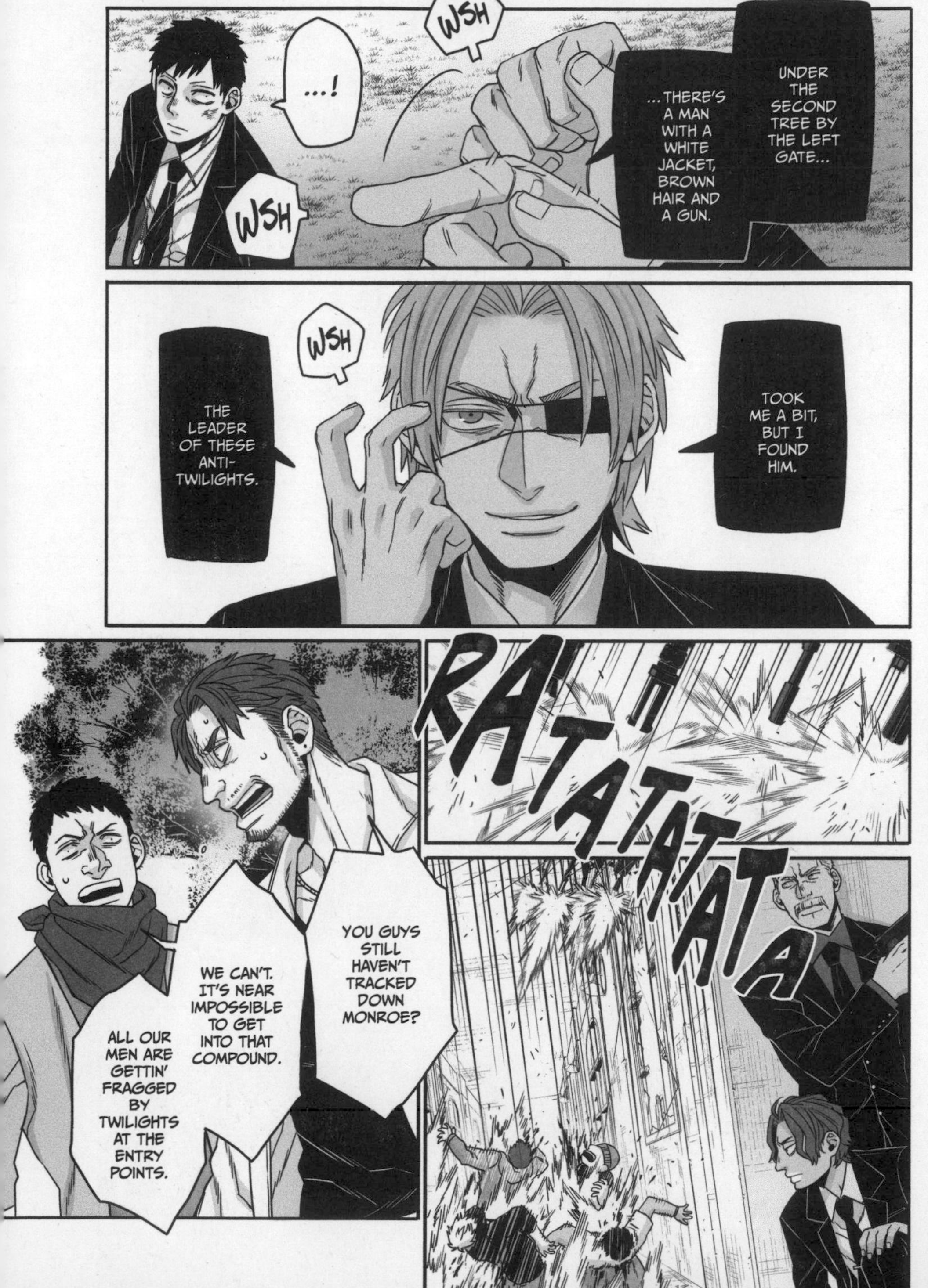
UNDER THE SECOND TREE BY THE LEFT GATE...
...THERE'S A MAN WITH A WHITE JACKET, BROWN HAIR AND A GUN.
WSH
...!
WSH
TOOK ME A BIT, BUT I FOUND HIM.
WSH
THE LEADER OF THESE ANTI-TWILIGHTS.
RATATATATATATA
YOU GUYS STILL HAVEN'T TRACKED DOWN MONROE?
WE CAN'T. IT'S NEAR IMPOSSIBLE TO GET INTO THAT COMPOUND.
ALL OUR MEN ARE GETTIN' FRAGGED BY TWILIGHTS AT THE ENTRY POINTS.

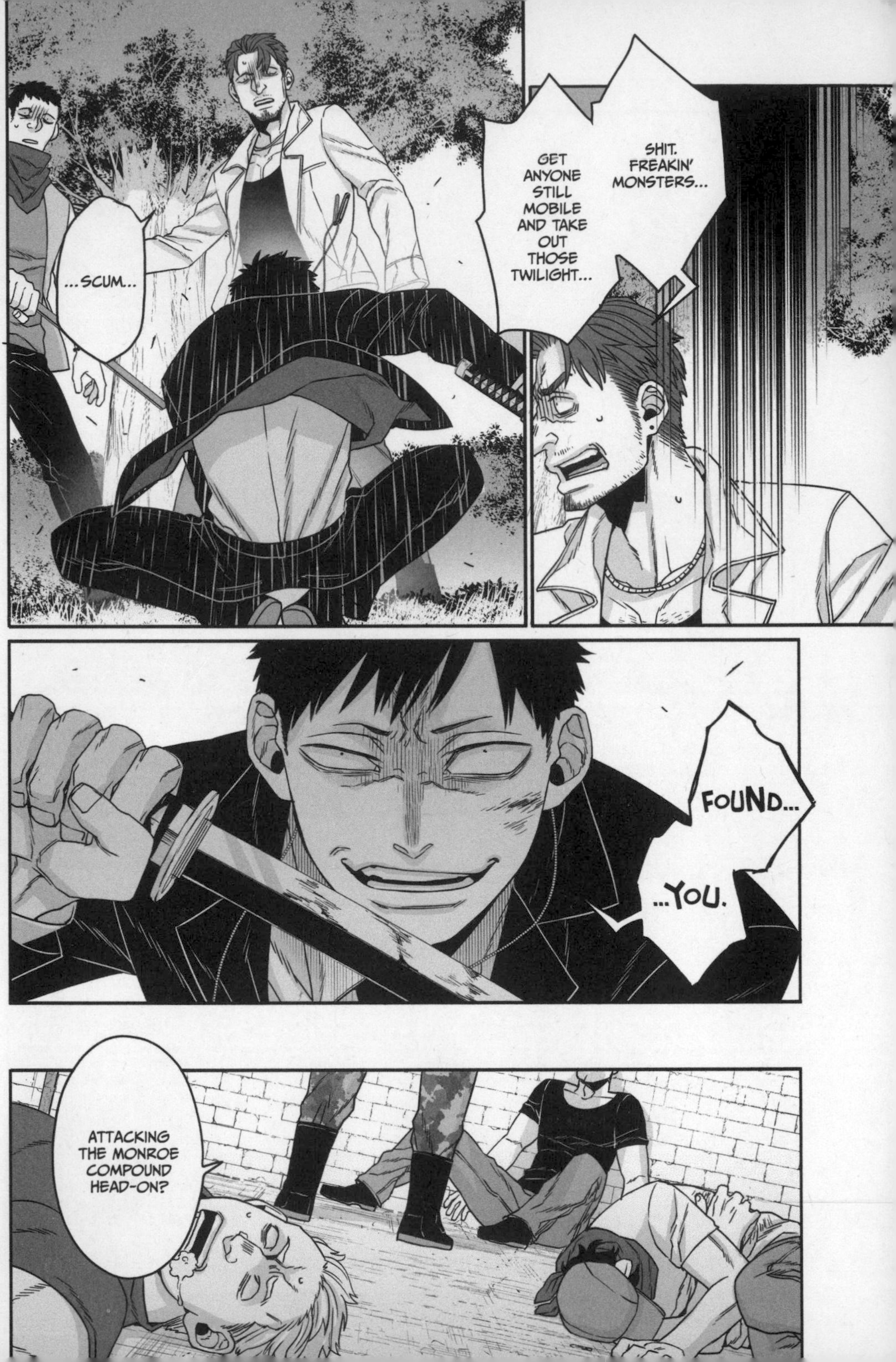
SHIT. FREAKIN' MONSTERS...
GET ANYONE STILL MOBILE AND TAKE OUT THOSE TWILIGHT...
...SCUM...
FOUND...
...YOU.
ATTACKING THE MONROE COMPOUND HEAD-ON?

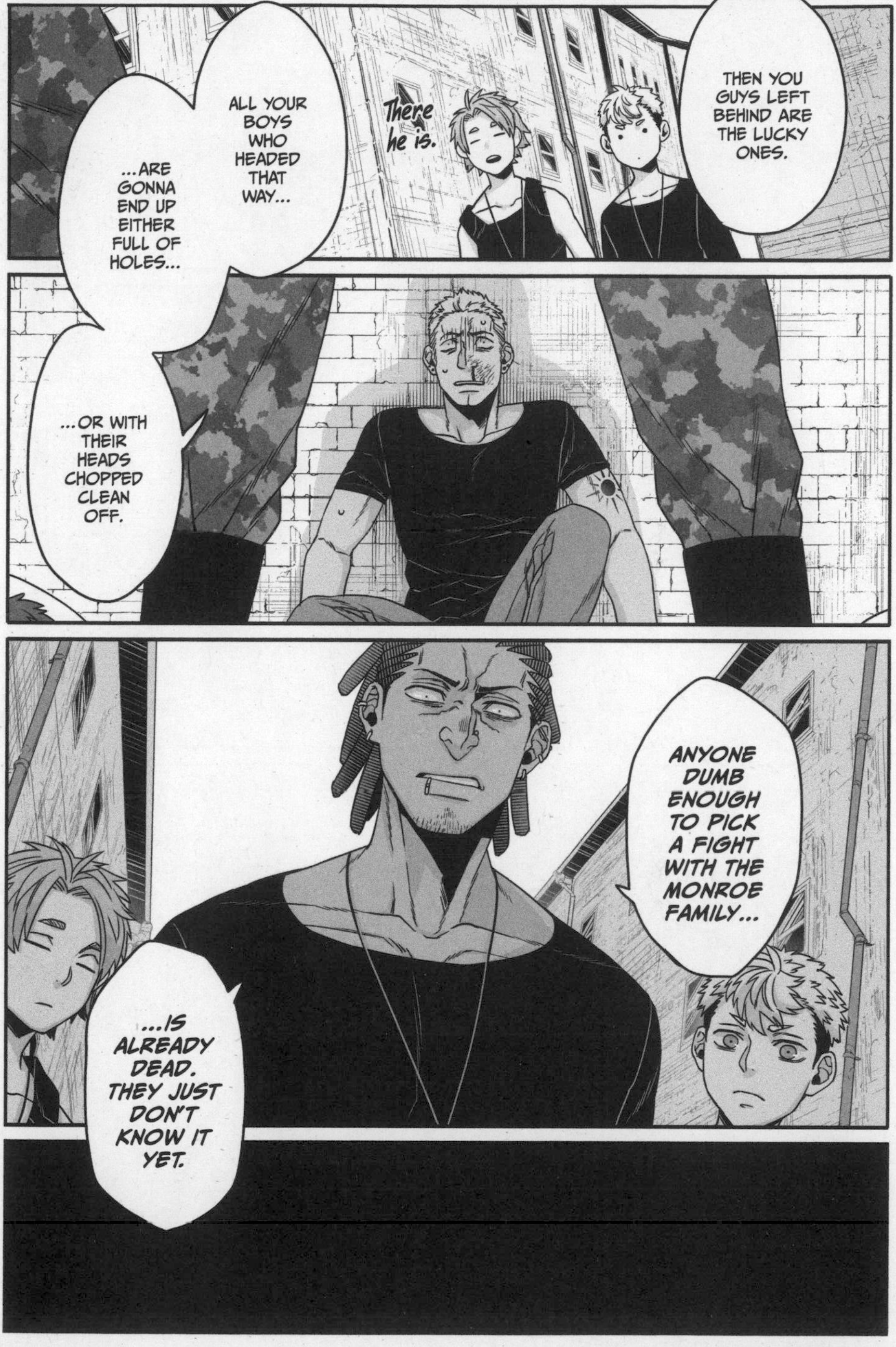
THEN YOU GUYS LEFT BEHIND ARE THE LUCKY ONES.
There he is.
ALL YOUR BOYS WHO HEADED THAT WAY...
...ARE GONNA END UP EITHER FULL OF HOLES...
...OR WITH THEIR HEADS CHOPPED CLEAN OFF.
ANYONE DUMB ENOUGH TO PICK A FIGHT WITH THE MONROE FAMILY...
...IS ALREADY DEAD. THEY JUST DON'T KNOW IT YET.

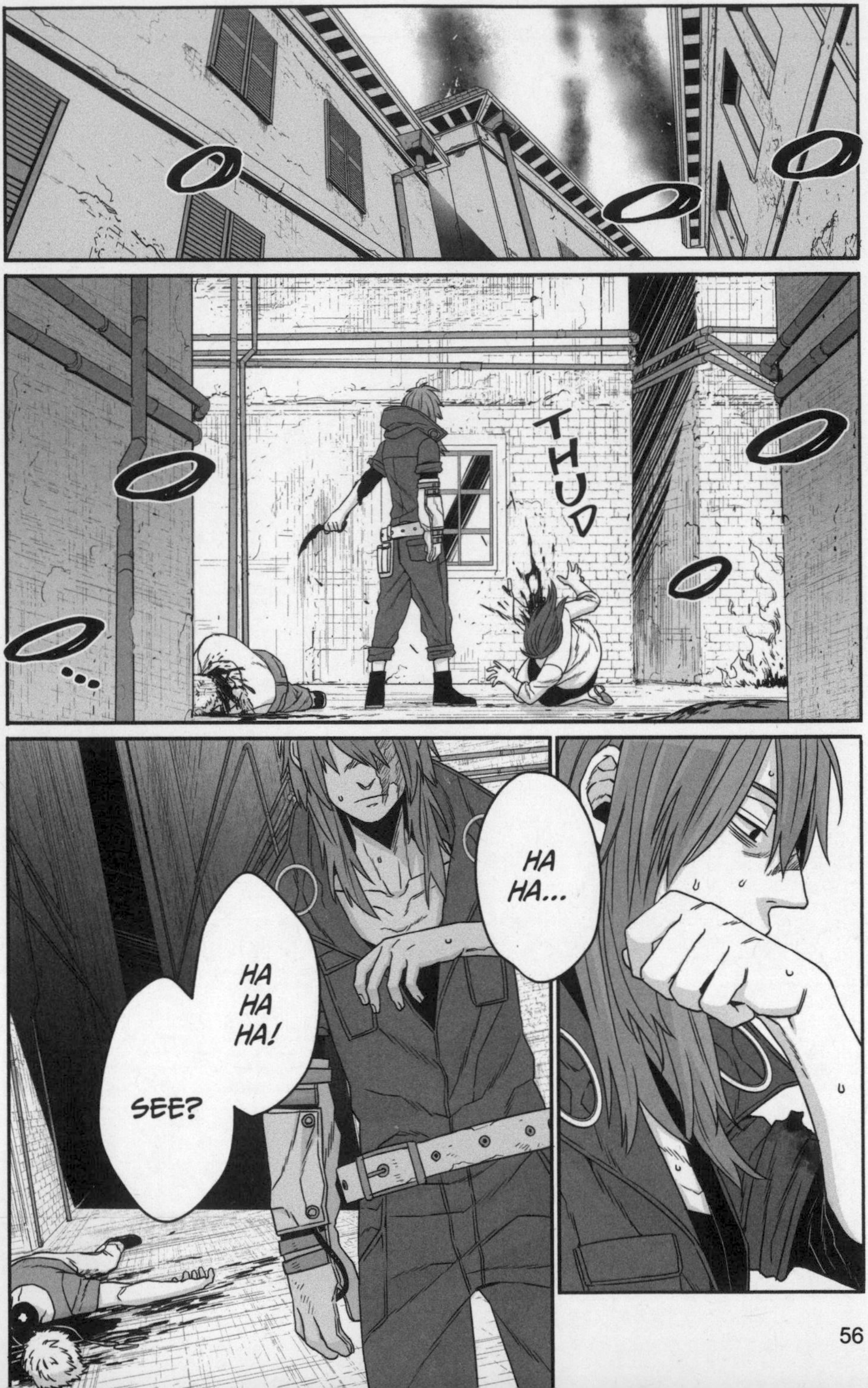
THUD
HA HA...
HA HA HA!
SEE?

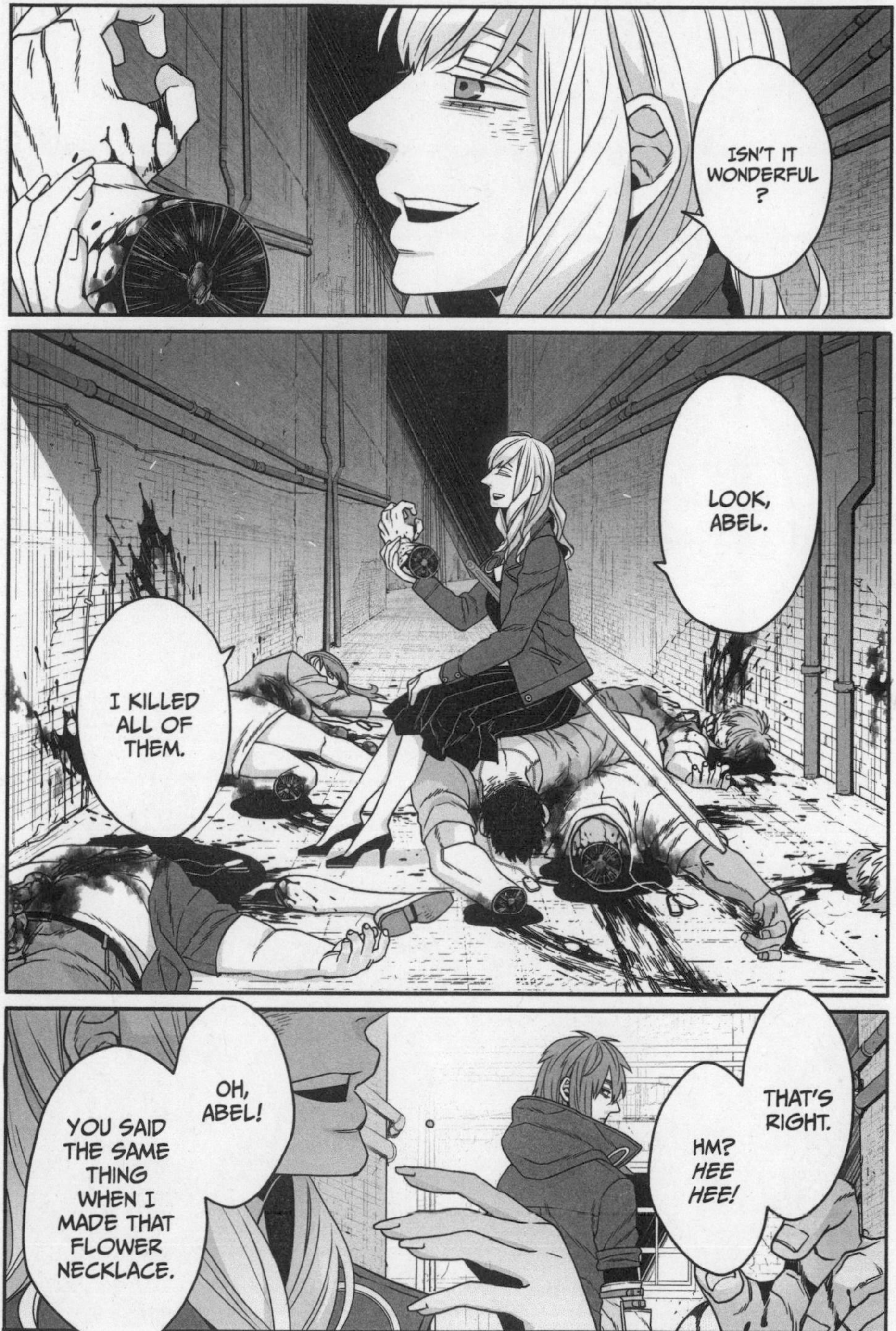
ISN'T IT WONDERFUL ?
LOOK, ABEL.
I KILLED ALL OF THEM.
THAT'S RIGHT. HM? HEE HEE!
OH, ABEL! YOU SAID THE SAME THING WHEN I MADE THAT FLOWER NECKLACE.

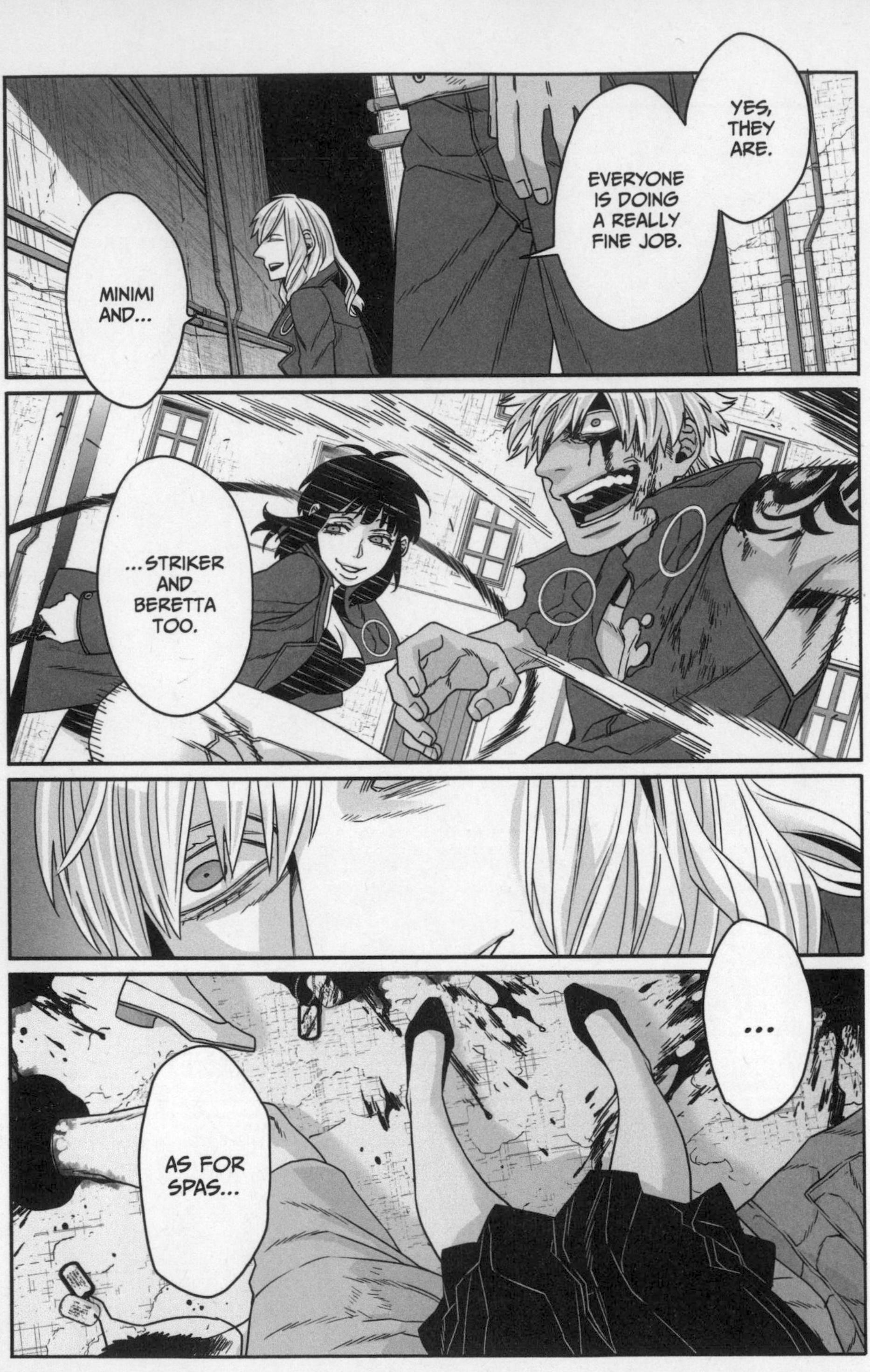
YES, THEY ARE.
EVERYONE IS DOING A REALLY FINE JOB.
MINIMI AND...
...STRIKER AND BERETTA TOO.
...
AS FOR SPAS...

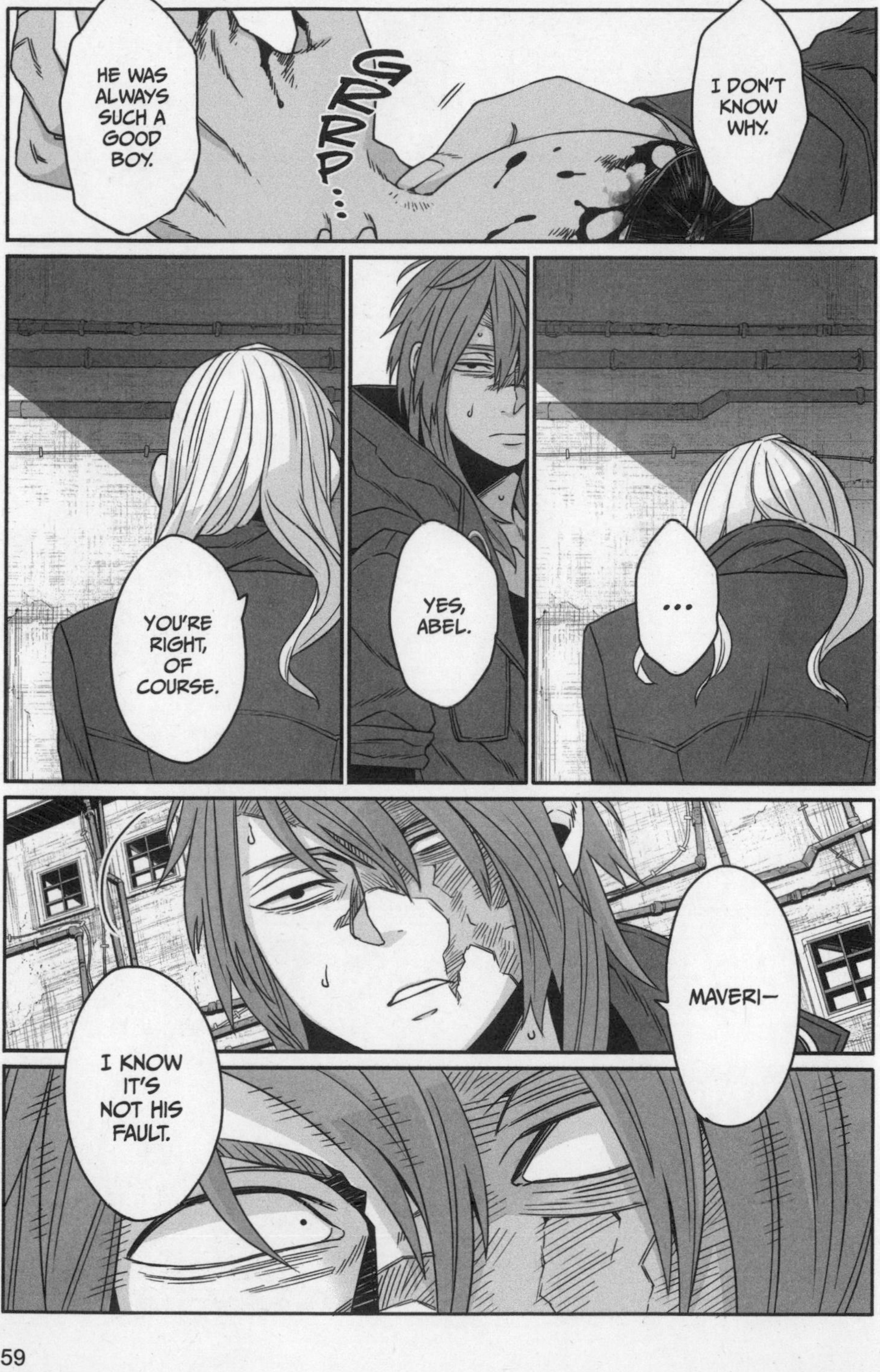
I DON'T KNOW WHY.
GRRP...
HE WAS ALWAYS SUCH A GOOD BOY.
...
YES, ABEL.
YOU'RE RIGHT, OF COURSE.
MAVERI—
I KNOW IT'S NOT HIS FAULT.

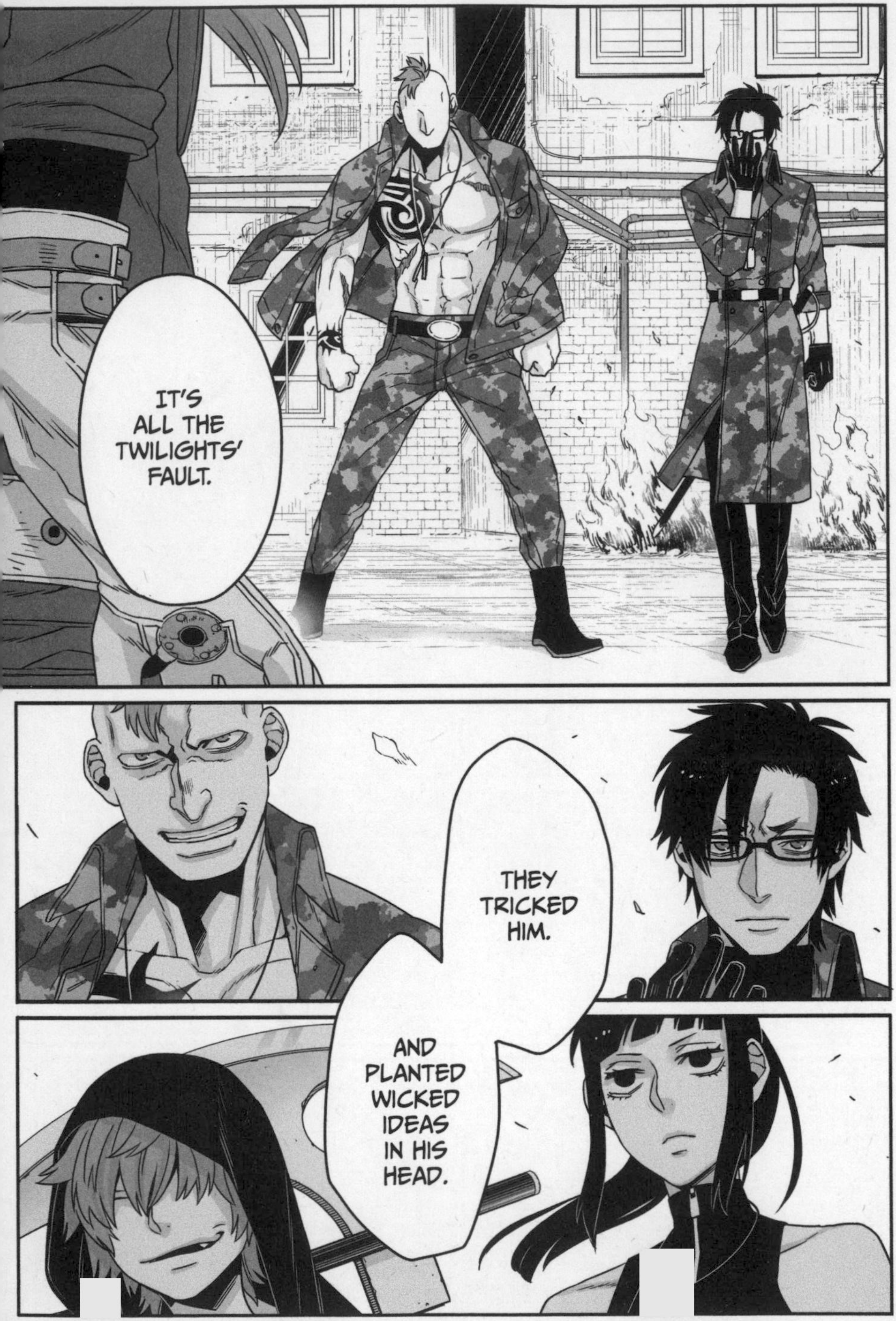
IT'S ALL THE TWILIGHTS' FAULT.
THEY TRICKED HIM.
AND PLANTED WICKED IDEAS IN HIS HEAD.

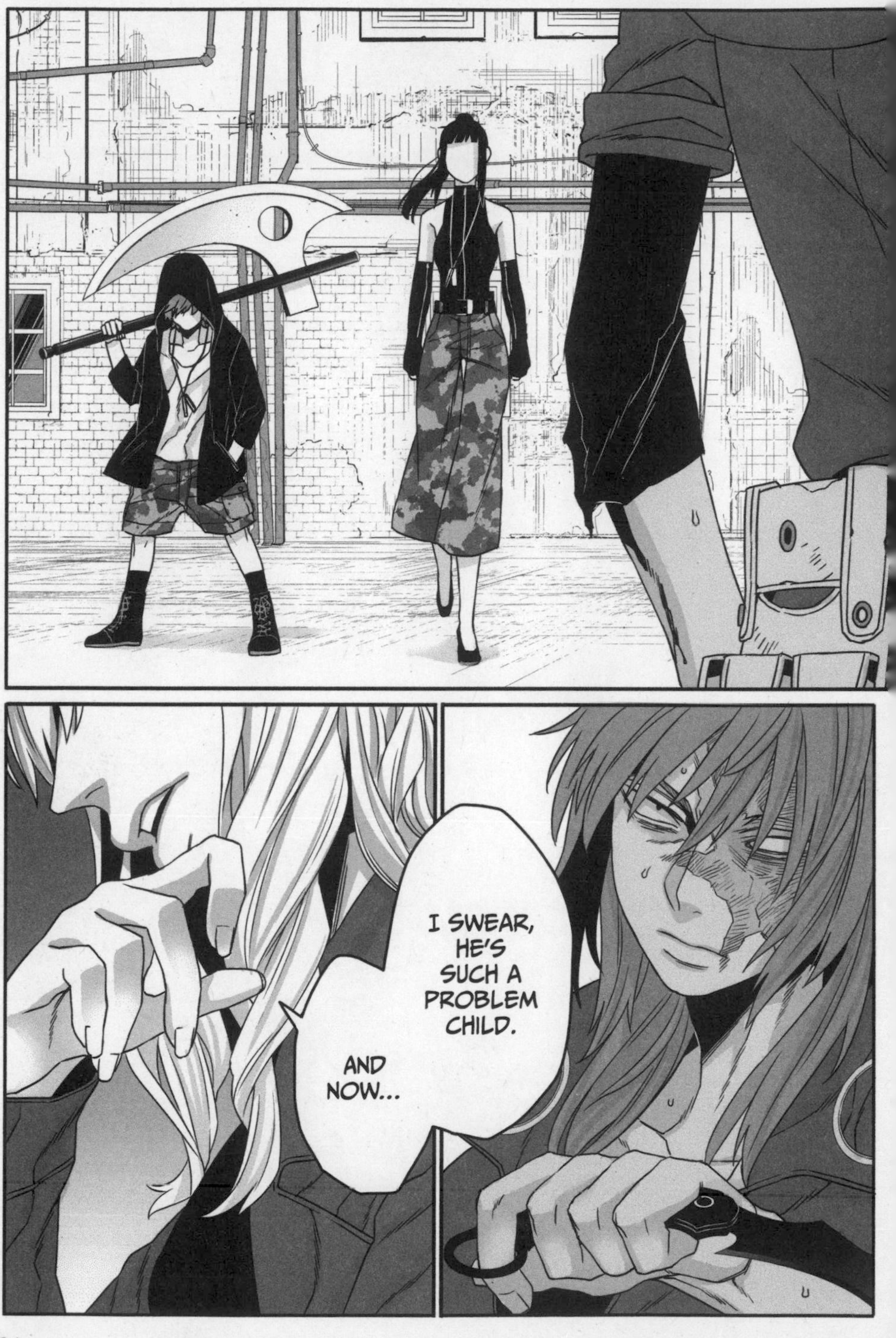
I SWEAR, HE'S SUCH A PROBLEM CHILD.
AND NOW...

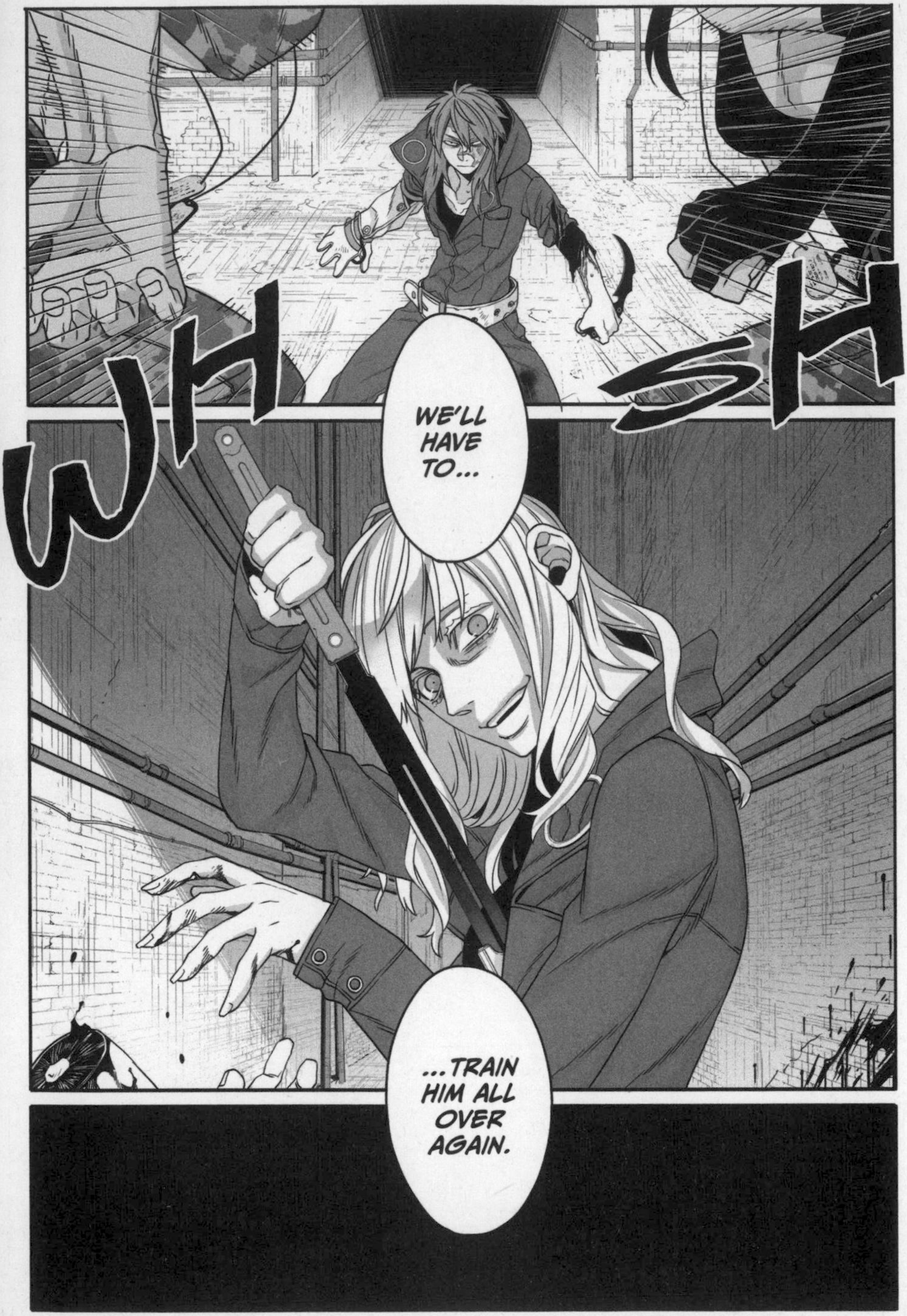
WHSH
WE'LL HAVE TO...
...TRAIN HIM ALL OVER AGAIN.

#07 END

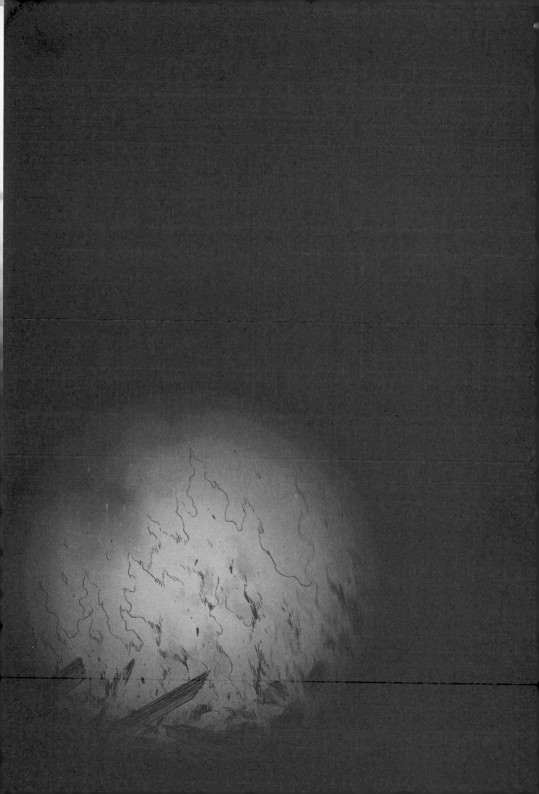

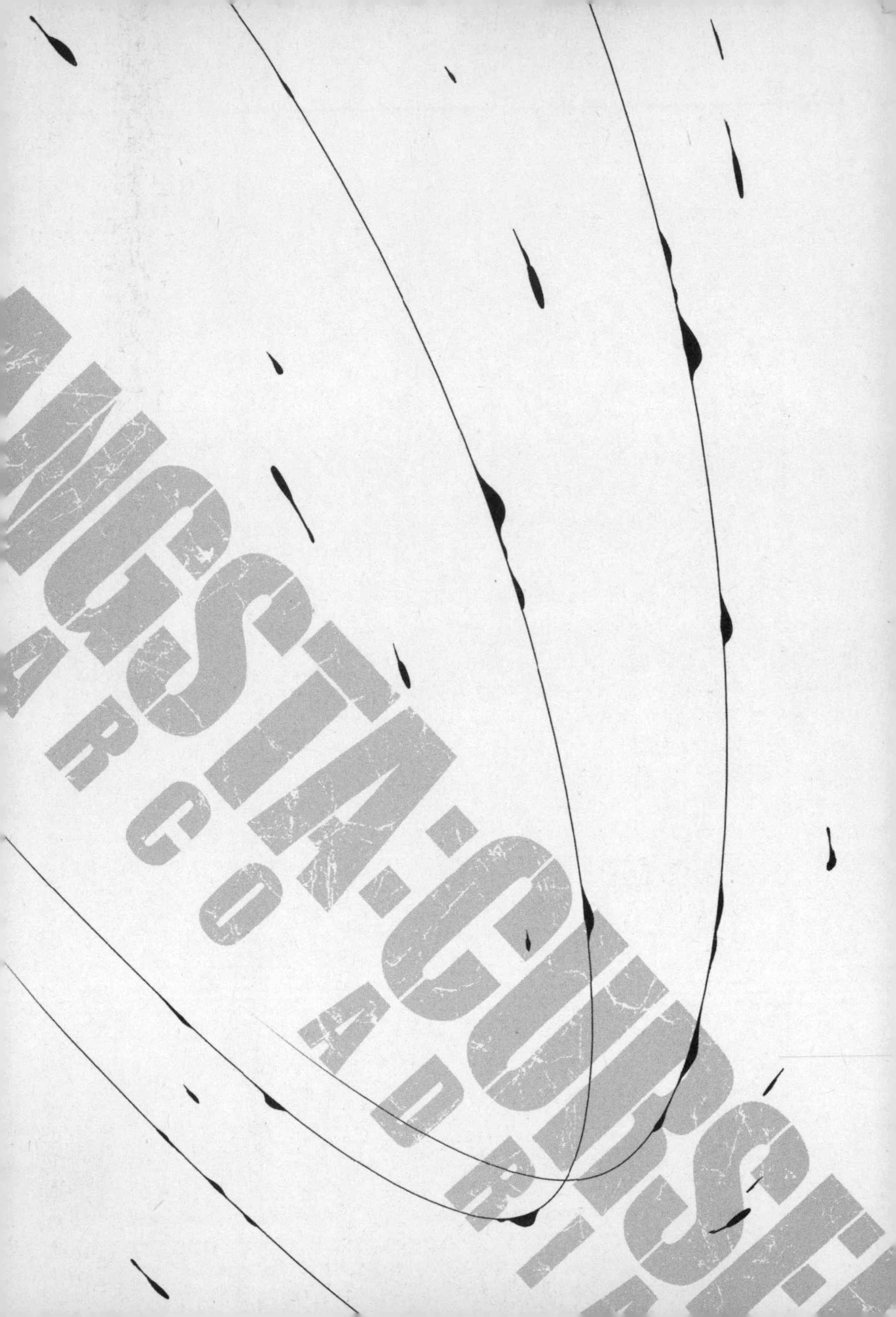

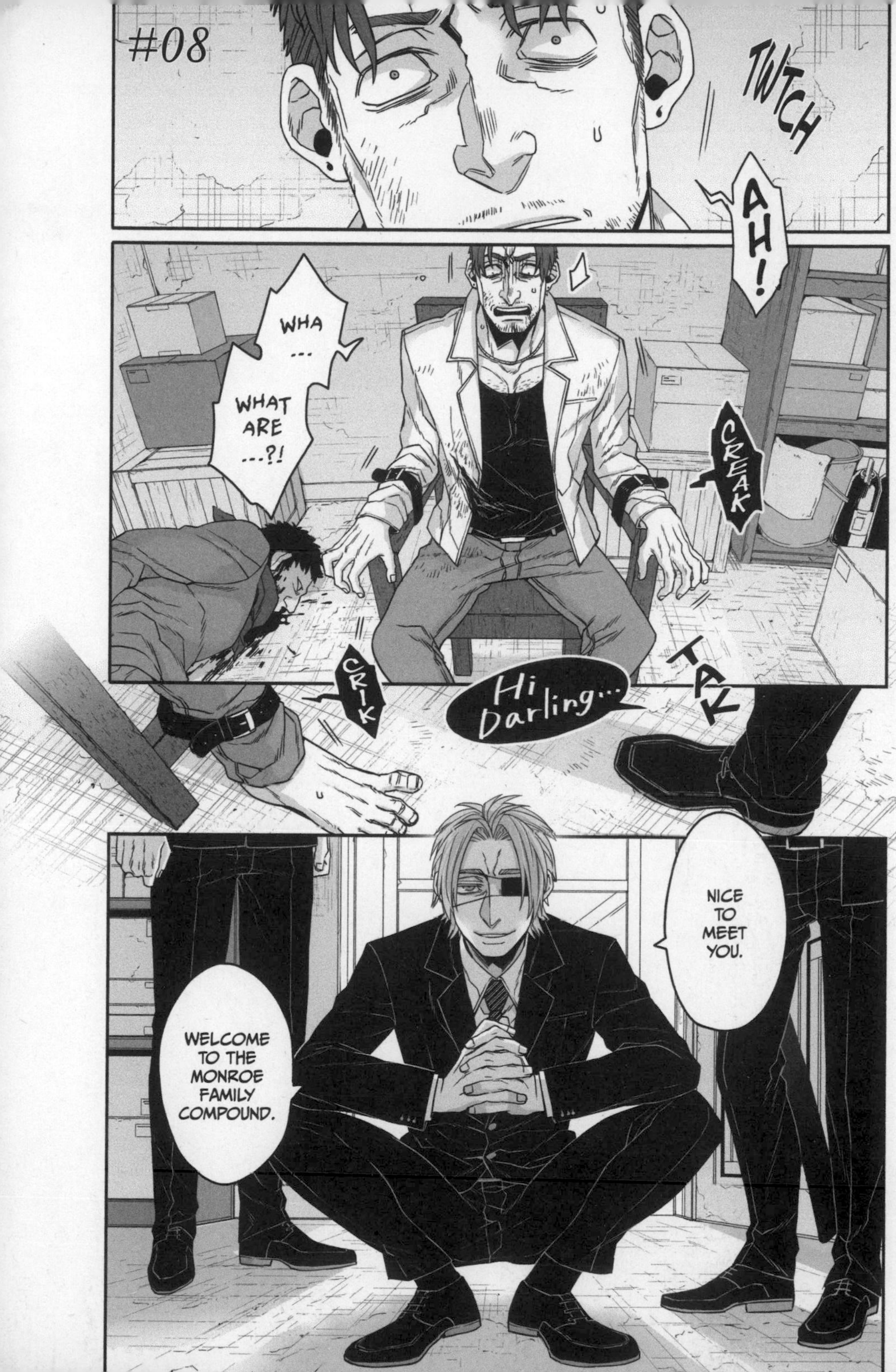
#08
TWTCH
AH!
CREAK
WHA...
WHAT ARE...?!
TAK
Hi Darling...
CRIK
NICE TO MEET YOU.
WELCOME TO THE MONROE FAMILY COMPOUND.

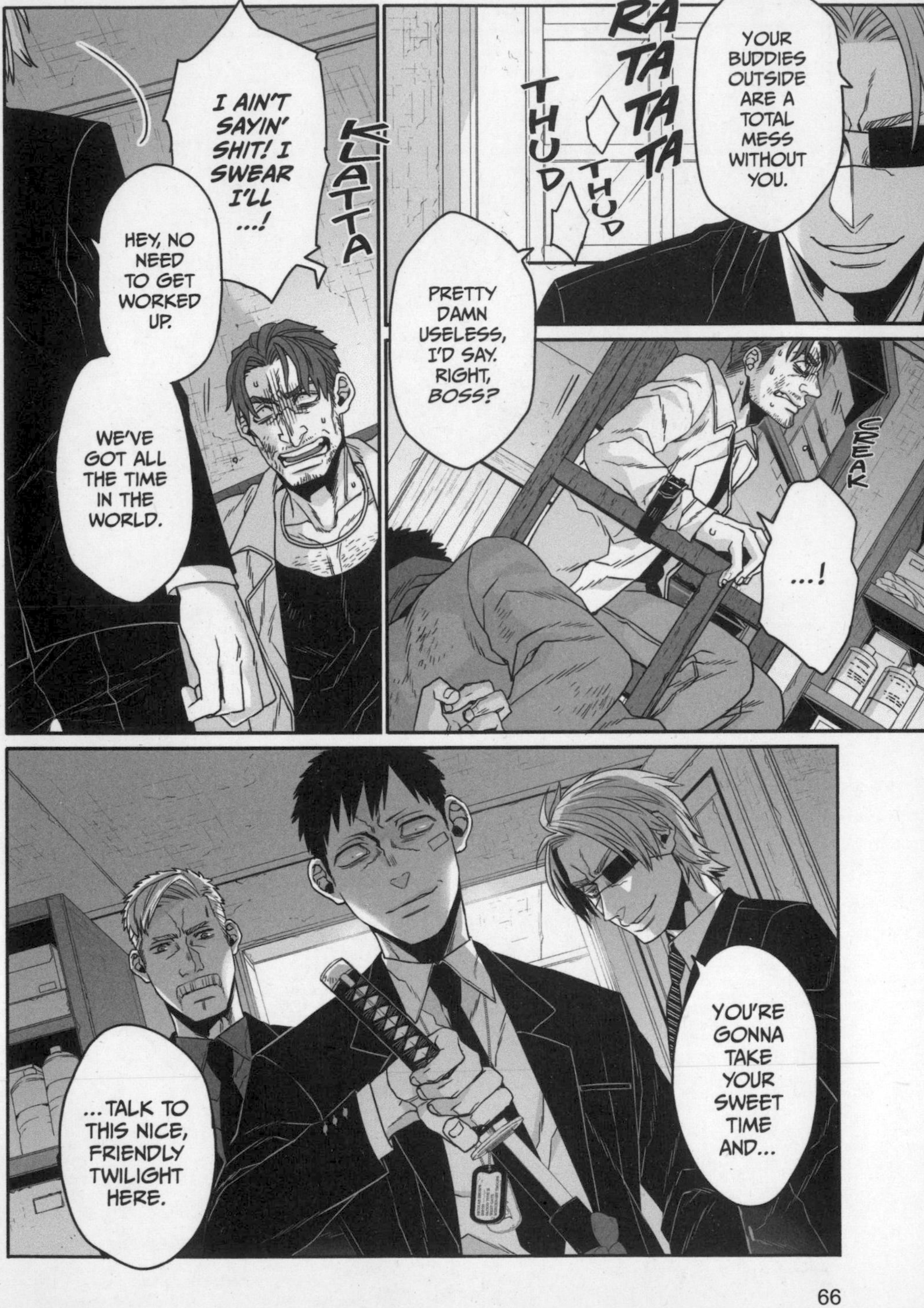
YOUR BUDDIES OUTSIDE ARE A TOTAL MESS WITHOUT YOU.
RATATATA
THUD
THUD
PRETTY DAMN USELESS, I'D SAY. RIGHT, *BOSS?*
CREAK
...!
I AIN'T SAYIN' SHIT! I SWEAR I'LL ...!
KLATTA
HEY, NO NEED TO GET WORKED UP.
WE'VE GOT ALL THE TIME IN THE WORLD.
YOU'RE GONNA TAKE YOUR SWEET TIME AND...
...TALK TO THIS NICE, FRIENDLY TWILIGHT HERE.

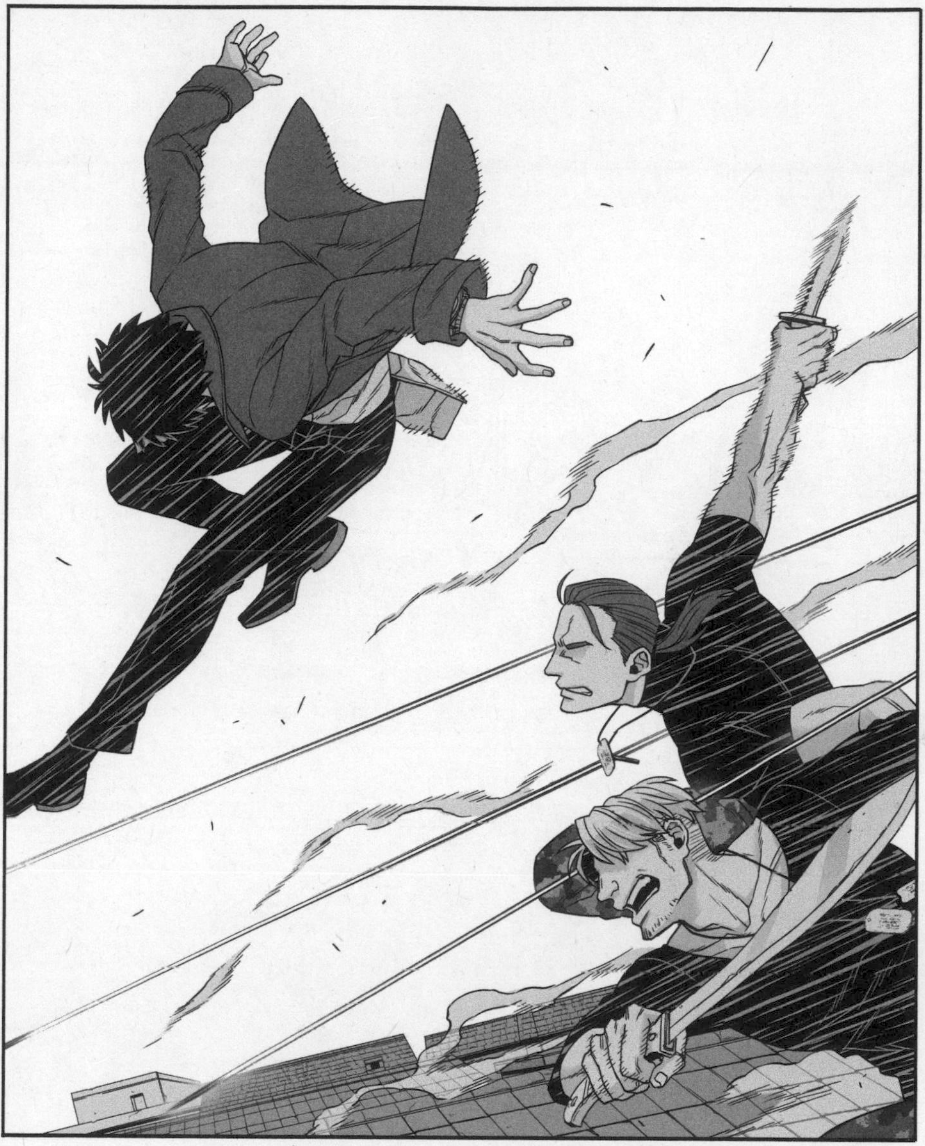

#08

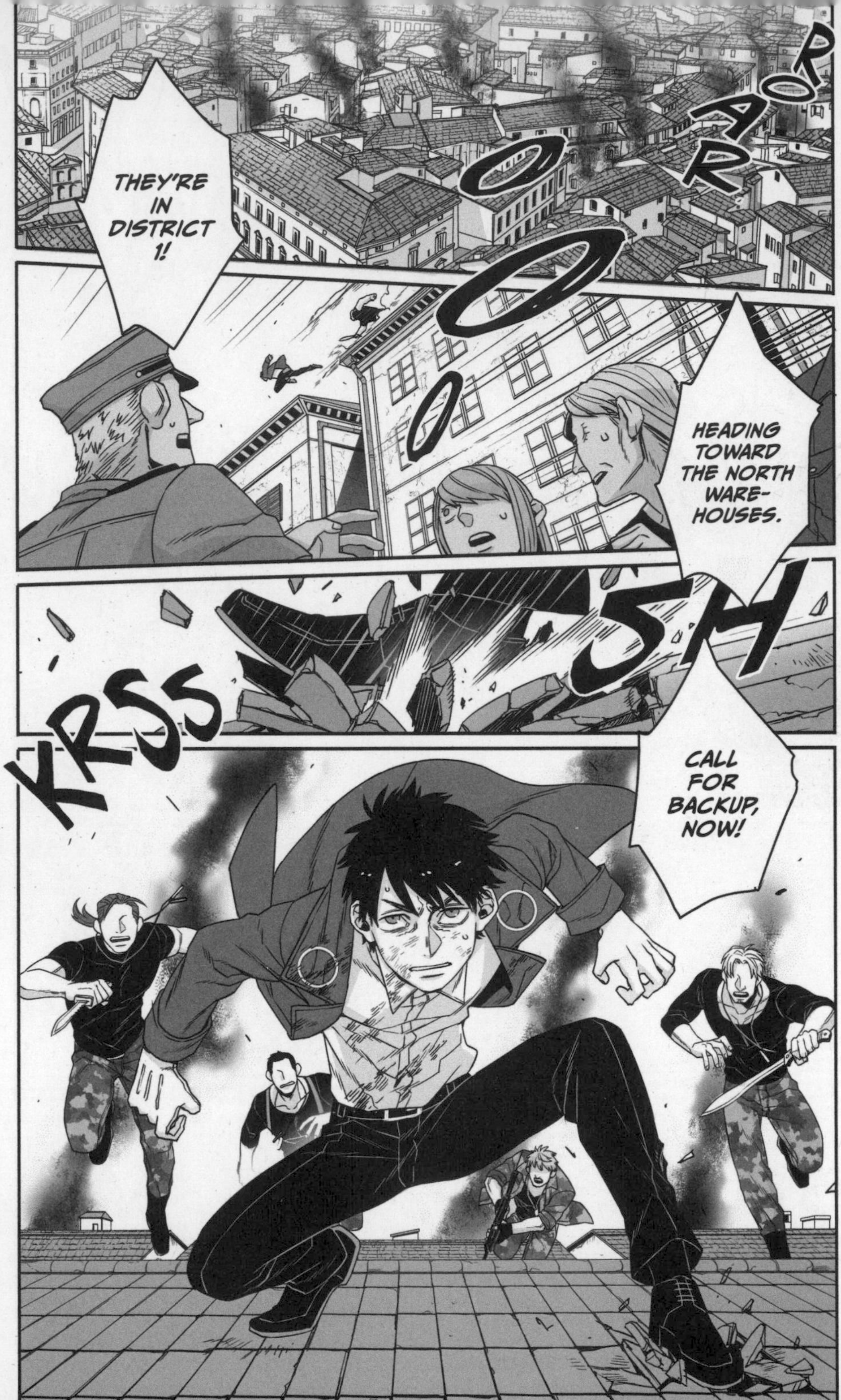
ROAR
OOOO
THEY'RE IN DISTRICT 1!
HEADING TOWARD THE NORTH WARE-HOUSES.
KRSS
SH
CALL FOR BACKUP, NOW!

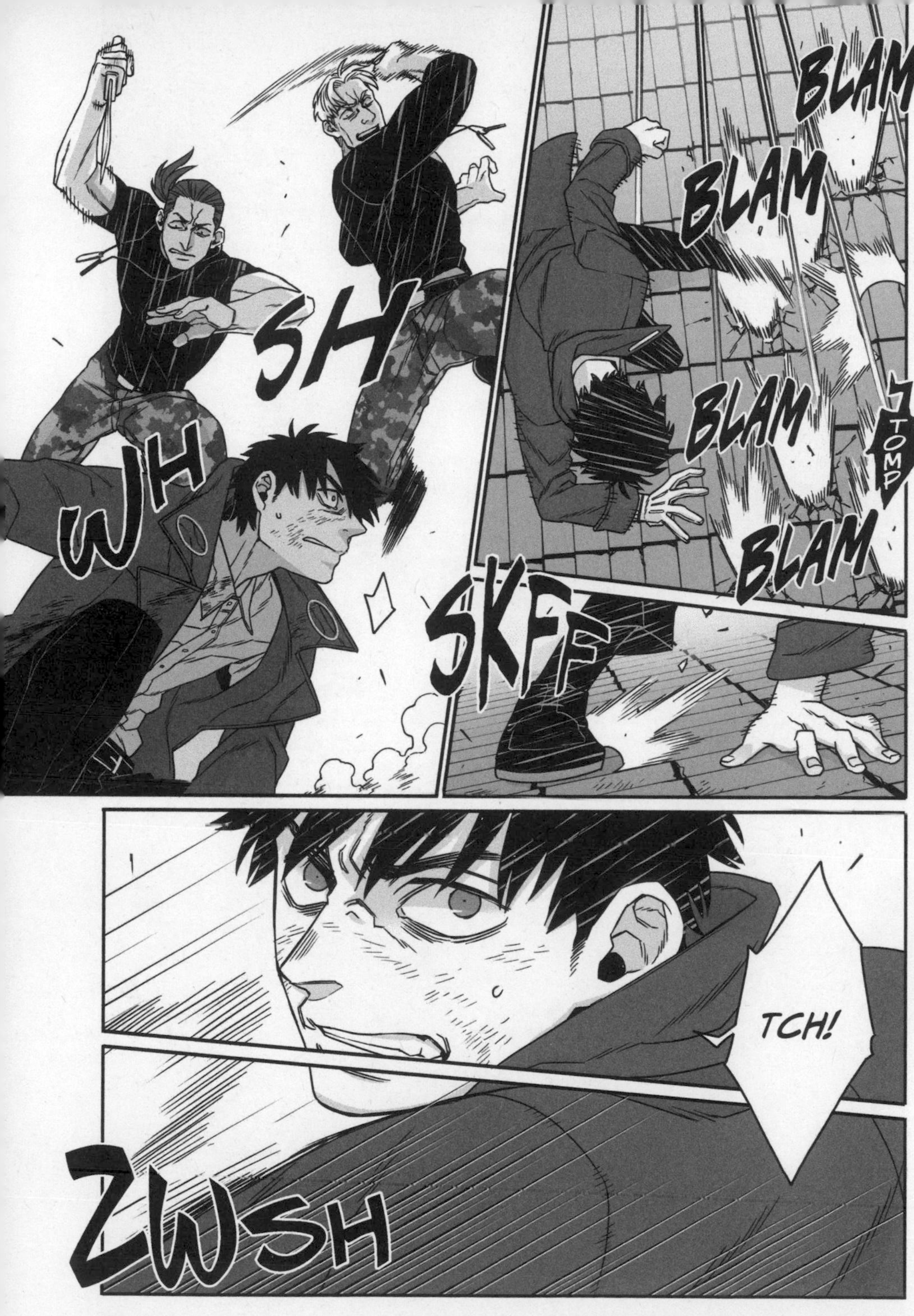
BLAM
BLAM
BLAM
STOMP
BLAM
SKFF
SH
WH
TCH!
ZWSH

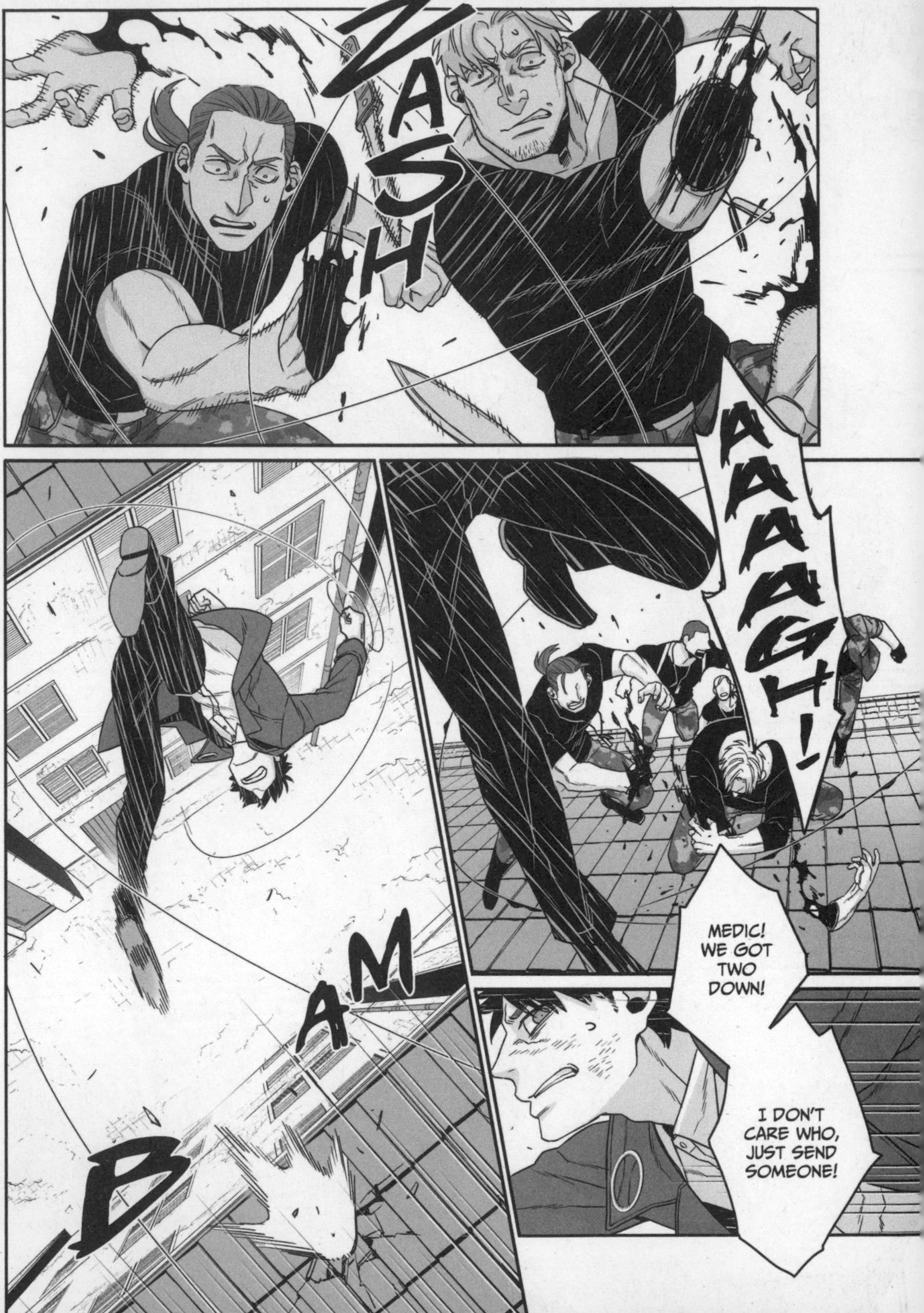
ZASH
AAAAGH!
MEDIC! WE GOT TWO DOWN!
I DON'T CARE WHO, JUST SEND SOMEONE!
BAM

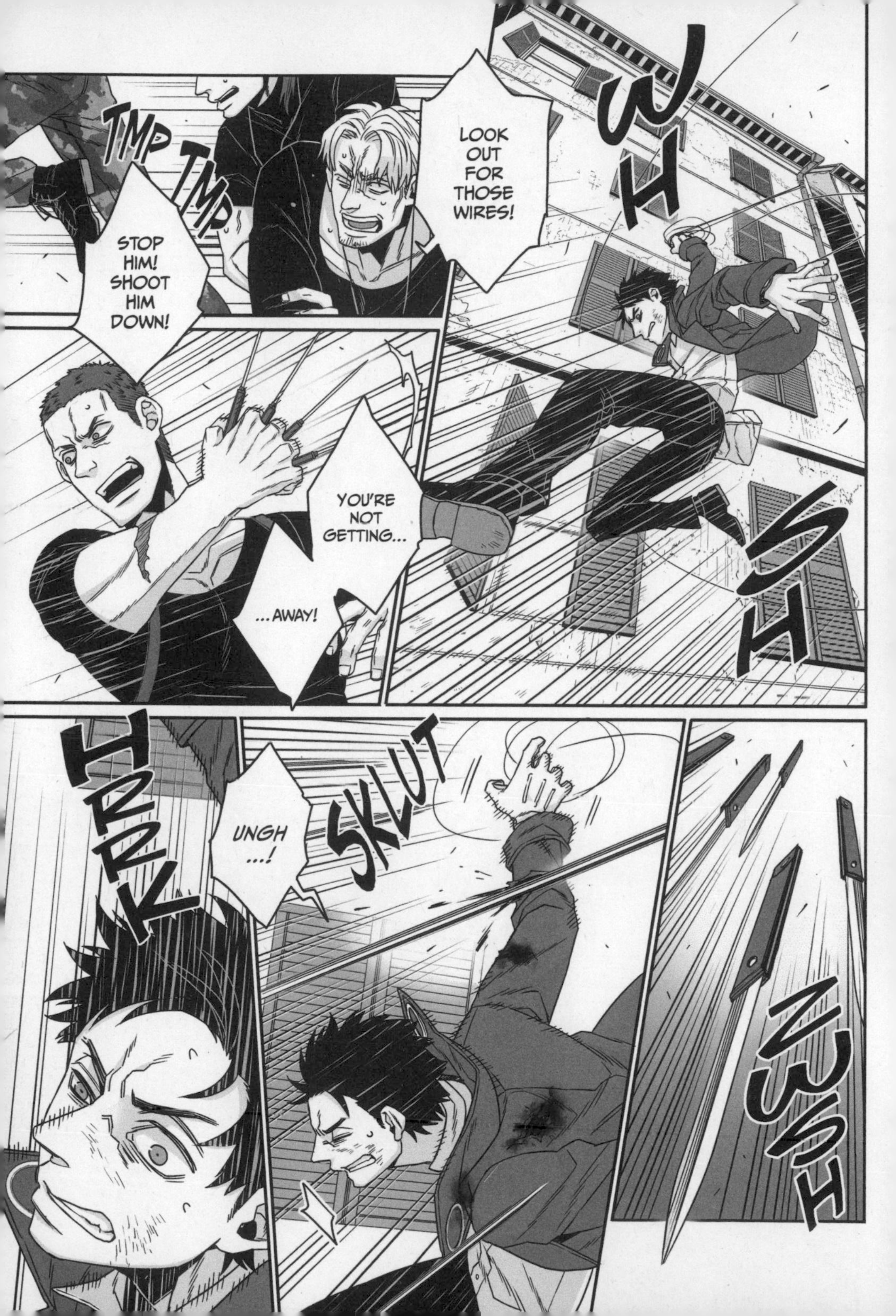
WH
SH
LOOK OUT FOR THOSE WIRES!
TMP TMP
STOP HIM! SHOOT HIM DOWN!
YOU'RE NOT GETTING...
...AWAY!
SKLUT
UNGH ...!
HRRK

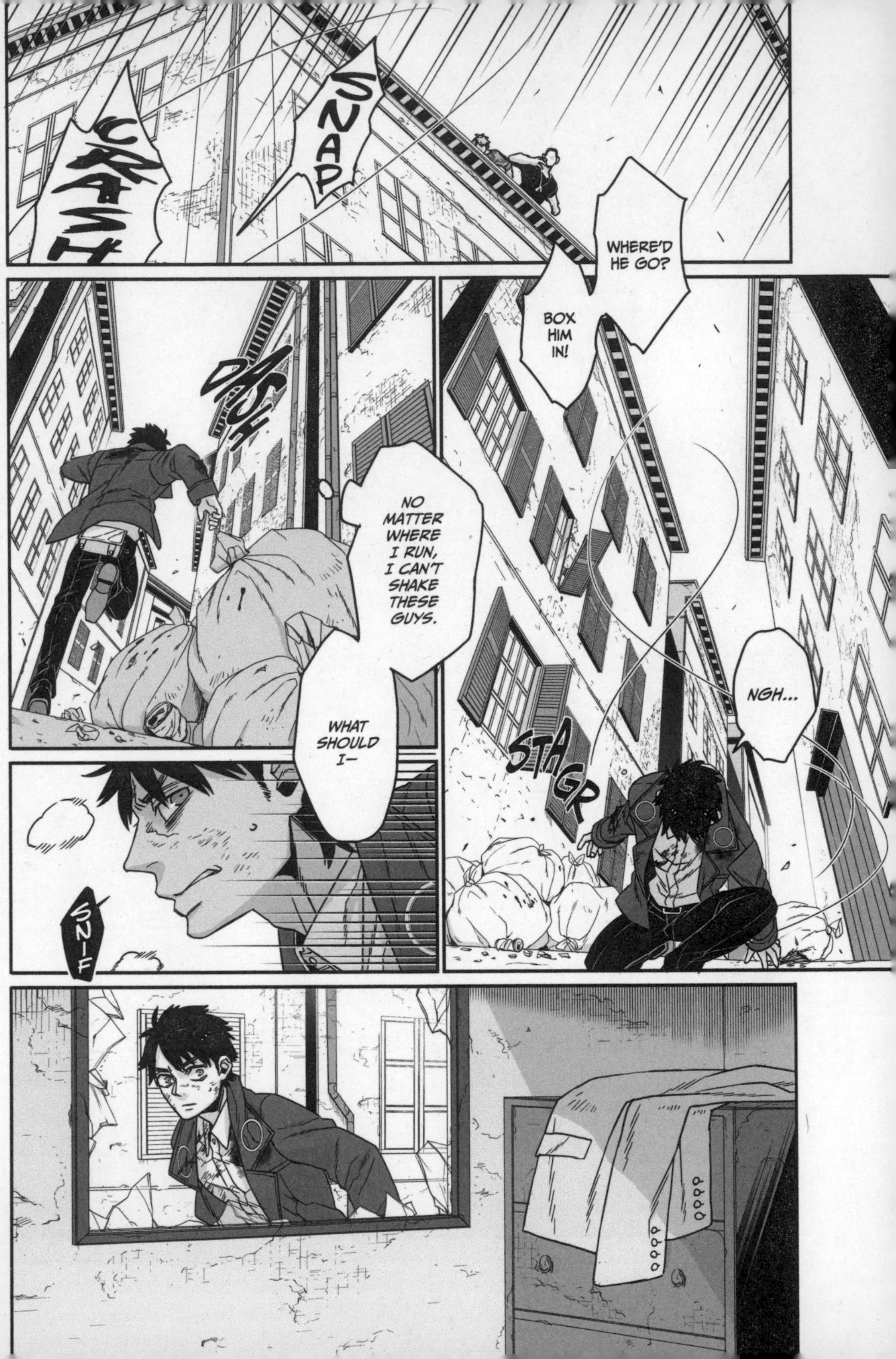
SNAP
CRASH
WHERE'D HE GO?
BOX HIM IN!
NGH...
STAGR
DASH
NO MATTER WHERE I RUN, I CAN'T SHAKE THESE GUYS.
WHAT SHOULD I—
SNIF

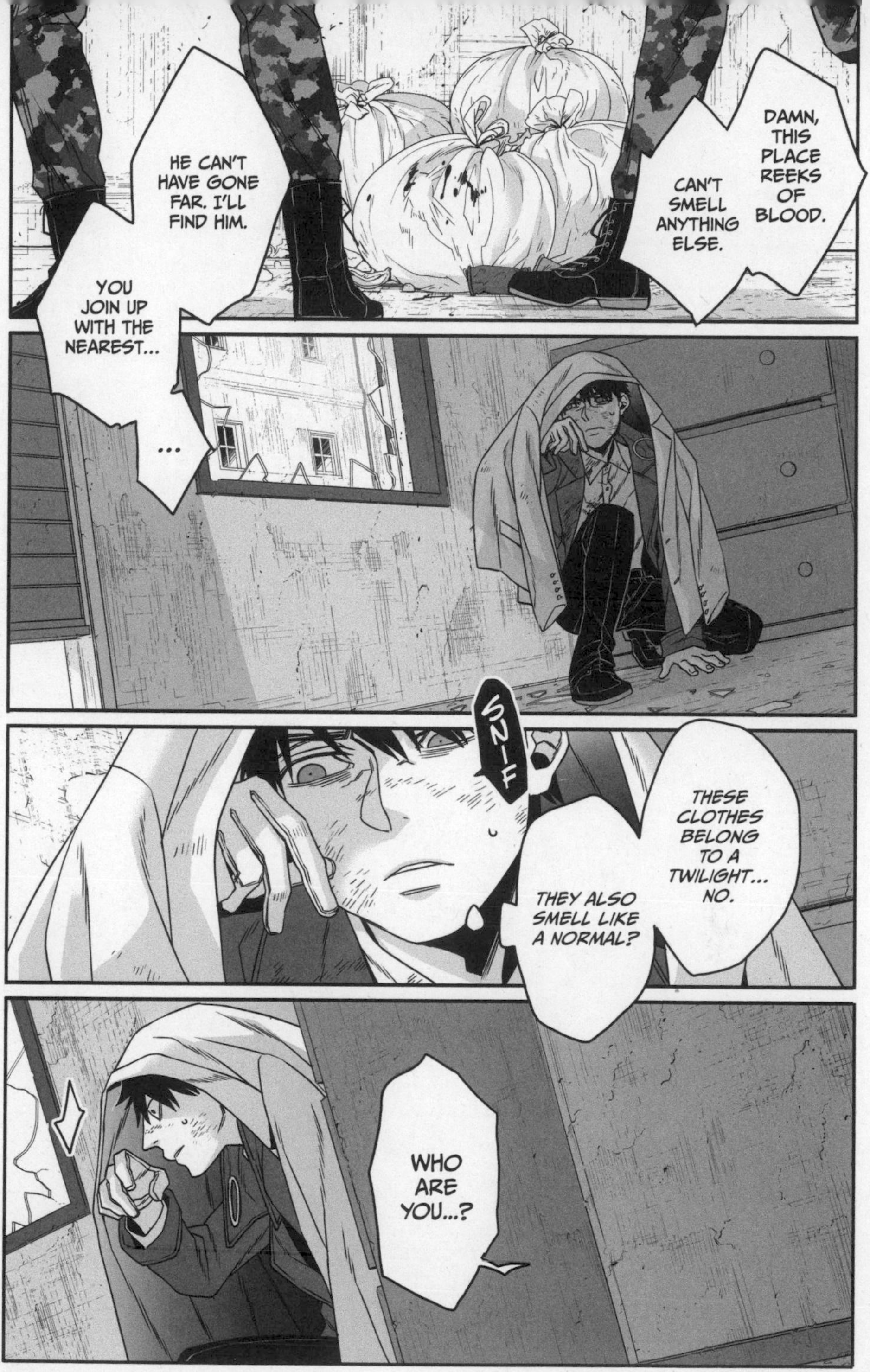
DAMN, THIS PLACE REEKS OF BLOOD.
CAN'T SMELL ANYTHING ELSE.
HE CAN'T HAVE GONE FAR. I'LL FIND HIM.
YOU JOIN UP WITH THE NEAREST...
...
SNIF
THESE CLOTHES BELONG TO A TWILIGHT... NO.
THEY ALSO SMELL LIKE A NORMAL?
WHO ARE YOU...?

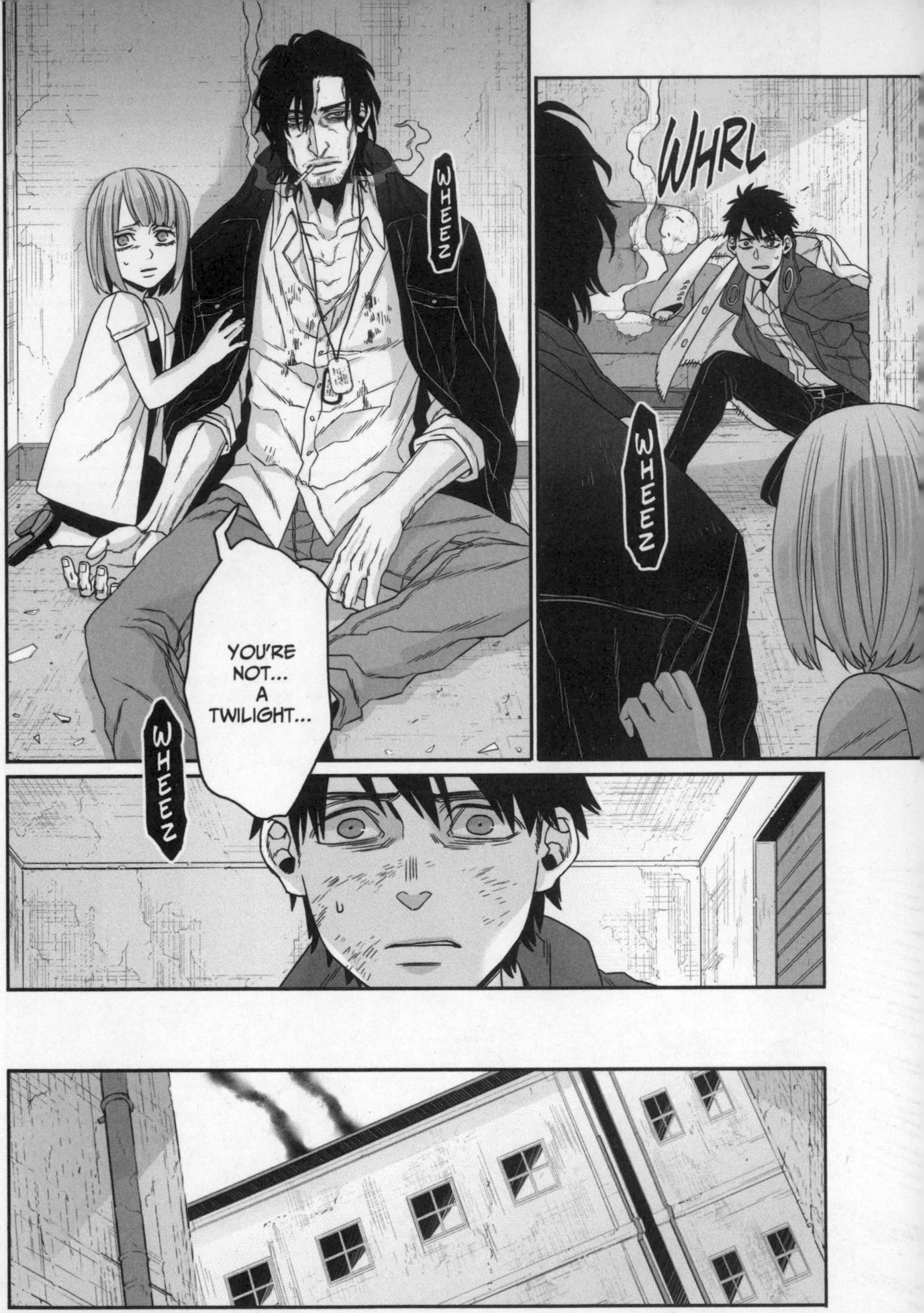
WHRL
WHEEZ
WHEEZ
YOU'RE NOT... A TWILIGHT...
WHEEZ

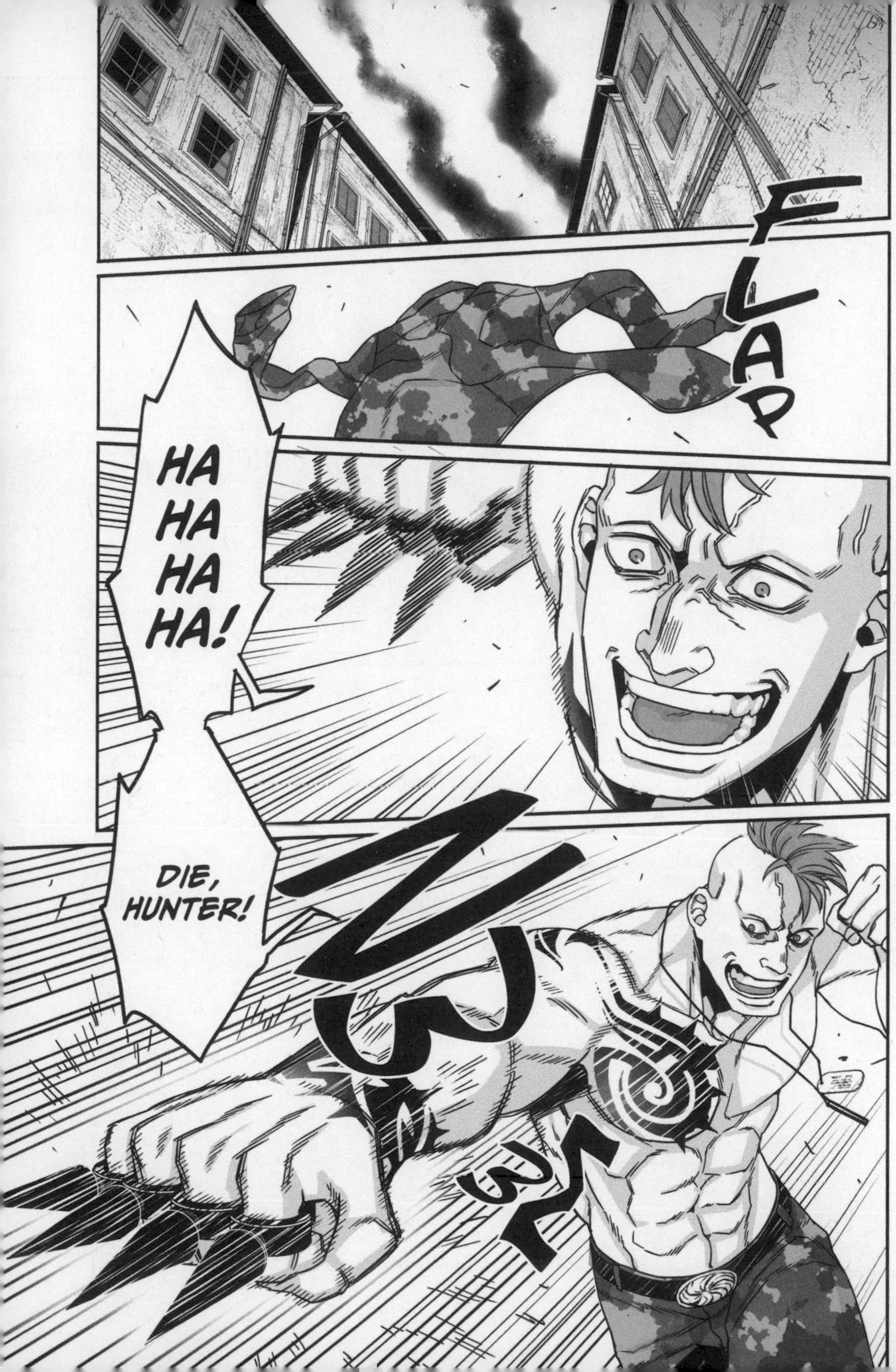
FLAP
HA HA HA HA!
DIE, HUNTER!

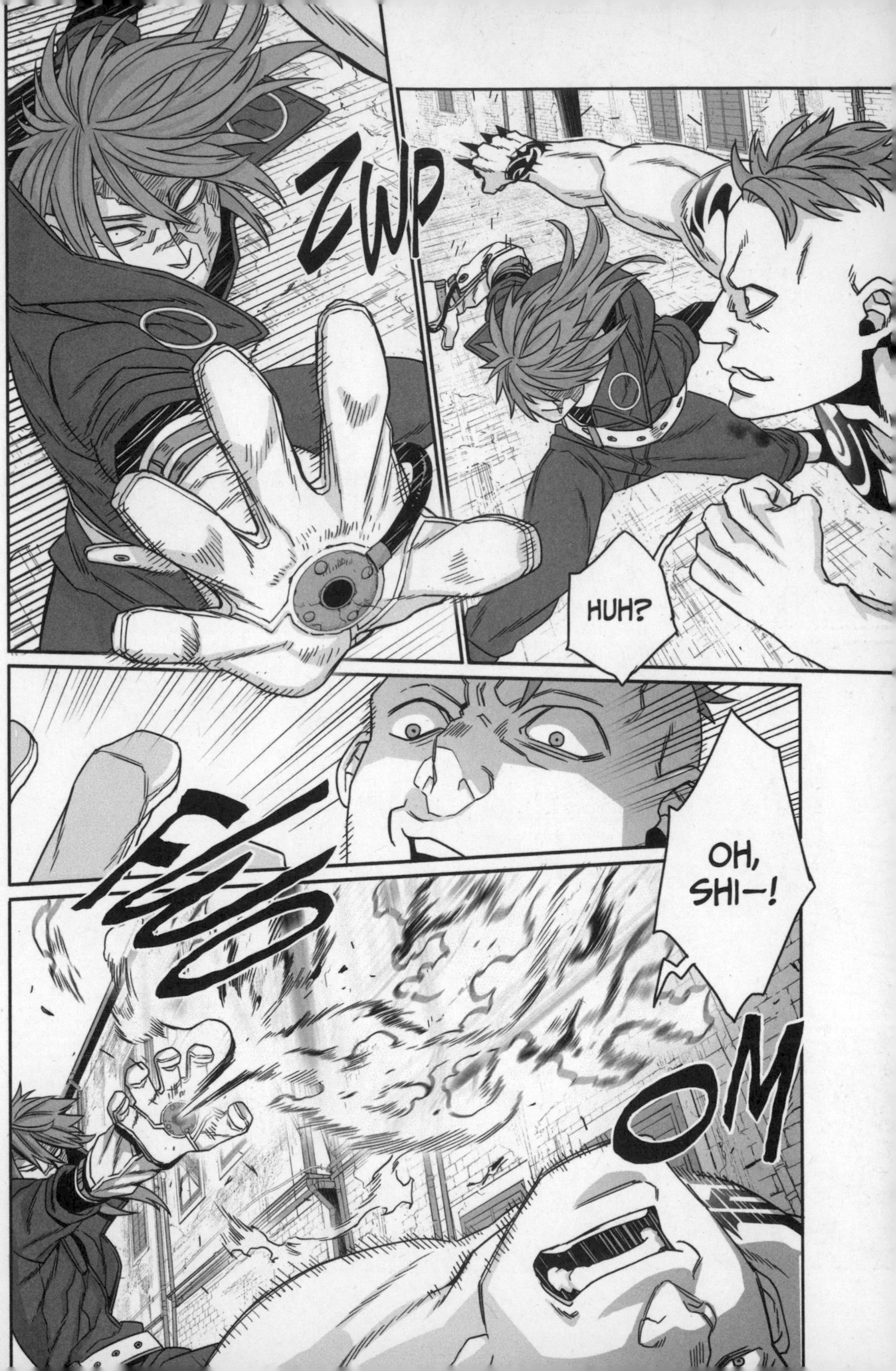
HUH?
ZWP
OH, SHI—!
FWOOM

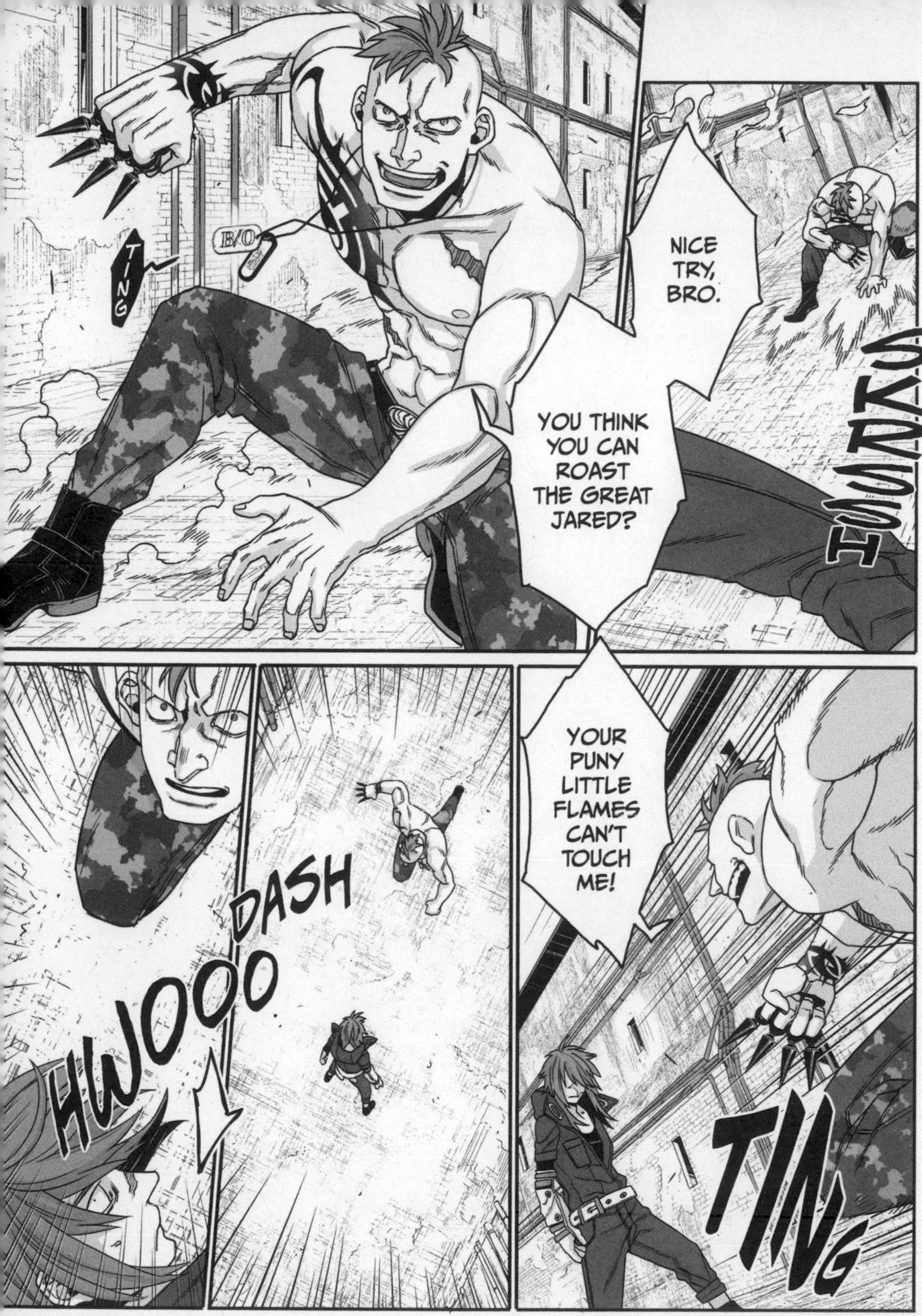
NICE TRY, BRO.
SKRSSH
YOU THINK YOU CAN ROAST THE GREAT JARED?
TING
YOUR PUNY LITTLE FLAMES CAN'T TOUCH ME!
TING
DASH
HWOOOO

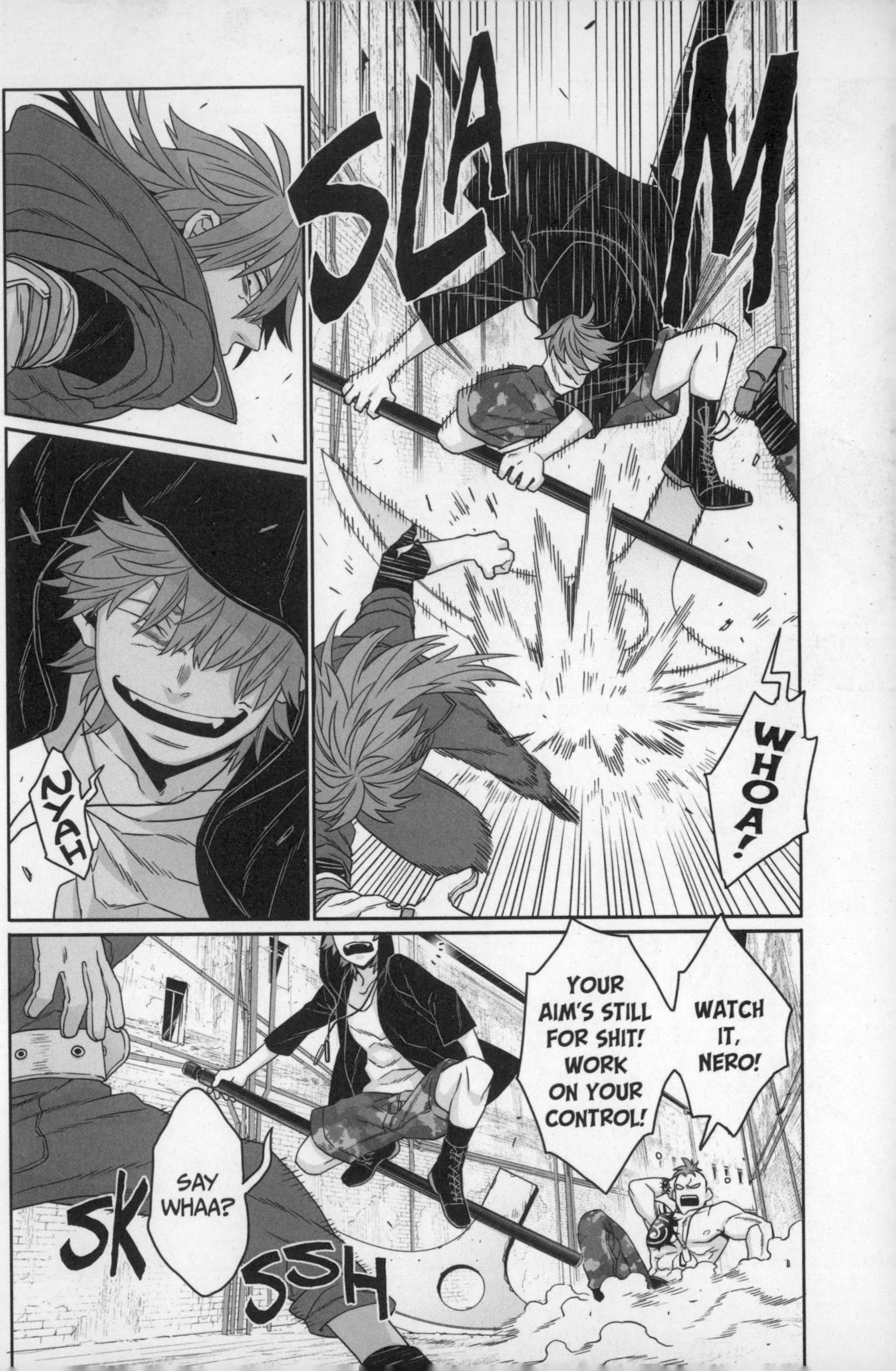
SLAM
WHOA!
NYAH
WATCH IT, NERO!
YOUR AIM'S STILL FOR SHIT! WORK ON YOUR CONTROL!
SAY WHAA?
SK SSH

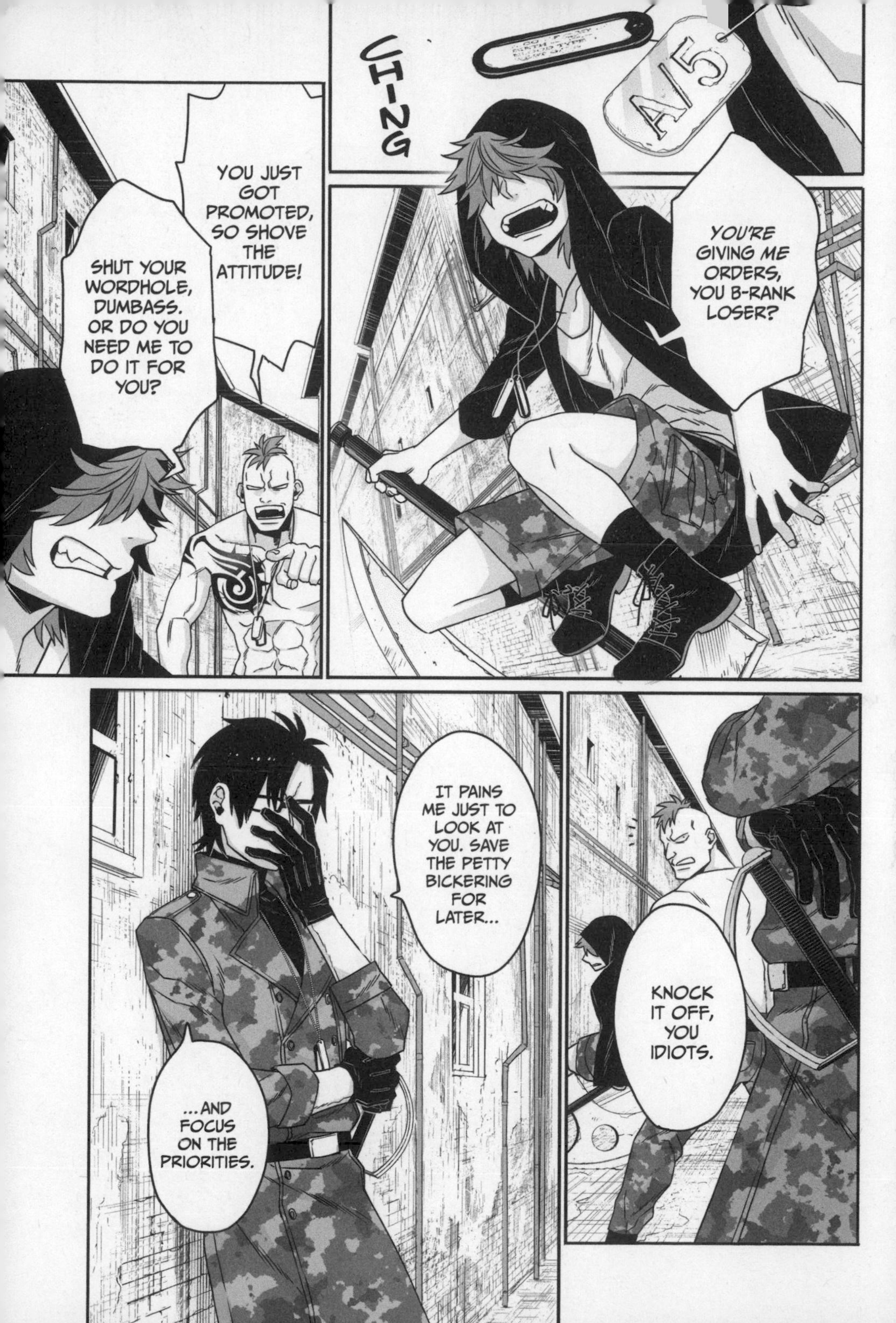
CHING
A/5
YOU'RE GIVING ME ORDERS, YOU B-RANK LOSER?
YOU JUST GOT PROMOTED, SO SHOVE THE ATTITUDE!
SHUT YOUR WORDHOLE, DUMBASS. OR DO YOU NEED ME TO DO IT FOR YOU?
KNOCK IT OFF, YOU IDIOTS.
IT PAINS ME JUST TO LOOK AT YOU. SAVE THE PETTY BICKERING FOR LATER...
...AND FOCUS ON THE PRIORITIES.

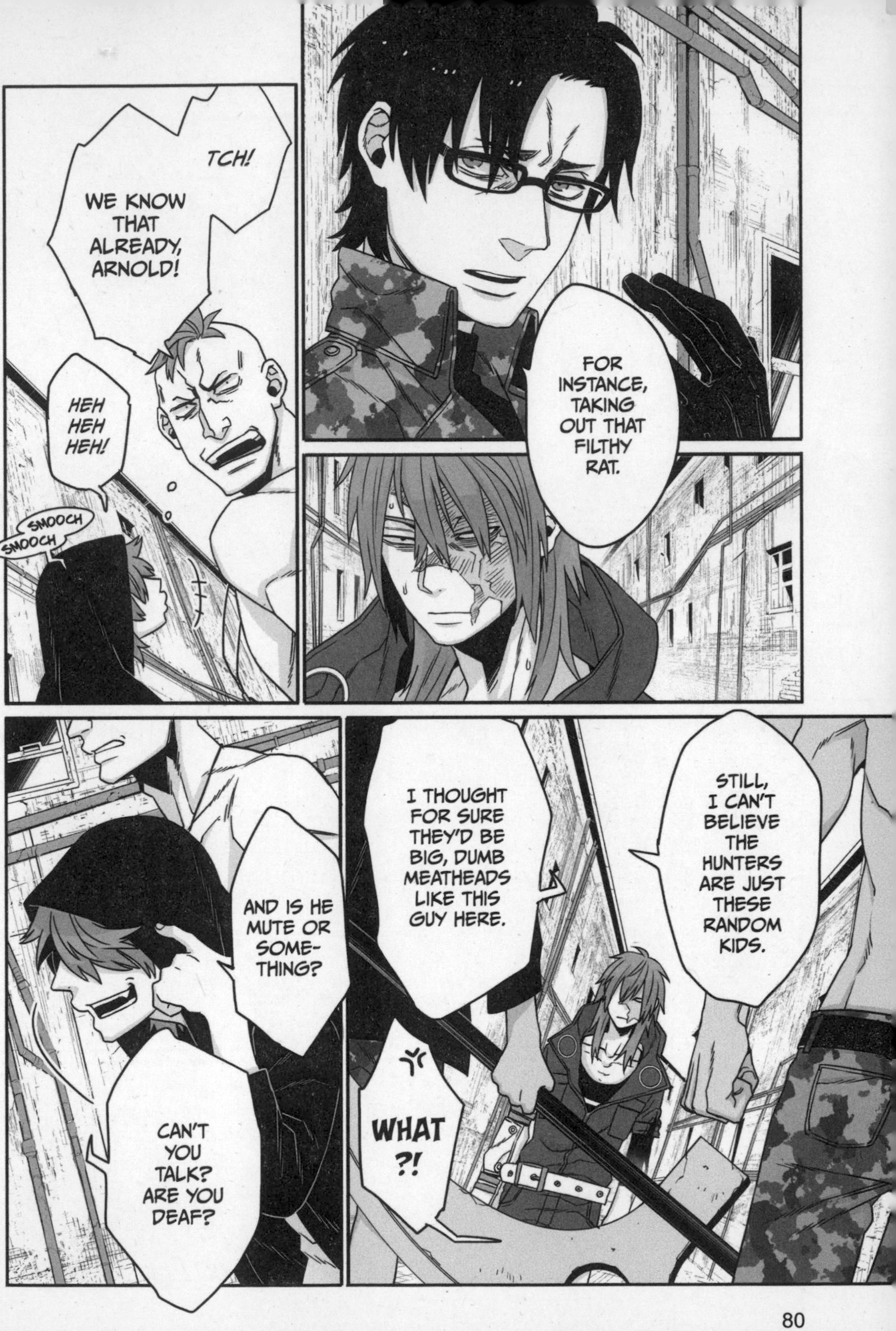
FOR INSTANCE, TAKING OUT THAT FILTHY RAT.
TCH!
WE KNOW THAT ALREADY, ARNOLD!
HEH HEH HEH!
SMOOCH SMOOCH
STILL, I CAN'T BELIEVE THE HUNTERS ARE JUST THESE RANDOM KIDS.
I THOUGHT FOR SURE THEY'D BE BIG, DUMB MEATHEADS LIKE THIS GUY HERE.
WHAT?!
AND IS HE MUTE OR SOME-THING?
CAN'T YOU TALK? ARE YOU DEAF?

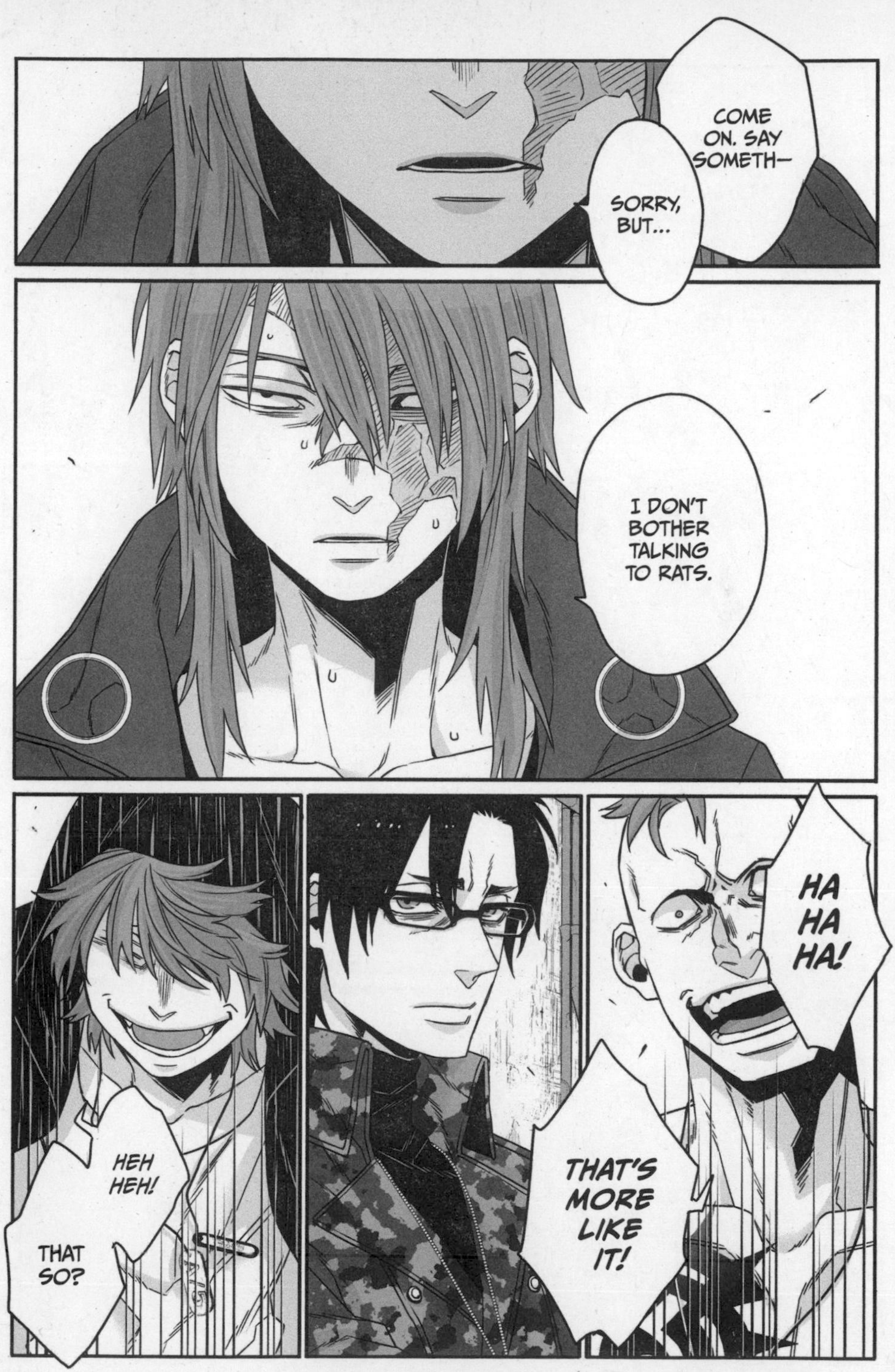
COME ON. SAY SOMETH—
SORRY, BUT...
I DON'T BOTHER TALKING TO RATS.
HA HA HA!
THAT'S MORE LIKE IT!
HEH HEH!
THAT SO?

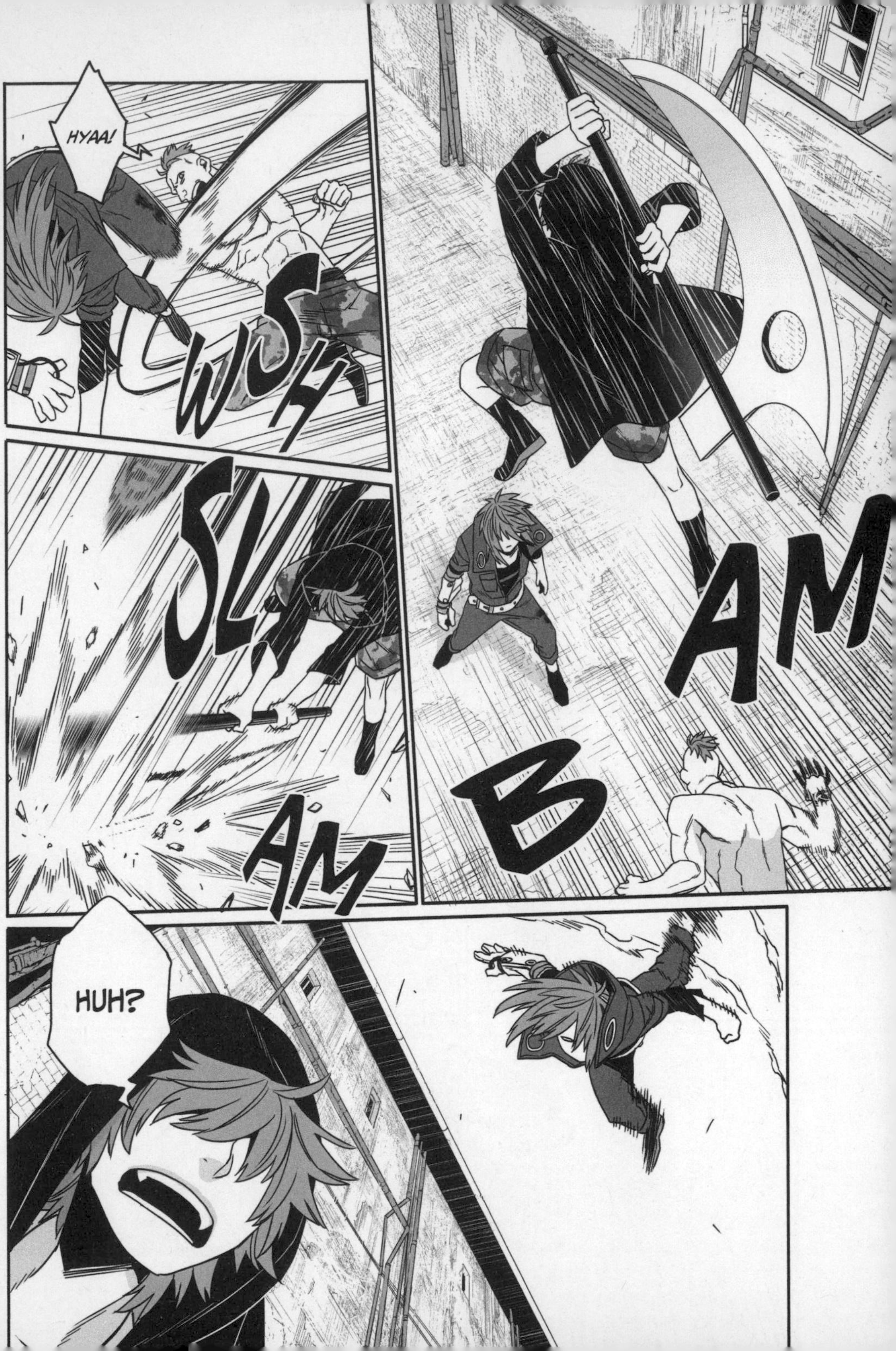
BAM
HYAA!
WSH
SLAM
HUH?

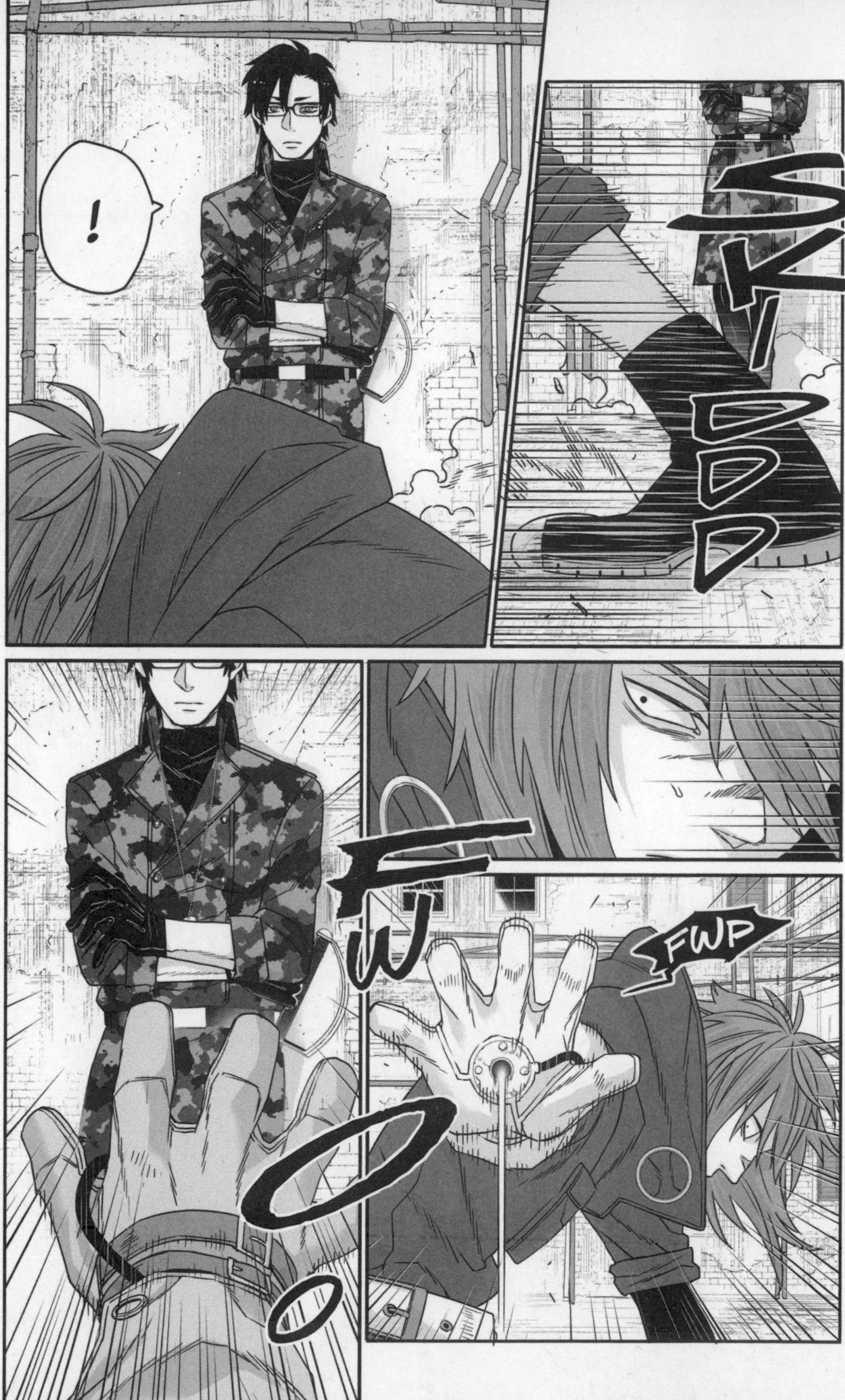
SKIDDD
!
FWP
FWOO

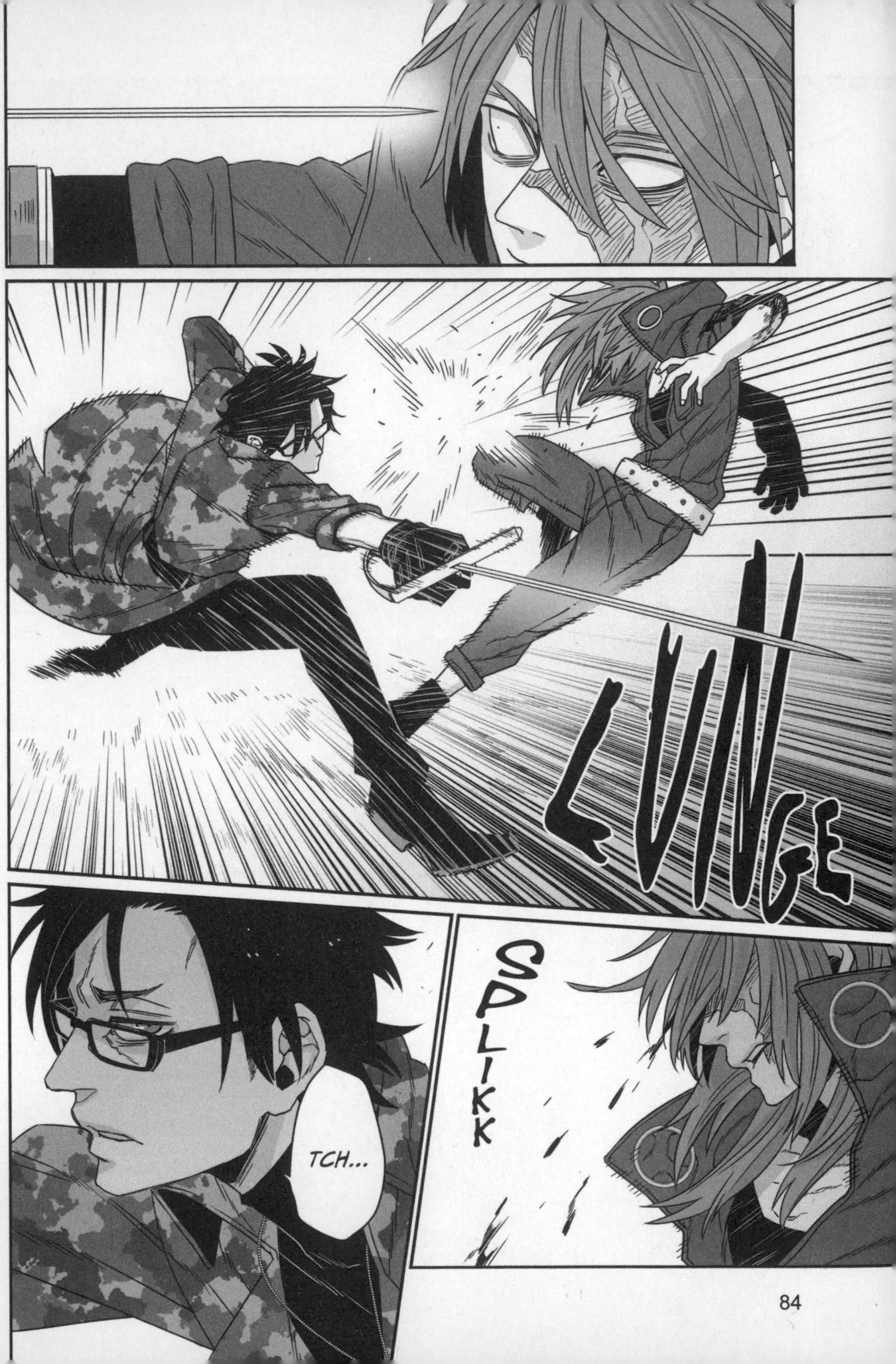
LUNGE
SPLIKK
TCH...

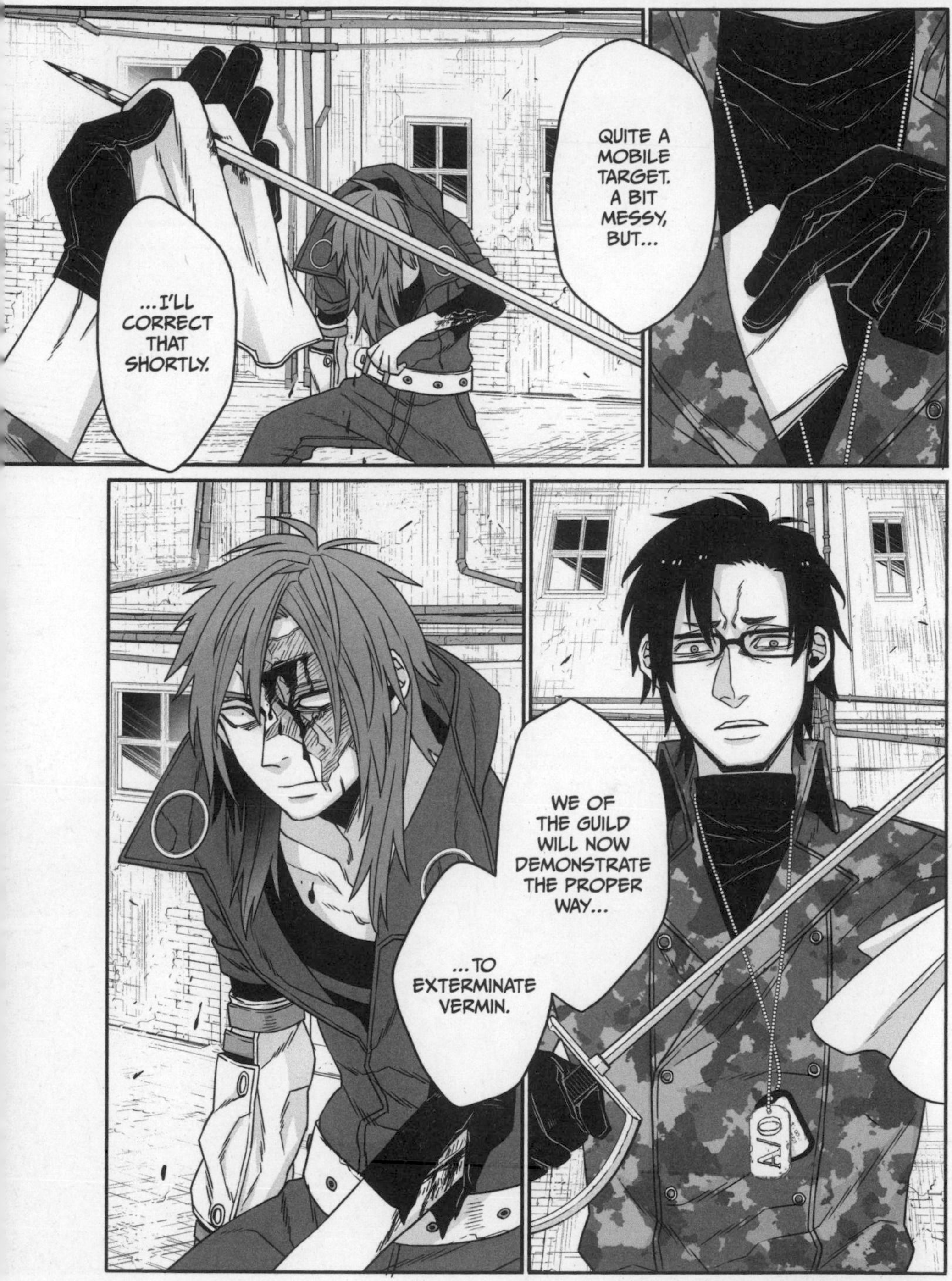
QUITE A MOBILE TARGET. A BIT MESSY, BUT...
...I'LL CORRECT THAT SHORTLY.
WE OF THE GUILD WILL NOW DEMONSTRATE THE PROPER WAY...
...TO EXTERMINATE VERMIN.
A/O

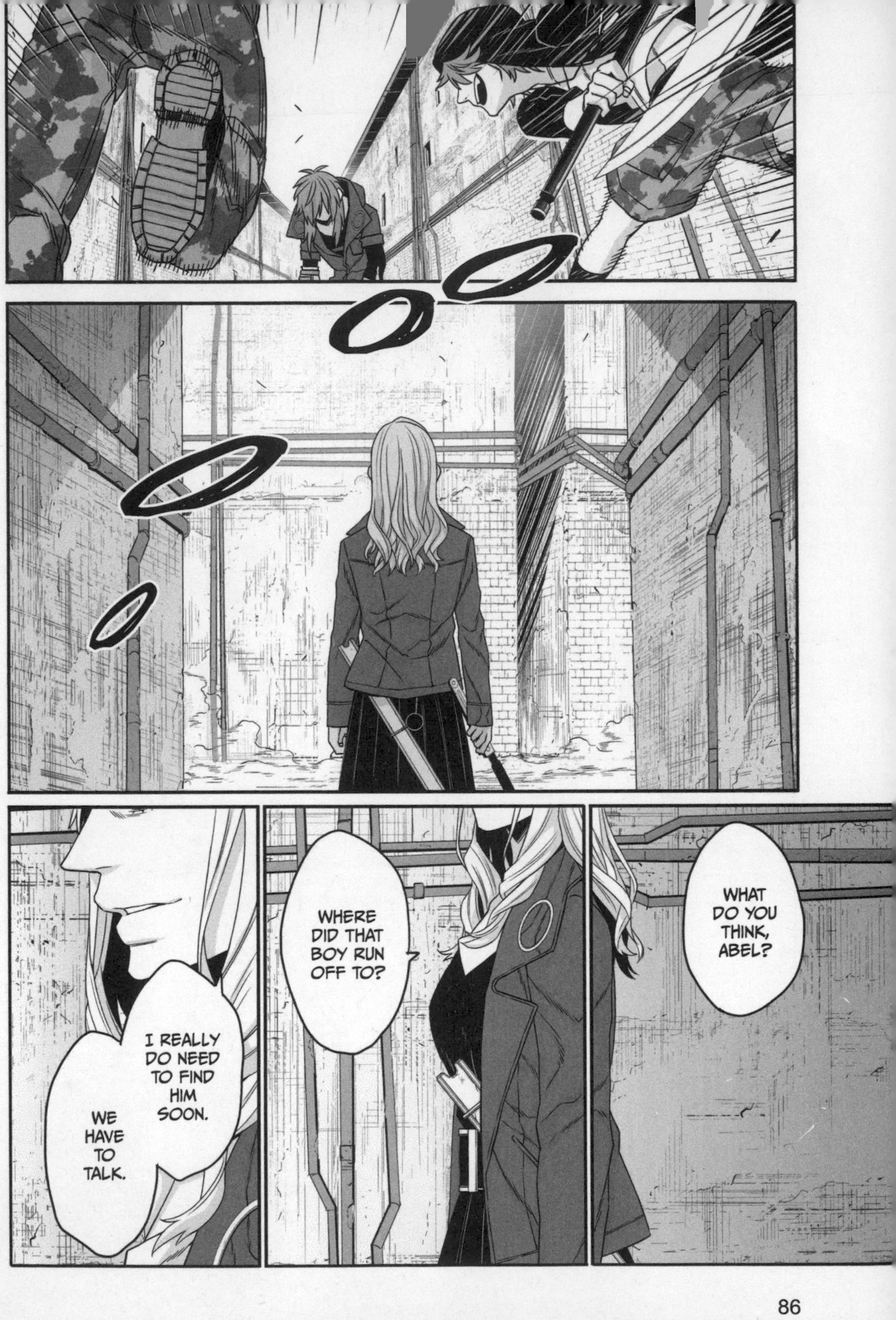
WHAT DO YOU THINK, ABEL?
WHERE DID THAT BOY RUN OFF TO?
I REALLY DO NEED TO FIND HIM SOON.
WE HAVE TO TALK.

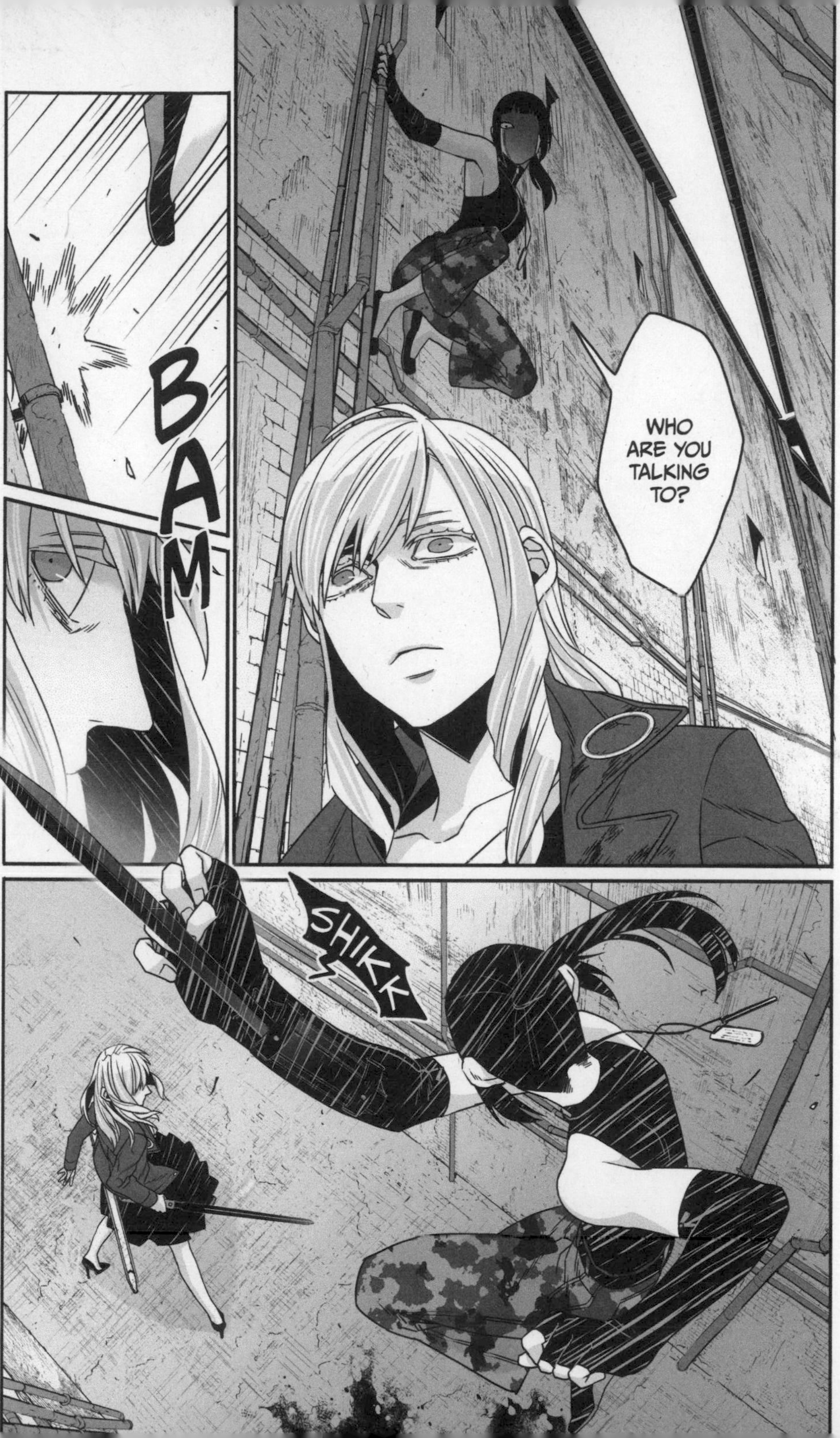
WHO ARE YOU TALKING TO?
BAM
SHIKK

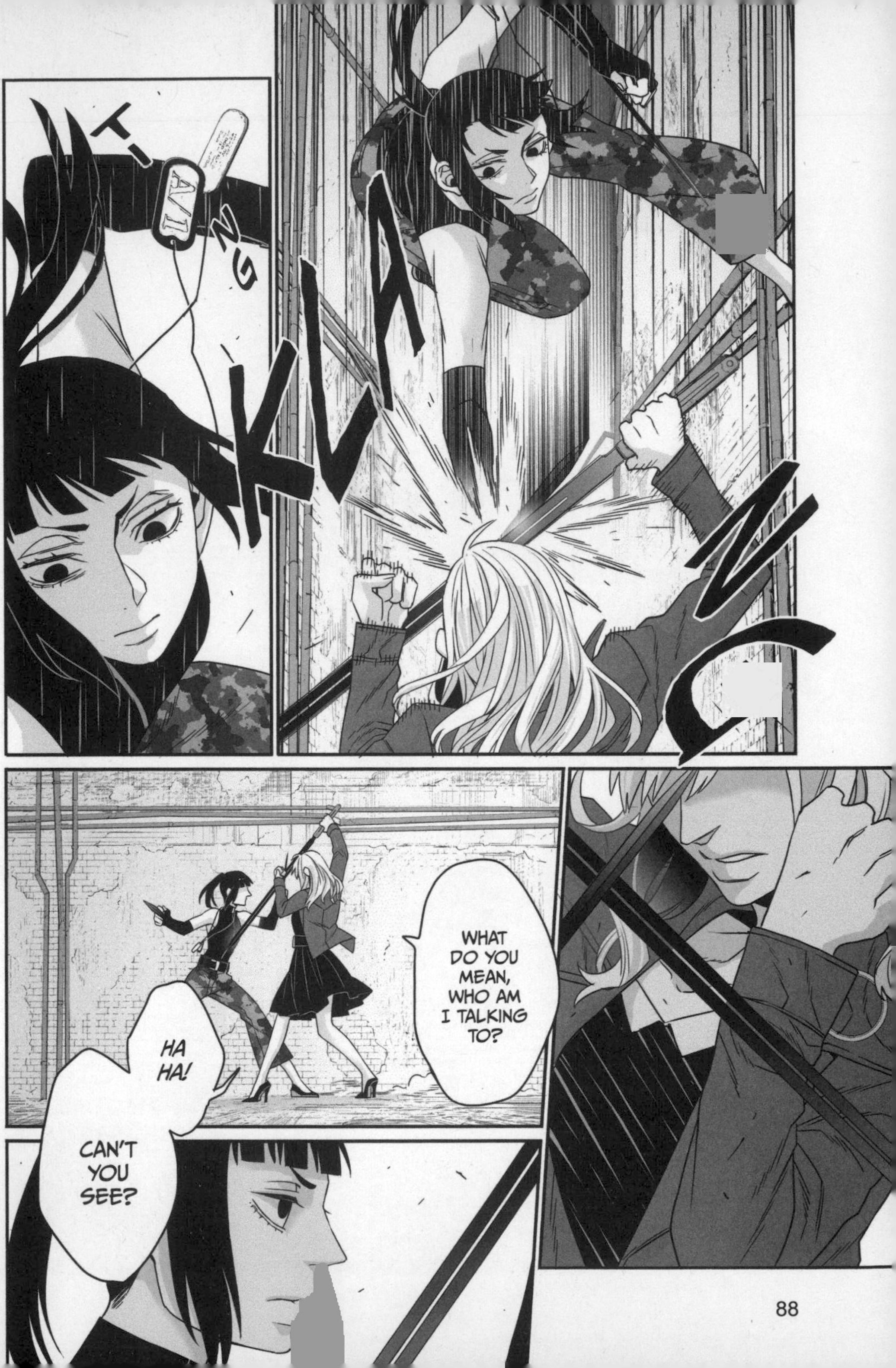
KLANG
T-ANG
WHAT DO YOU MEAN, WHO AM I TALKING TO?
HA HA!
CAN'T YOU SEE?

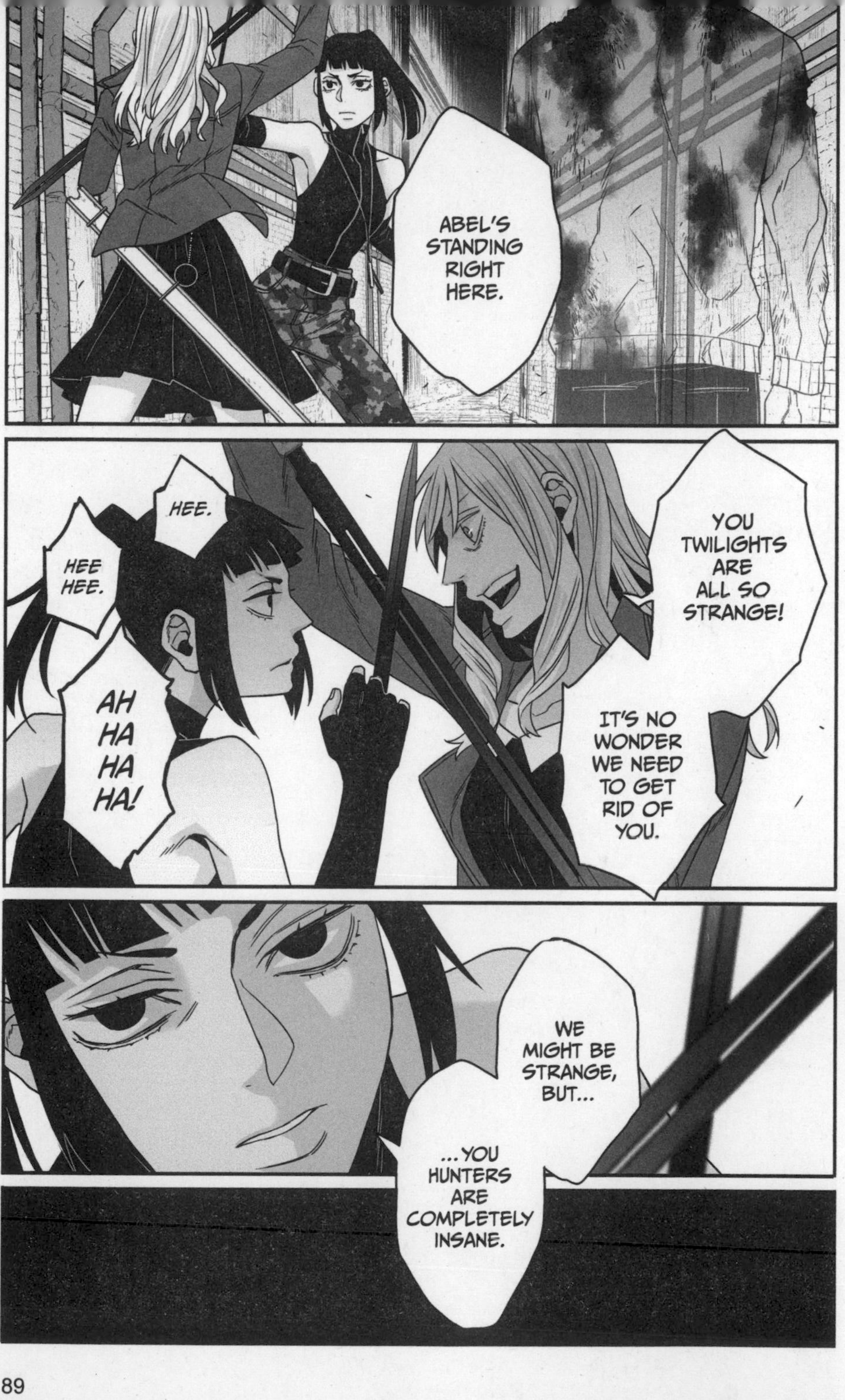
ABEL'S STANDING RIGHT HERE.
YOU TWILIGHTS ARE ALL SO STRANGE!
IT'S NO WONDER WE NEED TO GET RID OF YOU.
HEE.
HEE HEE.
AH HA HA HA!
WE MIGHT BE STRANGE, BUT...
...YOU HUNTERS ARE COMPLETELY INSANE.

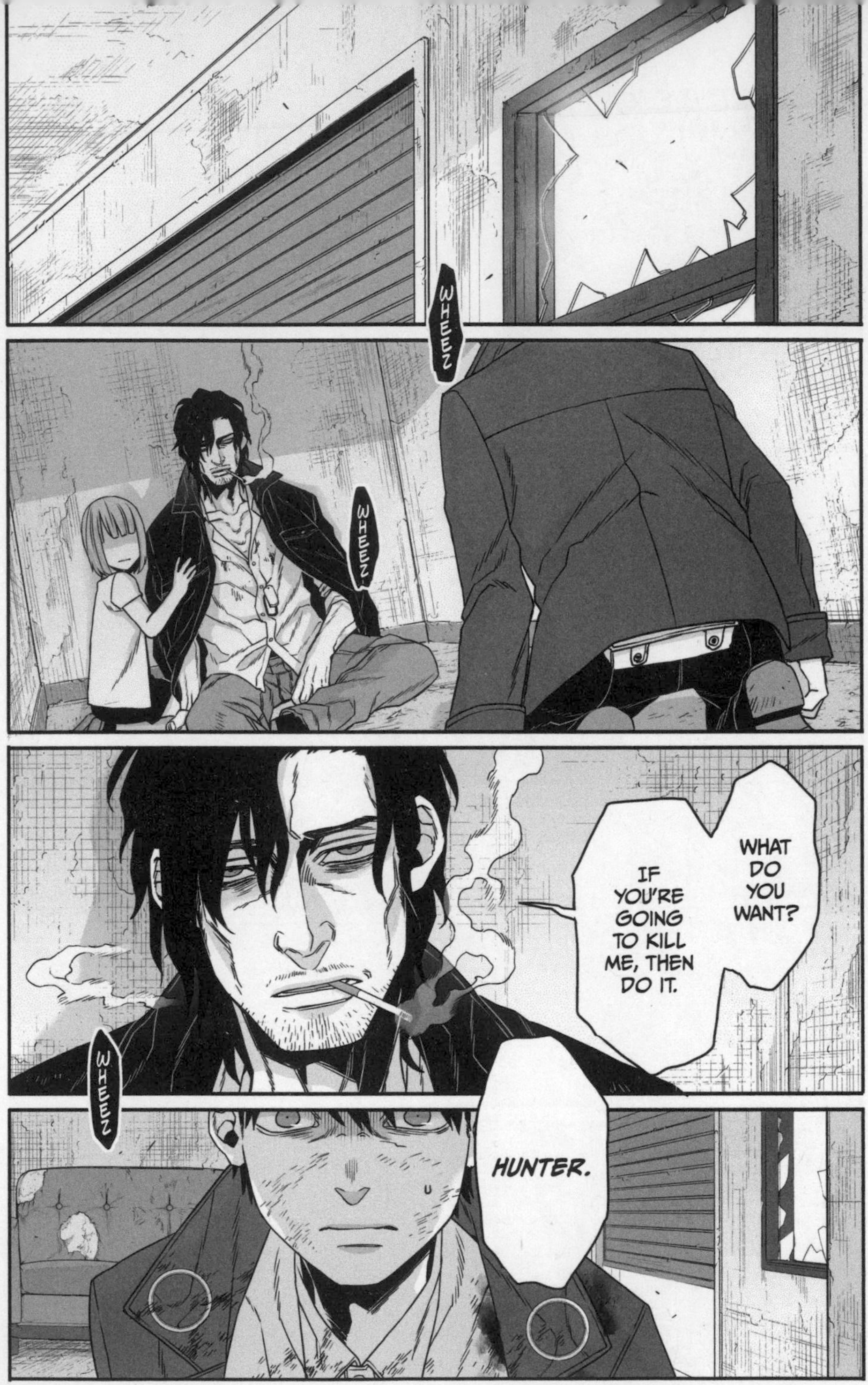
WHEEZ
WHEEZ
WHAT DO YOU WANT?
IF YOU'RE GOING TO KILL ME, THEN DO IT.
WHEEZ
HUNTER.

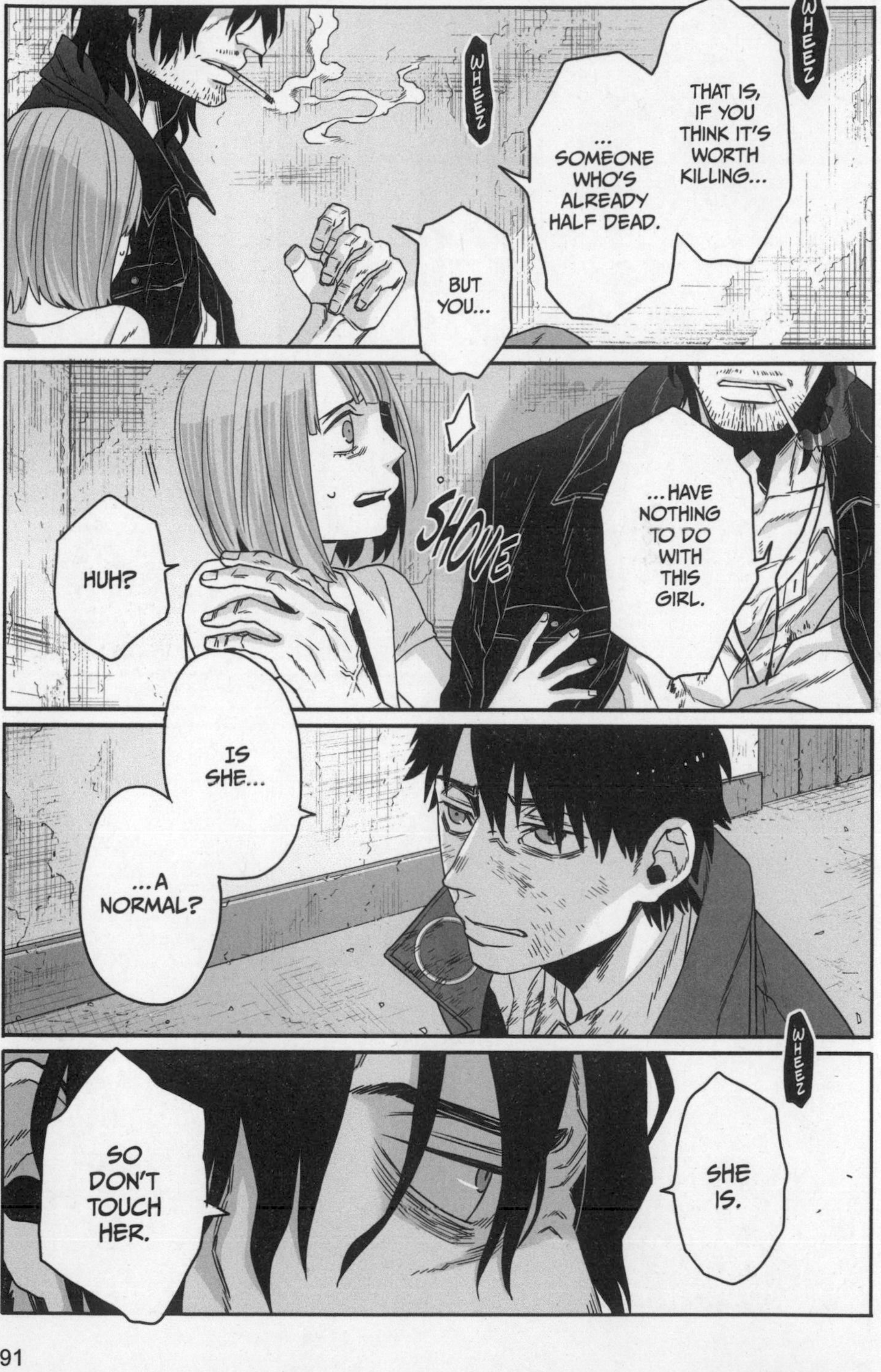
WHEEZ
THAT IS, IF YOU THINK IT'S WORTH KILLING...
WHEEZ
... SOMEONE WHO'S ALREADY HALF DEAD.
BUT YOU...
...HAVE NOTHING TO DO WITH THIS GIRL.
SHOVE
HUH?
IS SHE...
...A NORMAL?
WHEEZ
SHE IS.
SO DON'T TOUCH HER.

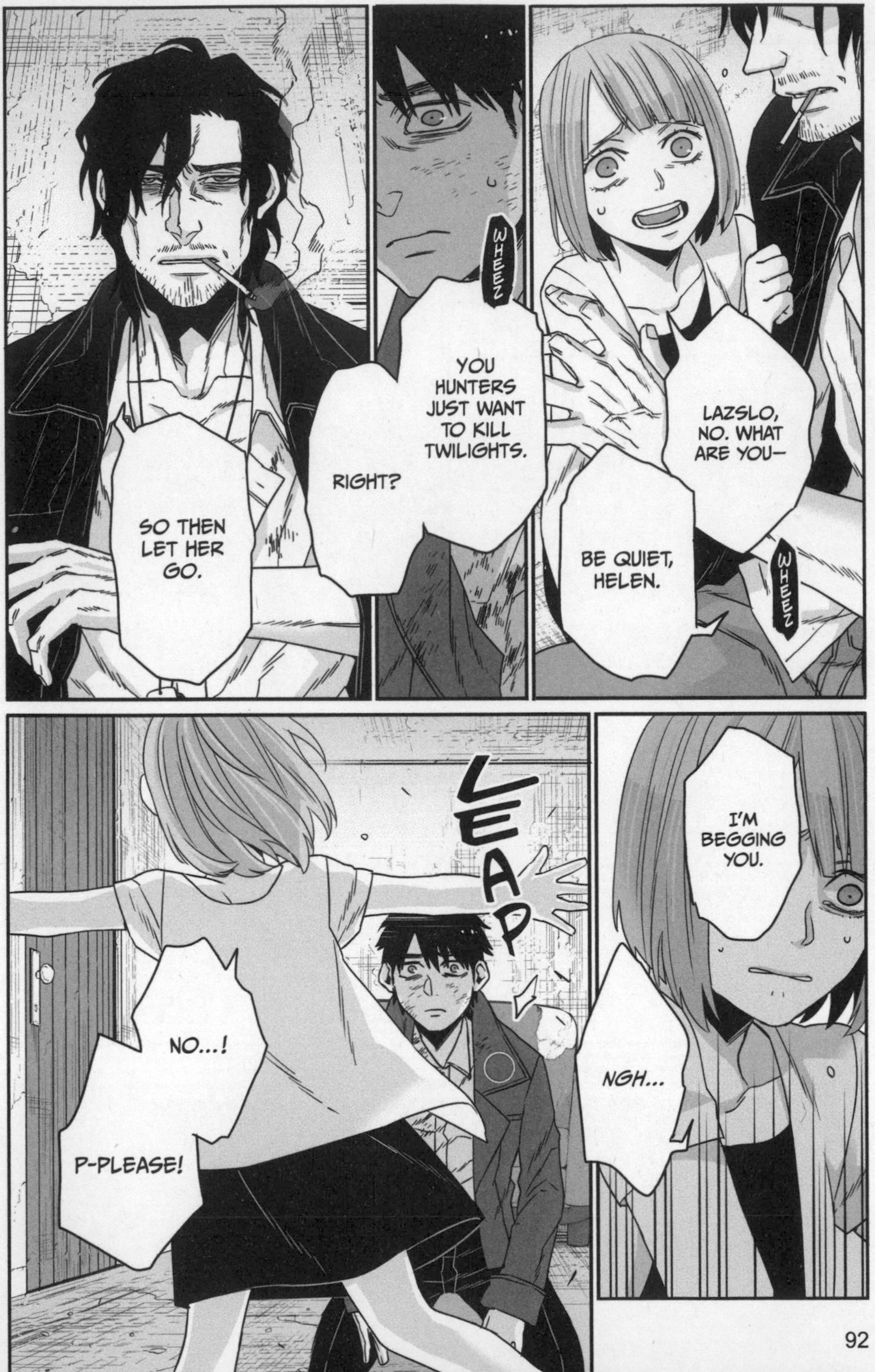

LAZSLO, NO. WHAT ARE YOU—
BE QUIET, HELEN.
WHEEZ
WHEEZ
YOU HUNTERS JUST WANT TO KILL TWILIGHTS.
RIGHT?
SO THEN LET HER GO.
I'M BEGGING YOU.
NGH...
LEAP
NO...!
P-PLEASE!

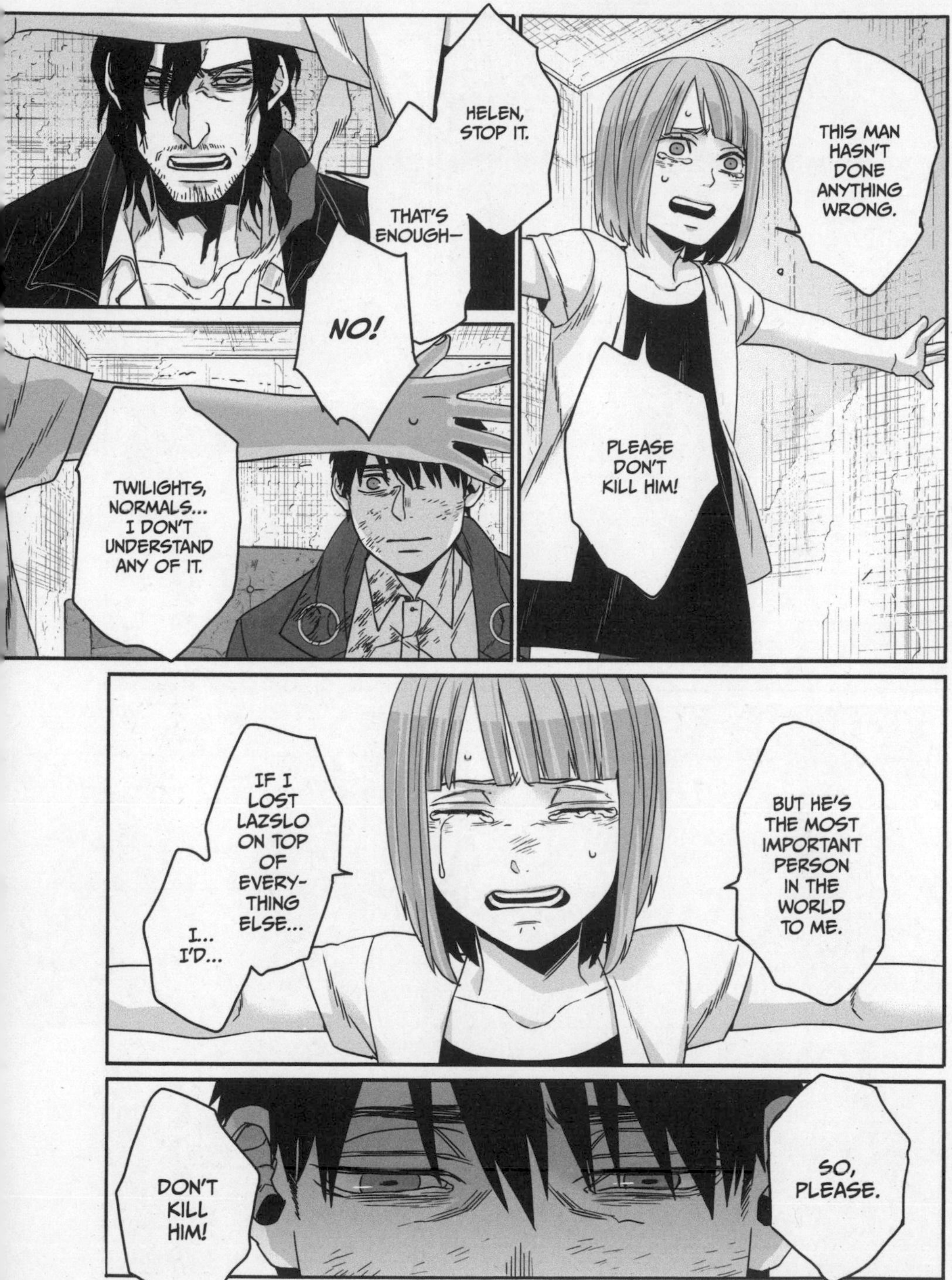
THIS MAN HASN'T DONE ANYTHING WRONG.
PLEASE DON'T KILL HIM!
HELEN, STOP IT.
THAT'S ENOUGH—
NO!
TWILIGHTS, NORMALS... I DON'T UNDERSTAND ANY OF IT.
BUT HE'S THE MOST IMPORTANT PERSON IN THE WORLD TO ME.
IF I LOST LAZSLO ON TOP OF EVERY-THING ELSE...
I... I'D...
SO, PLEASE.
DON'T KILL HIM!

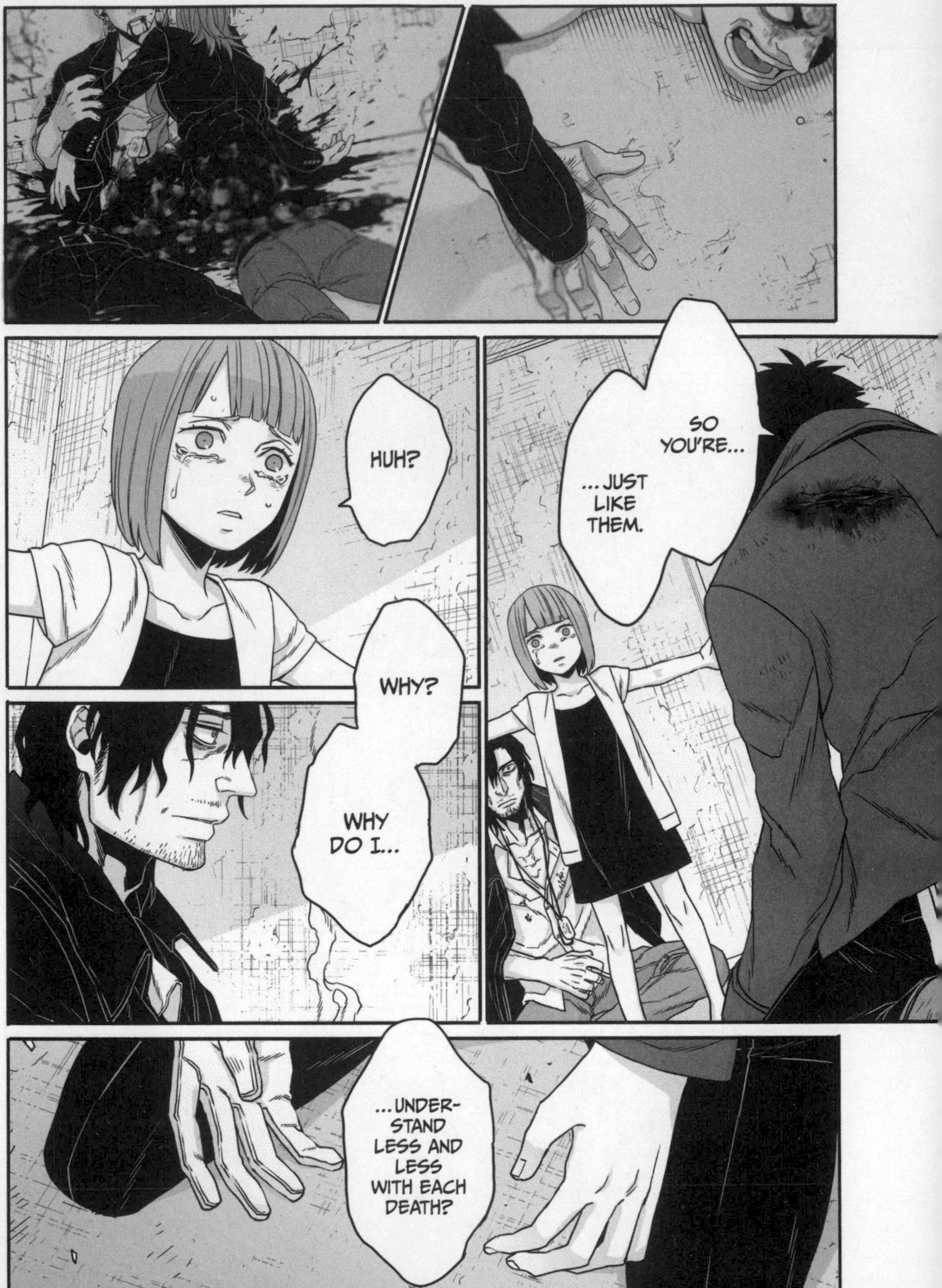
SO YOU'RE...
...JUST LIKE THEM.
HUH?
WHY?
WHY DO I...
...UNDER-STAND LESS AND LESS WITH EACH DEATH?

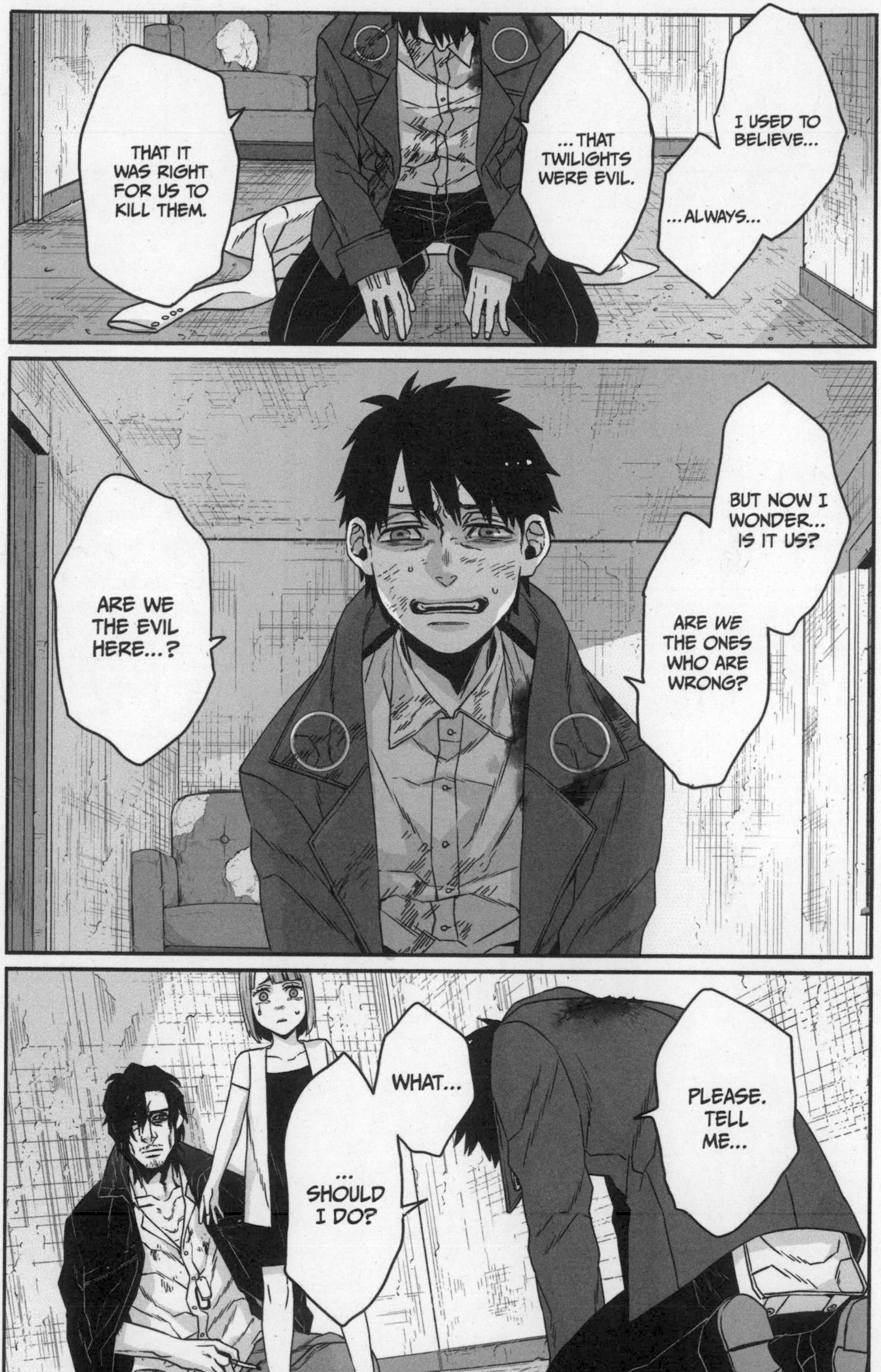
I USED TO BELIEVE...
...ALWAYS...
...THAT TWILIGHTS WERE EVIL.
THAT IT WAS RIGHT FOR US TO KILL THEM.
BUT NOW I WONDER... IS IT US?
ARE WE THE ONES WHO ARE WRONG?
ARE WE THE EVIL HERE...?
PLEASE. TELL ME...
WHAT...
...SHOULD I DO?

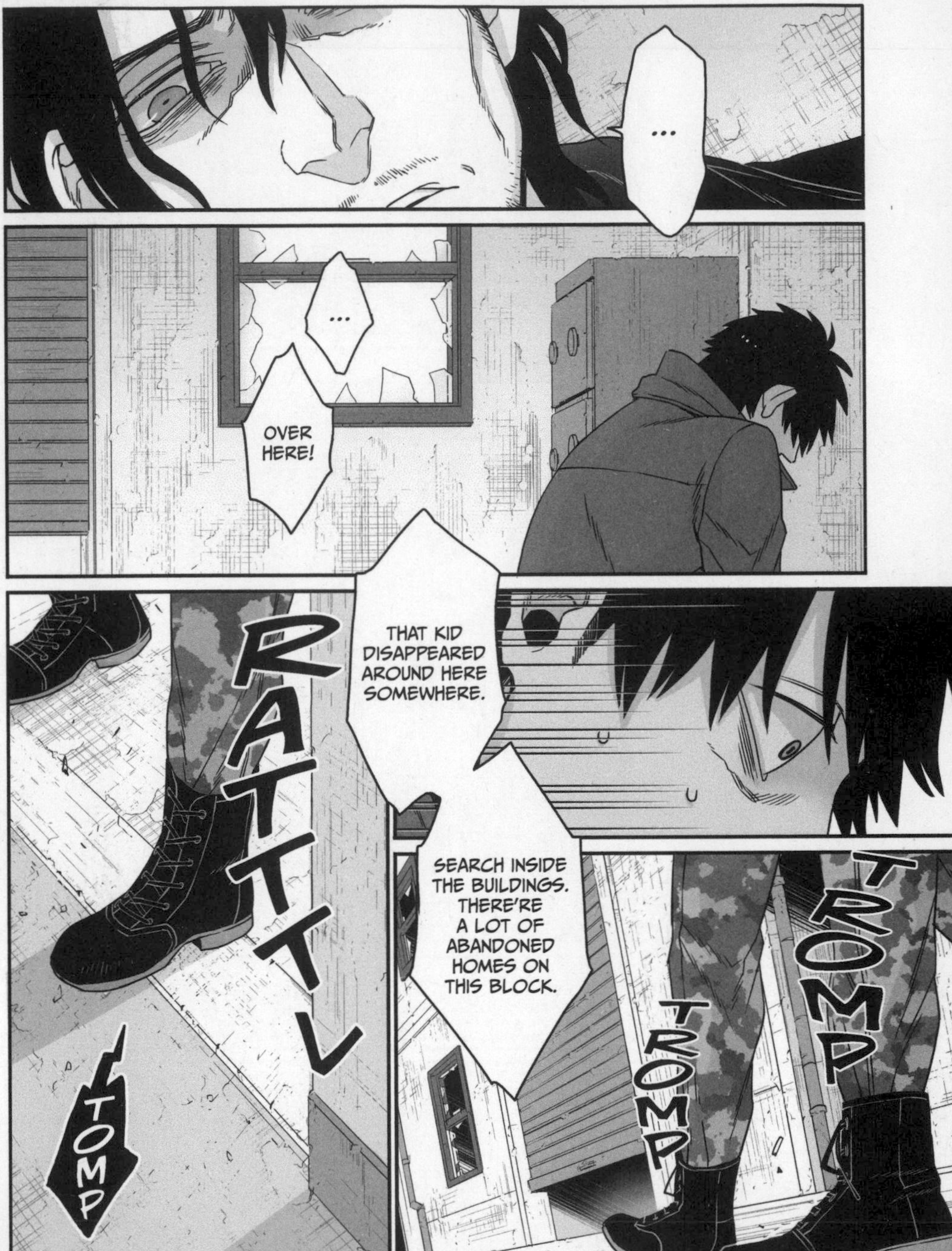
...
...
OVER HERE!
THAT KID DISAPPEARED AROUND HERE SOMEWHERE.
SEARCH INSIDE THE BUILDINGS. THERE'RE A LOT OF ABANDONED HOMES ON THIS BLOCK.
TROMP
TROMP
RATTTL
TOMP

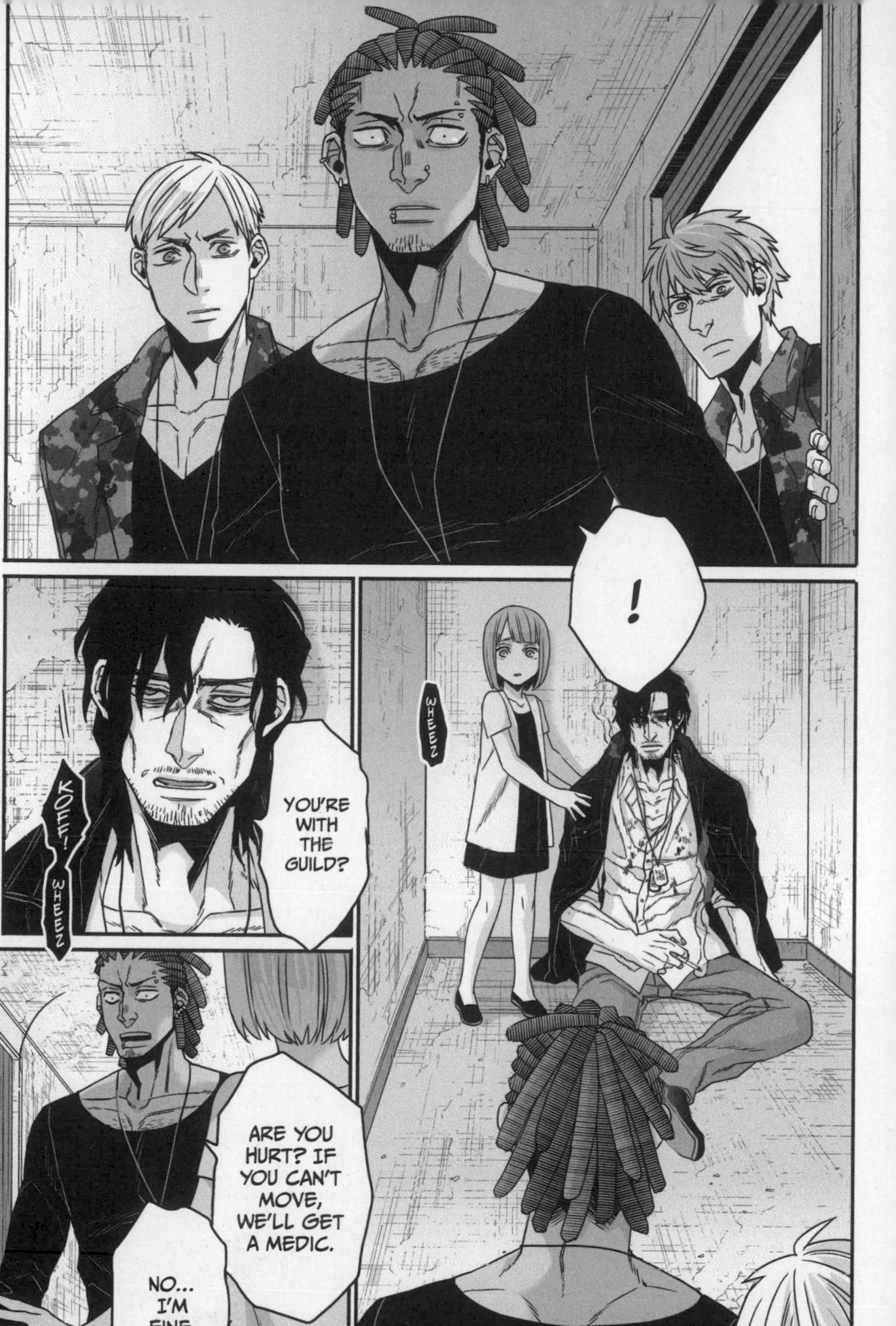
!
WHEEZ
KOFF!
WHEEZ
YOU'RE WITH THE GUILD?
ARE YOU HURT? IF YOU CAN'T MOVE, WE'LL GET A MEDIC.
NO... I'M FINE.

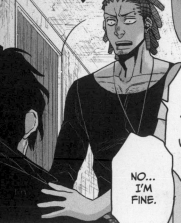

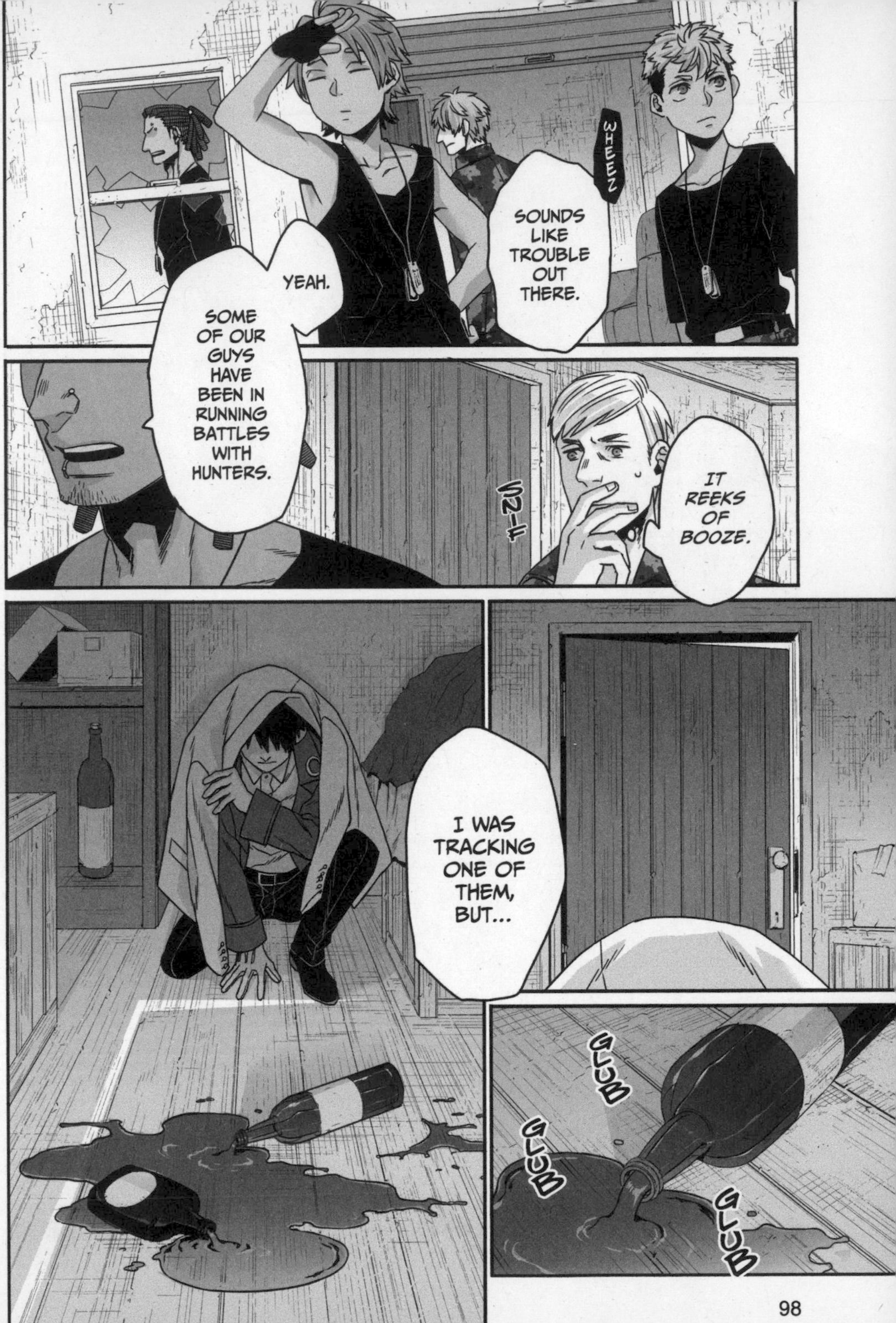
WHEEZ
SOUNDS LIKE TROUBLE OUT THERE.
YEAH.
SOME OF OUR GUYS HAVE BEEN IN RUNNING BATTLES WITH HUNTERS.
IT REEKS OF BOOZE.
SNIF
I WAS TRACKING ONE OF THEM, BUT...
GLUB
GLUB
GLUB

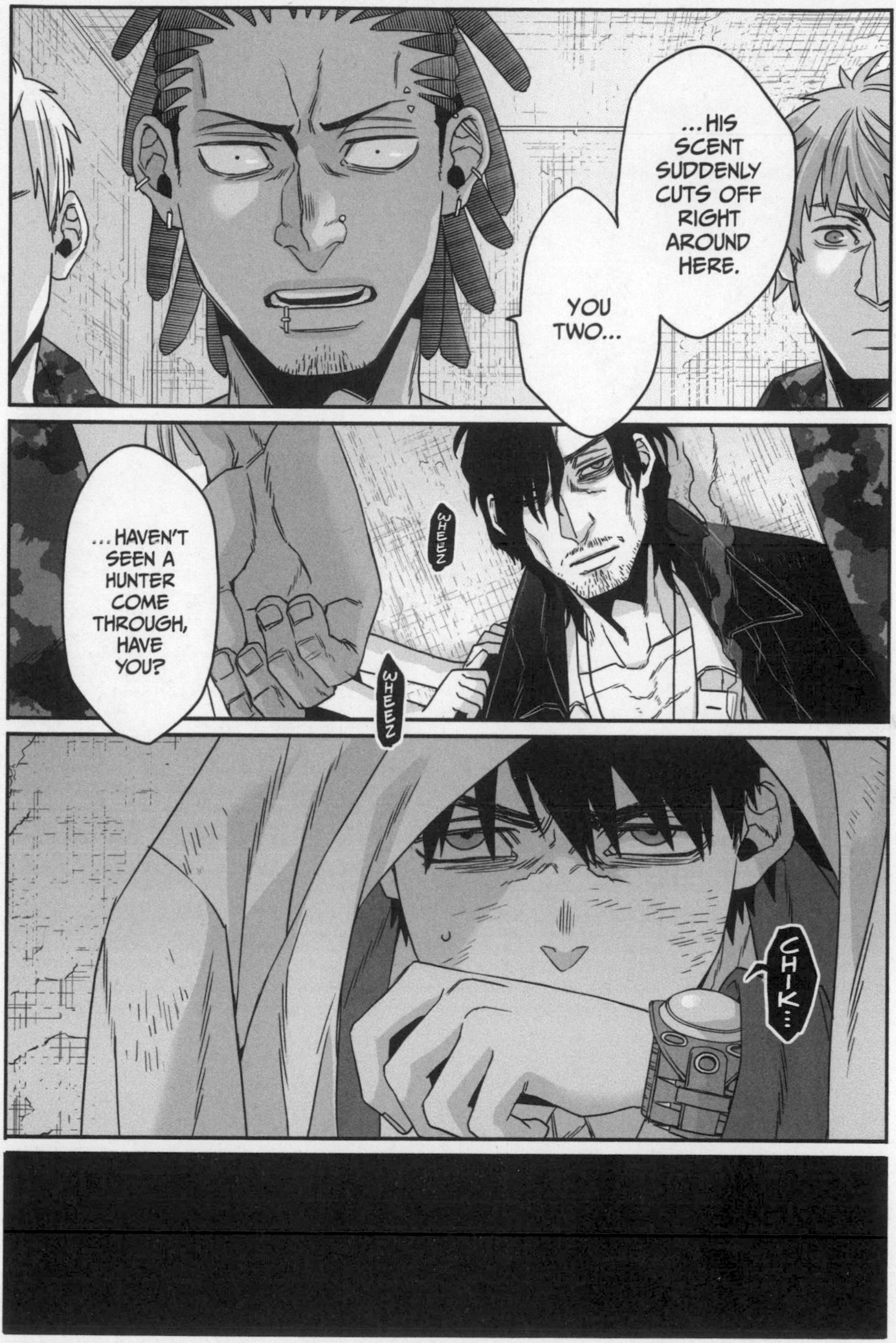
...HIS SCENT SUDDENLY CUTS OFF RIGHT AROUND HERE.
YOU TWO...
...HAVEN'T SEEN A HUNTER COME THROUGH, HAVE YOU?
WHEEZ
WHEEZ
CHIK...

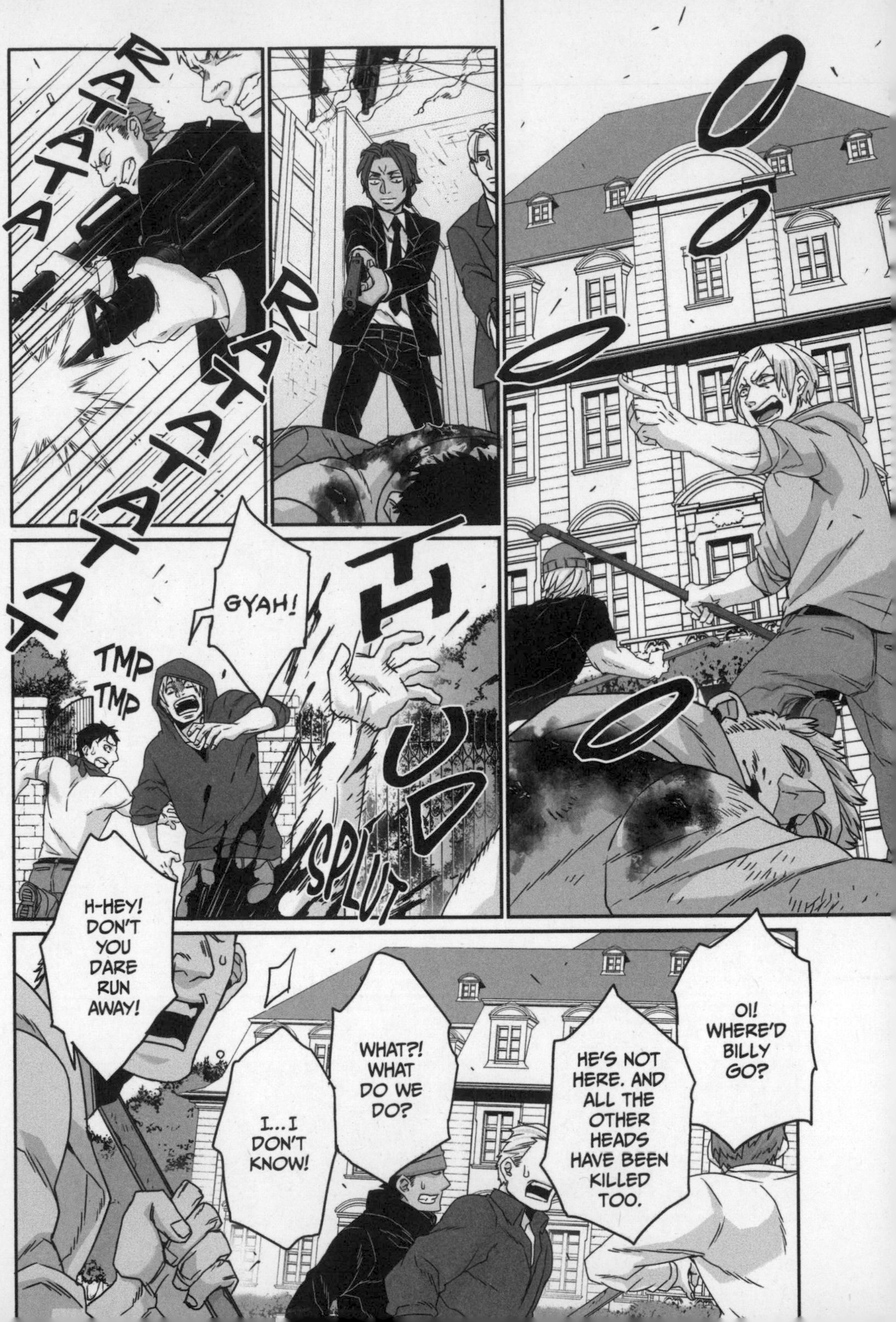
OOOOO
RATATATATA
RATATATATAT
THUD
GYAH!
TMP TMP
SPLUT
OI! WHERE'D BILLY GO?
HE'S NOT HERE. AND ALL THE OTHER HEADS HAVE BEEN KILLED TOO.
WHAT?! WHAT DO WE DO?
I...I DON'T KNOW!
H-HEY! DON'T YOU DARE RUN AWAY!

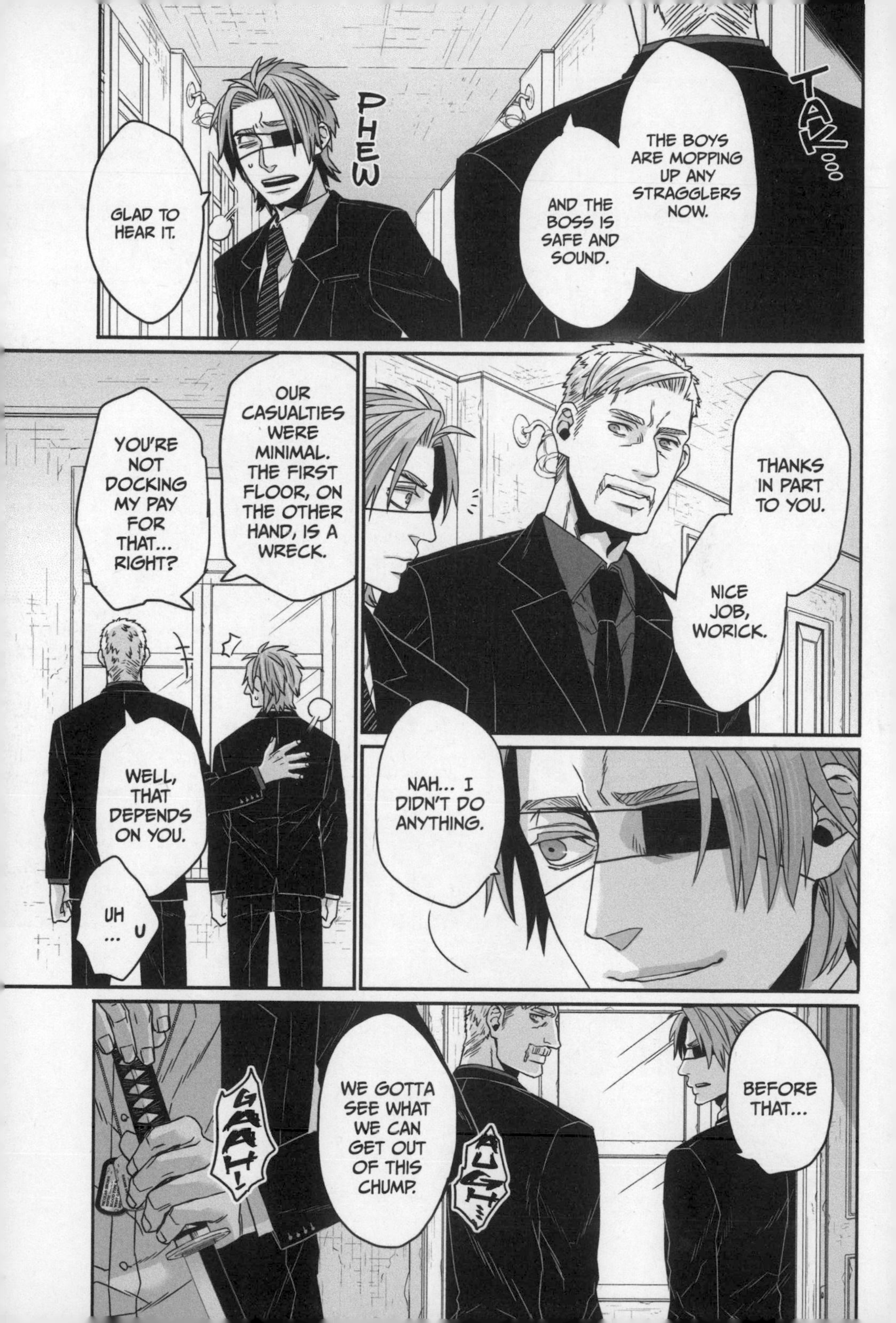
TAK...
THE BOYS ARE MOPPING UP ANY STRAGGLERS NOW.
AND THE BOSS IS SAFE AND SOUND.
PHEW
GLAD TO HEAR IT.
THANKS IN PART TO YOU.
NICE JOB, WORICK.
NAH... I DIDN'T DO ANYTHING.
OUR CASUALTIES WERE MINIMAL. THE FIRST FLOOR, ON THE OTHER HAND, IS A WRECK.
YOU'RE NOT DOCKING MY PAY FOR THAT... RIGHT?
WELL, THAT DEPENDS ON YOU.
UH ... U
BEFORE THAT...
WE GOTTA SEE WHAT WE CAN GET OUT OF THIS CHUMP.
AUGH!!
GAAH!

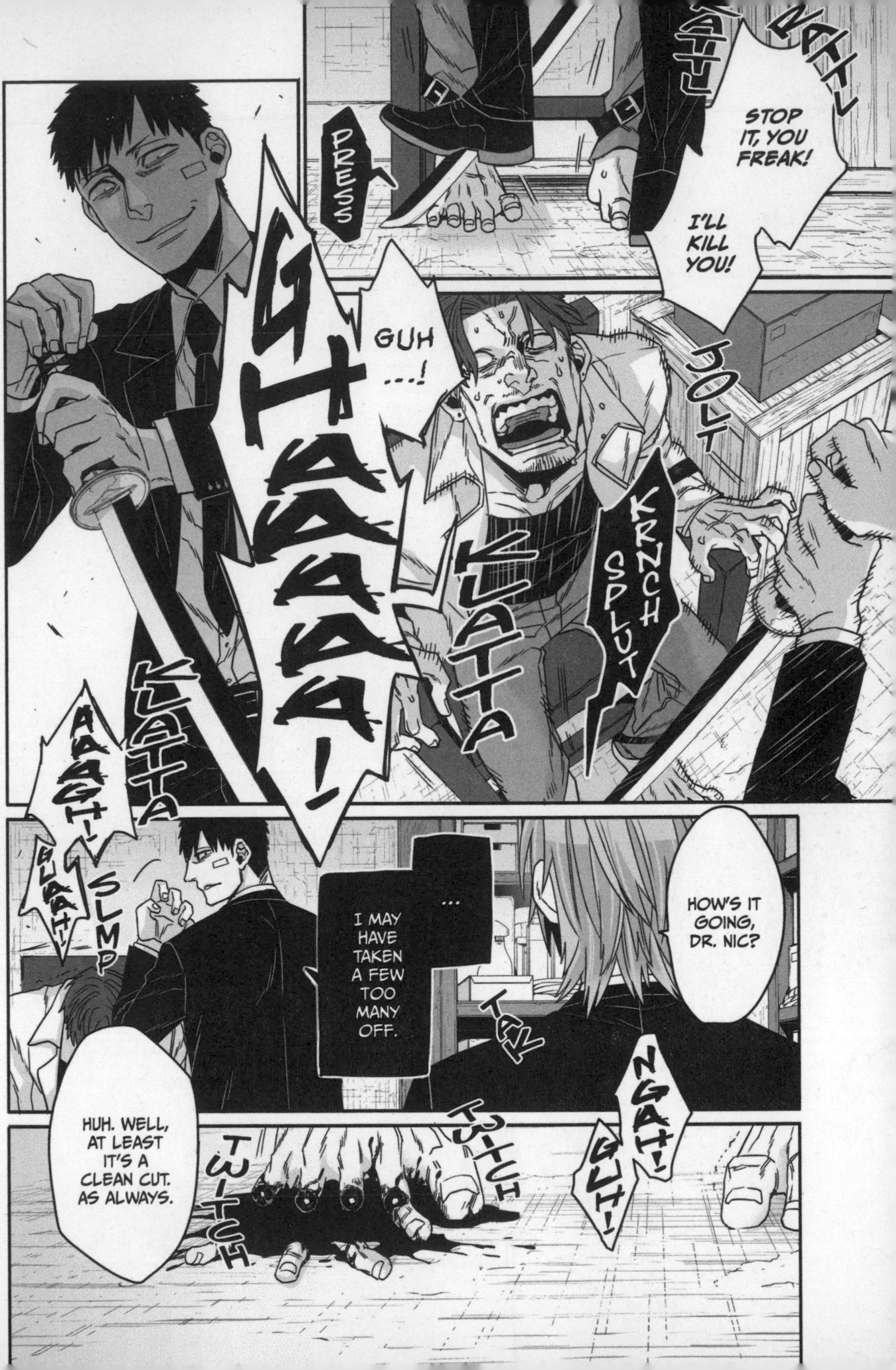
STOP IT, YOU FREAK!
I'LL KILL YOU!
PRESS
JOLT
GUH ...!
GHAAAAA!
KRNCH SPLUT
KLATTA
KLATTA
AAAGH!
GUAAH!
SLMP
HOW'S IT GOING, DR. NIC?
...
I MAY HAVE TAKEN A FEW TOO MANY OFF.
TAY
NGAH!
GUH!
TWITCH
TWITCH
HUH. WELL, AT LEAST IT'S A CLEAN CUT. AS ALWAYS.

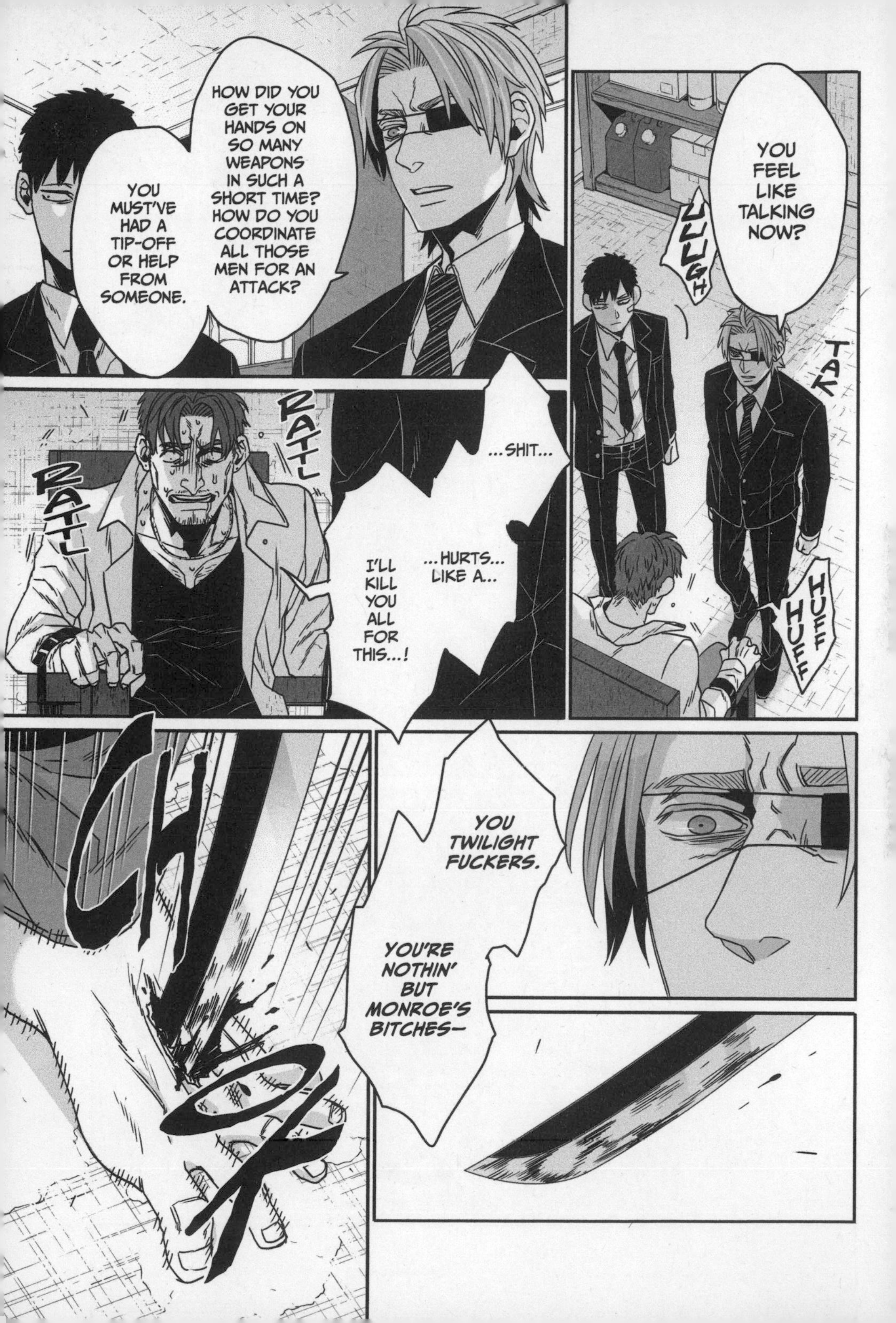

YOU FEEL LIKE TALKING NOW?
UUUGH
TAK
HUFF HUFF
HOW DID YOU GET YOUR HANDS ON SO MANY WEAPONS IN SUCH A SHORT TIME? HOW DO YOU COORDINATE ALL THOSE MEN FOR AN ATTACK?
YOU MUST'VE HAD A TIP-OFF OR HELP FROM SOMEONE.
RATTL
RATTL
...SHIT...
...HURTS... LIKE A...
I'LL KILL YOU ALL FOR THIS...!
YOU TWILIGHT FUCKERS.
YOU'RE NOTHIN' BUT MONROE'S BITCHES—
CHOP

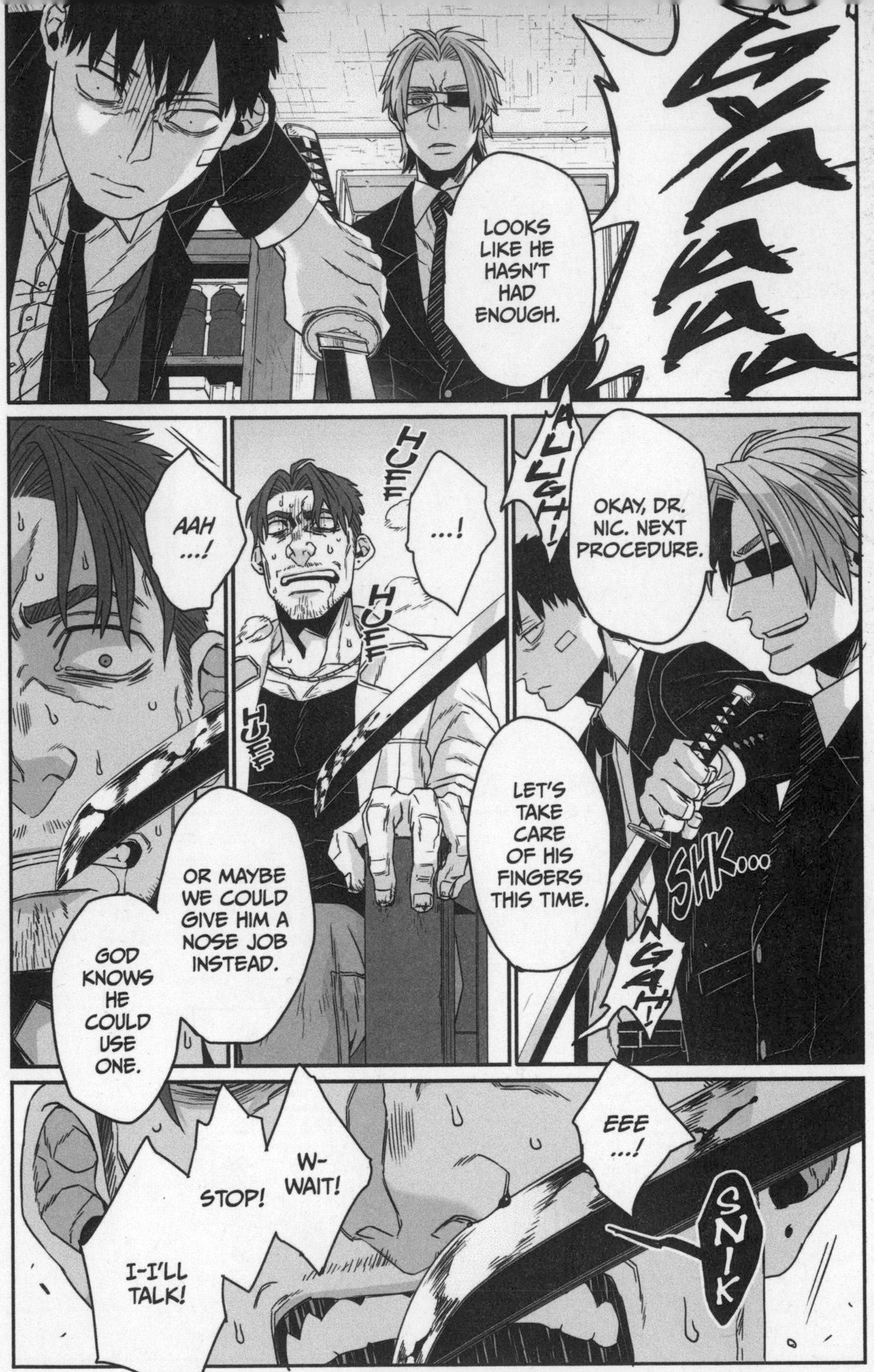
LOOKS LIKE HE HASN'T HAD ENOUGH.
AAUGH!
OKAY, DR. NIC. NEXT PROCEDURE.
LET'S TAKE CARE OF HIS FINGERS THIS TIME.
SHK...
NGAH!
HUFF
...!
HUFF
HUFF
AAH ...!
OR MAYBE WE COULD GIVE HIM A NOSE JOB INSTEAD.
GOD KNOWS HE COULD USE ONE.
EEE ...!
SNIK
W-WAIT!
STOP!
I-I'LL TALK!

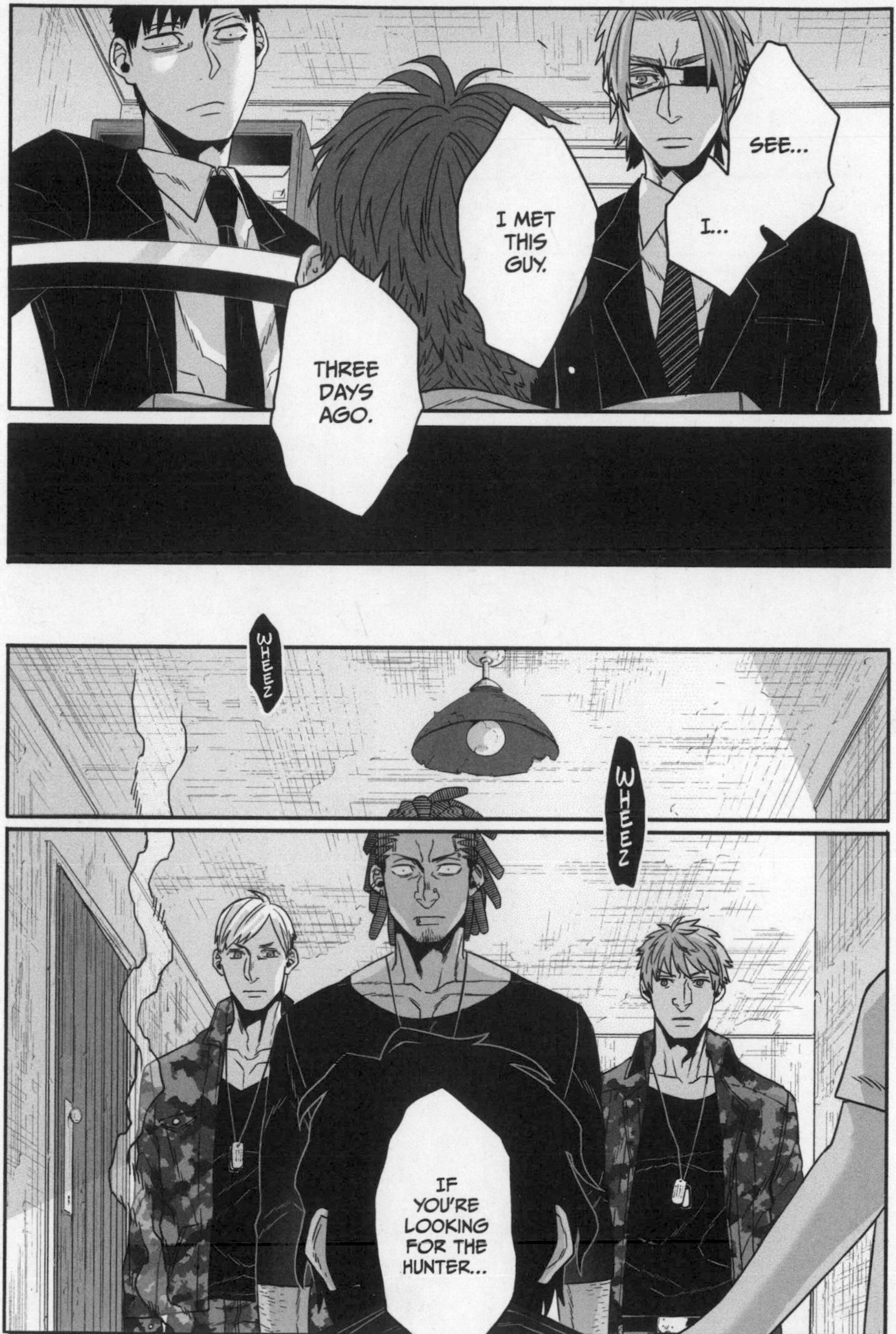
SEE... I...
I MET THIS GUY.
THREE DAYS AGO.
WHEEZ
WHEEZ
IF YOU'RE LOOKING FOR THE HUNTER...

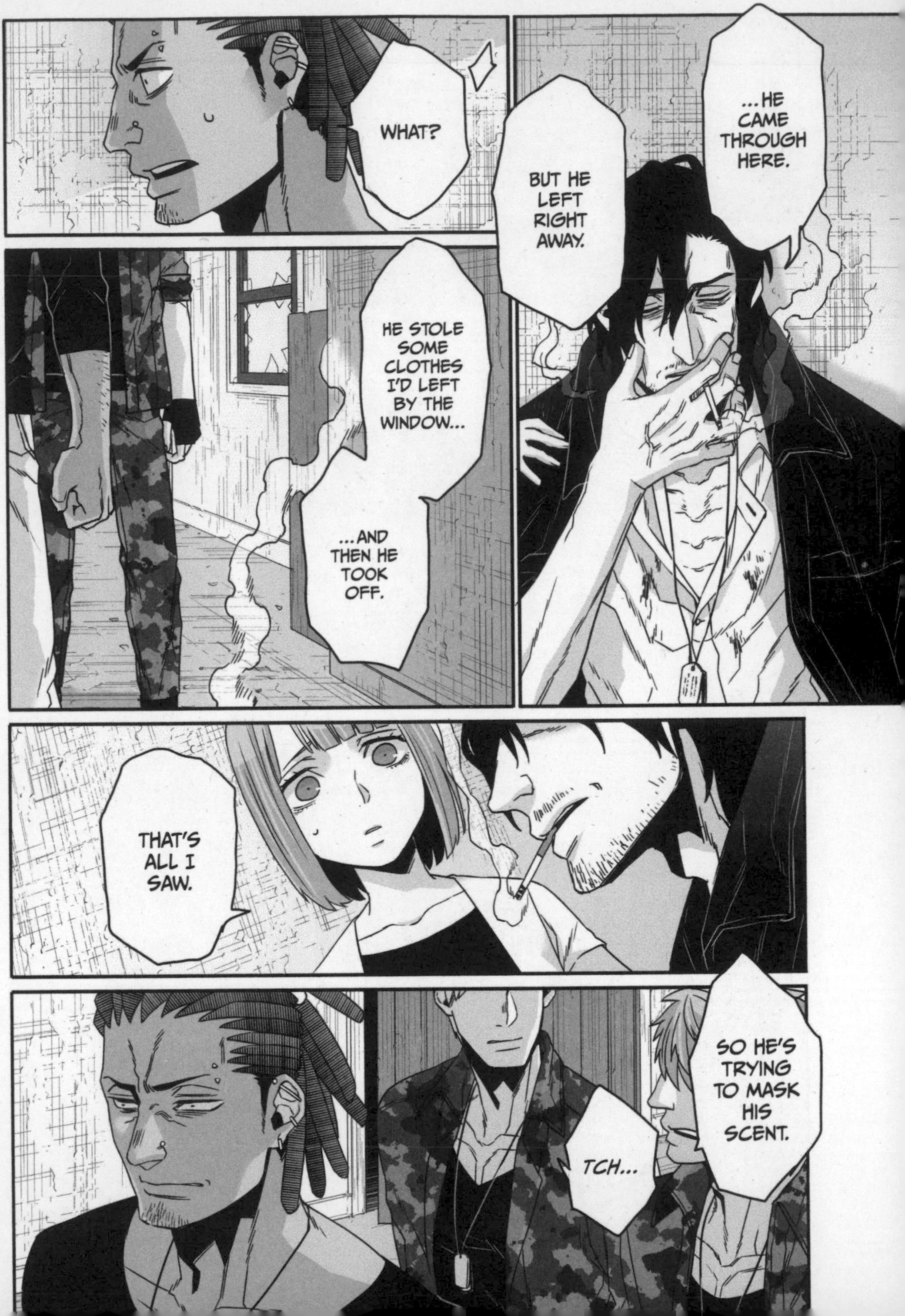
...HE CAME THROUGH HERE.
BUT HE LEFT RIGHT AWAY.
WHAT?
HE STOLE SOME CLOTHES I'D LEFT BY THE WINDOW...
...AND THEN HE TOOK OFF.
THAT'S ALL I SAW.
SO HE'S TRYING TO MASK HIS SCENT.
TCH...

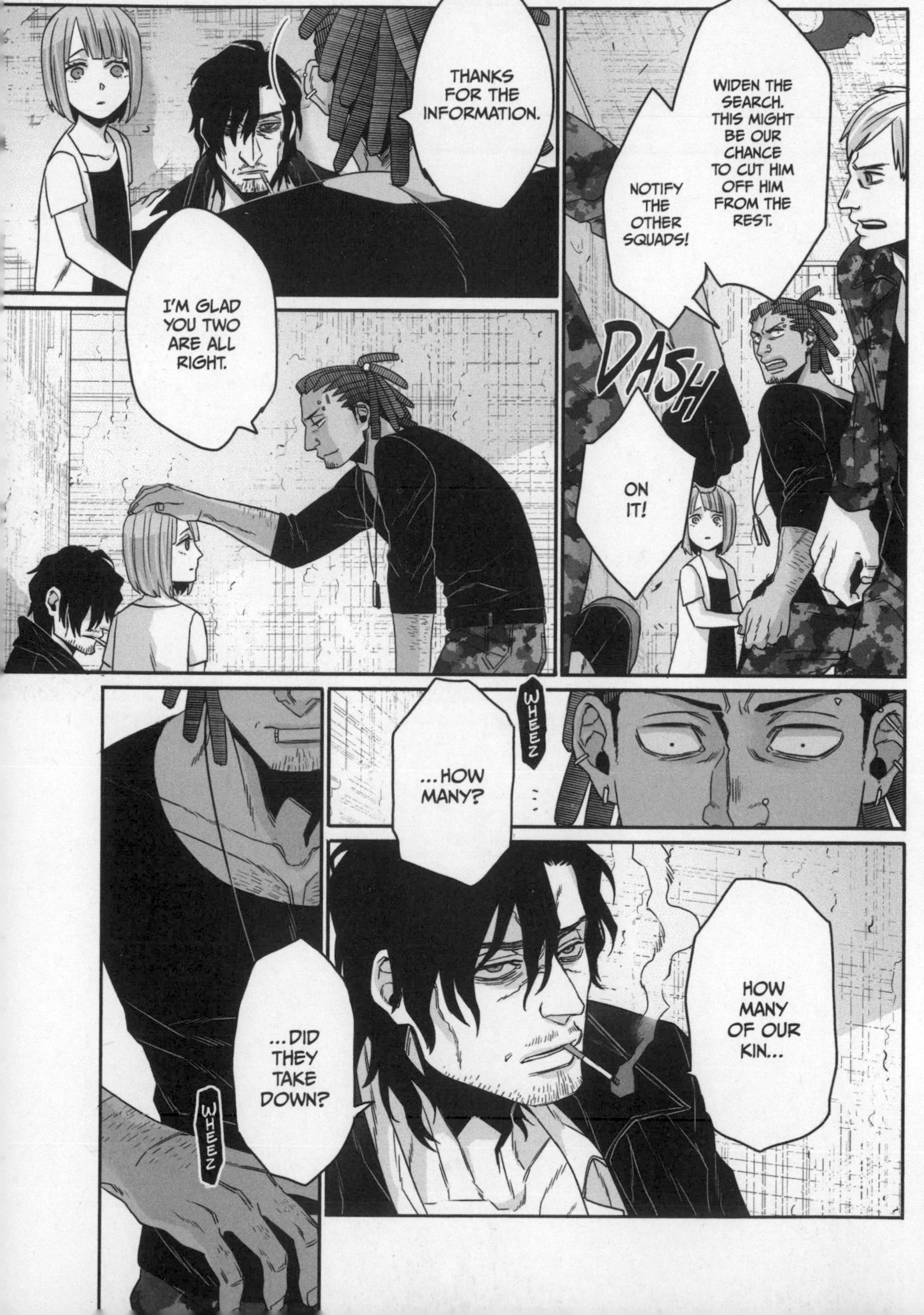
WIDEN THE SEARCH. THIS MIGHT BE OUR CHANCE TO CUT HIM OFF HIM FROM THE REST.
NOTIFY THE OTHER SQUADS!
DASH
ON IT!
THANKS FOR THE INFORMATION.
I'M GLAD YOU TWO ARE ALL RIGHT.
WHEEZ
...HOW MANY?
...
HOW MANY OF OUR KIN...
...DID THEY TAKE DOWN?
WHEEZ

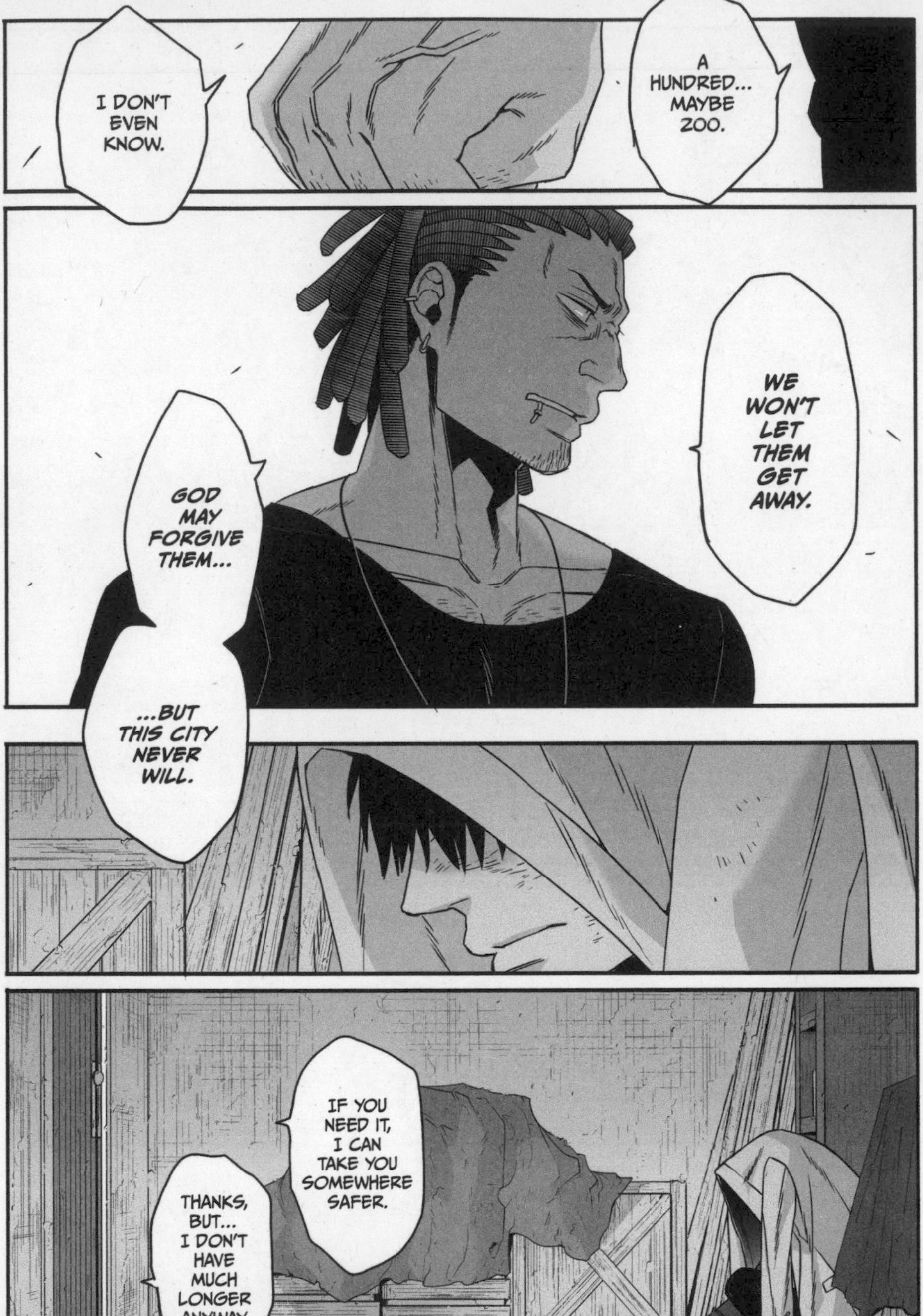
A HUNDRED... MAYBE 200.
I DON'T EVEN KNOW.
WE WON'T LET THEM GET AWAY.
GOD MAY FORGIVE THEM...
...BUT THIS CITY NEVER WILL.
IF YOU NEED IT, I CAN TAKE YOU SOMEWHERE SAFER.
THANKS, BUT... I DON'T HAVE MUCH LONGER ANYWAY.

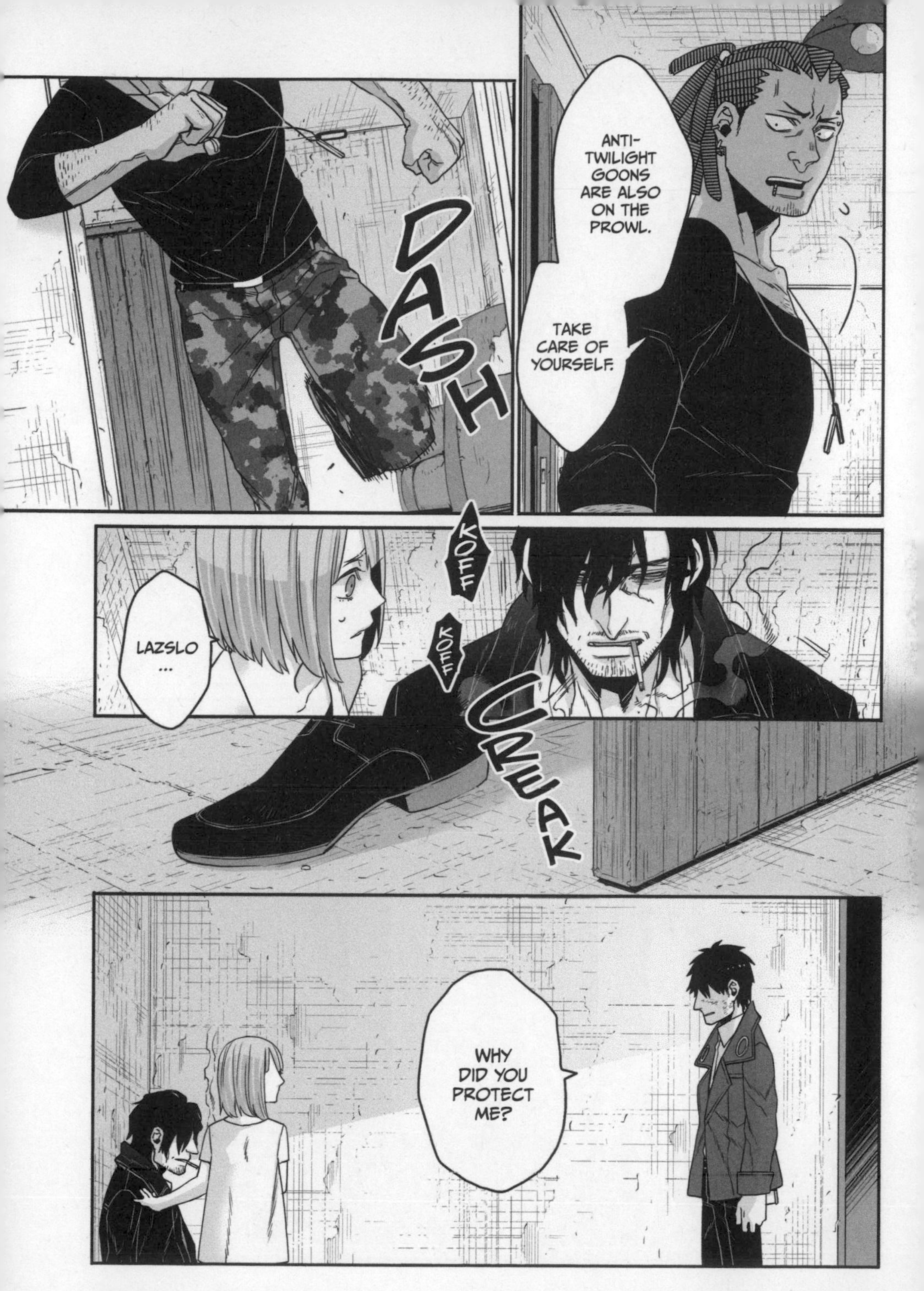
ANTI-TWILIGHT GOONS ARE ALSO ON THE PROWL.
TAKE CARE OF YOURSELF.
DASH
KOFF
KOFF
LAZSLO ...
CREAK
WHY DID YOU PROTECT ME?

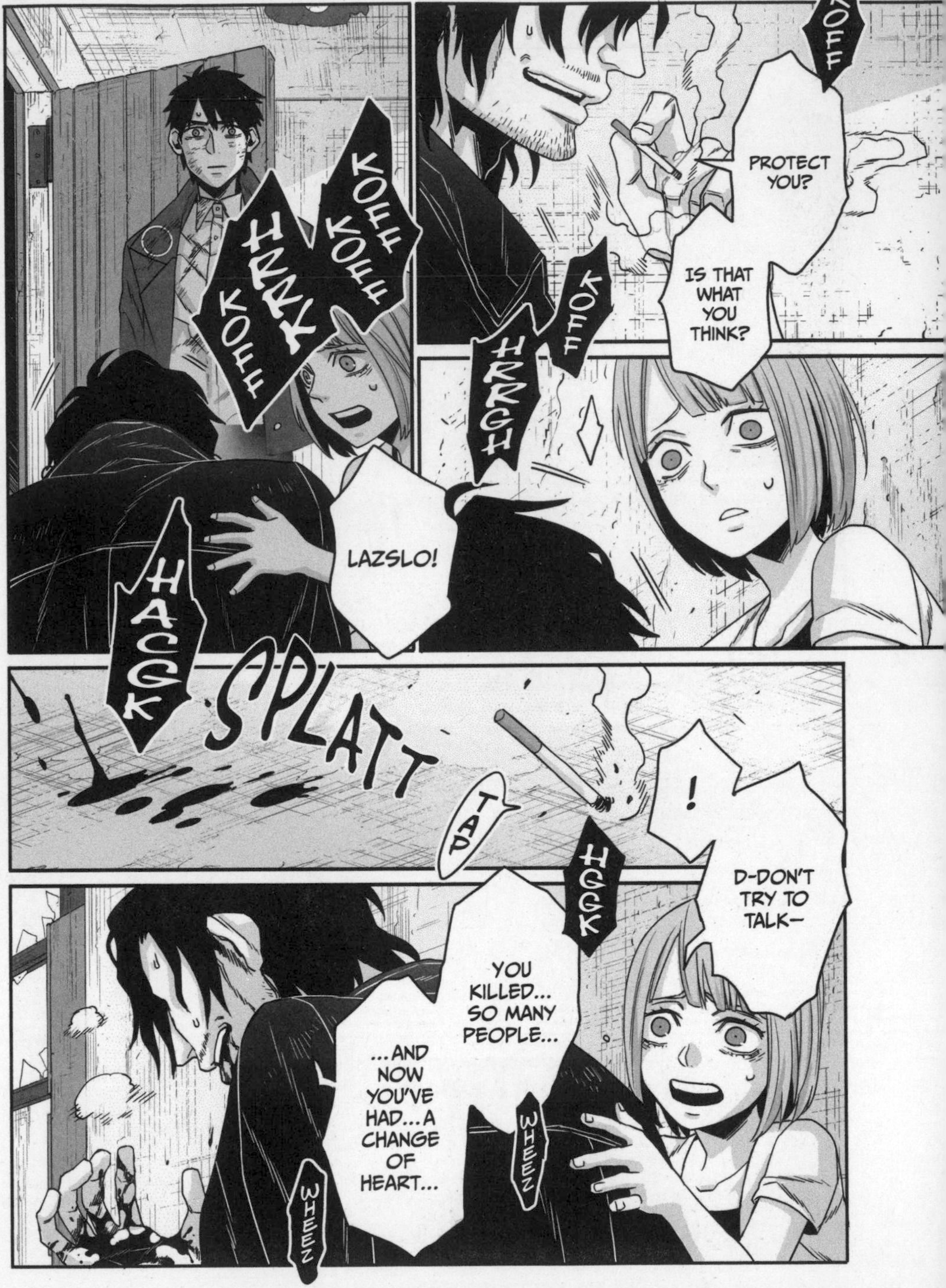
KOFF
PROTECT YOU?
IS THAT WHAT YOU THINK?
KOFF
HRRGH
KOFF KOFF
HRRK
KOFF
LAZSLO!
HACGK
!
TAP
SPLATT
D-DON'T TRY TO TALK—
HGGK
YOU KILLED... SO MANY PEOPLE...
...AND NOW YOU'VE HAD... A CHANGE OF HEART...
WHEEZ
WHEEZ

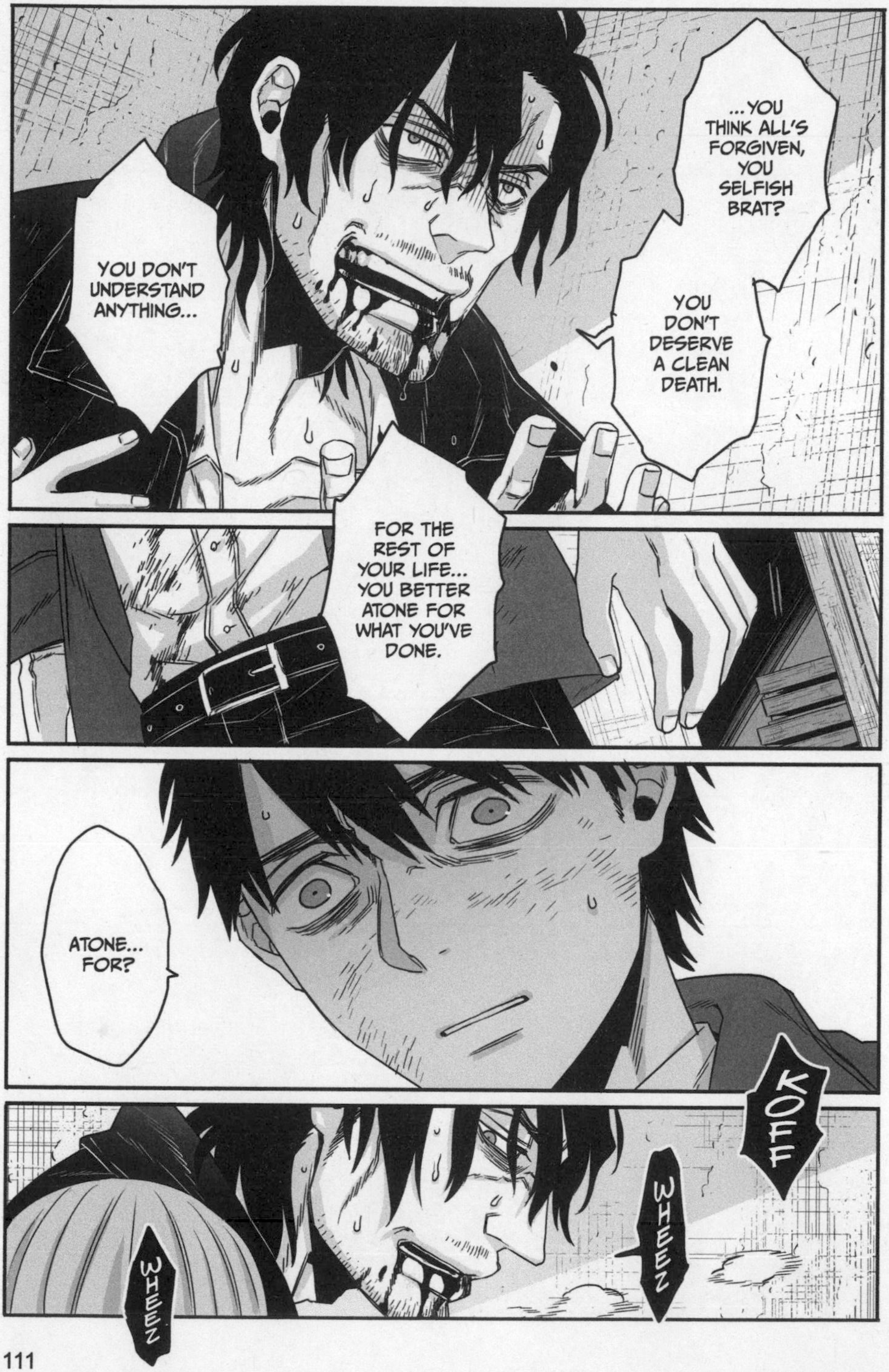
...YOU THINK ALL'S FORGIVEN, YOU SELFISH BRAT?
YOU DON'T DESERVE A CLEAN DEATH.
YOU DON'T UNDERSTAND ANYTHING...
FOR THE REST OF YOUR LIFE... YOU BETTER ATONE FOR WHAT YOU'VE DONE.
ATONE... FOR?
KOFF
WHEEZ
WHEEZ

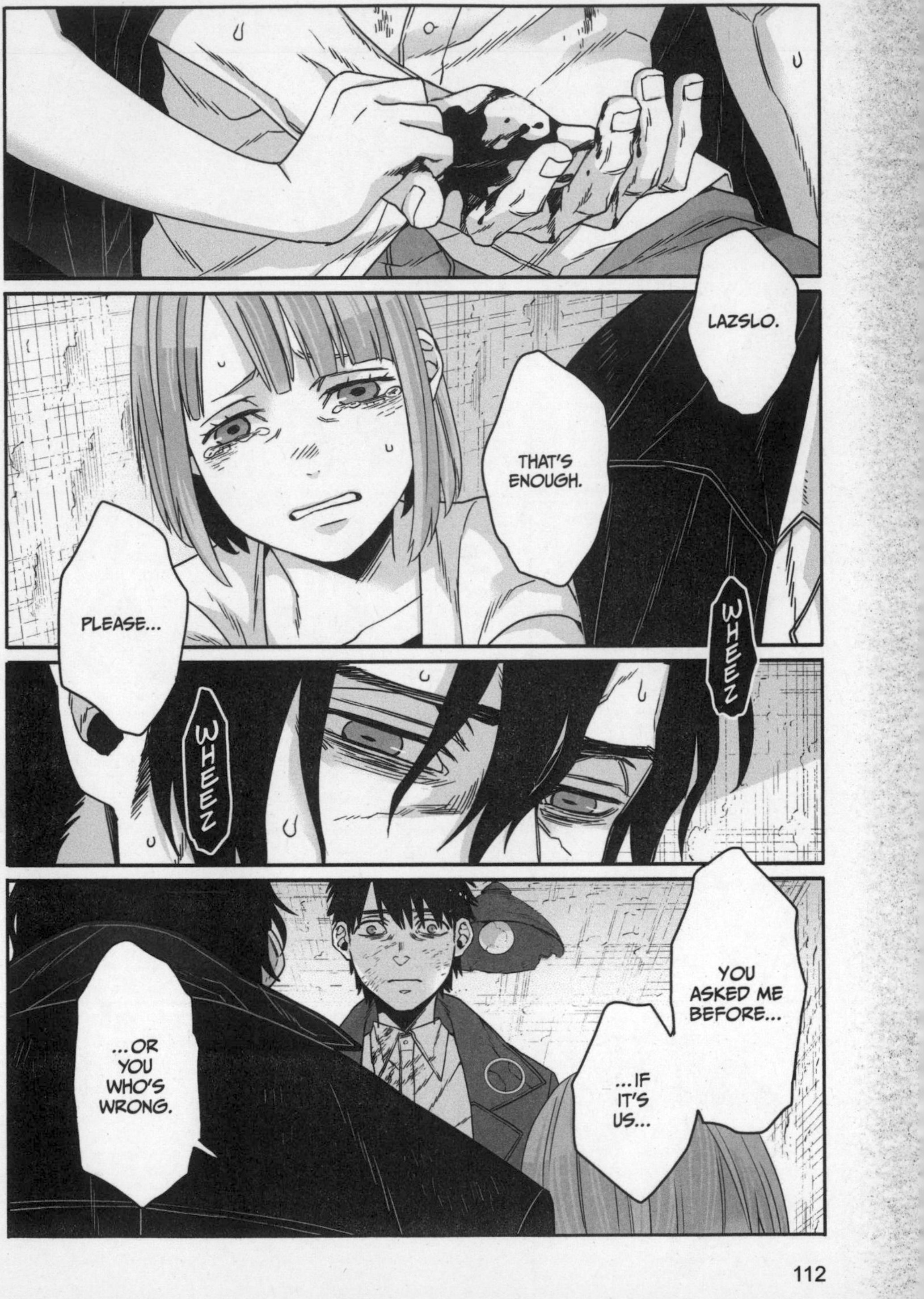
LAZSLO.
THAT'S ENOUGH.
PLEASE...
WHEEZ
WHEEZ
YOU ASKED ME BEFORE...
...IF IT'S US...
...OR YOU WHO'S WRONG.

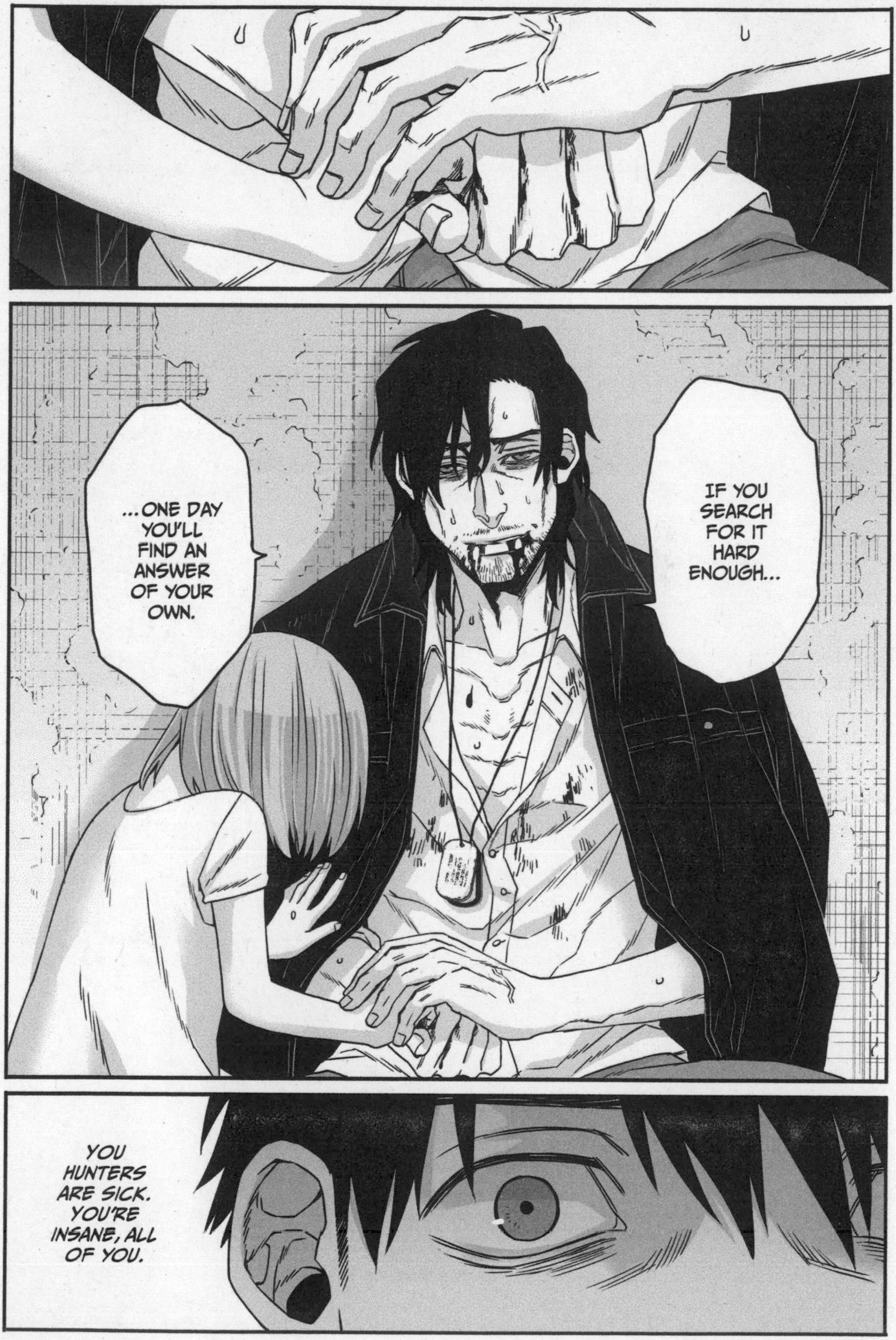
IF YOU SEARCH FOR IT HARD ENOUGH...
...ONE DAY YOU'LL FIND AN ANSWER OF YOUR OWN.
YOU HUNTERS ARE SICK. YOU'RE INSANE, ALL OF YOU.

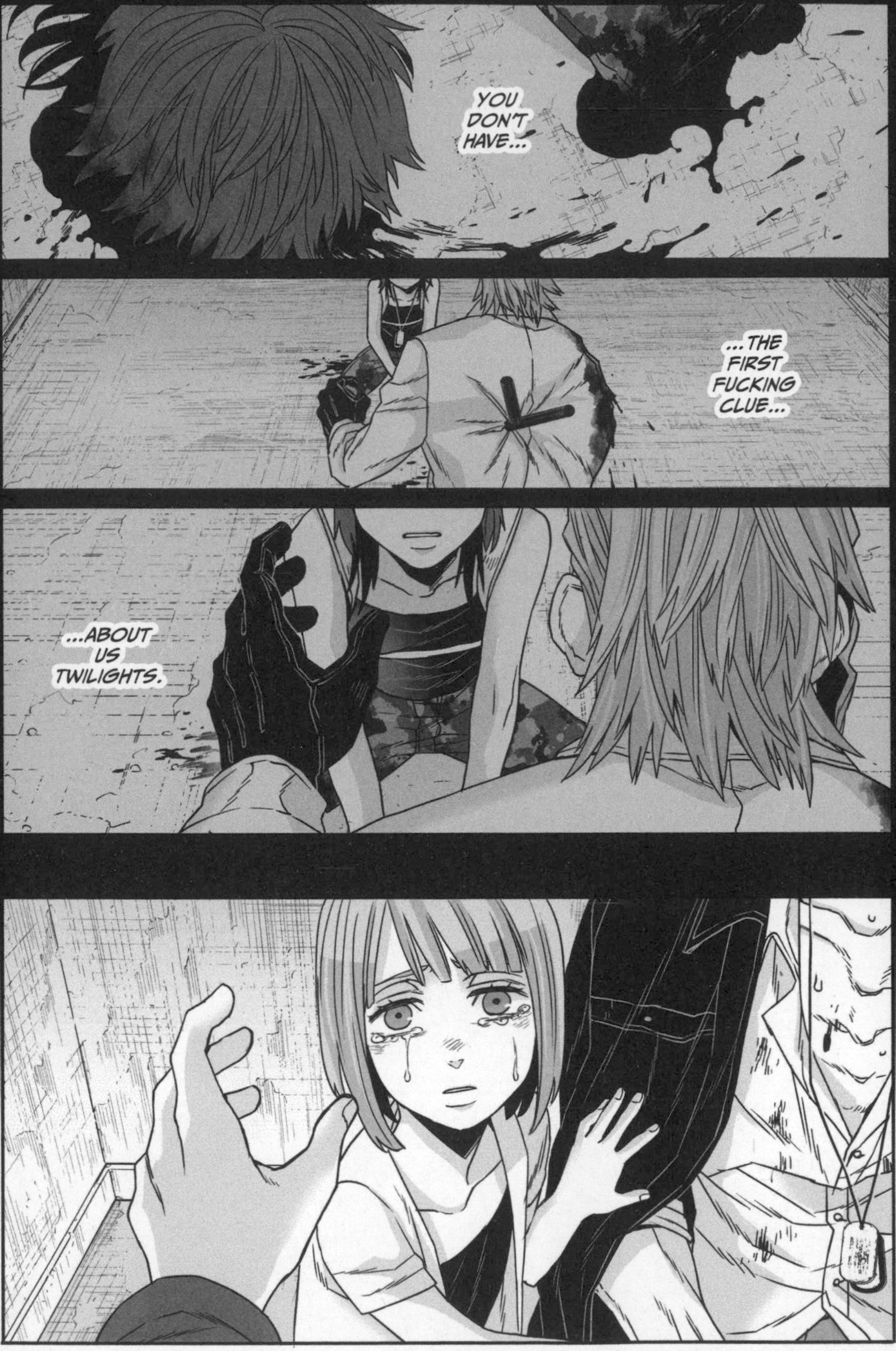
YOU DON'T HAVE...
...THE FIRST FUCKING CLUE...
...ABOUT US TWILIGHTS.

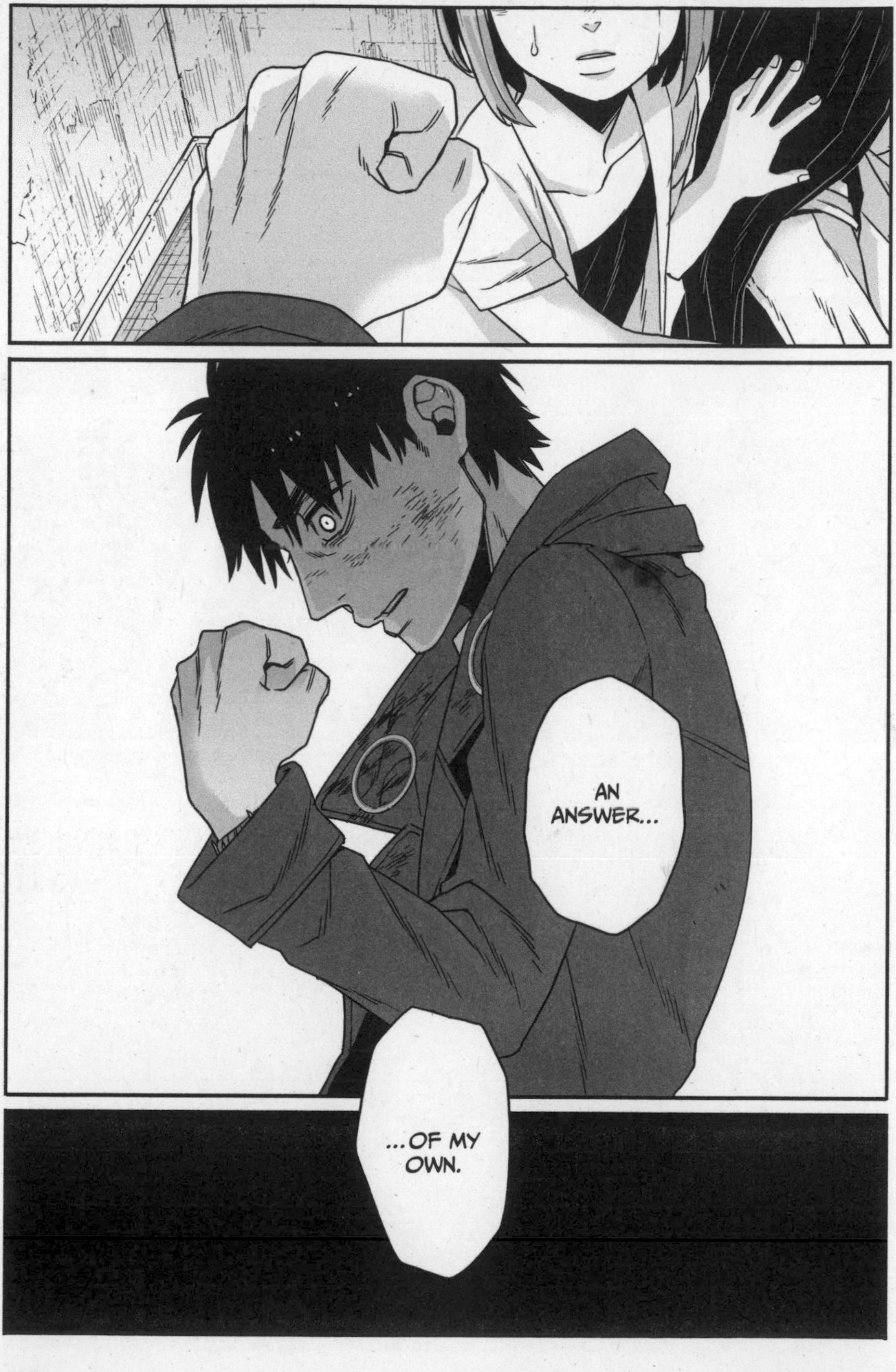
AN ANSWER...
...OF MY OWN.

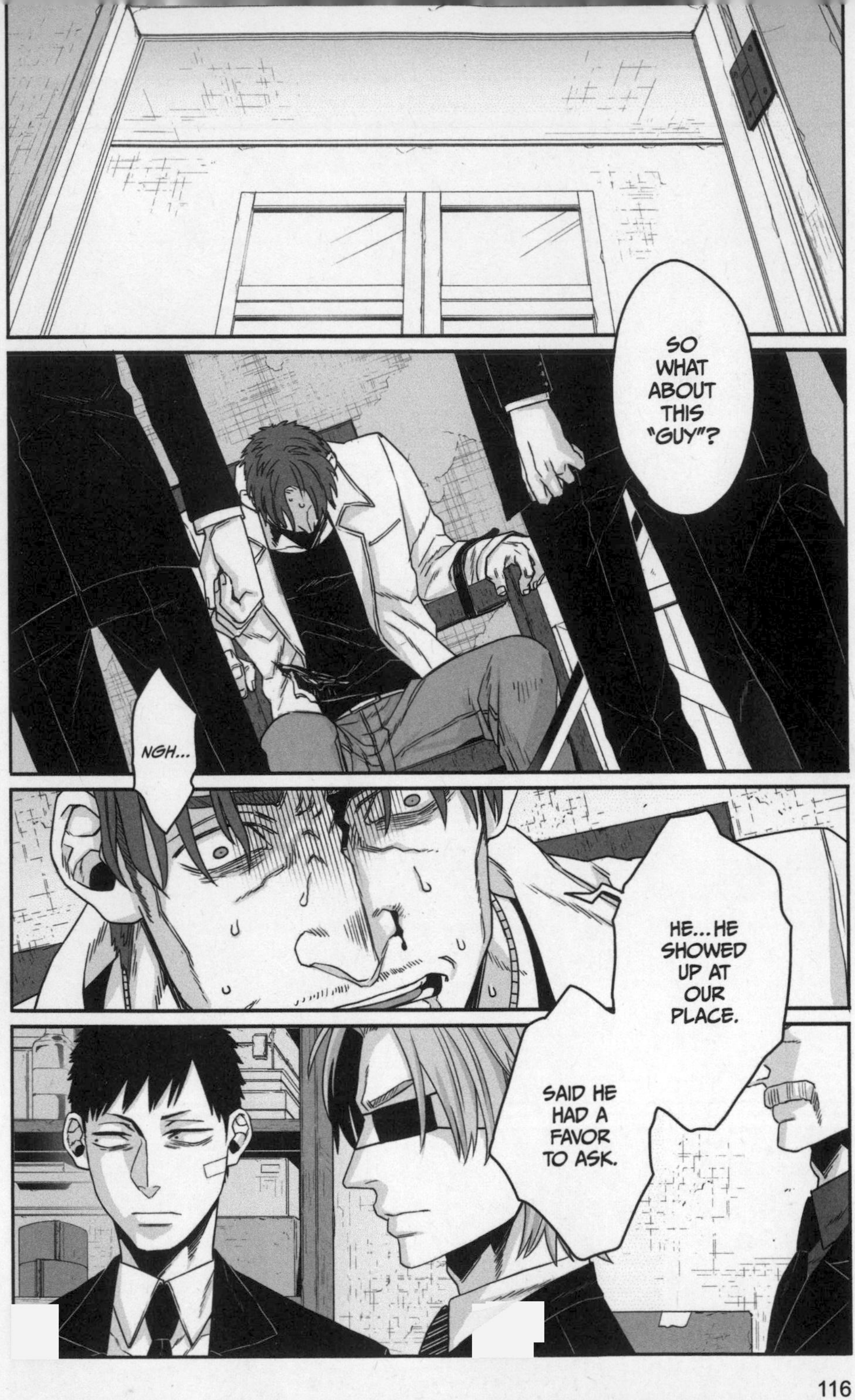
SO WHAT ABOUT THIS "GUY"?
NGH...
HE... HE SHOWED UP AT OUR PLACE.
SAID HE HAD A FAVOR TO ASK.

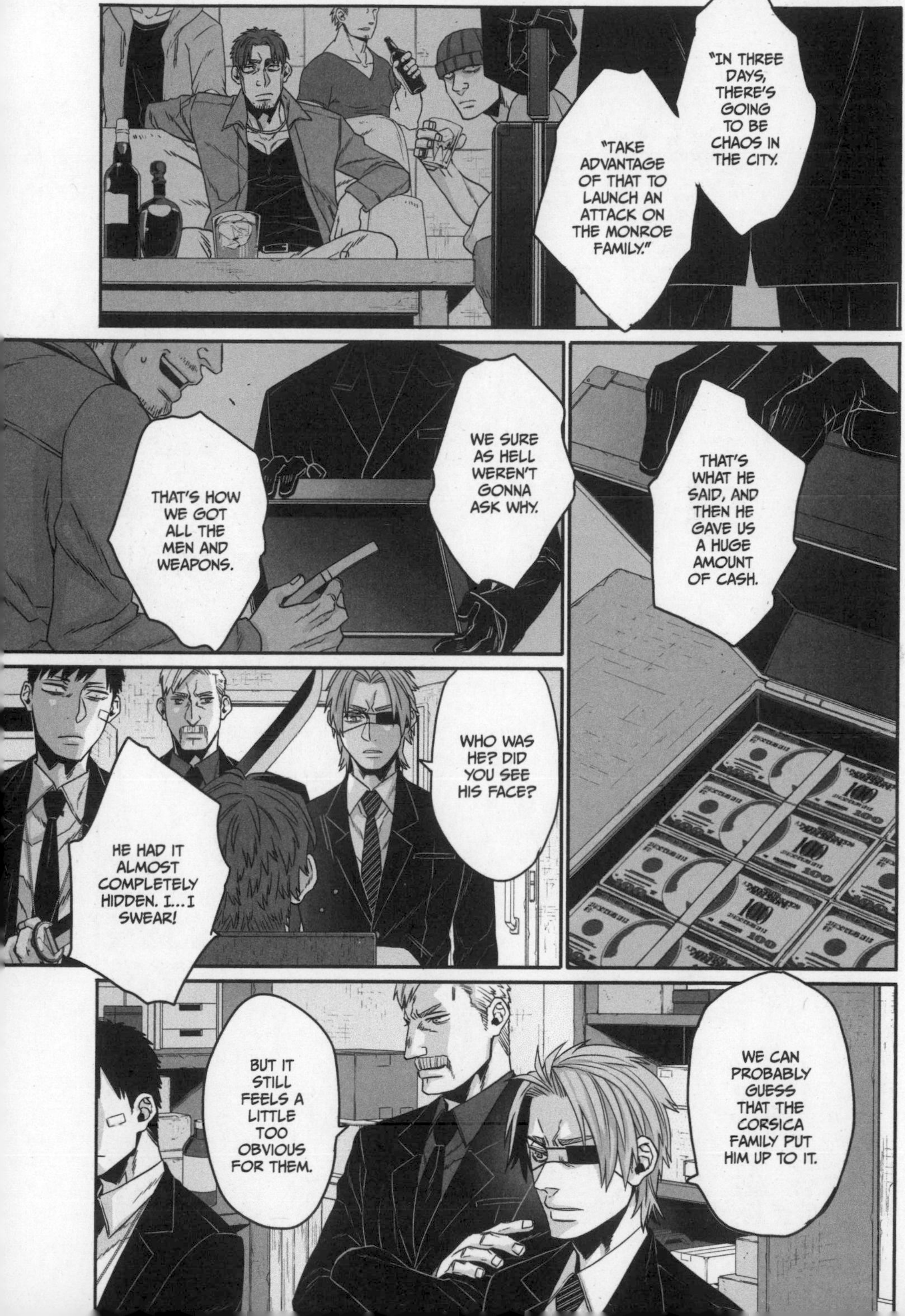
"IN THREE DAYS, THERE'S GOING TO BE CHAOS IN THE CITY.
"TAKE ADVANTAGE OF THAT TO LAUNCH AN ATTACK ON THE MONROE FAMILY."
THAT'S WHAT HE SAID, AND THEN HE GAVE US A HUGE AMOUNT OF CASH.
WE SURE AS HELL WEREN'T GONNA ASK WHY.
THAT'S HOW WE GOT ALL THE MEN AND WEAPONS.
WHO WAS HE? DID YOU SEE HIS FACE?
HE HAD IT ALMOST COMPLETELY HIDDEN. I...I SWEAR!
WE CAN PROBABLY GUESS THAT THE CORSICA FAMILY PUT HIM UP TO IT.
BUT IT STILL FEELS A LITTLE TOO OBVIOUS FOR THEM.

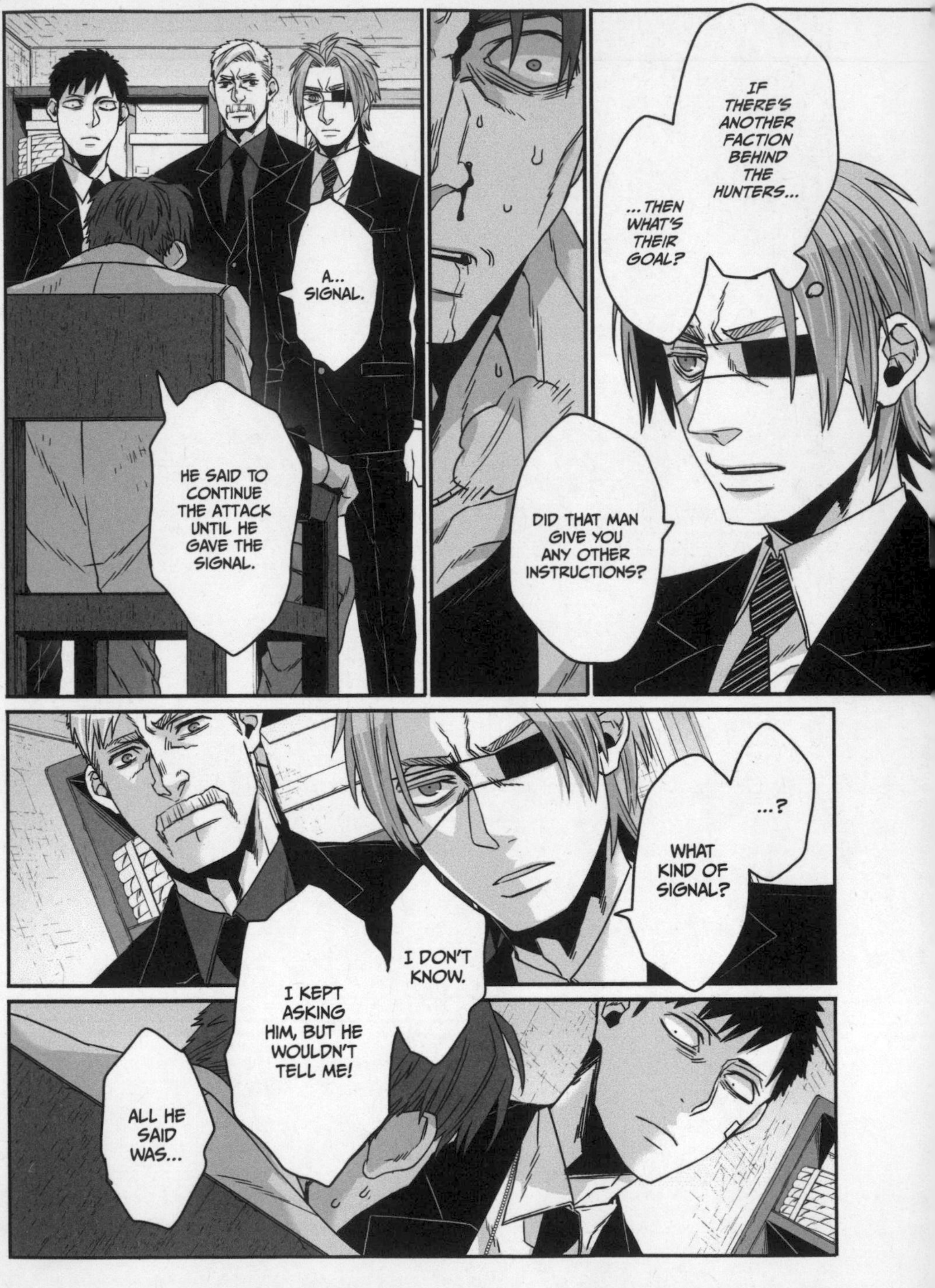
IF THERE'S ANOTHER FACTION BEHIND THE HUNTERS...
...THEN WHAT'S THEIR GOAL?
DID THAT MAN GIVE YOU ANY OTHER INSTRUCTIONS?
A... SIGNAL.
HE SAID TO CONTINUE THE ATTACK UNTIL HE GAVE THE SIGNAL.
...?
WHAT KIND OF SIGNAL?
I DON'T KNOW.
I KEPT ASKING HIM, BUT HE WOULDN'T TELL ME!
ALL HE SAID WAS...

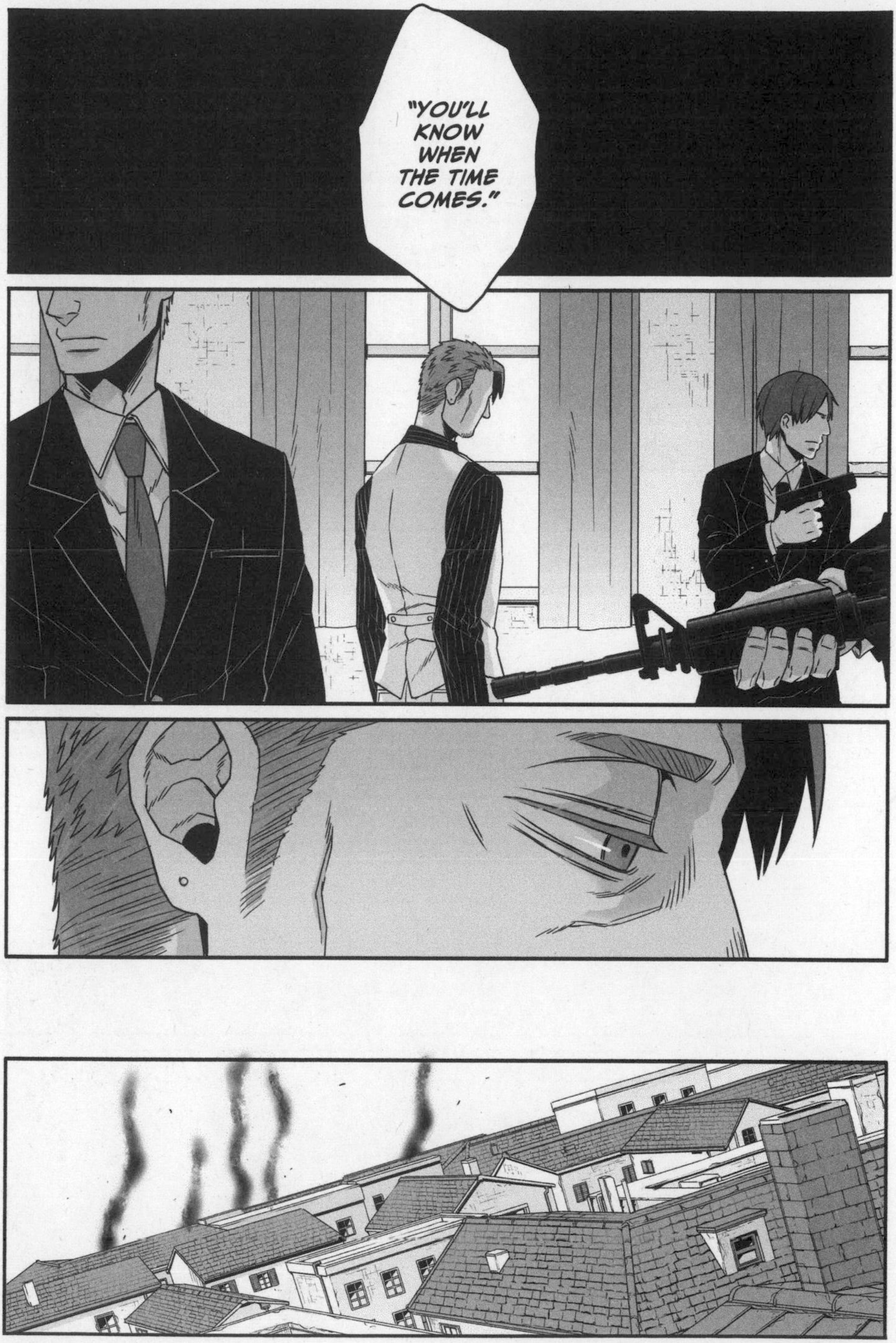
"YOU'LL KNOW WHEN THE TIME COMES."

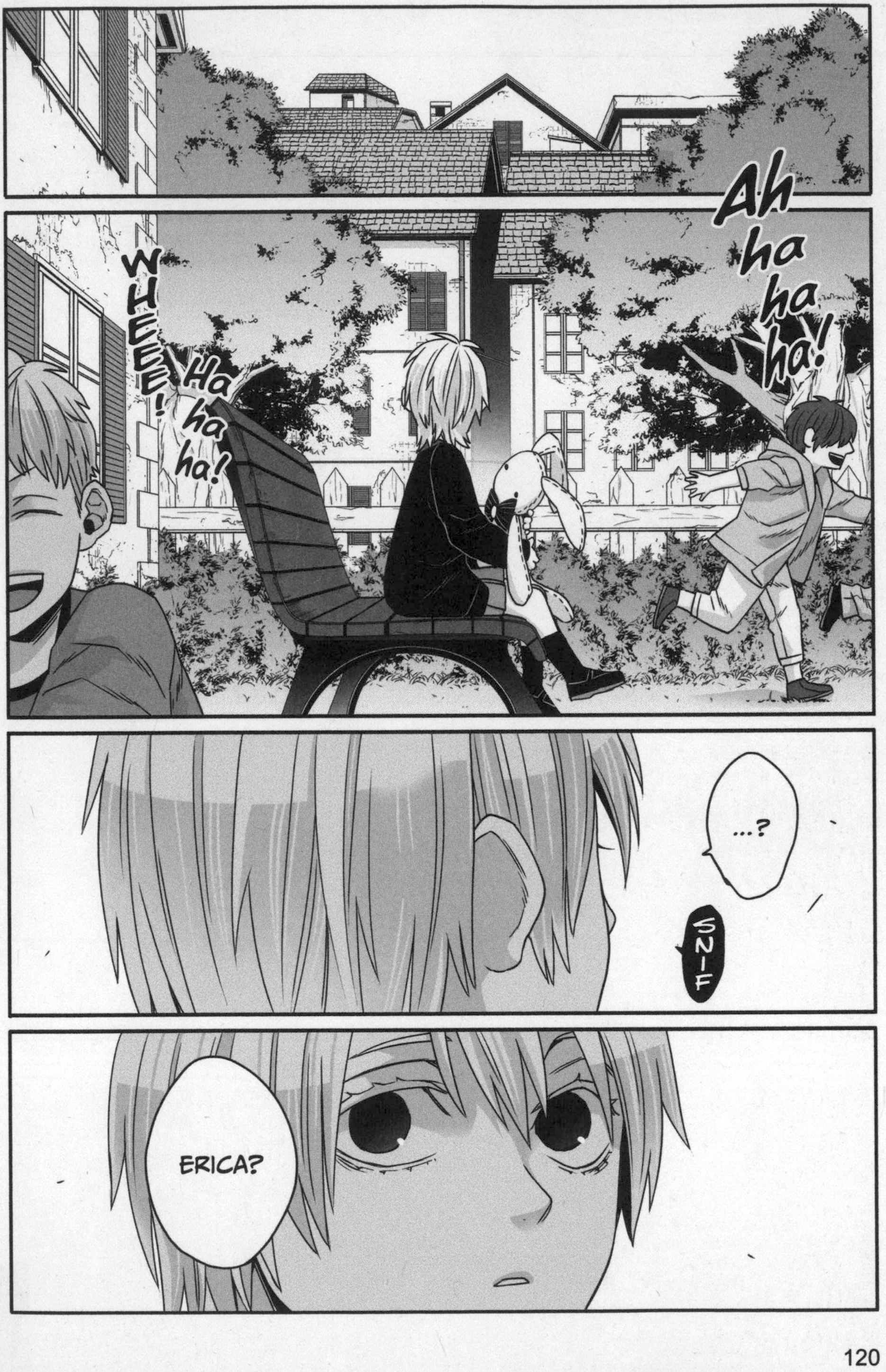
Ah ha ha ha!
Ha ha ha!
WHEEE!
...?
SNIF
ERICA?

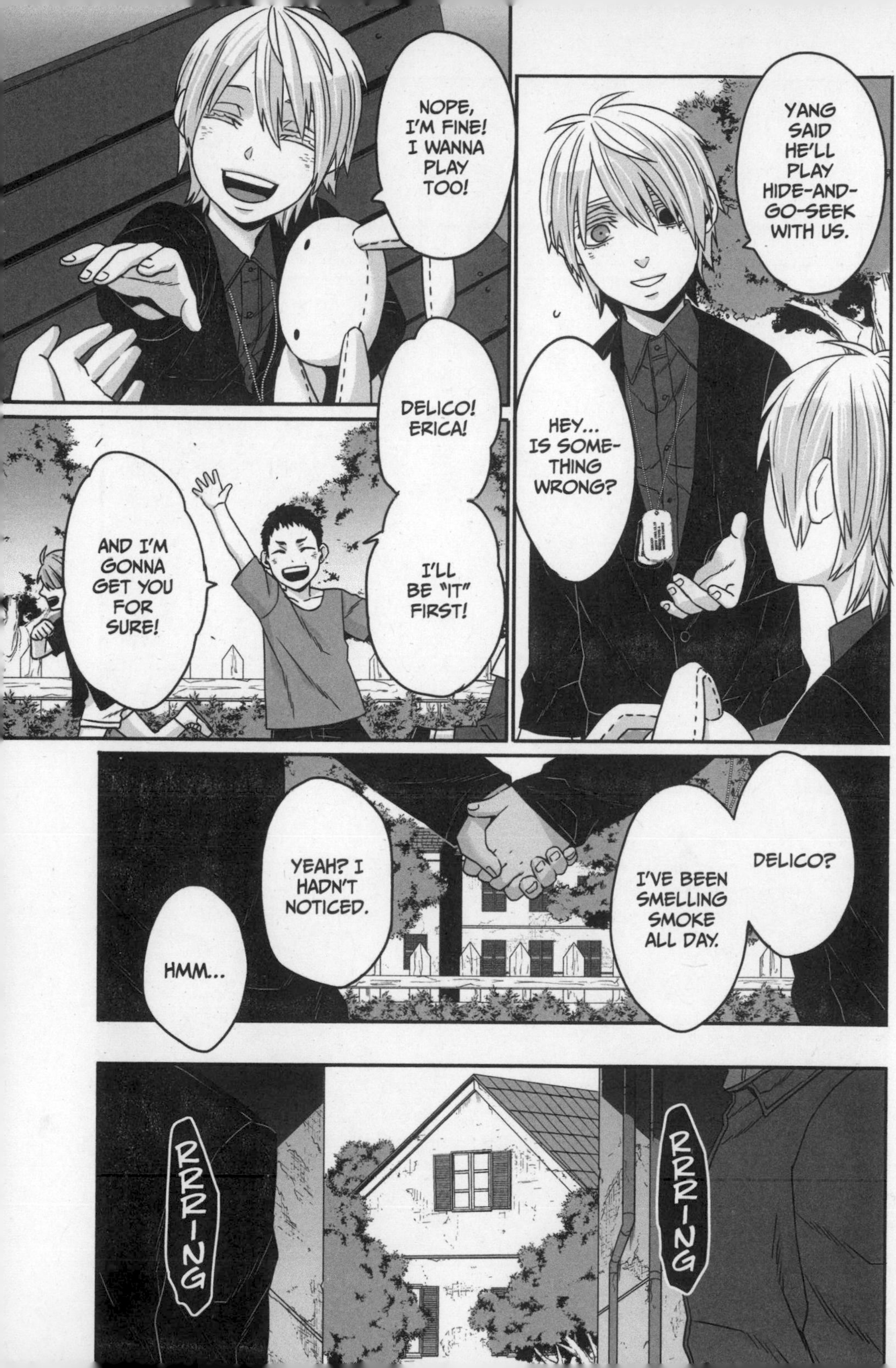
YANG SAID HE'LL PLAY HIDE-AND-GO-SEEK WITH US.
HEY... IS SOME-THING WRONG?
NOPE, I'M FINE! I WANNA PLAY TOO!
DELICO! ERICA!
I'LL BE "IT" FIRST!
AND I'M GONNA GET YOU FOR SURE!
DELICO?
I'VE BEEN SMELLING SMOKE ALL DAY.
YEAH? I HADN'T NOTICED.
HMM...
RRRING
RRRING

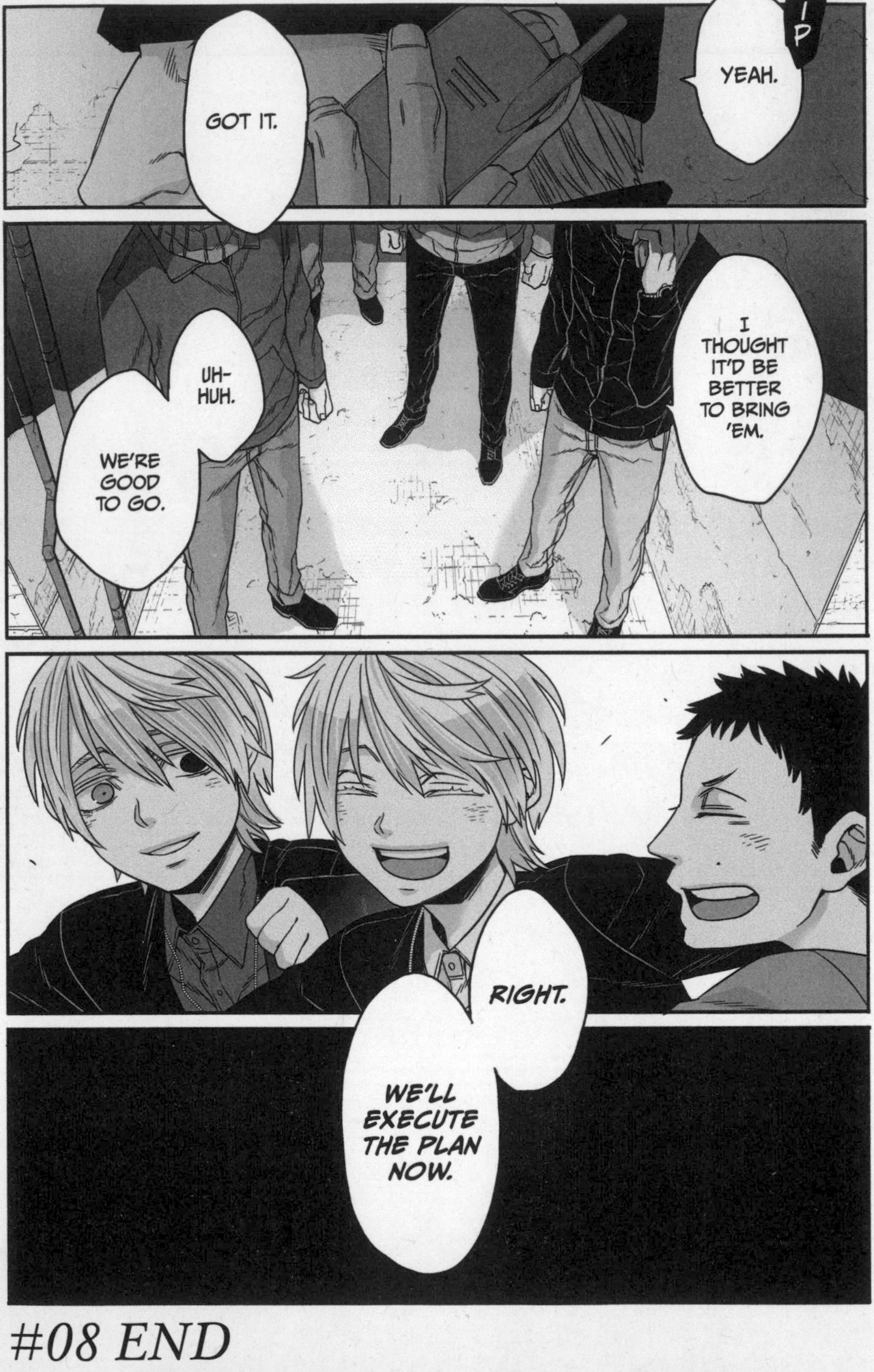
BIP
YEAH.
GOT IT.
I THOUGHT IT'D BE BETTER TO BRING 'EM.
UH-HUH.
WE'RE GOOD TO GO.
RIGHT.
WE'LL EXECUTE THE PLAN NOW.

#08 END

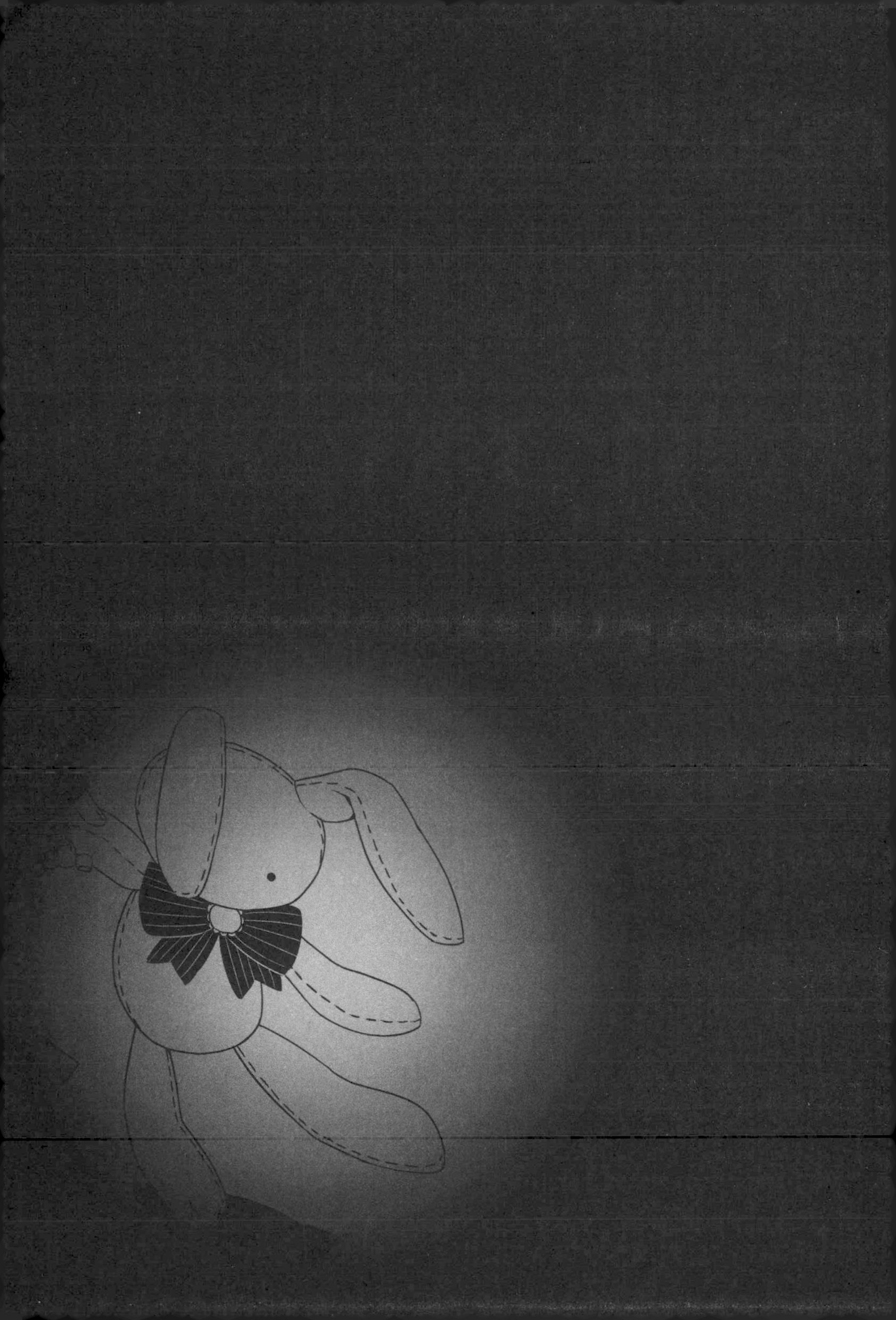

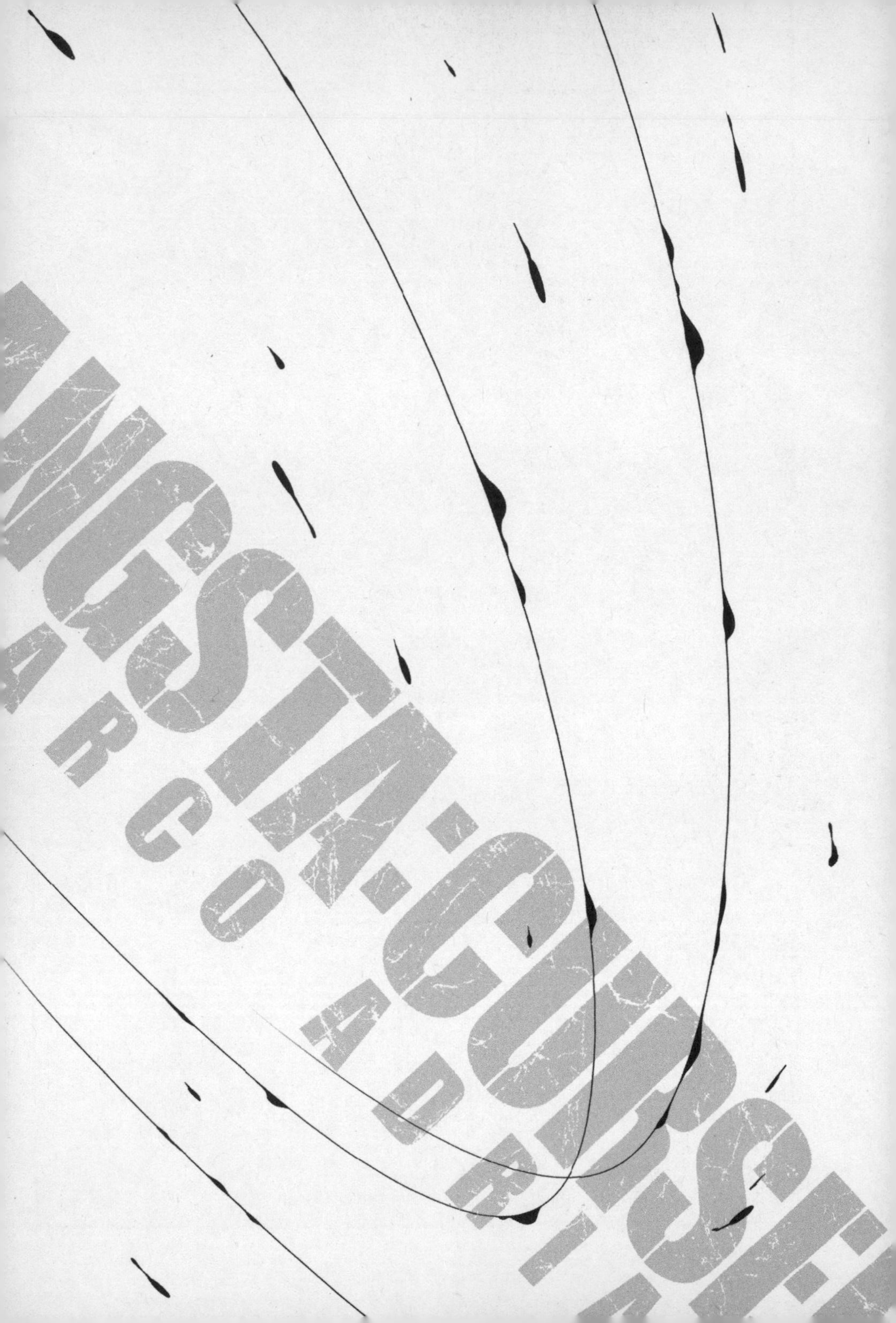

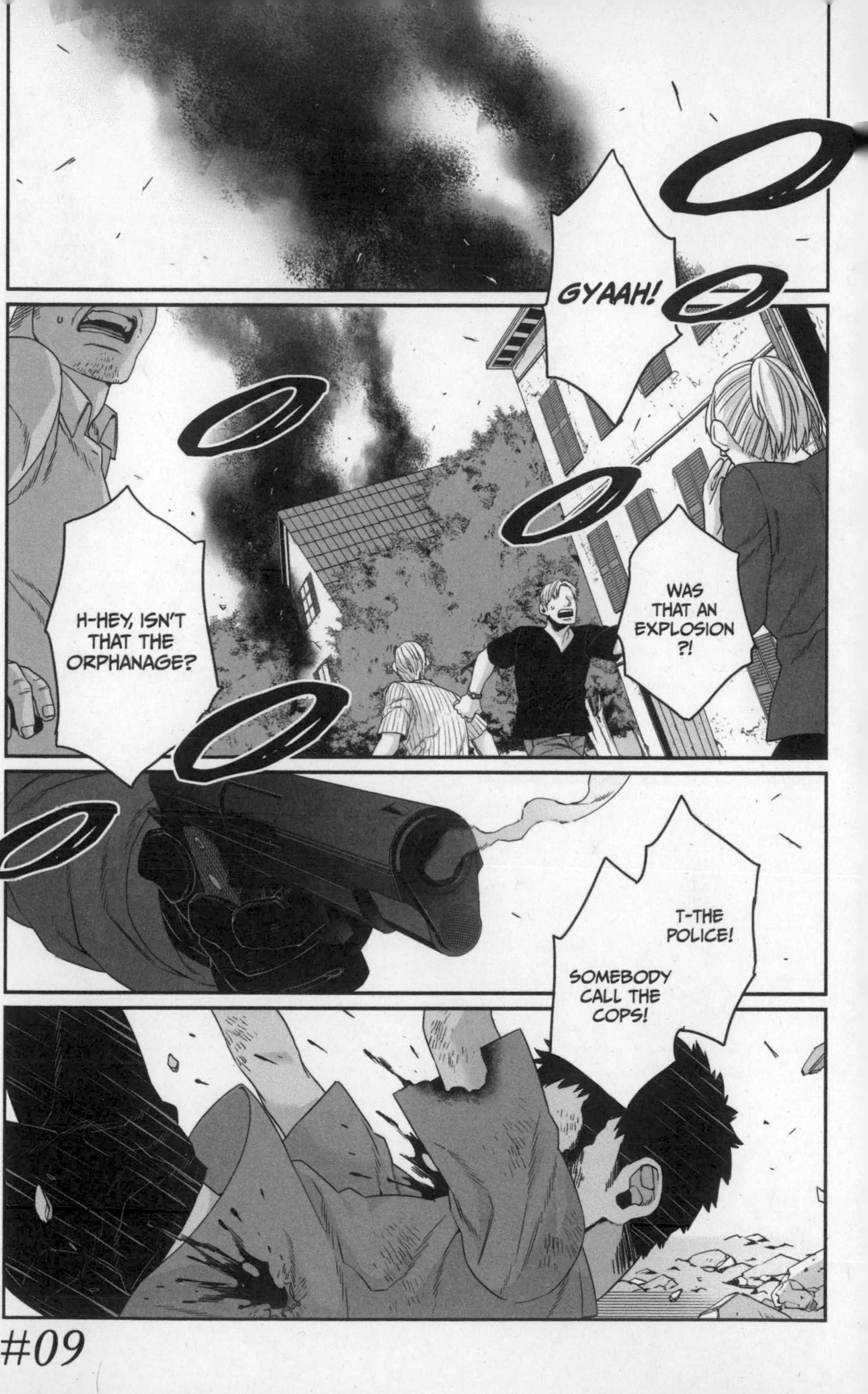
GYAAH!
WAS THAT AN EXPLOSION ?!
H-HEY, ISN'T THAT THE ORPHANAGE?
T-THE POLICE!
SOMEBODY CALL THE COPS!

#09

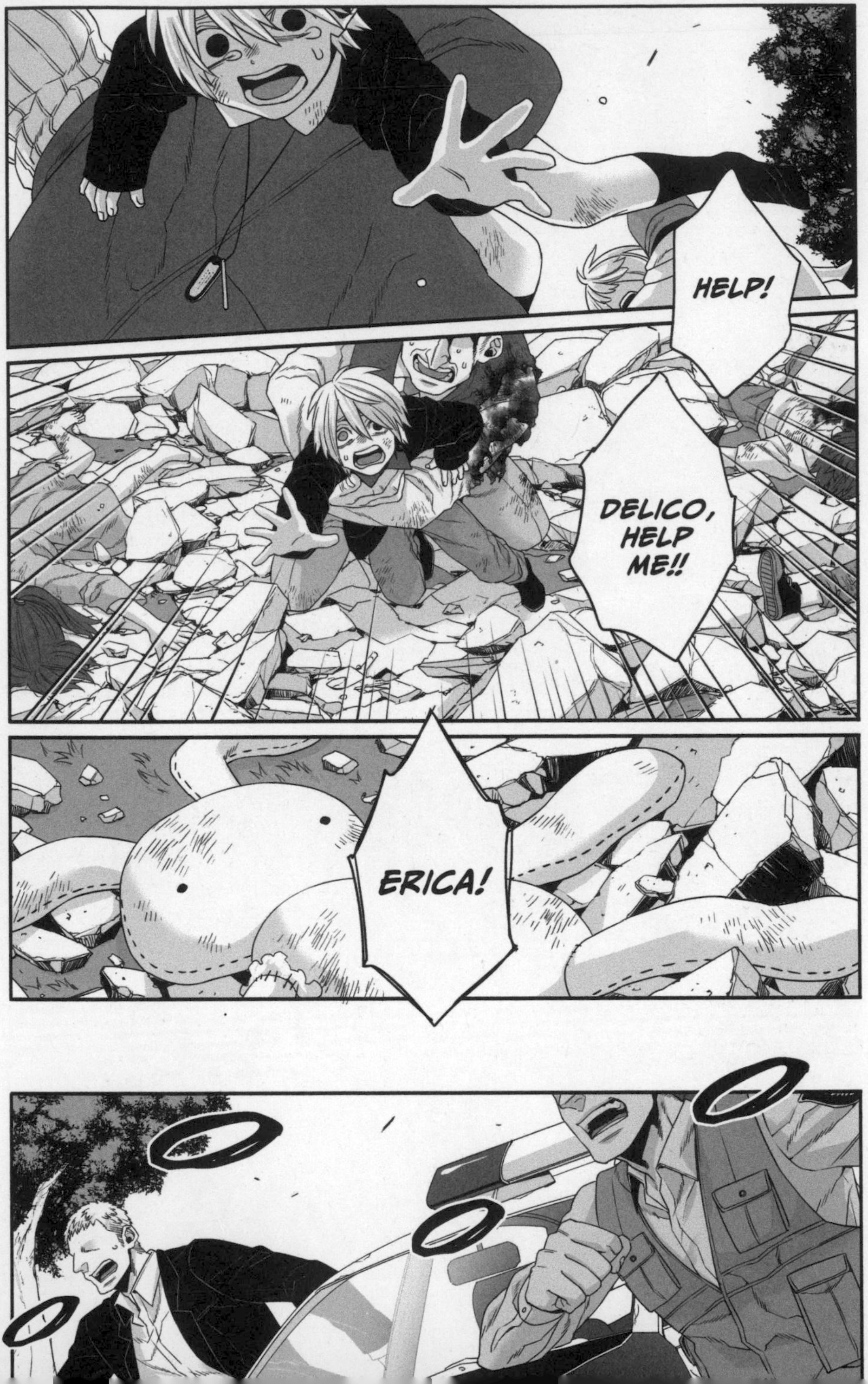
HELP!
DELICO, HELP ME!!
ERICA!

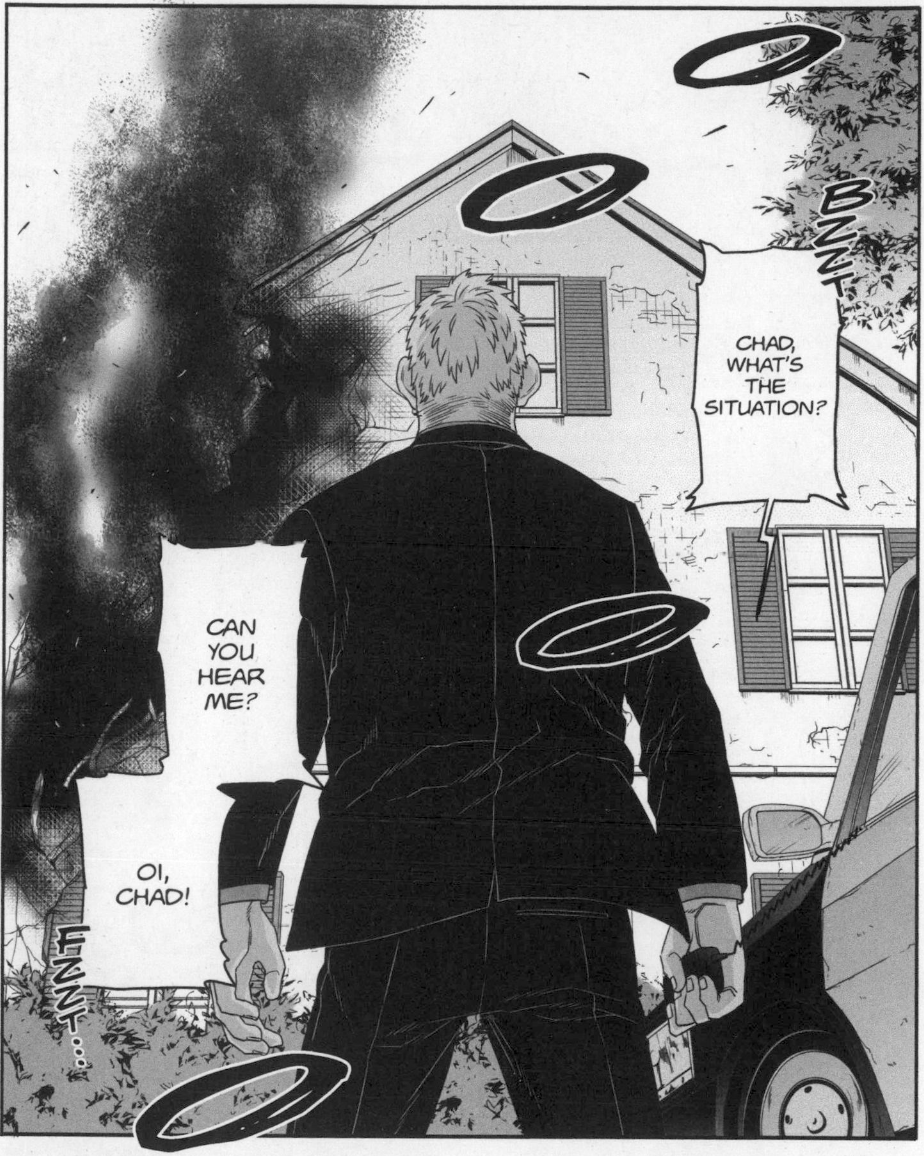
BZZZT
CHAD, WHAT'S THE SITUATION?
CAN YOU HEAR ME?
OI, CHAD!
FZZZT...

#09

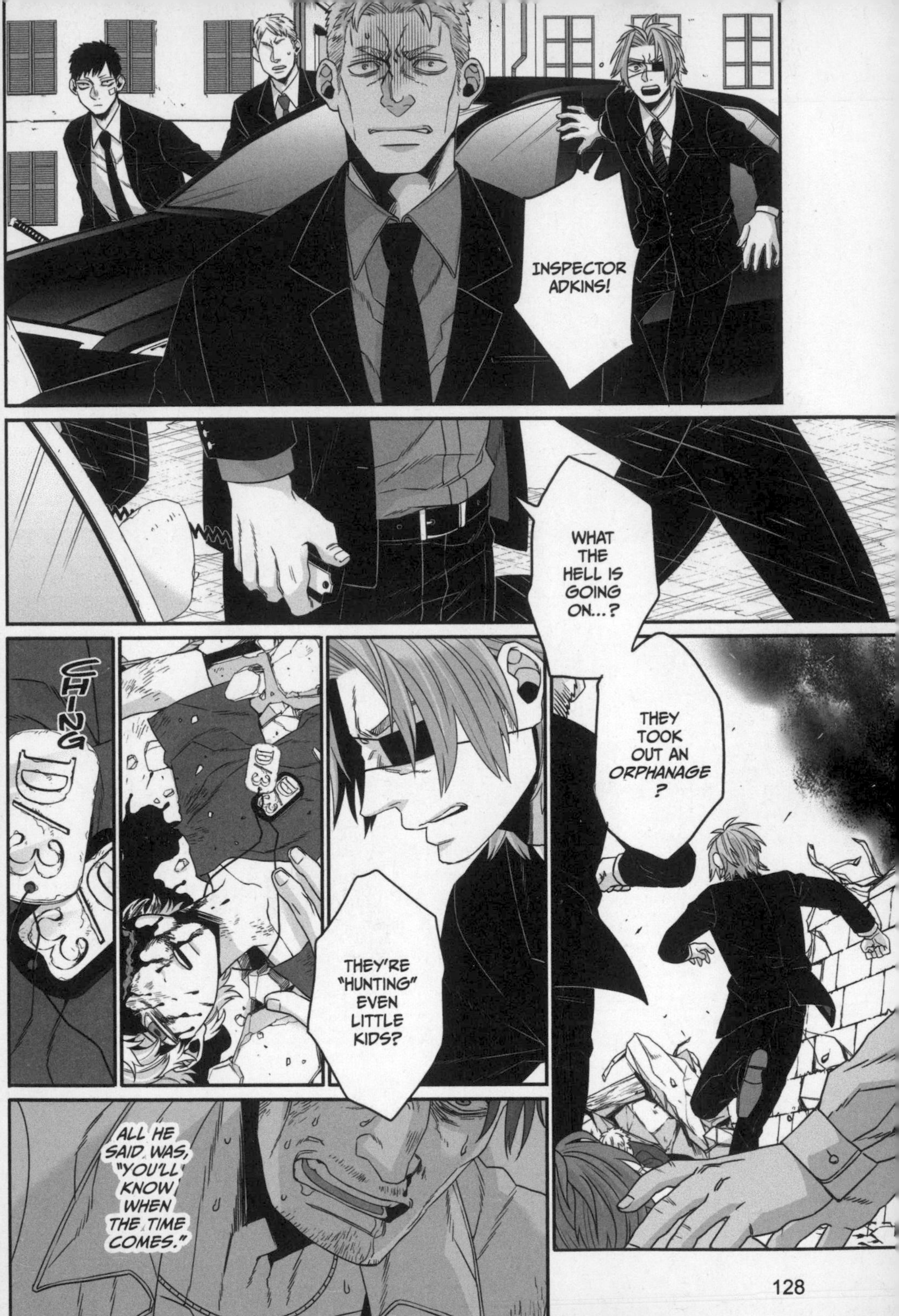
INSPECTOR ADKINS!
WHAT THE HELL IS GOING ON...?
THEY TOOK OUT AN ORPHANAGE?
THEY'RE "HUNTING" EVEN LITTLE KIDS?
CHING
ALL HE SAID WAS, "YOU'LL KNOW WHEN THE TIME COMES."

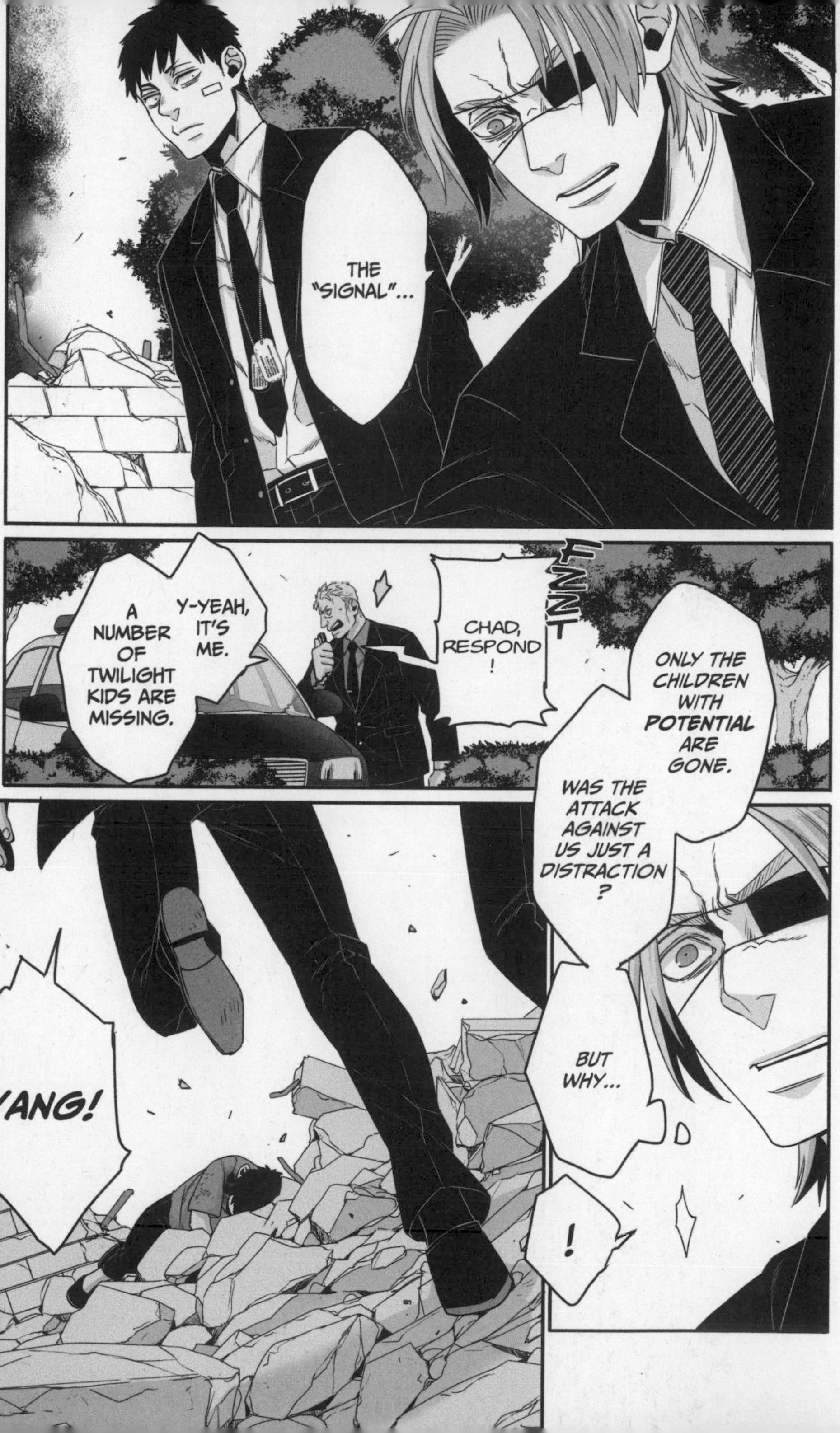
THE "SIGNAL"...
FZZT
CHAD, RESPOND!
Y-YEAH, IT'S ME.
A NUMBER OF TWILIGHT KIDS ARE MISSING.
ONLY THE CHILDREN WITH **POTENTIAL** ARE GONE.
WAS THE ATTACK AGAINST US JUST A DISTRACTION?
BUT WHY...
!
YANG!

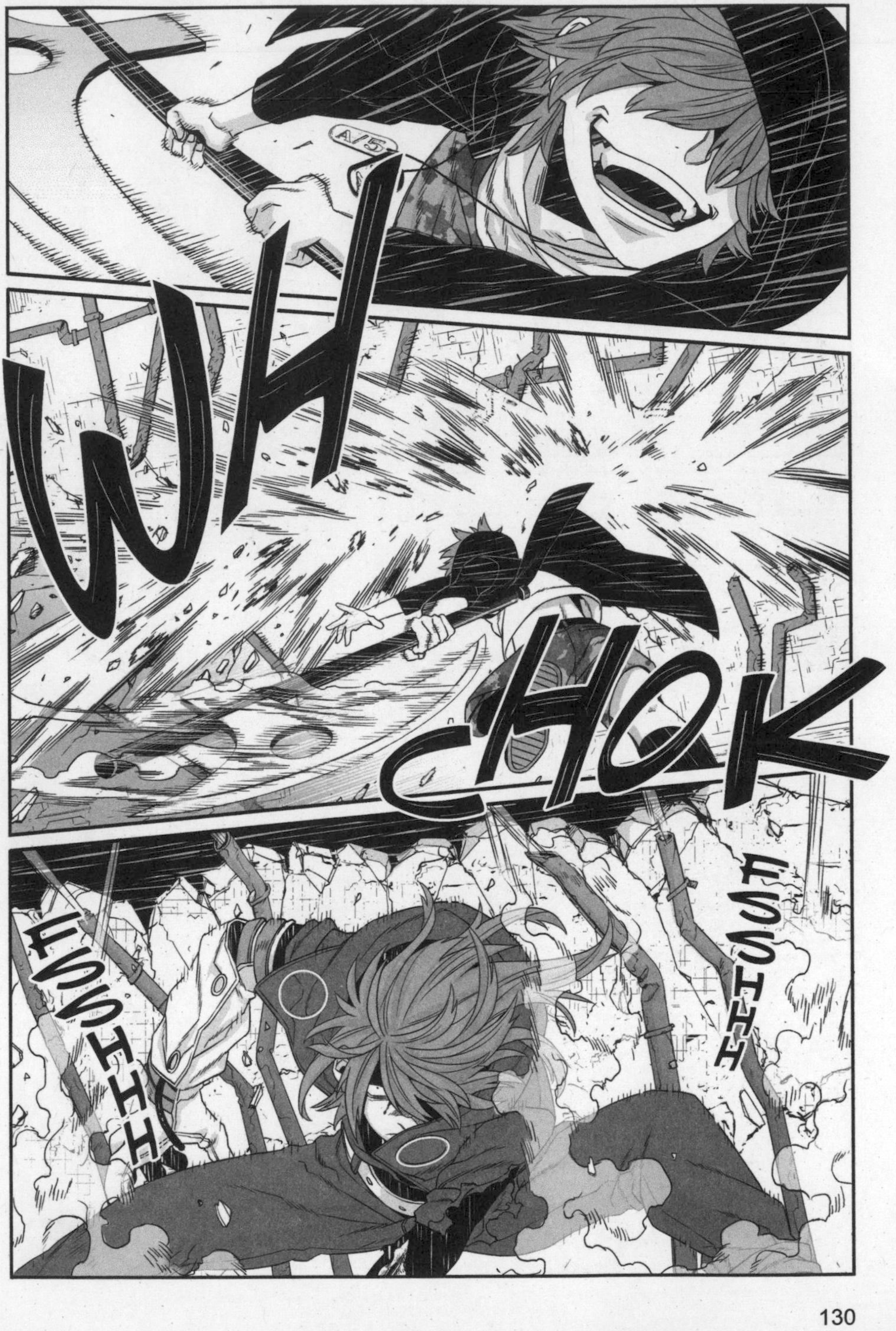
A/5
WH
CHOK
FSSHHH
FSSHHH

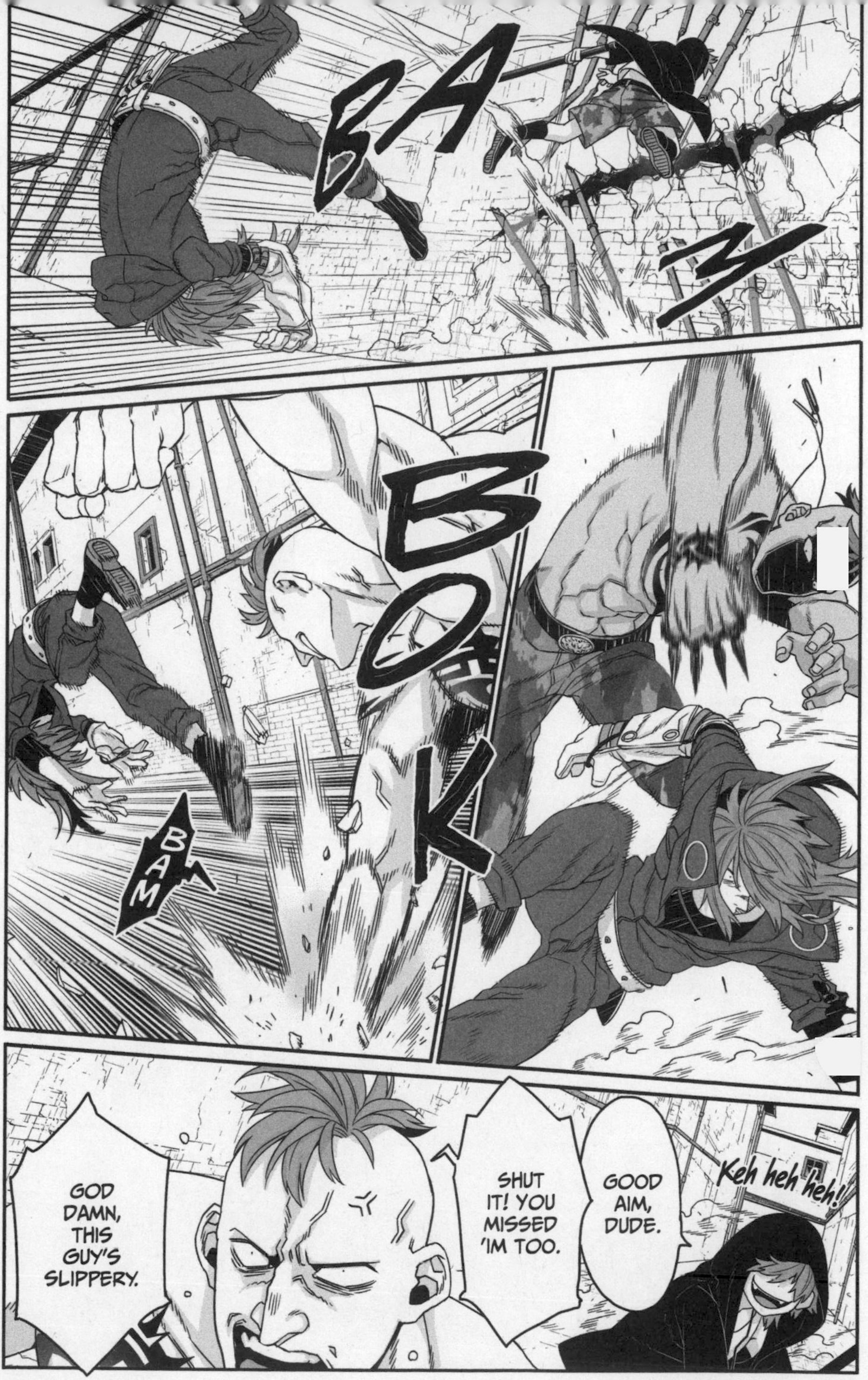
BAM
BOOK
BAM
Keh heh heh!!
GOOD AIM, DUDE.
SHUT IT! YOU MISSED 'IM TOO.
GOD DAMN, THIS GUY'S SLIPPERY.

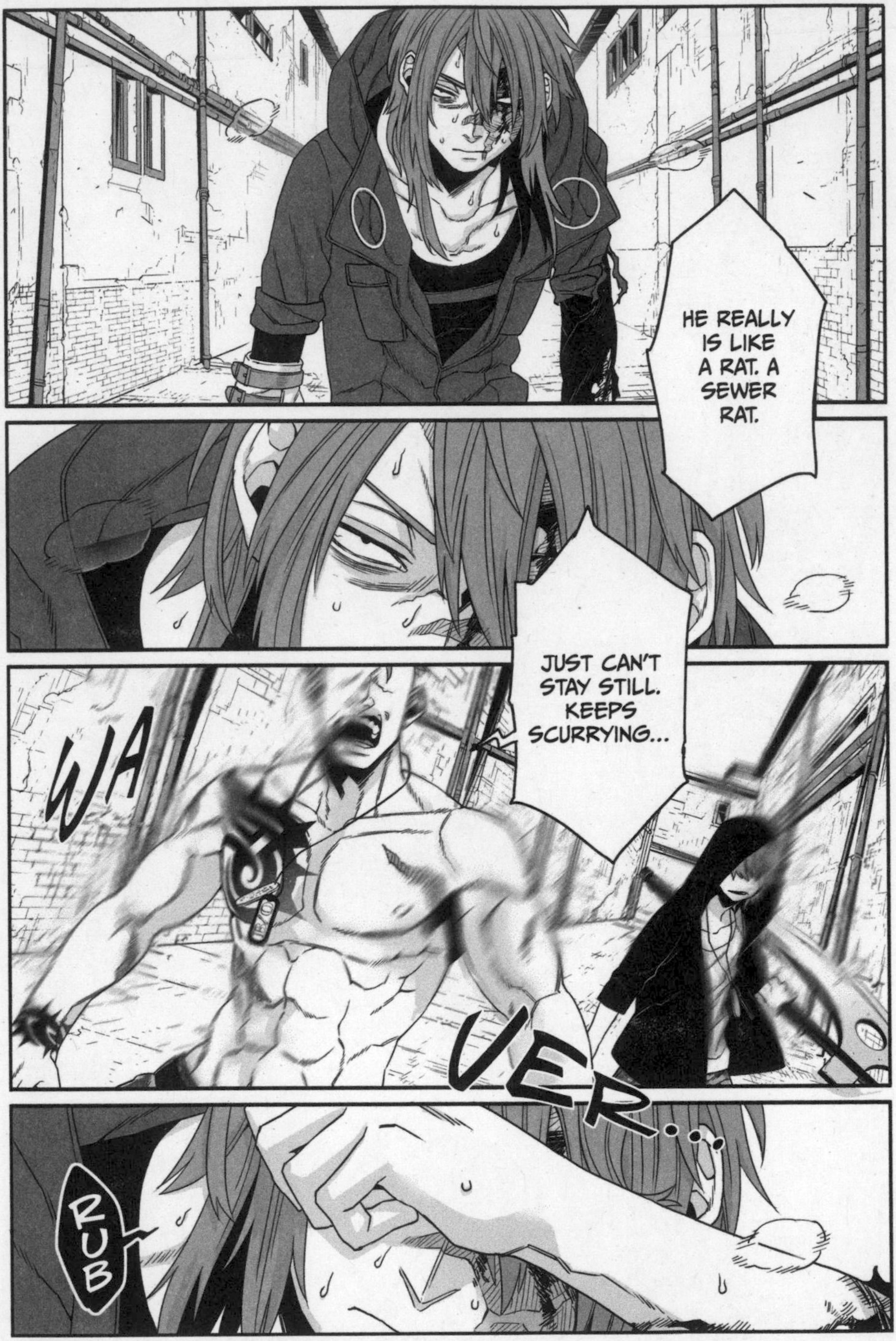
HE REALLY IS LIKE A RAT. A SEWER RAT.
JUST CAN'T STAY STILL. KEEPS SCURRYING...
WAVER...
RUB

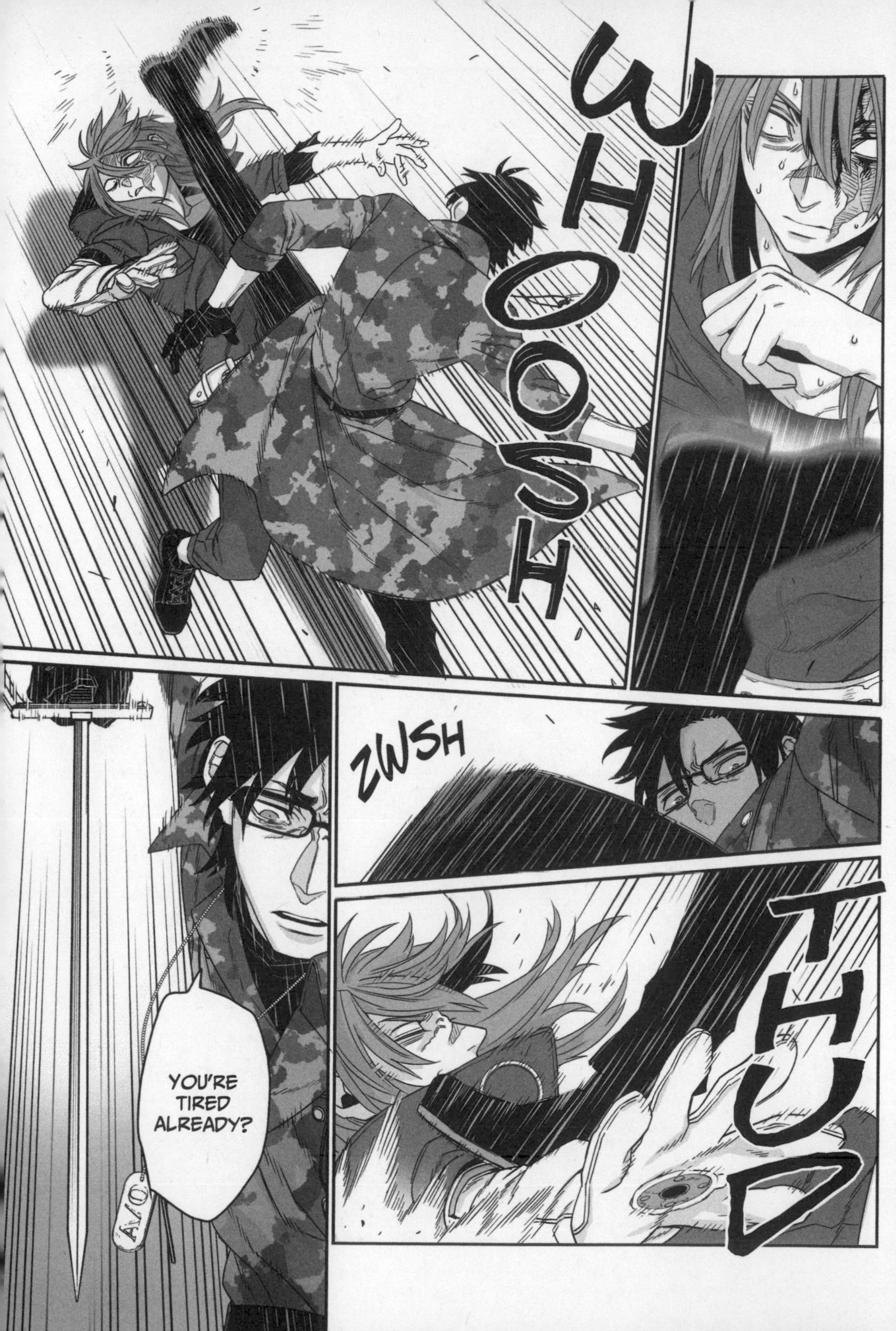
WHOOSH
ZWSH
THUD
YOU'RE TIRED ALREADY?

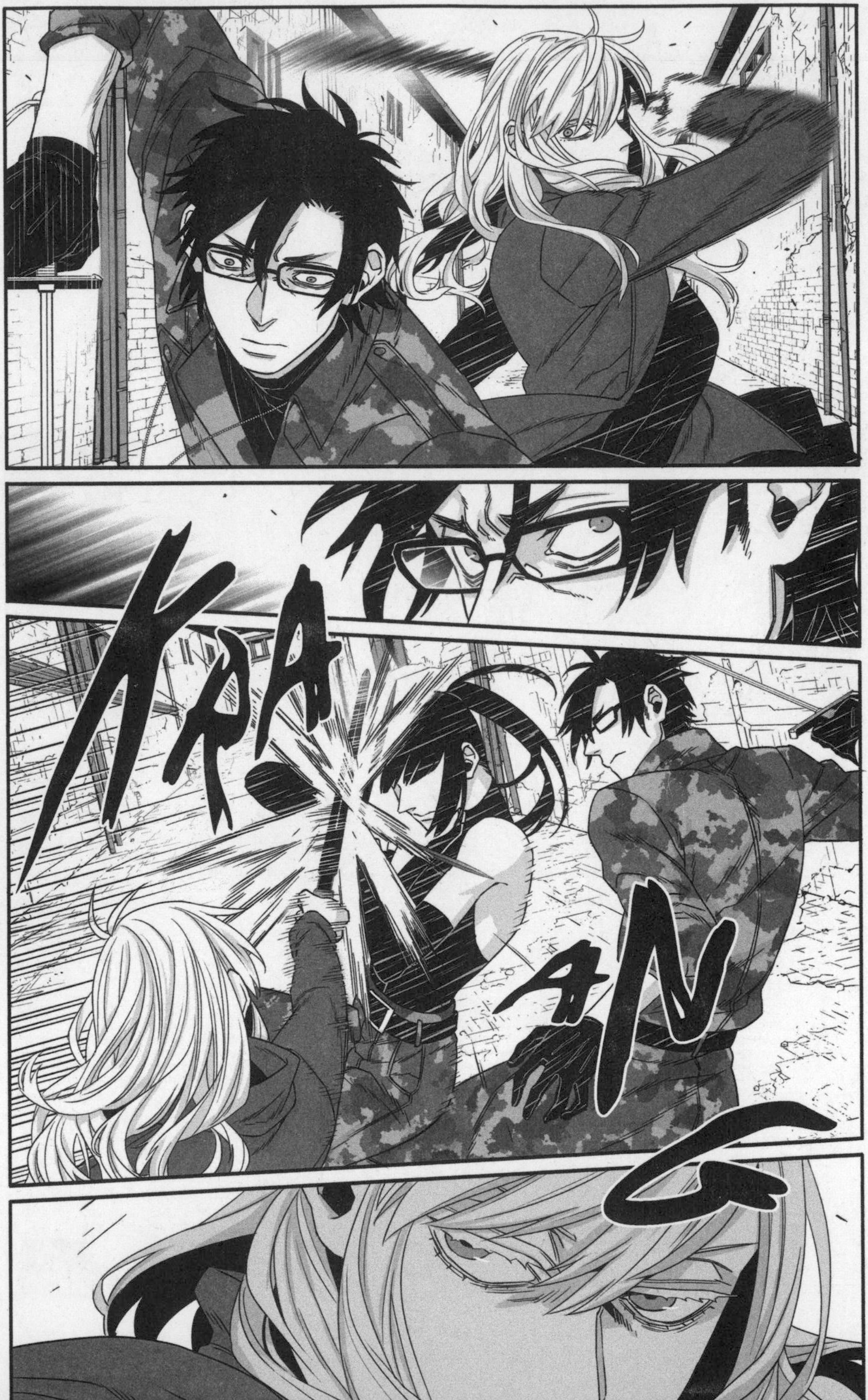
KRAAANG

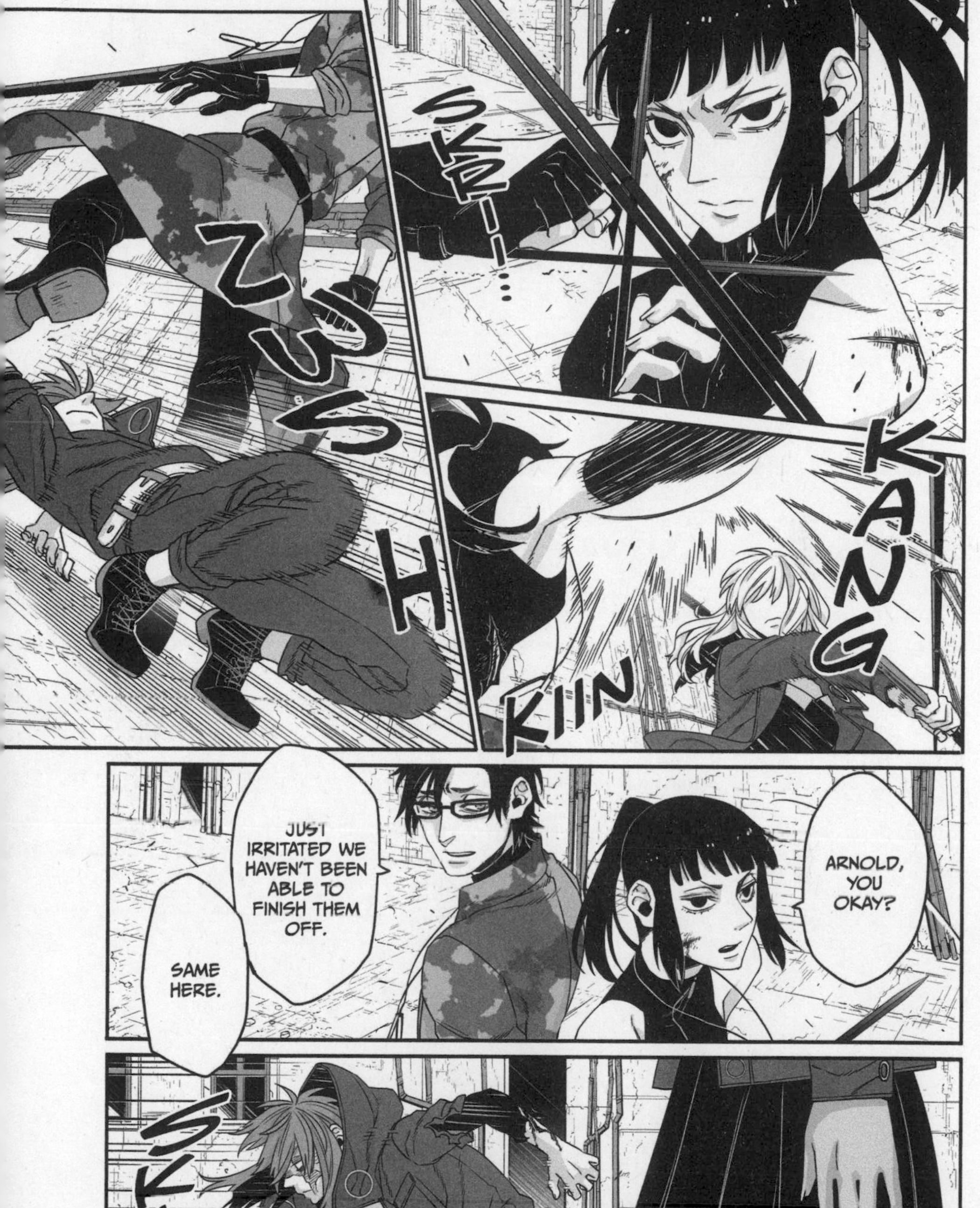
SKRII...
KANG
KIIN
ZWSH
ARNOLD, YOU OKAY?
JUST IRRITATED WE HAVEN'T BEEN ABLE TO FINISH THEM OFF.
SAME HERE.
SKIDD

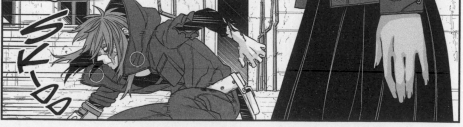

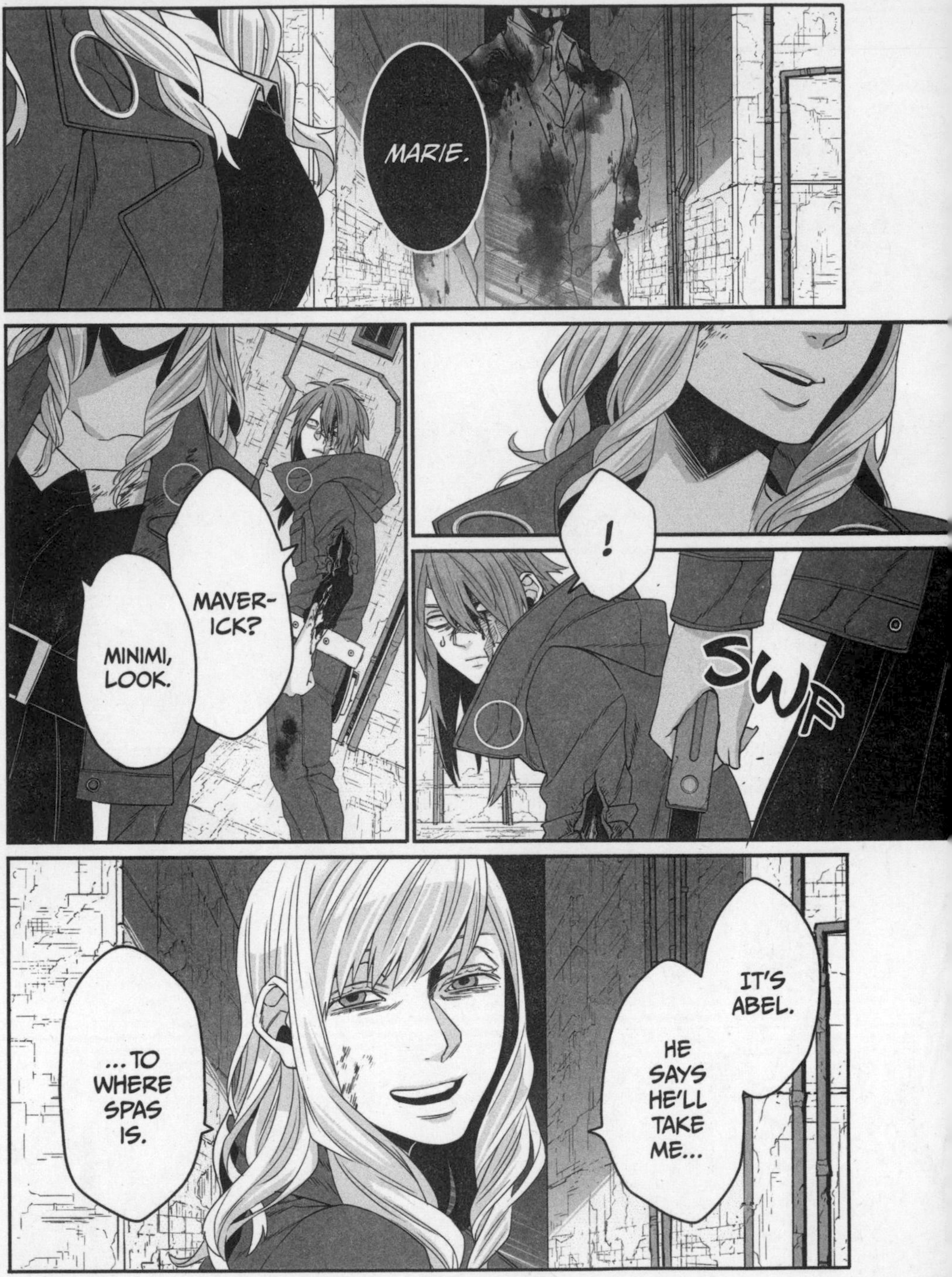
MARIE.
!
SWF
MAVER-ICK?
MINIMI, LOOK.
IT'S ABEL.
HE SAYS HE'LL TAKE ME...
...TO WHERE SPAS IS.

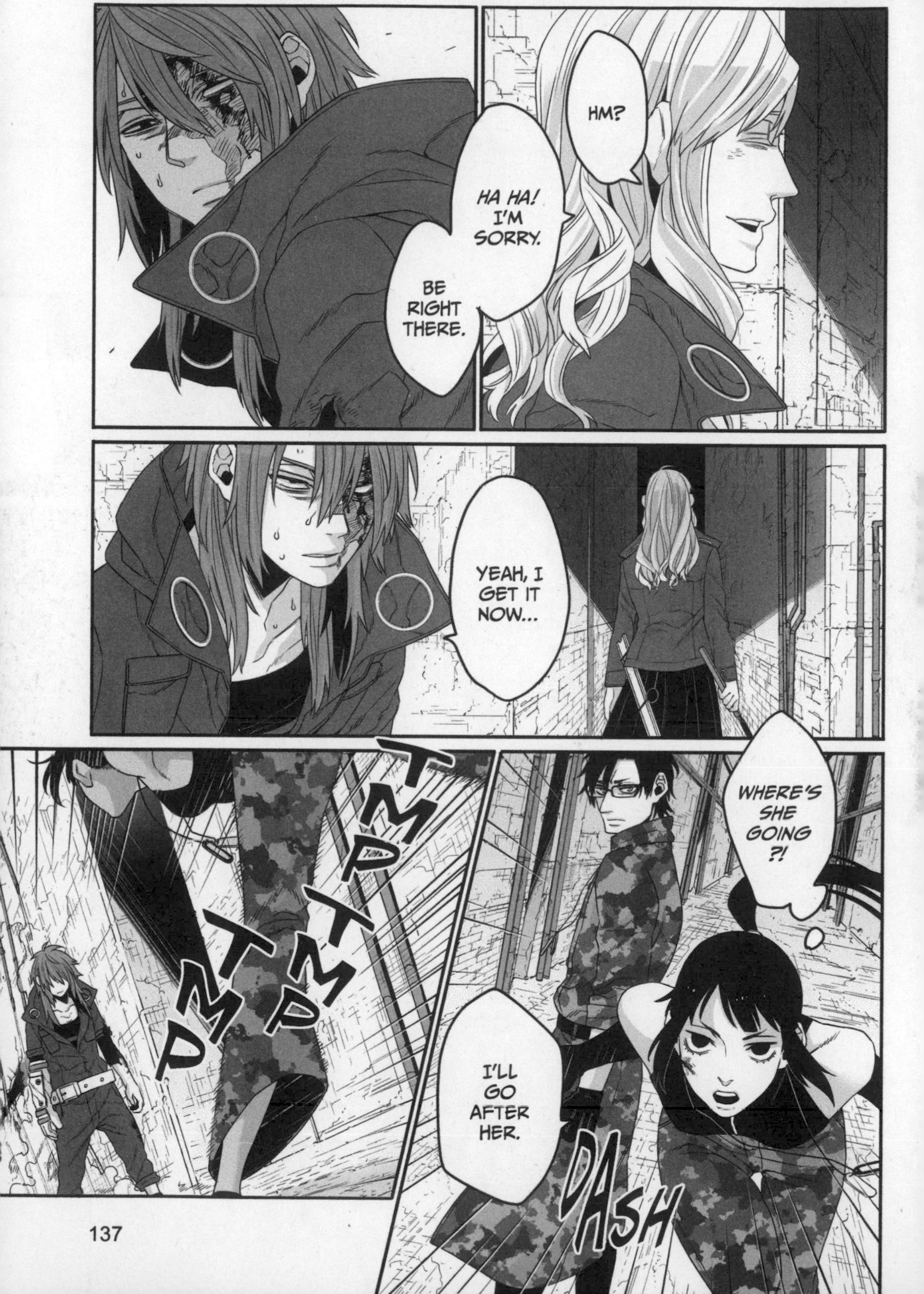
HM?
HA HA! I'M SORRY.
BE RIGHT THERE.
YEAH, I GET IT NOW...
WHERE'S SHE GOING?!
I'LL GO AFTER HER.
DASH
TMP TMP
TMP TMP

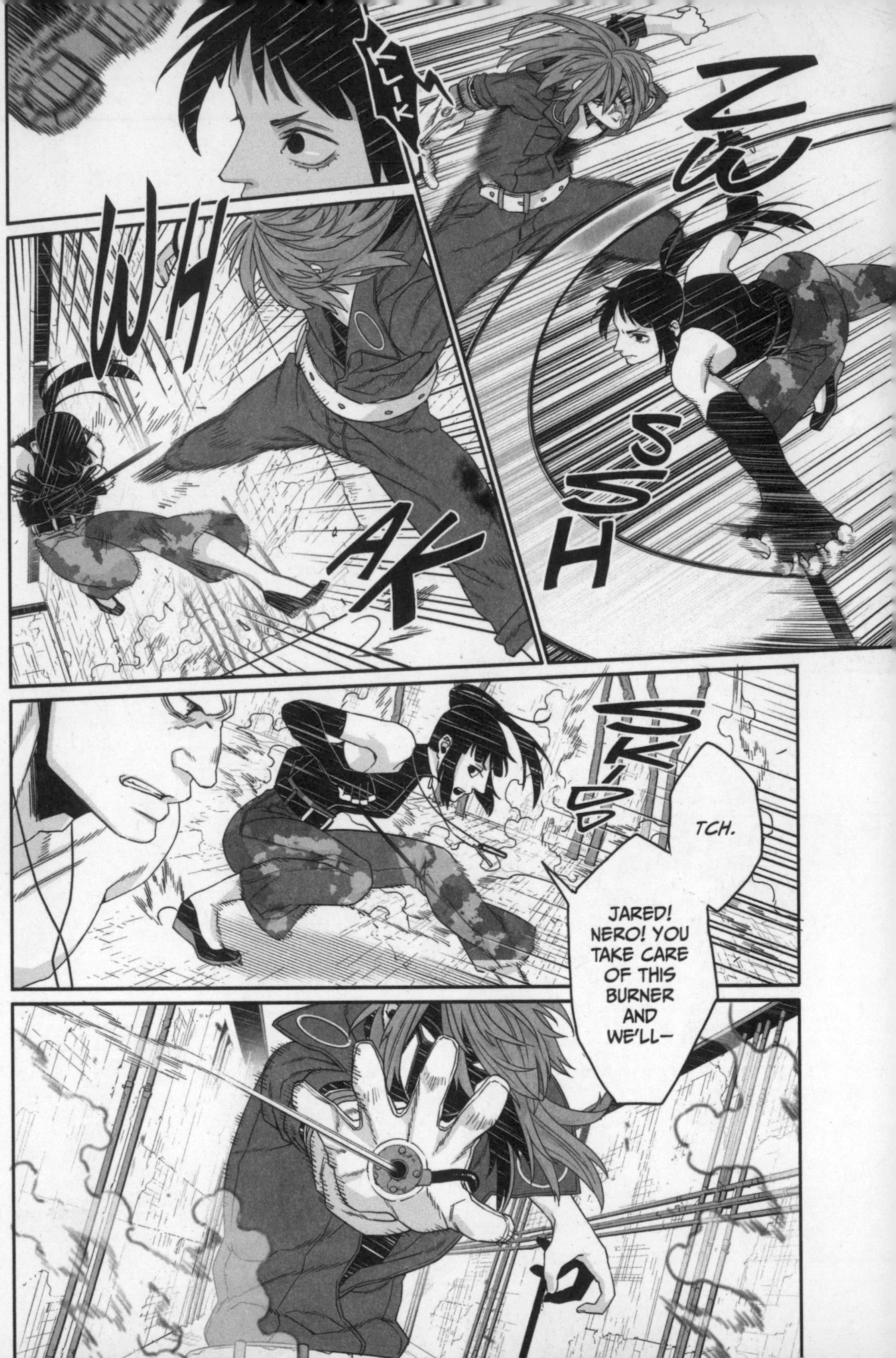
ZUSSH
KLIK
WHAK
SKID
TCH.
JARED! NERO! YOU TAKE CARE OF THIS BURNER AND WE'LL—

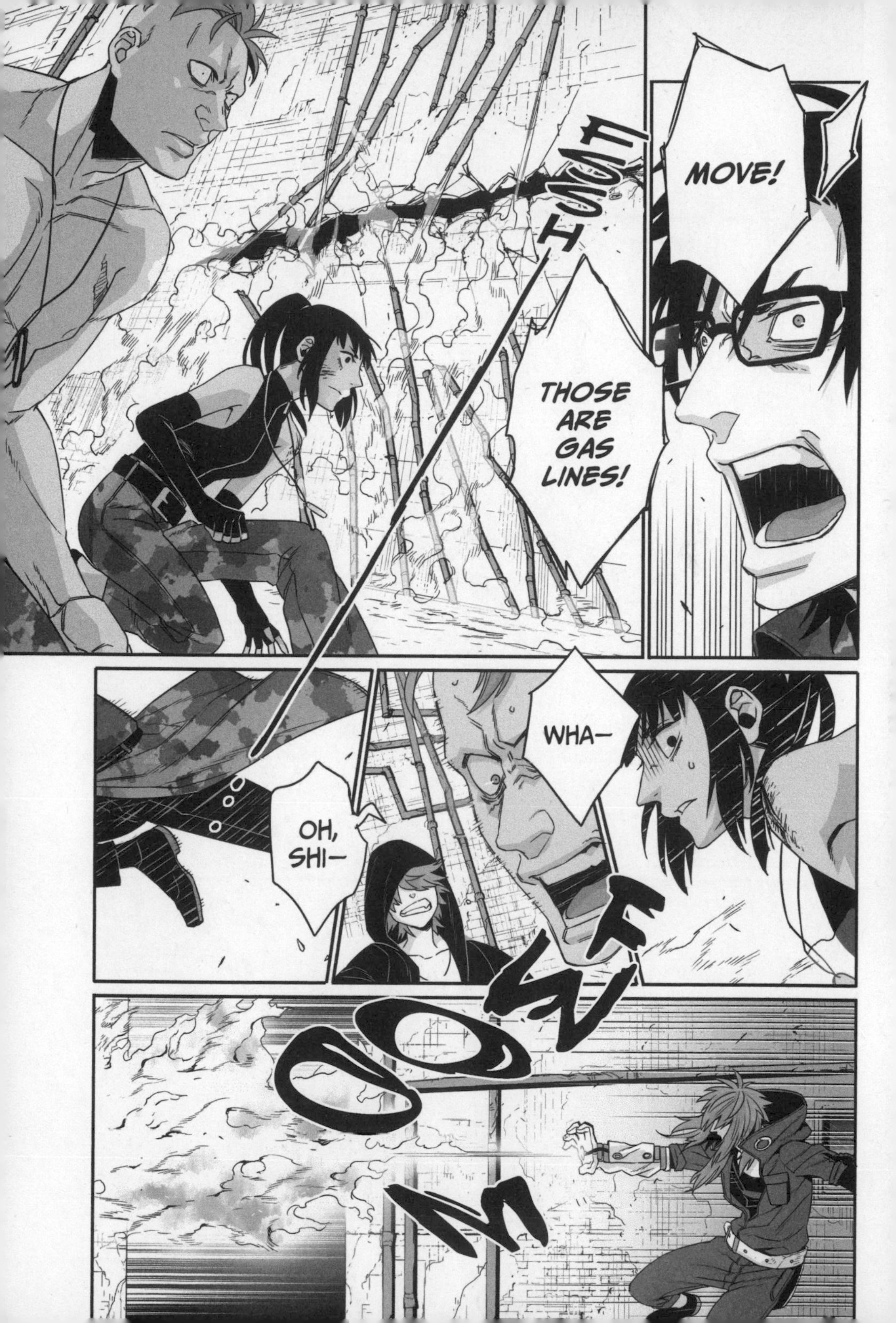
MOVE!
THOSE ARE GAS LINES!
FSSH
WHA-
OH, SHI-
FWOOM

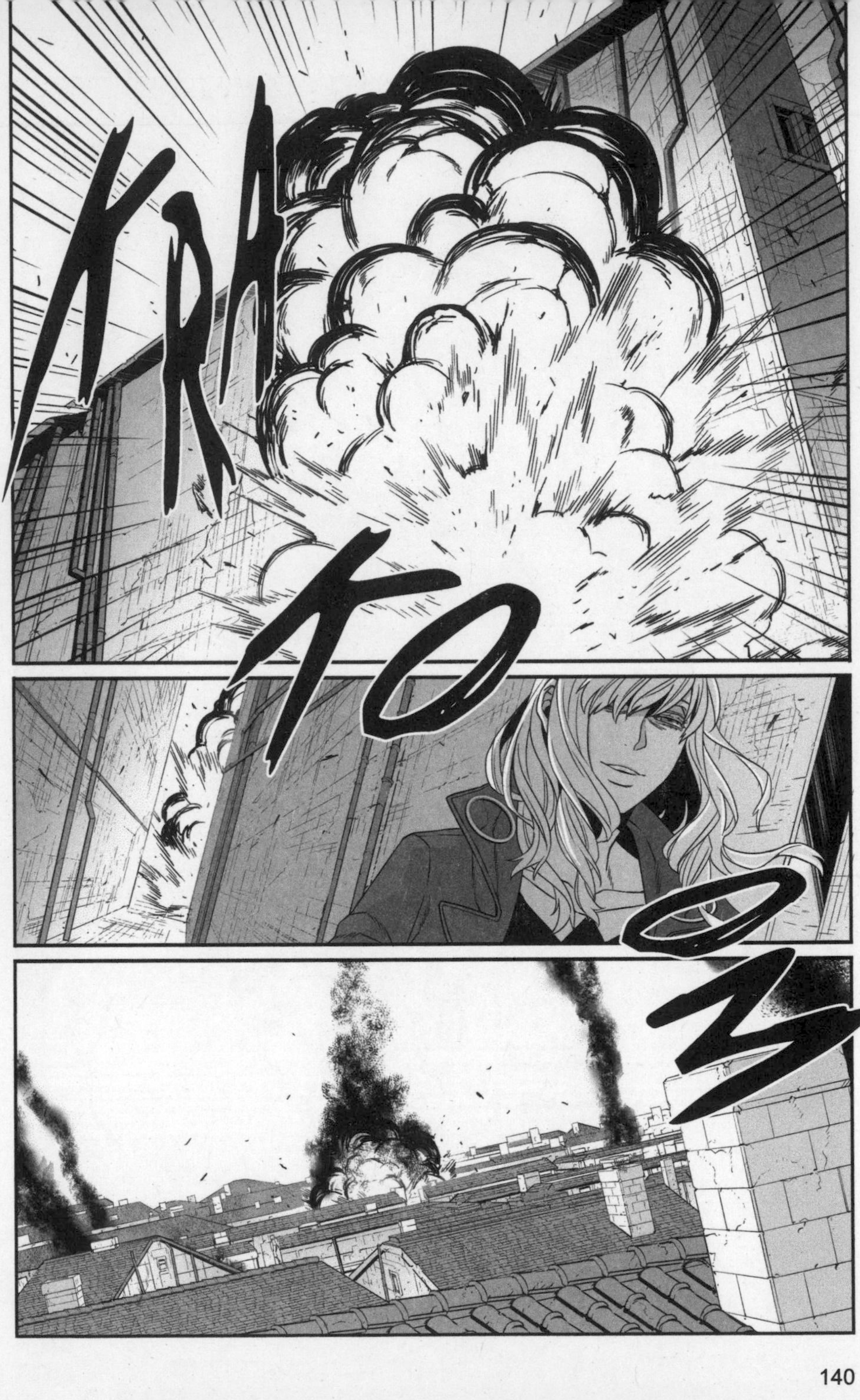
KRAKOOM

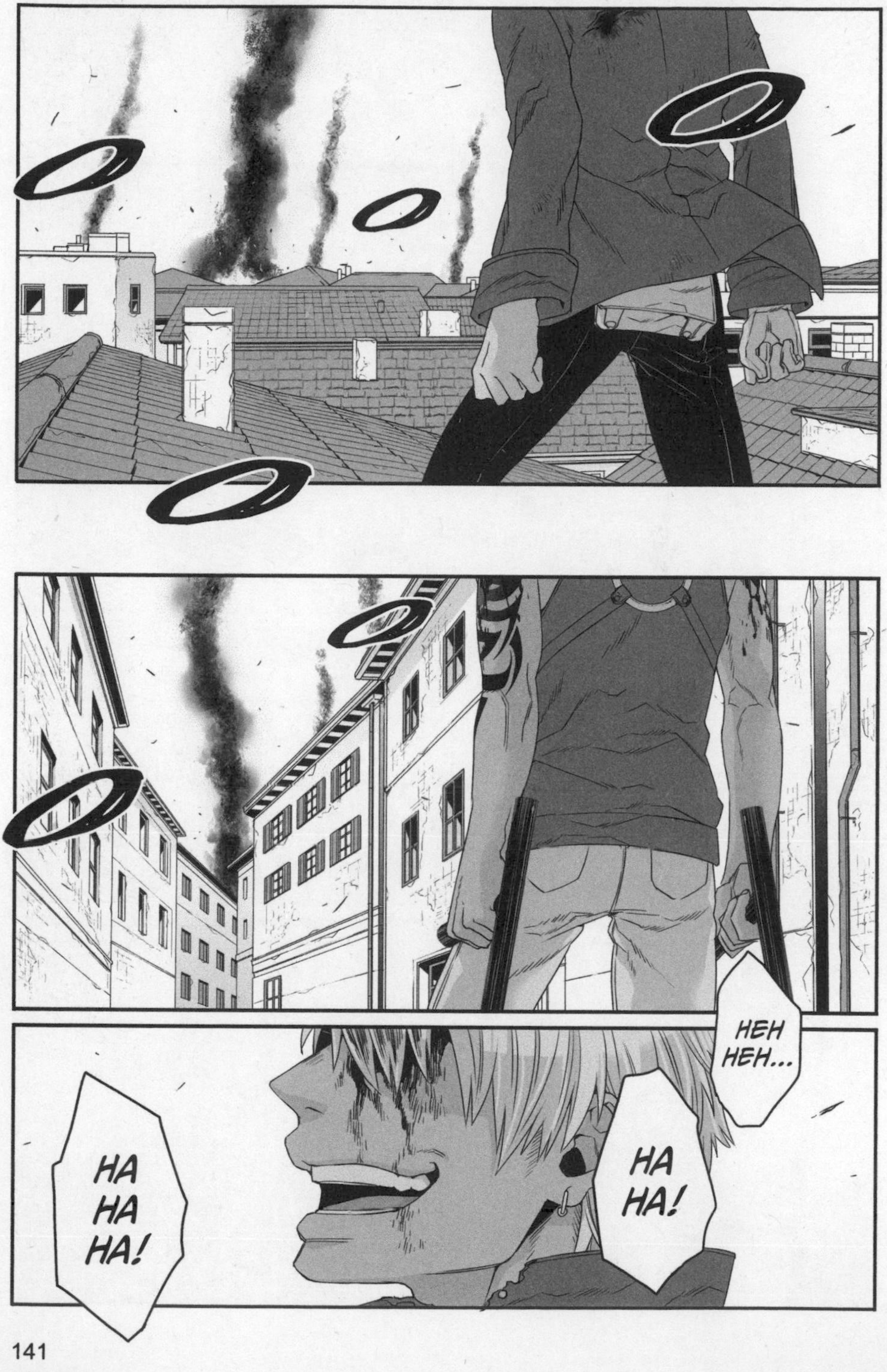
HEH HEH...
HA HA!
HA HA HA HA!

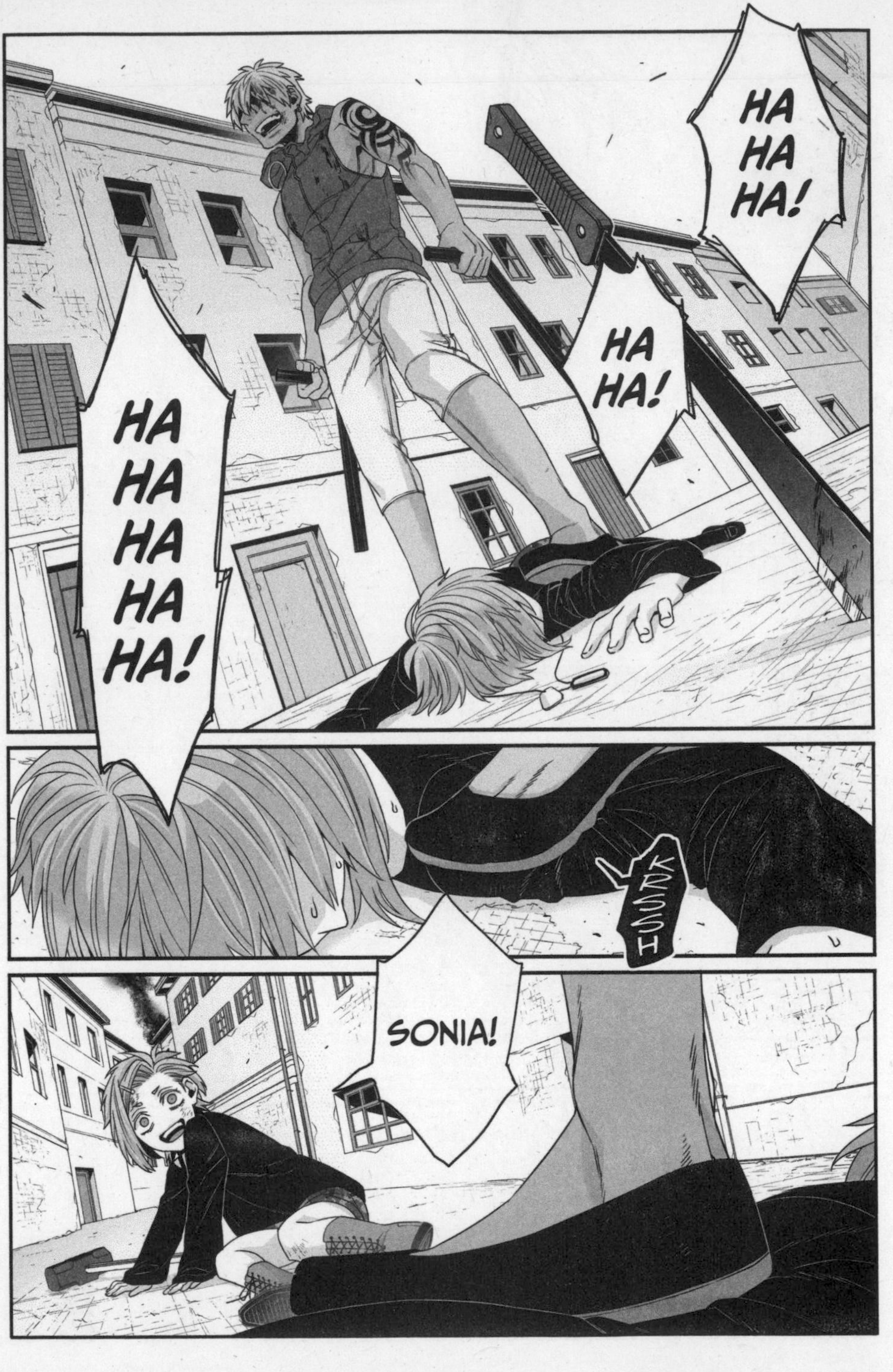
HA HA HA!
HA HA!
HA HA HA HA HA!
KRSSH
SONIA!

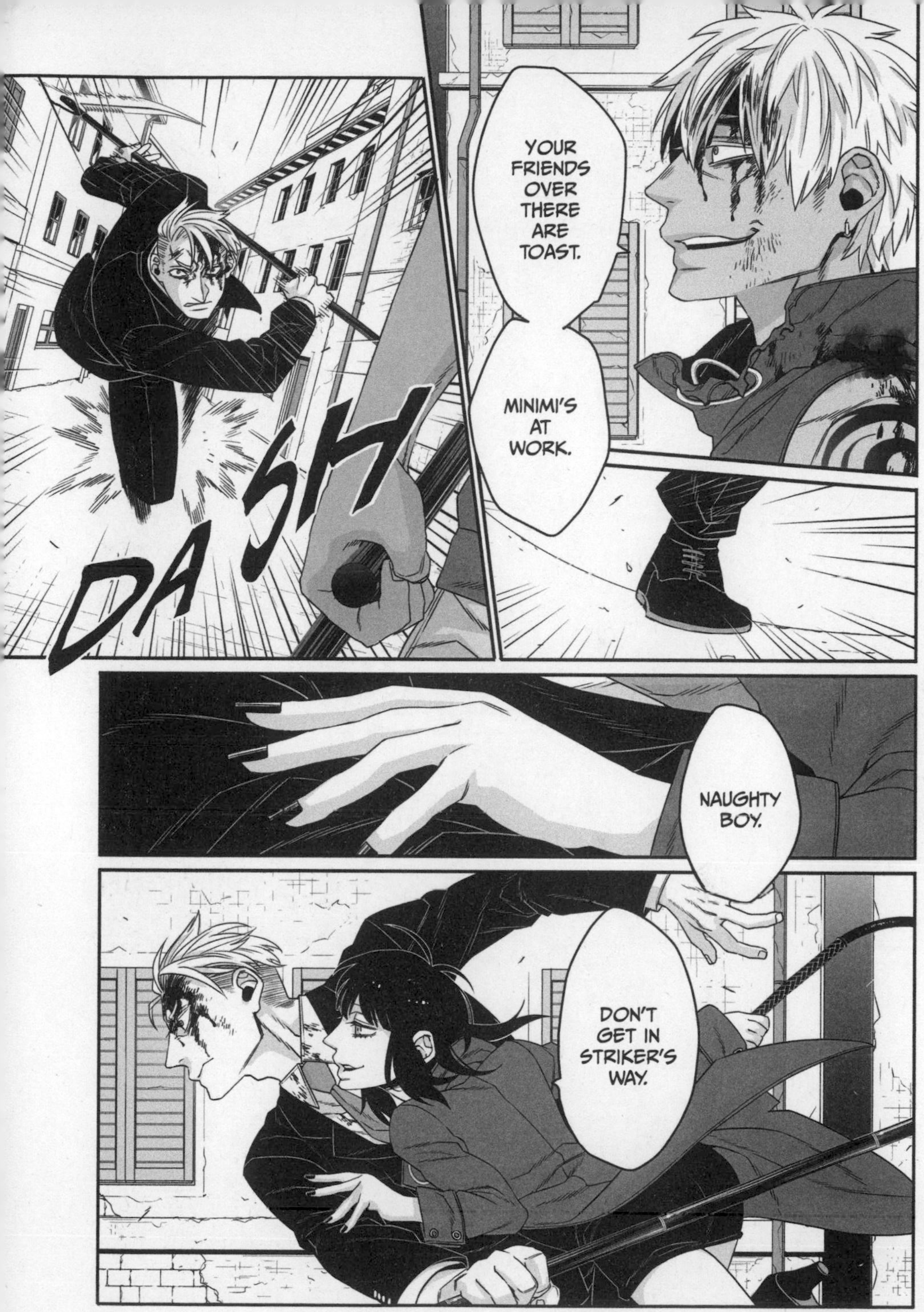
YOUR FRIENDS OVER THERE ARE TOAST.
MINIMI'S AT WORK.
DASH
NAUGHTY BOY.
DON'T GET IN STRIKER'S WAY.

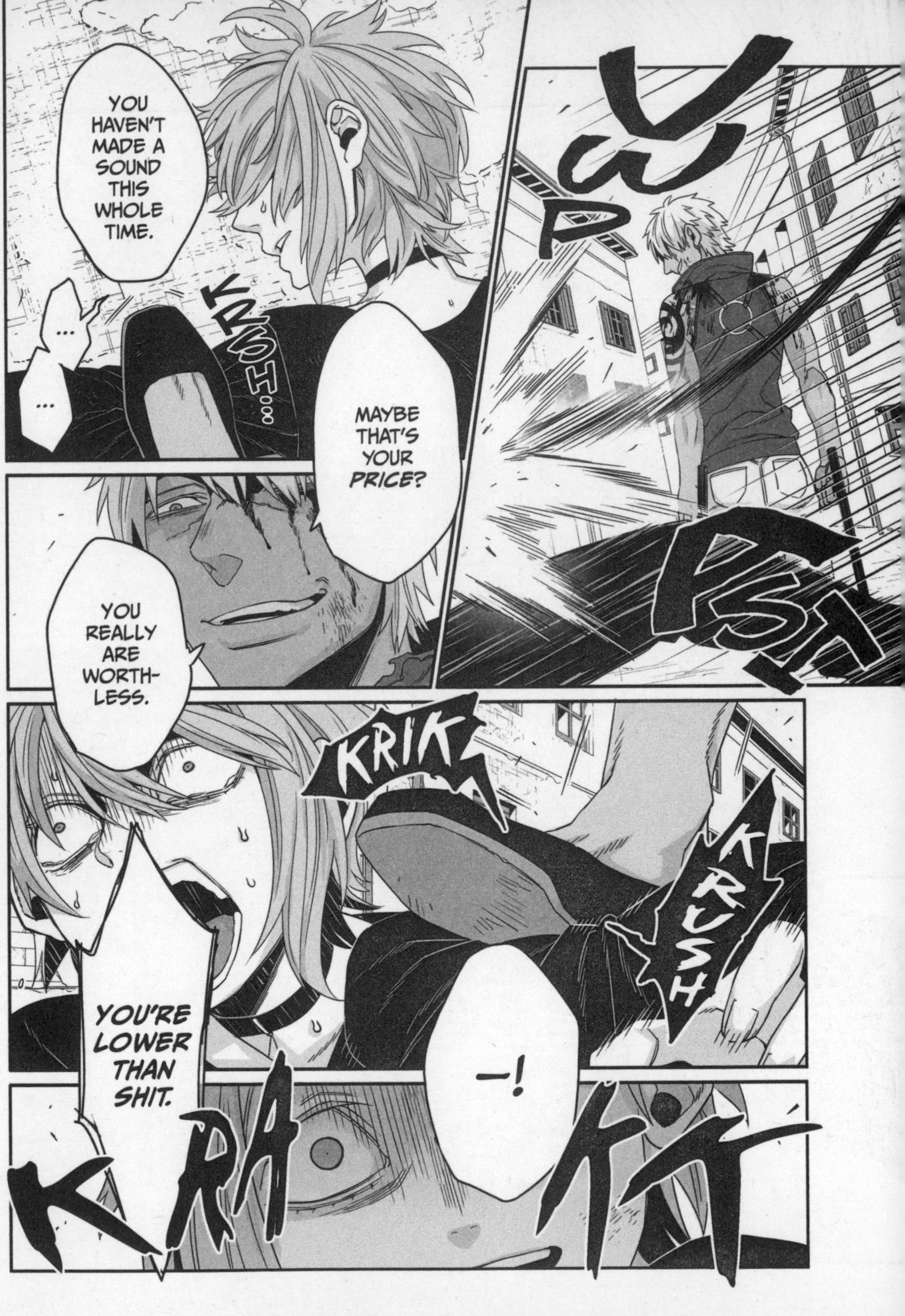
YAP
PST
YOU HAVEN'T MADE A SOUND THIS WHOLE TIME.
...
...
KRSH...
MAYBE THAT'S YOUR PRICE?
YOU REALLY ARE WORTH-LESS.
KRIK
KRUSH
YOU'RE LOWER THAN SHIT.
—!
KRAKT

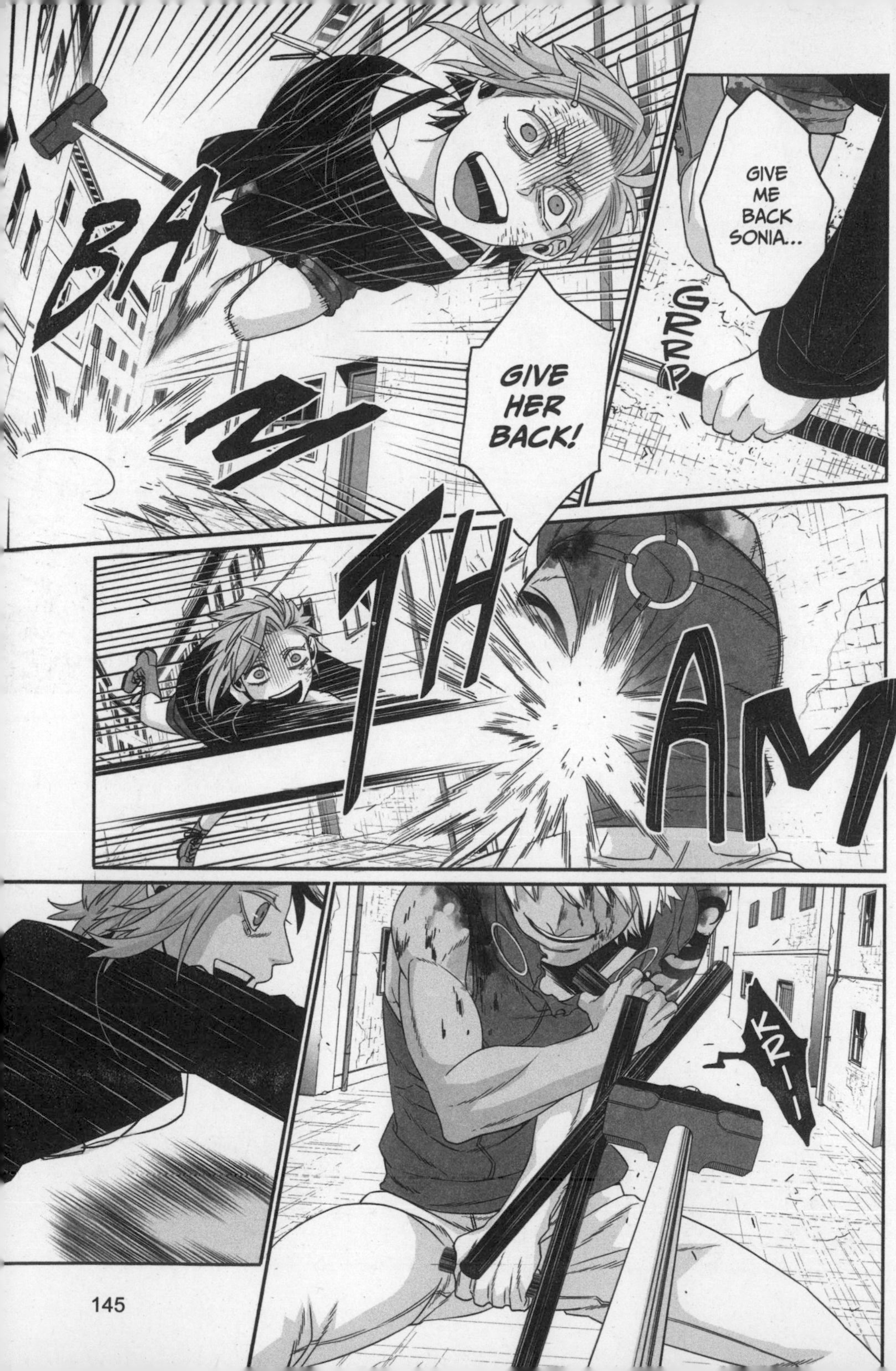
GIVE ME BACK SONIA...
GRRP
BA
GIVE HER BACK!
THAM
KR—

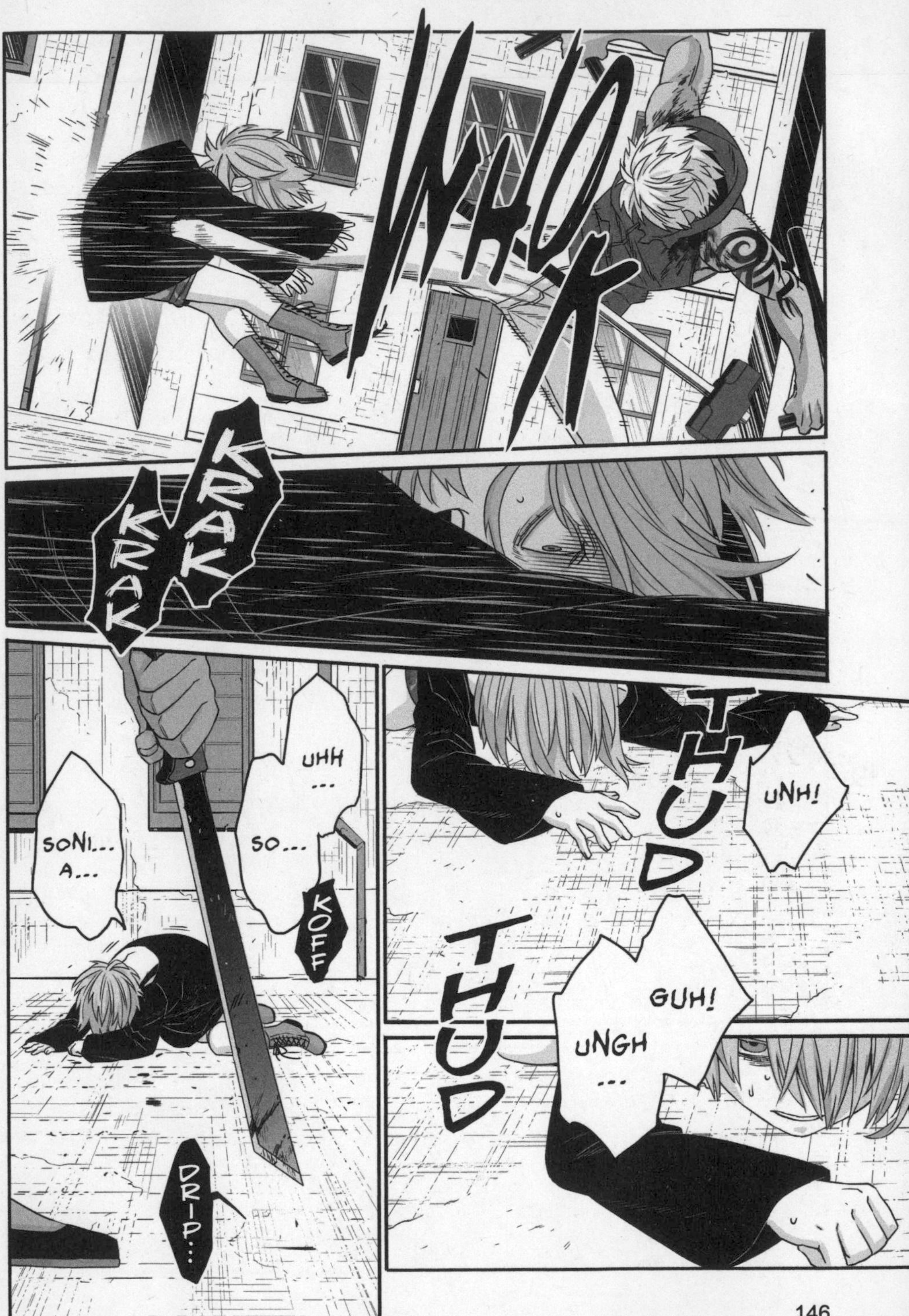
KRAK
KRAK
THUD
UNH!
THUD
GUH!
UNGH ...
UHH ...
SO...
KOFF
SONI... A...
DRIP...

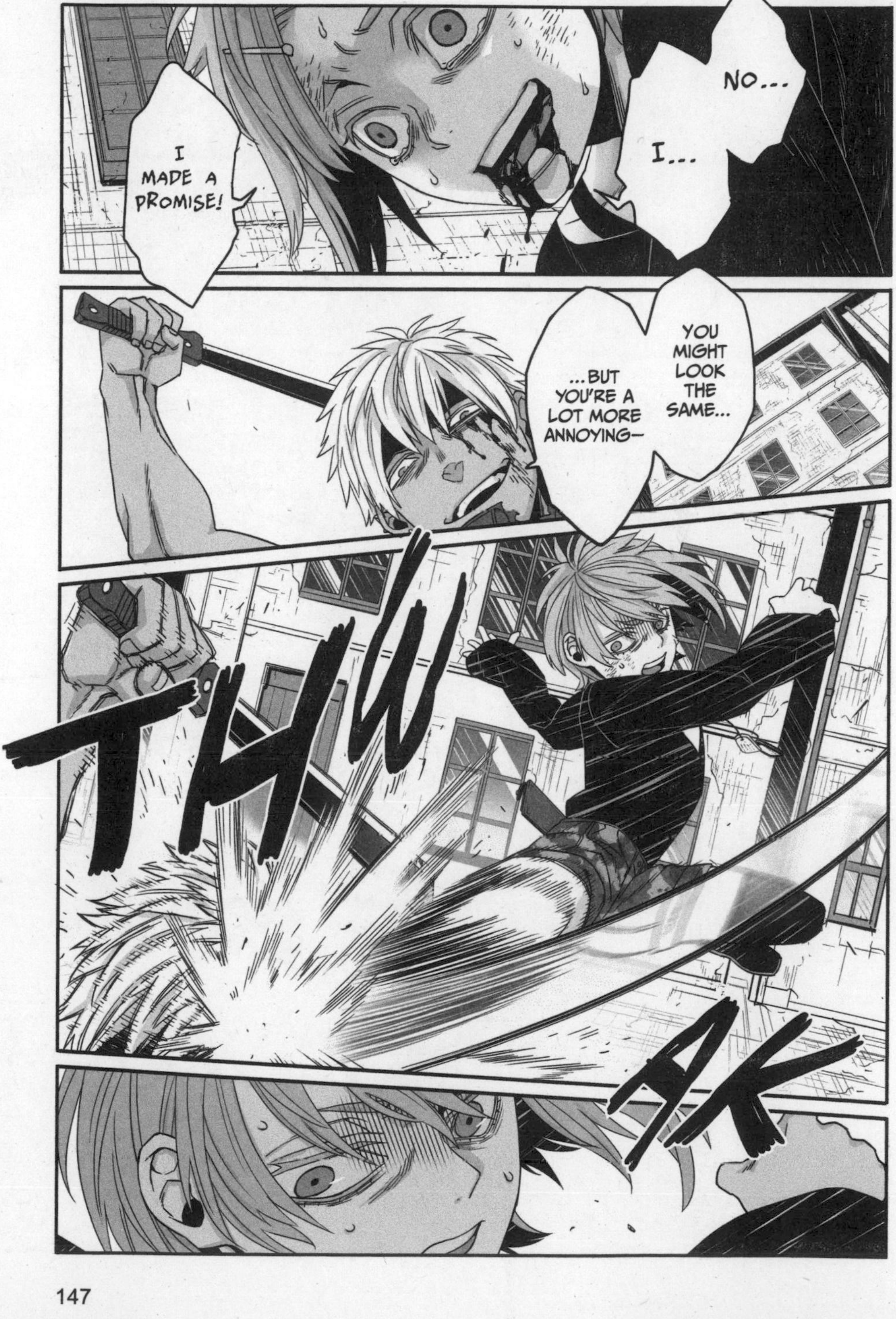
NO... I...
I MADE A PROMISE!
YOU MIGHT LOOK THE SAME...
...BUT YOU'RE A LOT MORE ANNOYING—
THWAK

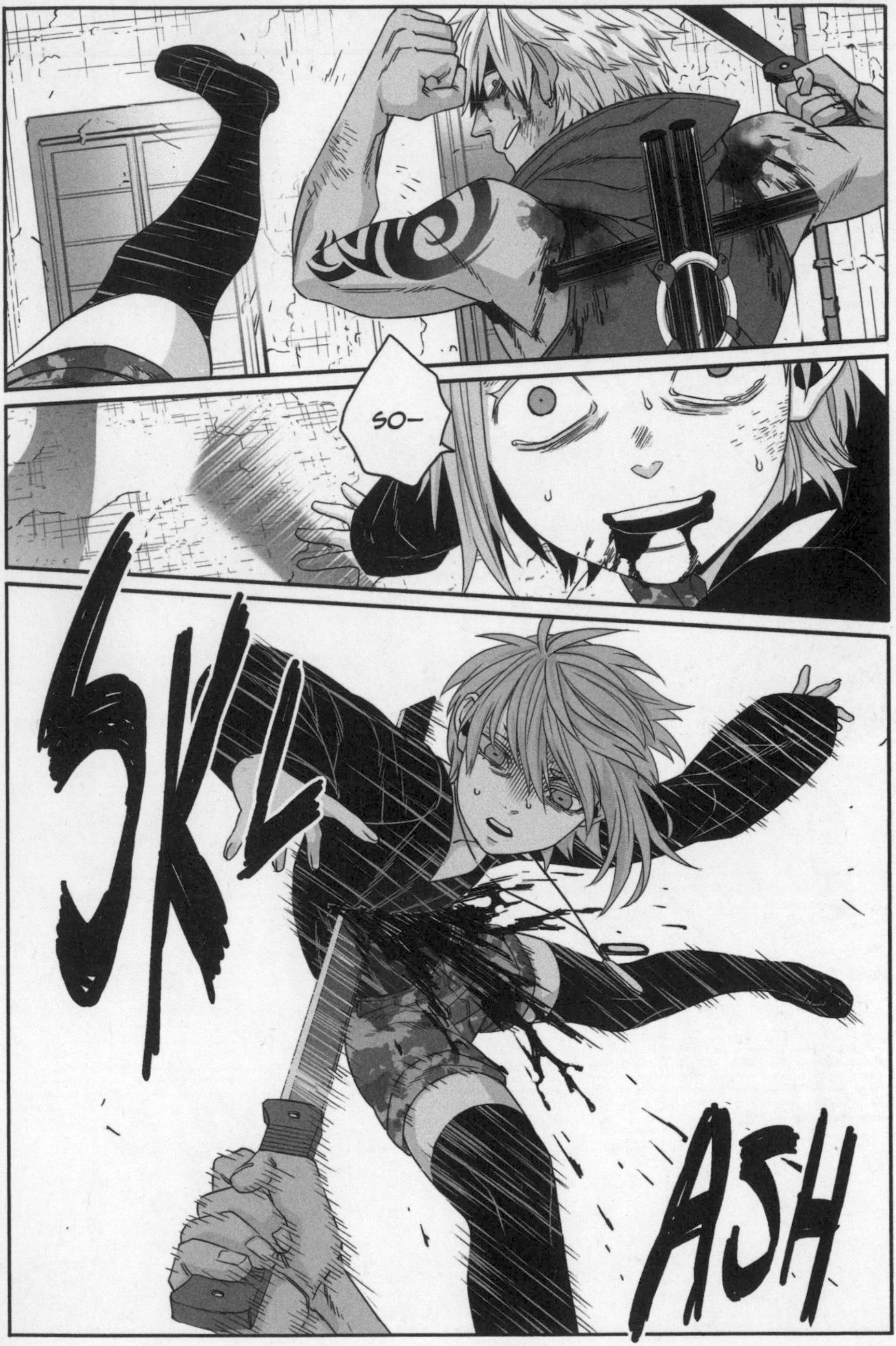
SO–
SKL
ASH

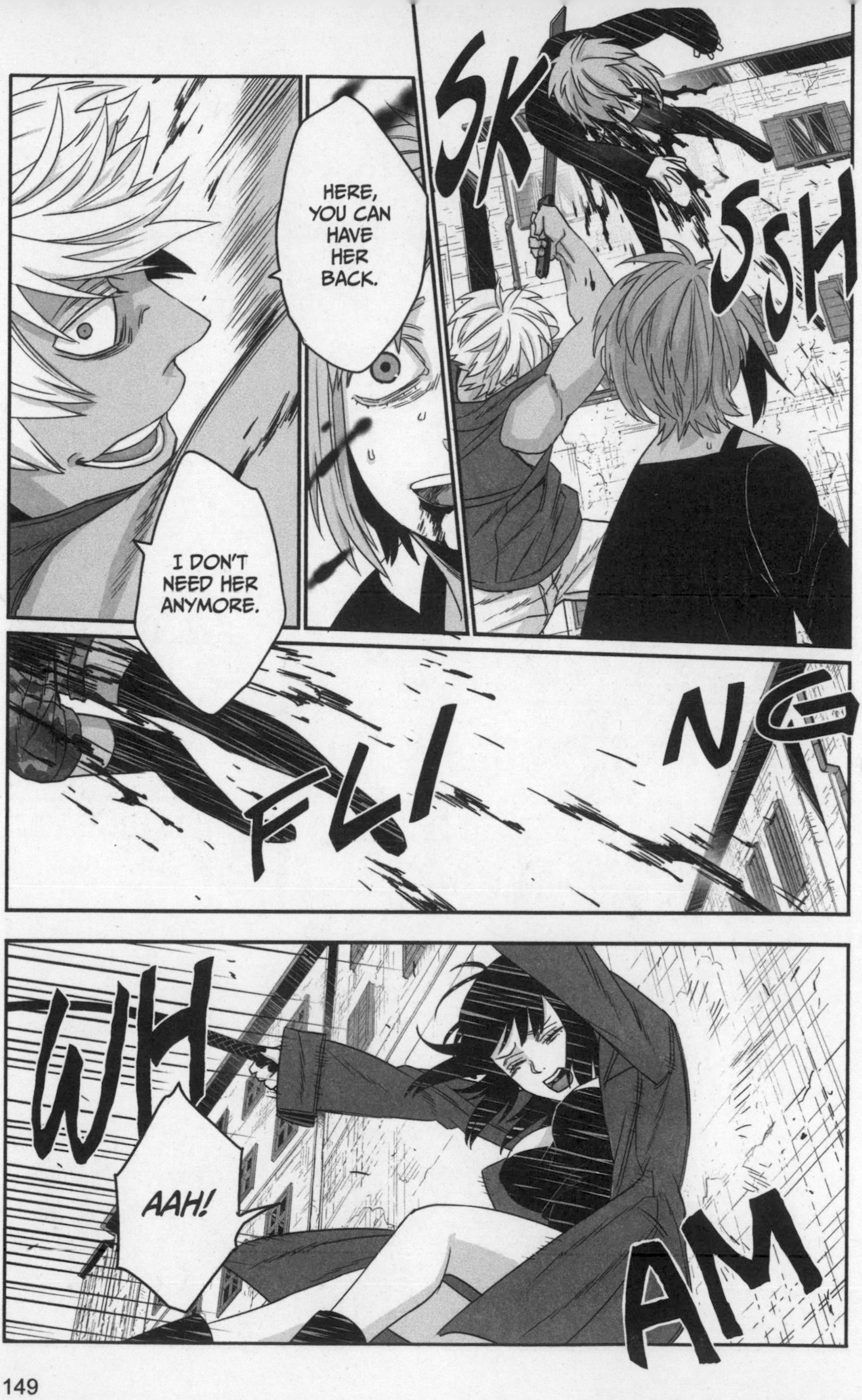
SK
SSH
HERE, YOU CAN HAVE HER BACK.
I DON'T NEED HER ANYMORE.
FLI
NG
WH
AM
AAH!

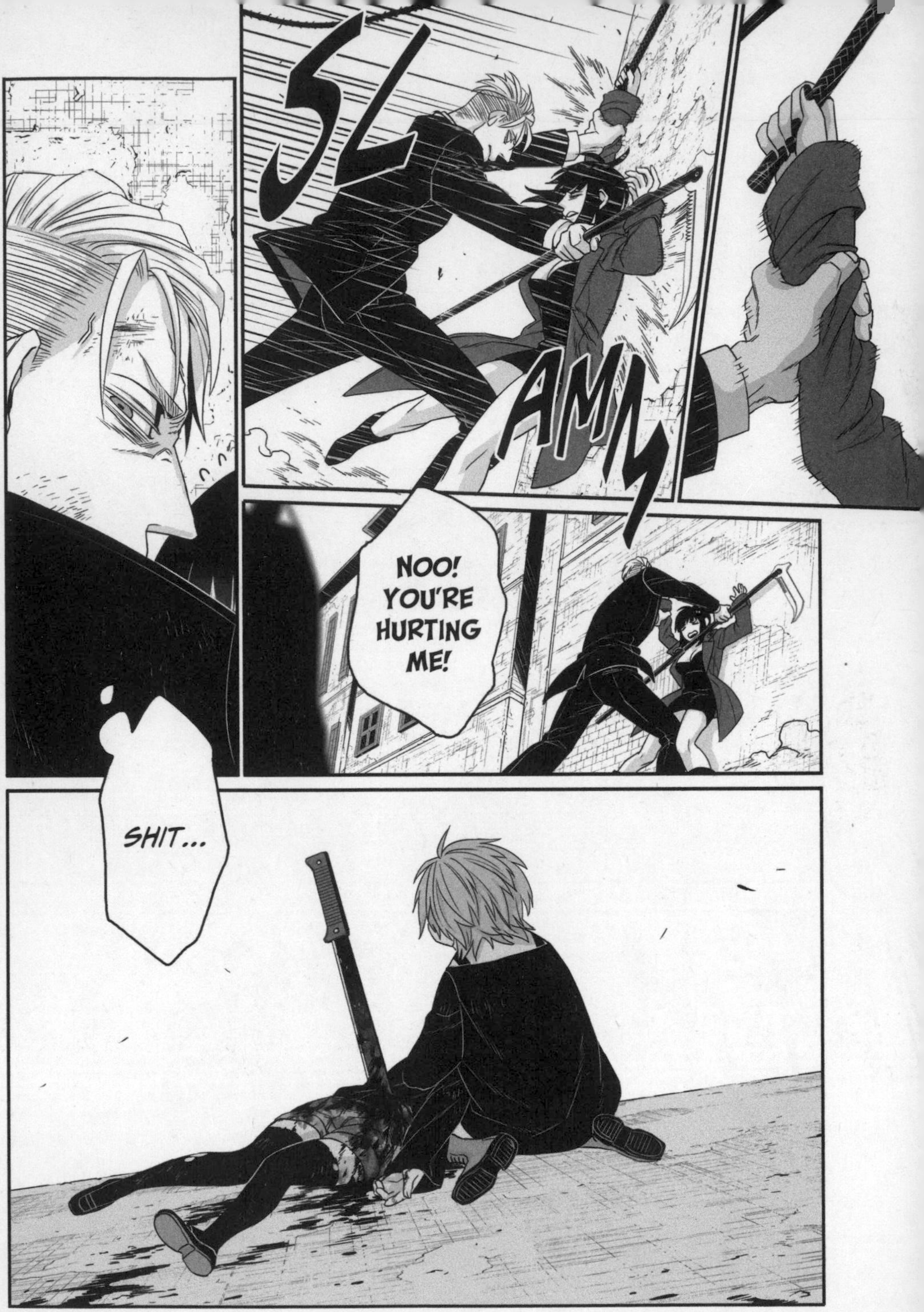
SLAMM
NOO! YOU'RE HURTING ME!
SHIT...

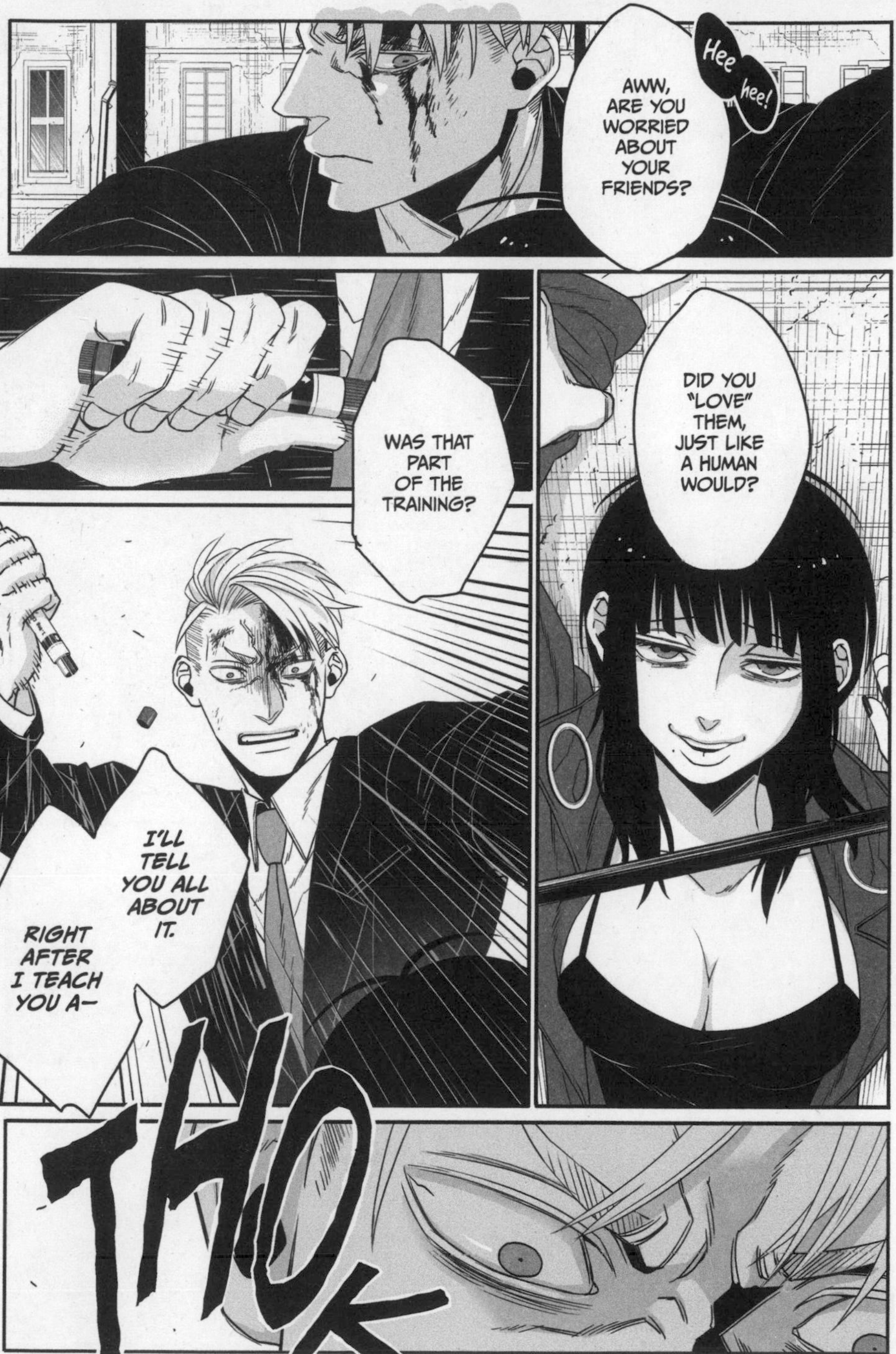
Hee hee!
AWW, ARE YOU WORRIED ABOUT YOUR FRIENDS?
DID YOU "LOVE" THEM, JUST LIKE A HUMAN WOULD?
WAS THAT PART OF THE TRAINING?
I'LL TELL YOU ALL ABOUT IT.
RIGHT AFTER I TEACH YOU A—
THOK

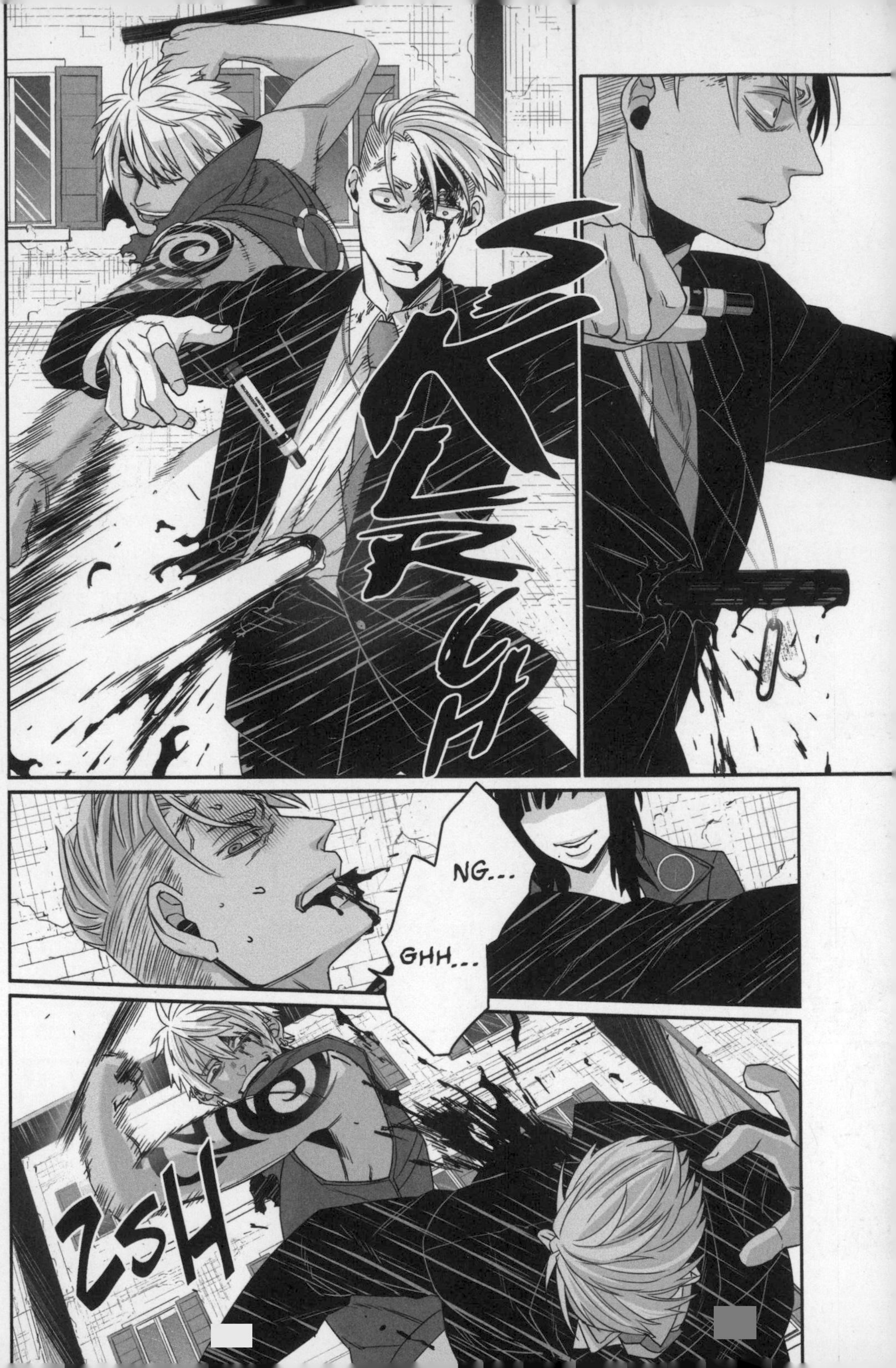
NG...
GHH...
ZSH

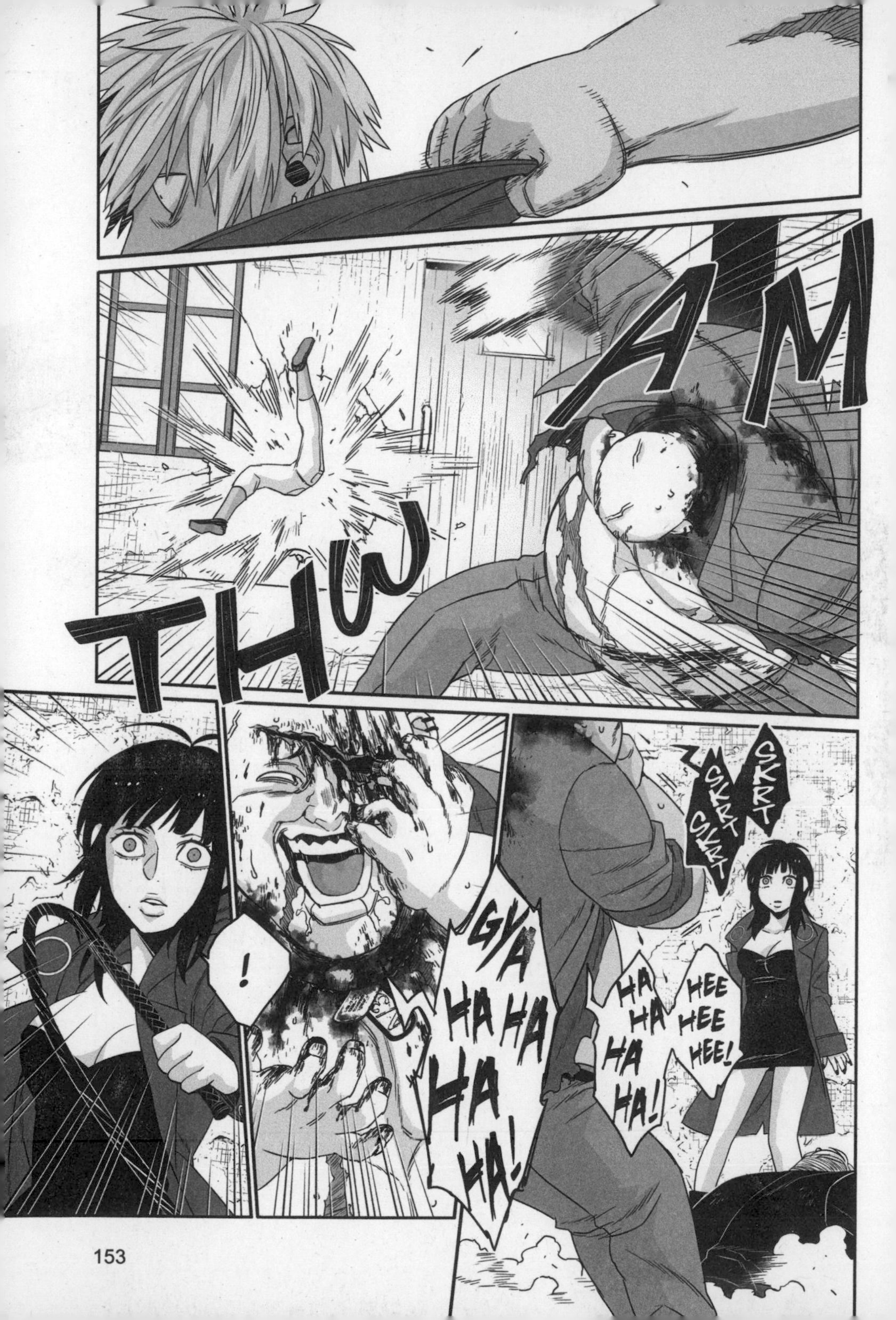
THWAM
SKRT
SKRT SKRT
HEE HEE HEE!
HA HA HA HA!
GYA HA HA HA HA HA HA!
!

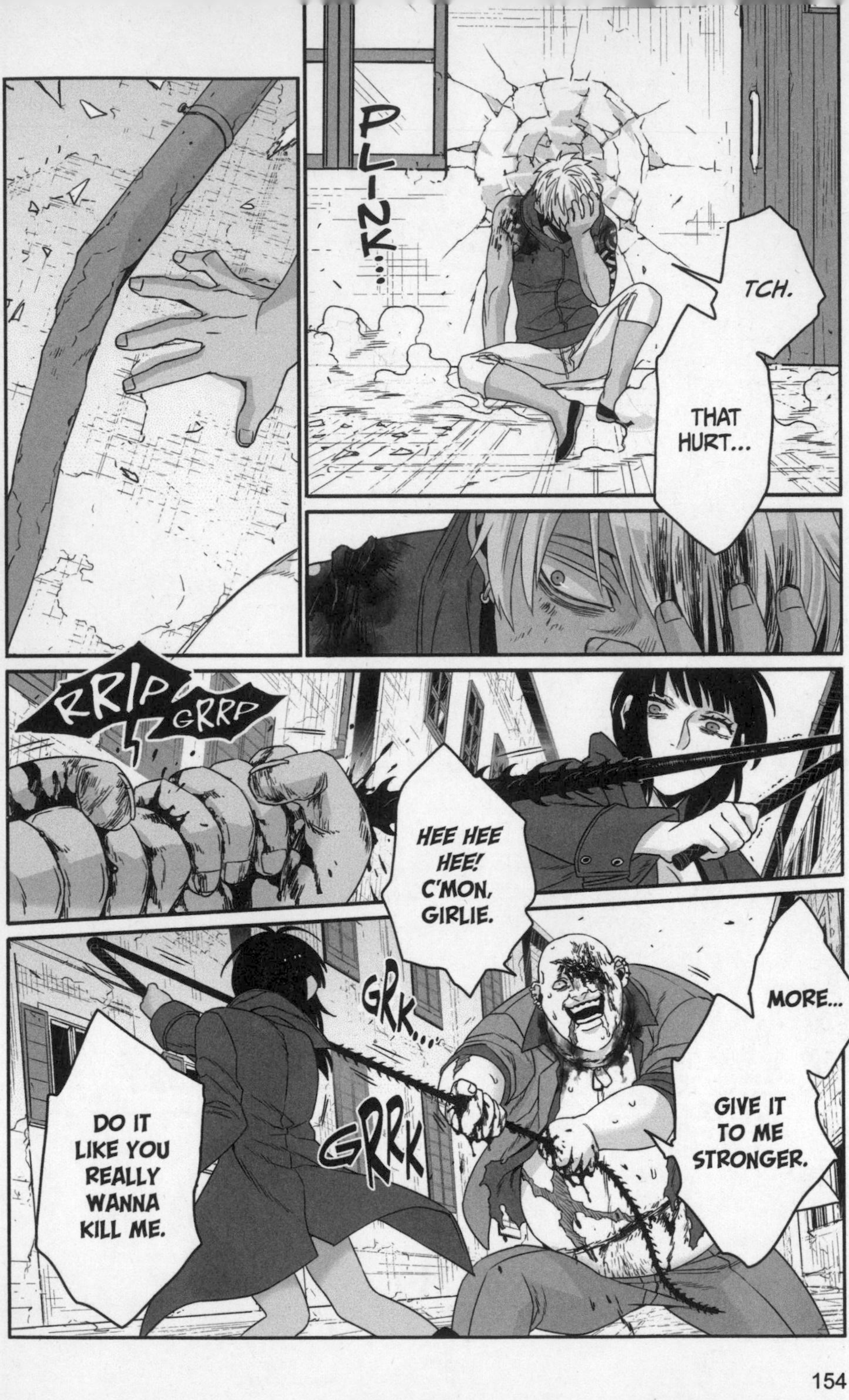
PLINK...
TCH.
THAT HURT...
HEE HEE HEE! C'MON, GIRLIE.
RRIP GRRP
MORE...
GIVE IT TO ME STRONGER.
GRK...
GRRK
DO IT LIKE YOU REALLY WANNA KILL ME.

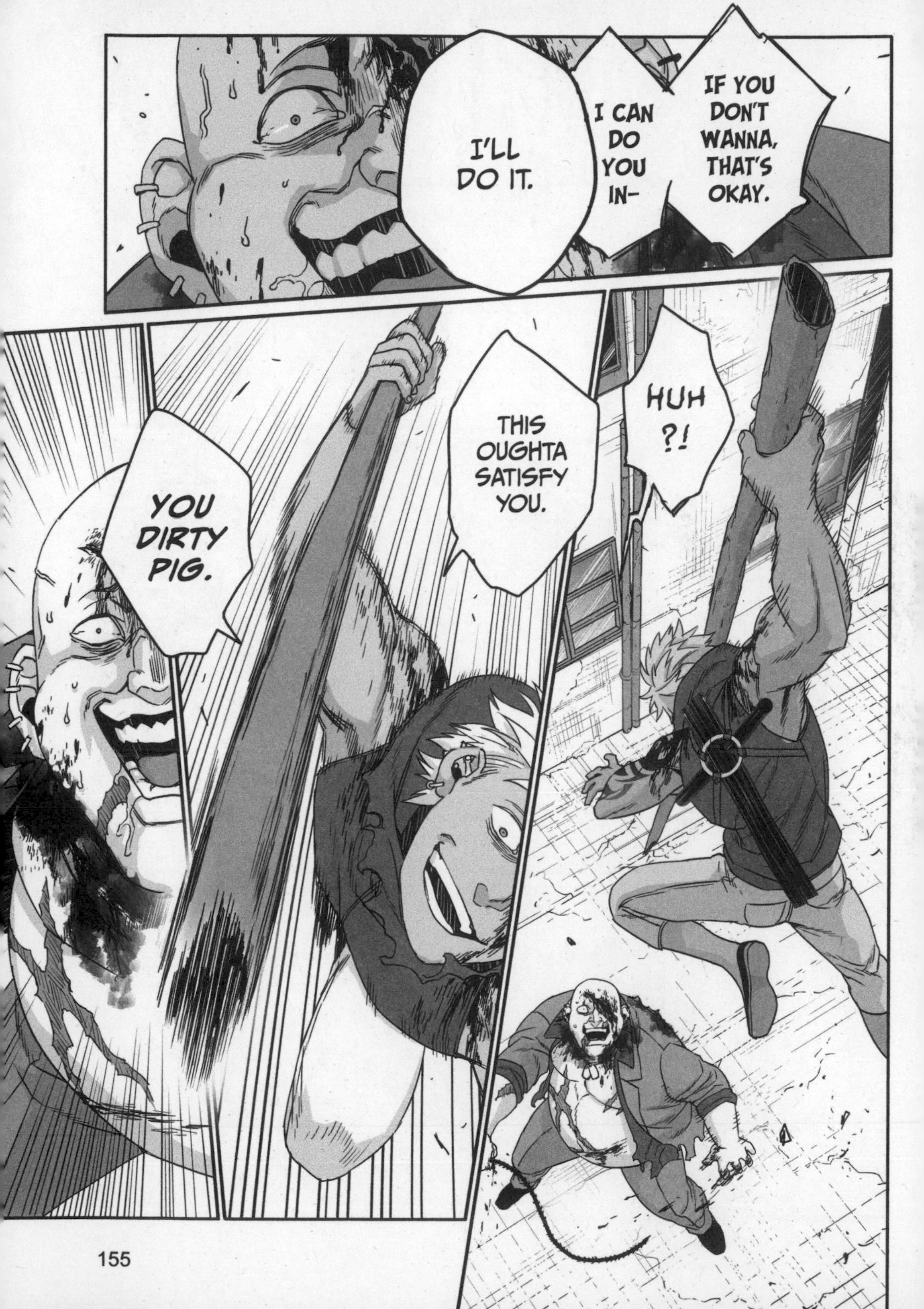
IF YOU DON'T WANNA, THAT'S OKAY.
I CAN DO YOU IN-
I'LL DO IT.
HUH ?!
THIS OUGHTA SATISFY YOU.
YOU DIRTY PIG.

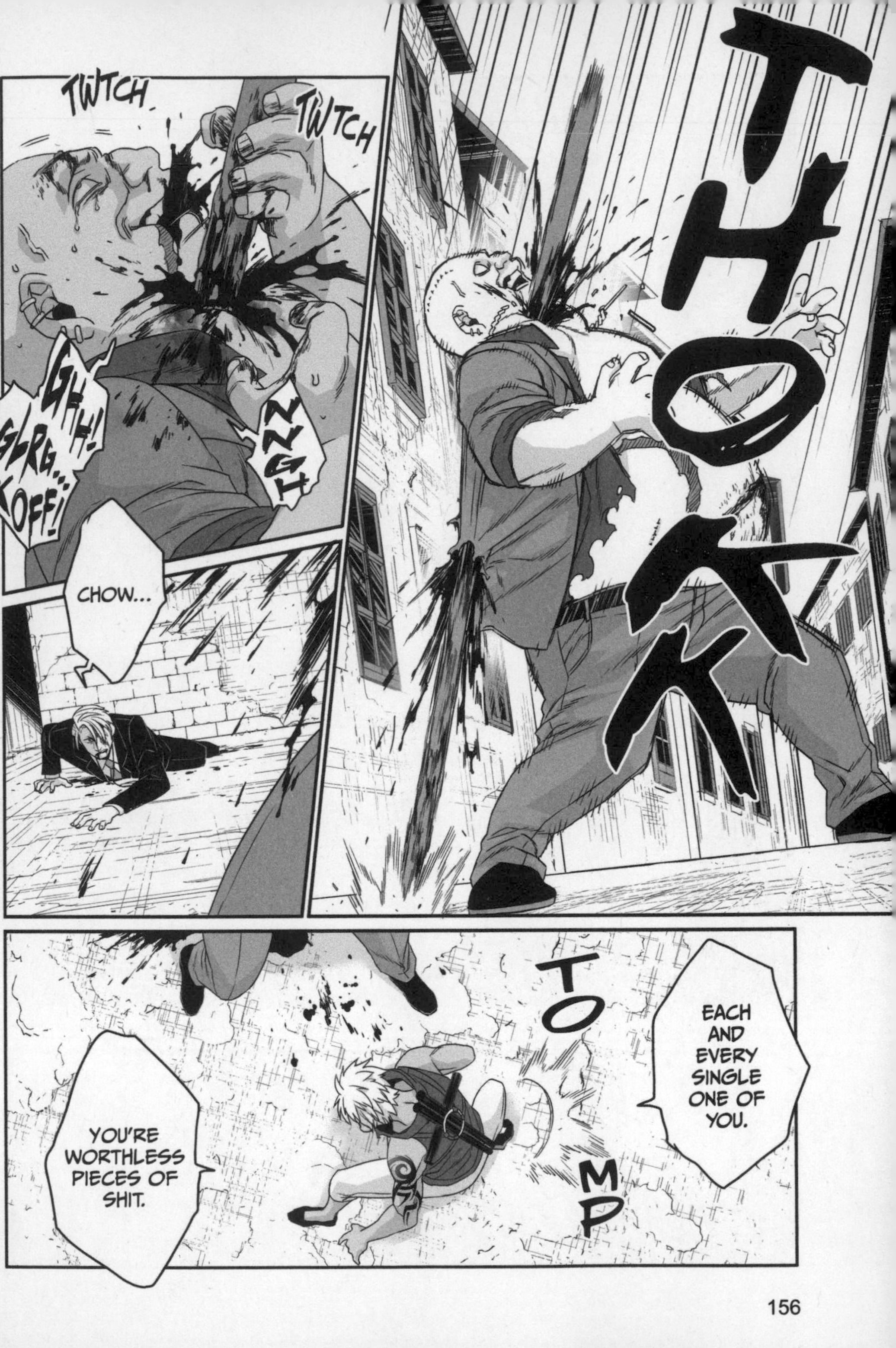
THOCK
TWTCH
TWTCH
GHH! GLRG... KOFF!
NNGH
CHOW...
EACH AND EVERY SINGLE ONE OF YOU.
TOMP
YOU'RE WORTHLESS PIECES OF SHIT.

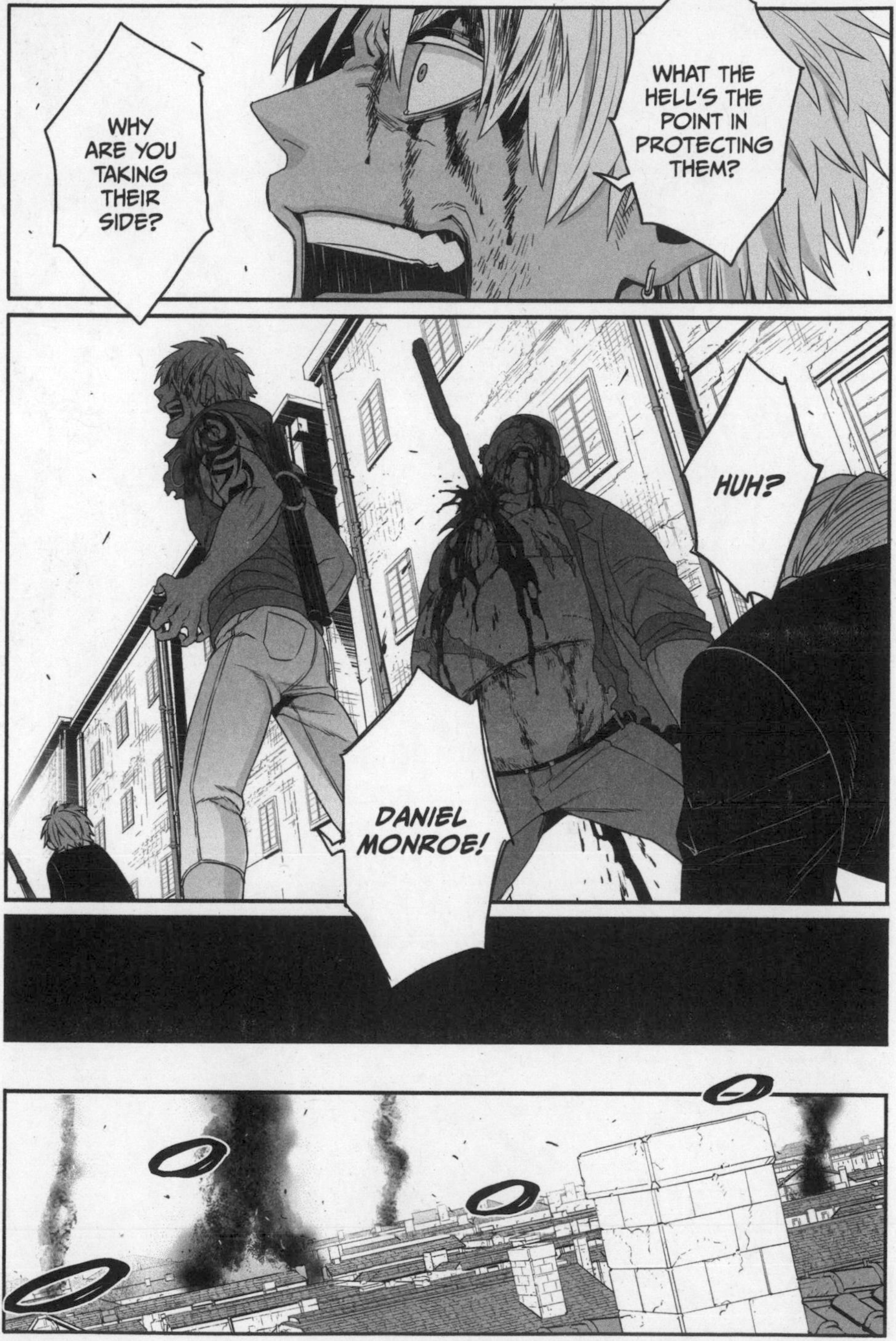
WHAT THE HELL'S THE POINT IN PROTECTING THEM?
WHY ARE YOU TAKING THEIR SIDE?
HUH?
DANIEL MONROE!

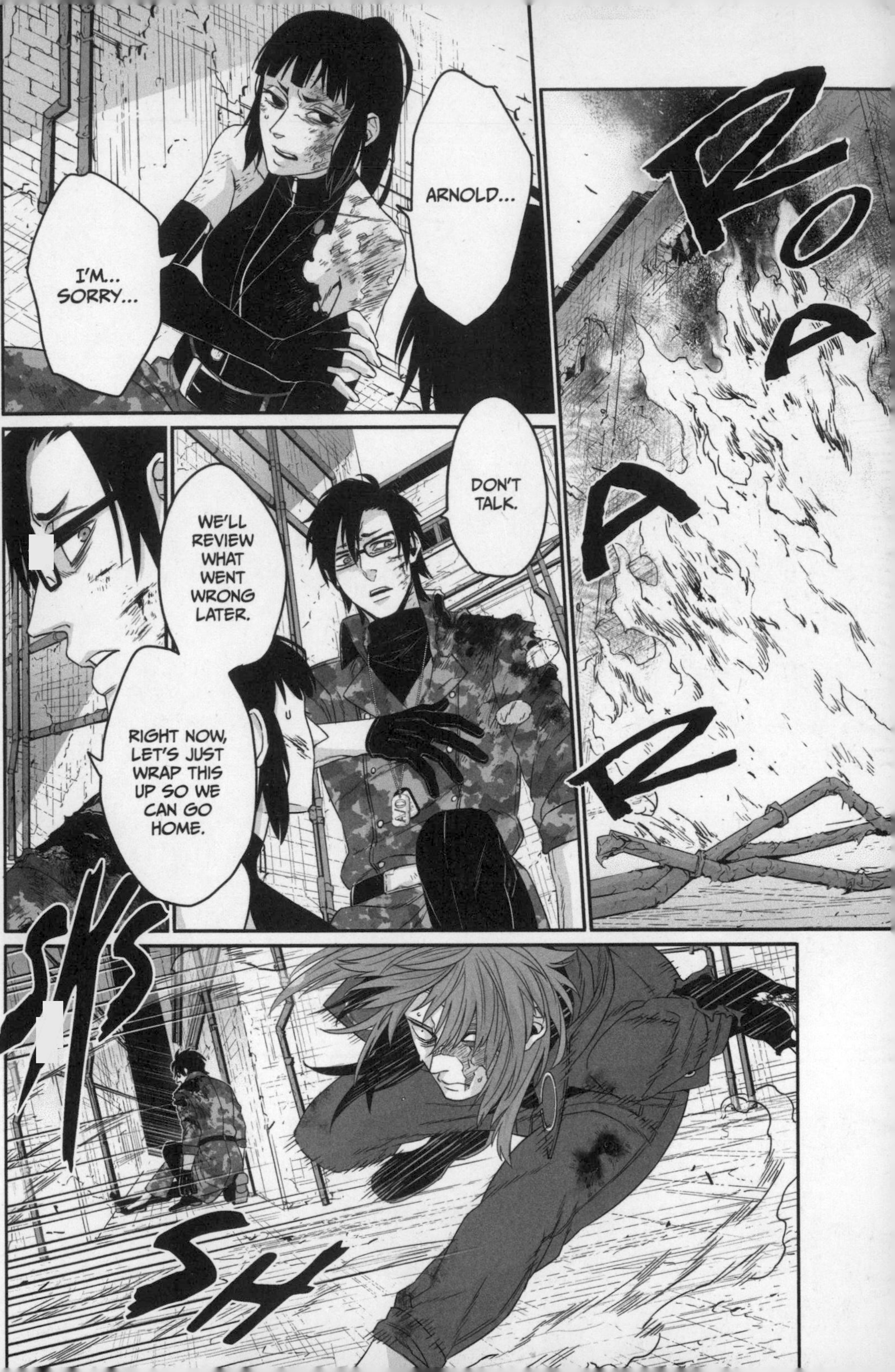
ROAAR
ARNOLD...
I'M... SORRY...
DON'T TALK.
WE'LL REVIEW WHAT WENT WRONG LATER.
RIGHT NOW, LET'S JUST WRAP THIS UP SO WE CAN GO HOME.
SHS
SH

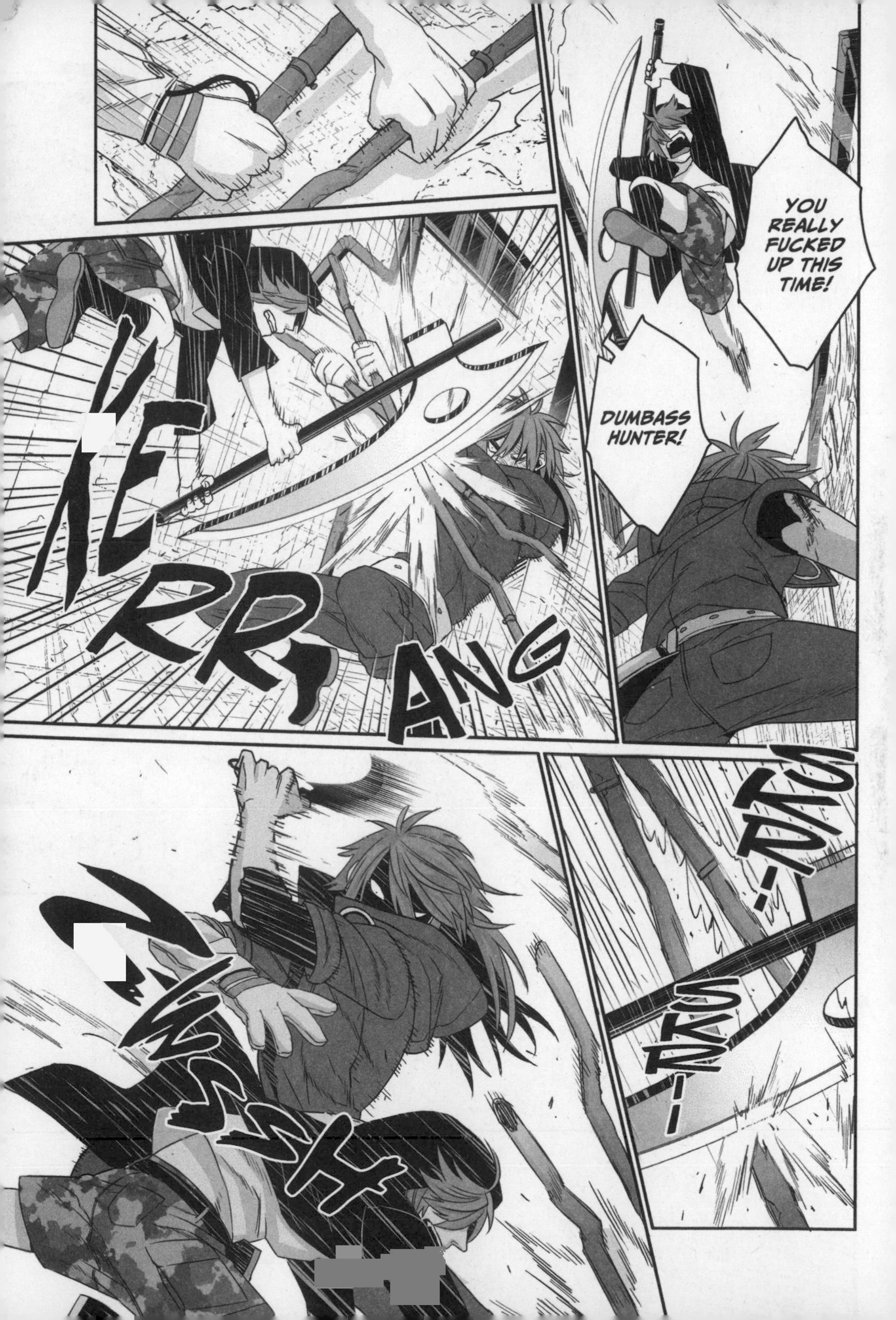
YOU REALLY FUCKED UP THIS TIME!
DUMBASS HUNTER!
KERRANG
SKRI!!
SKRI!!
WHSSH

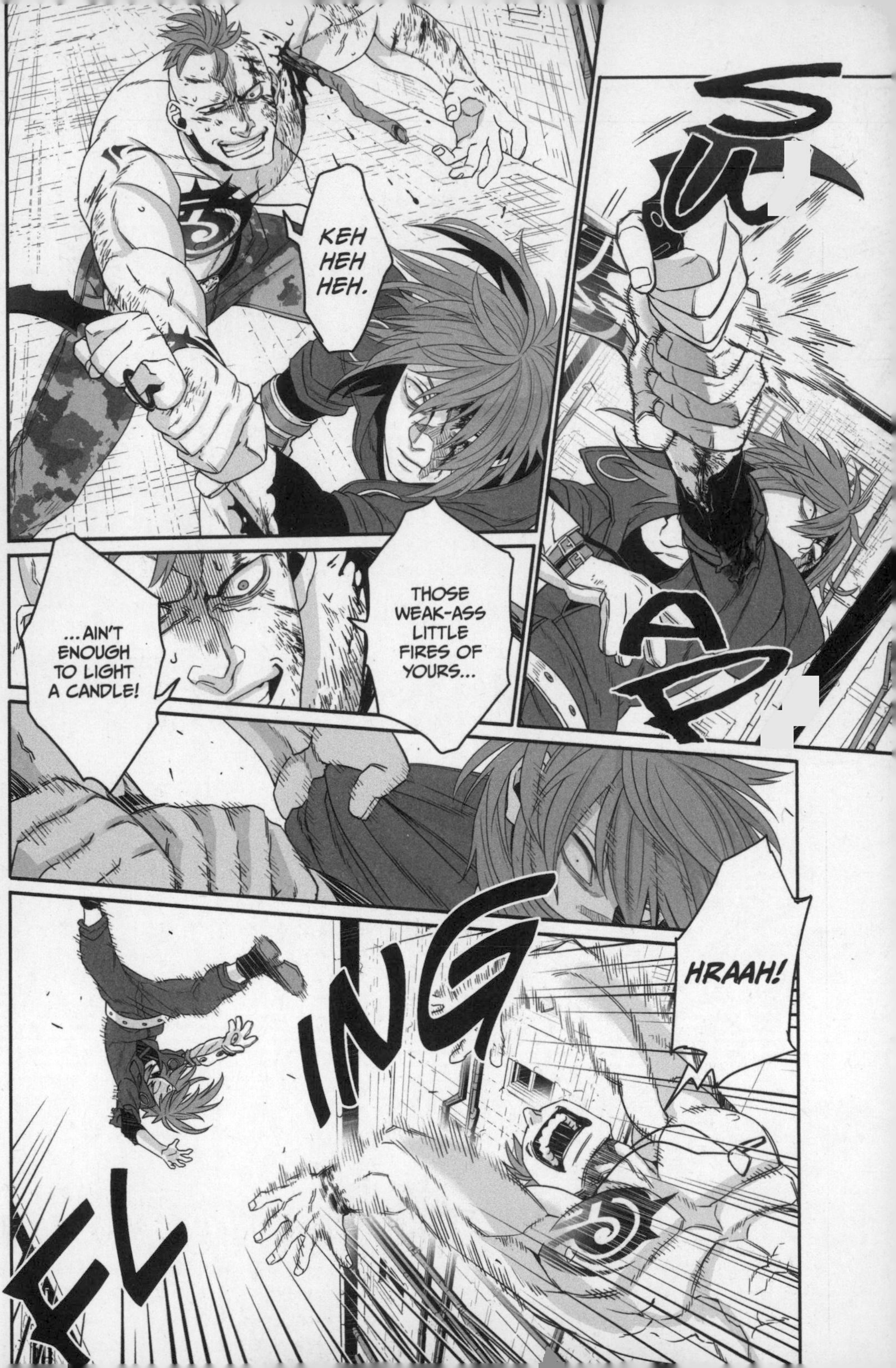
SU
AP
KEH HEH HEH.
THOSE WEAK-ASS LITTLE FIRES OF YOURS...
...AIN'T ENOUGH TO LIGHT A CANDLE!
HRAAH!
FL
ING

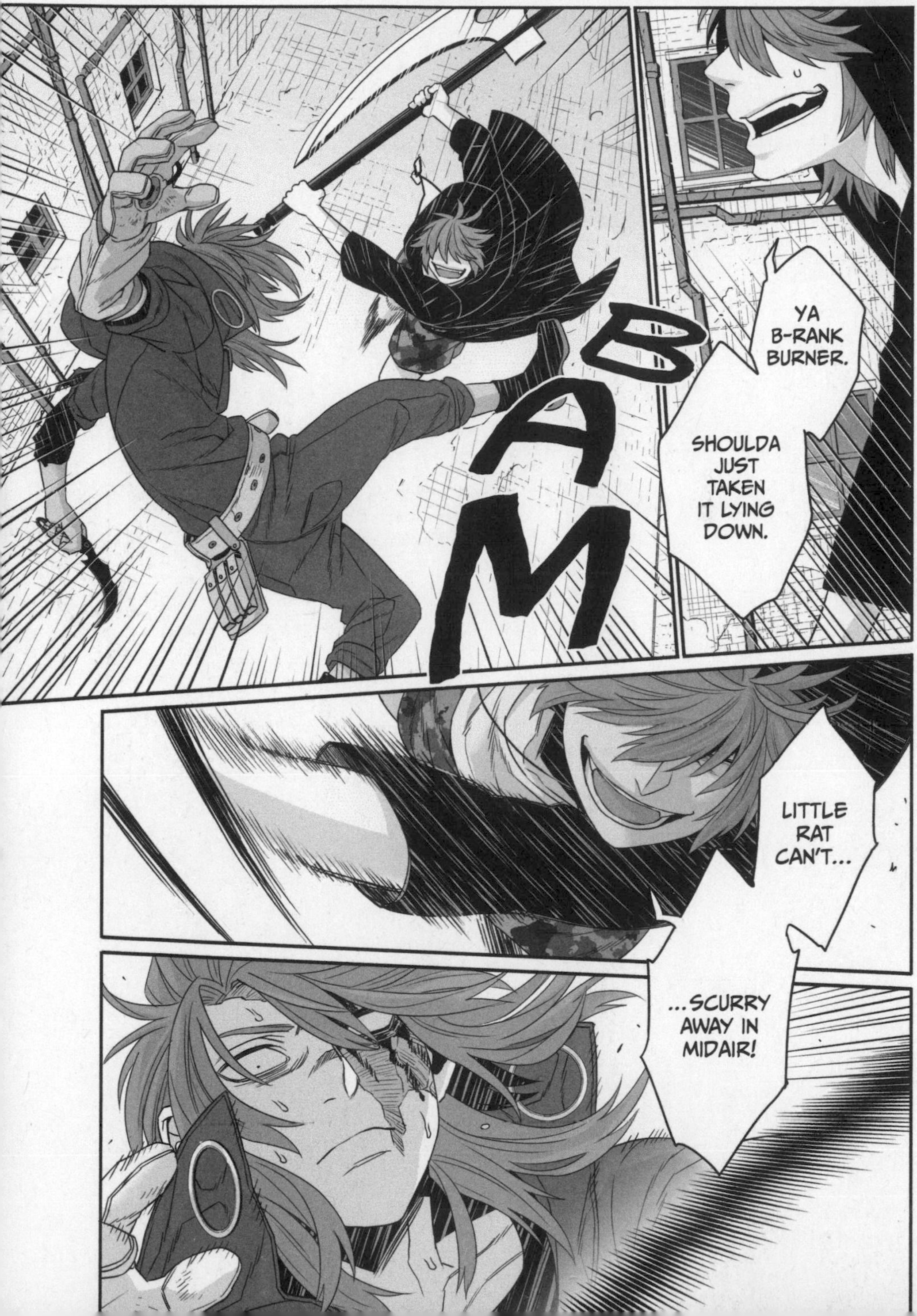
YA B-RANK BURNER.
SHOULDA JUST TAKEN IT LYING DOWN.
BAM
LITTLE RAT CAN'T...
...SCURRY AWAY IN MIDAIR!

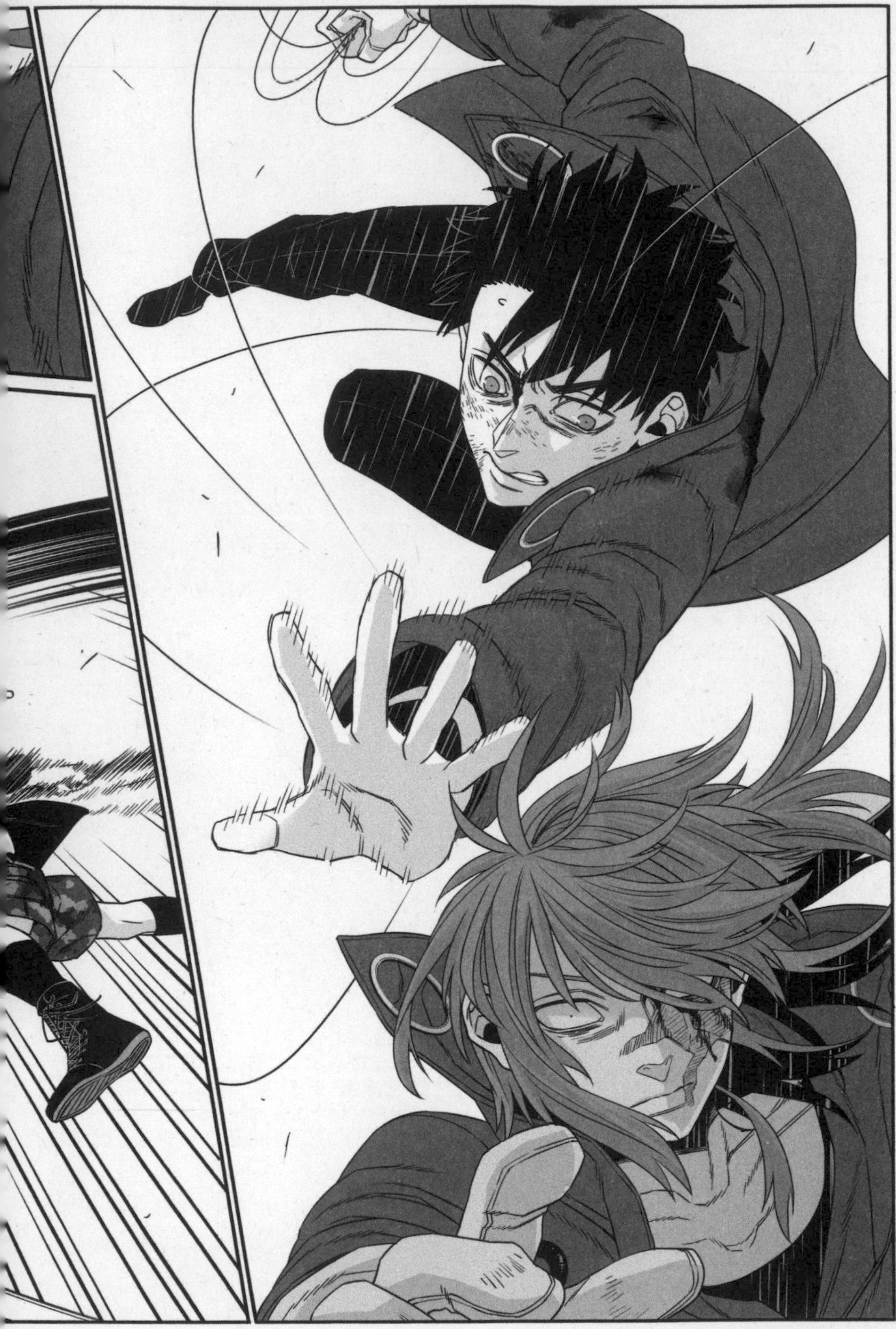

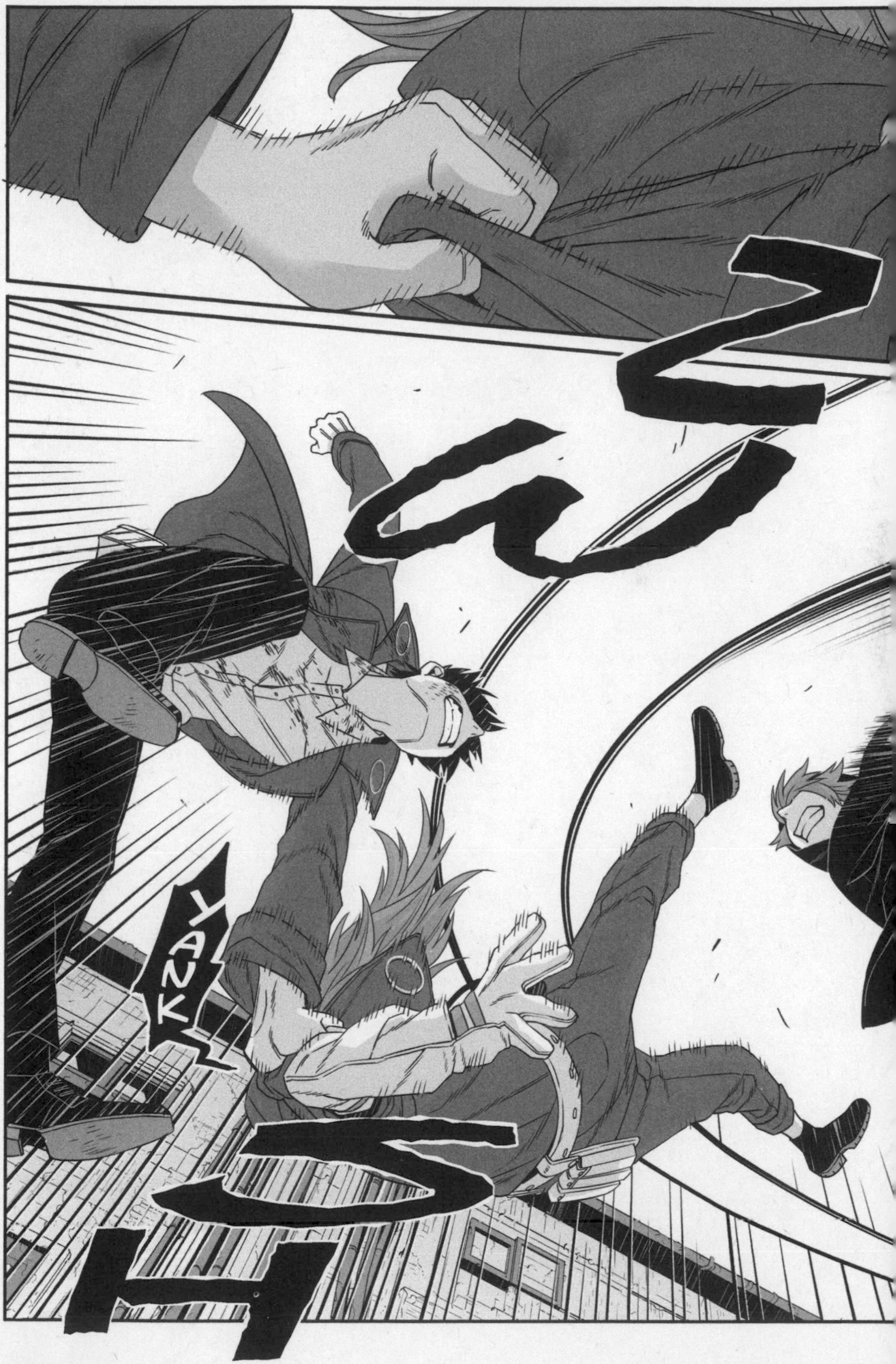
YANK

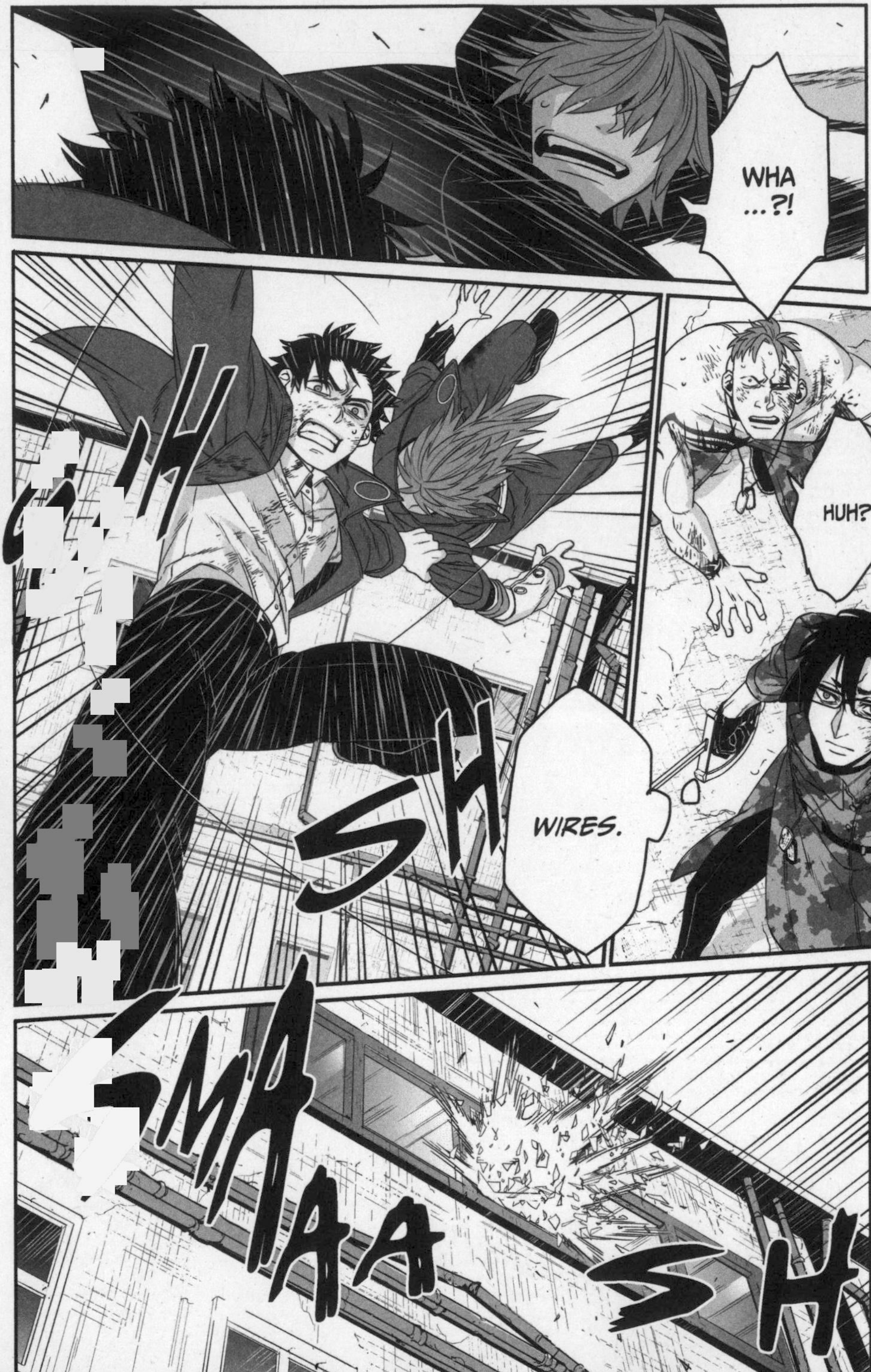
WHA ...?!
HUH?
WIRES.
SMAAASH

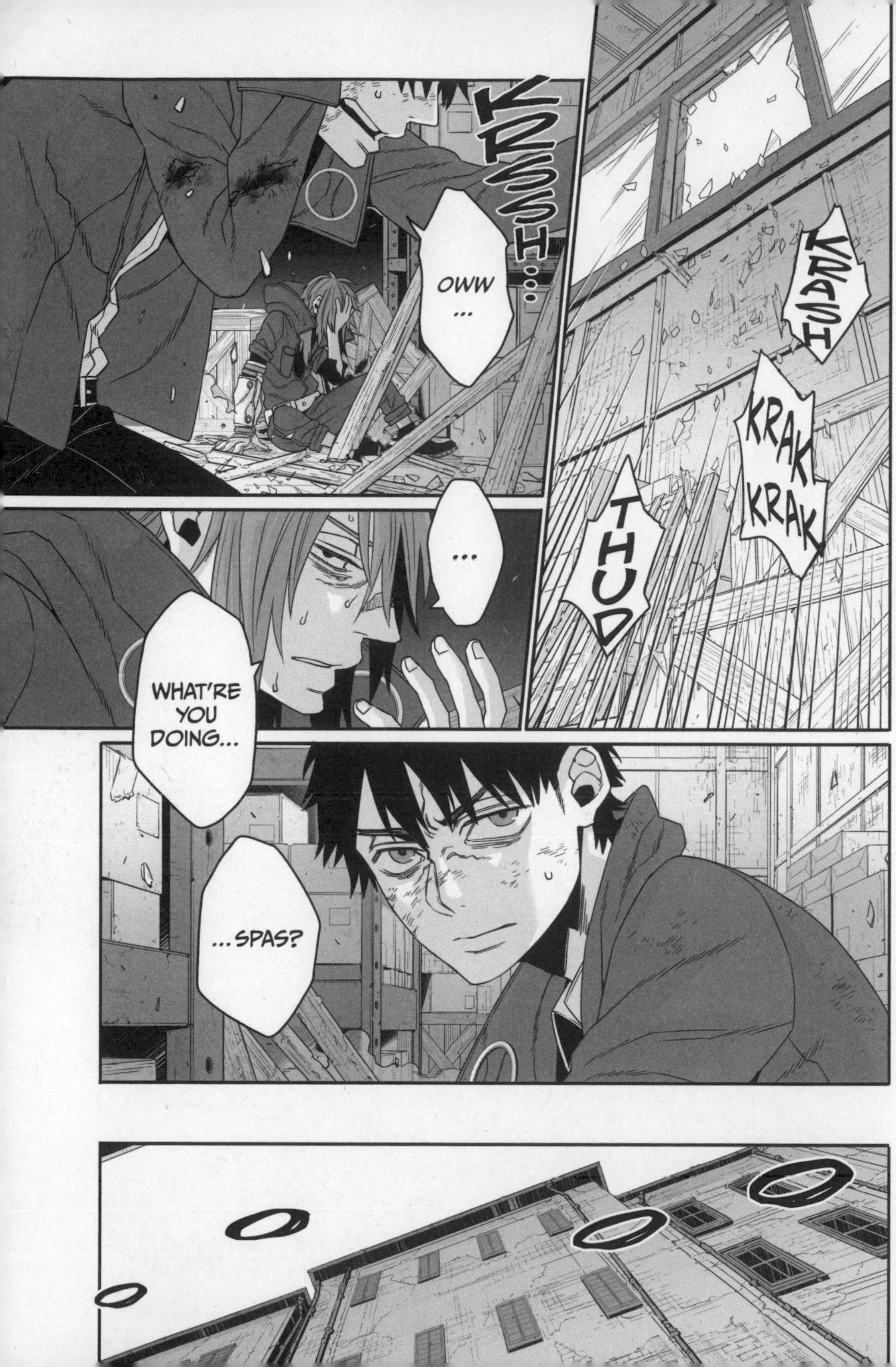
KRASH
KRAK KRAK
THUD
KRSSH...
OWW...
...
WHAT'RE YOU DOING...
...SPAS?

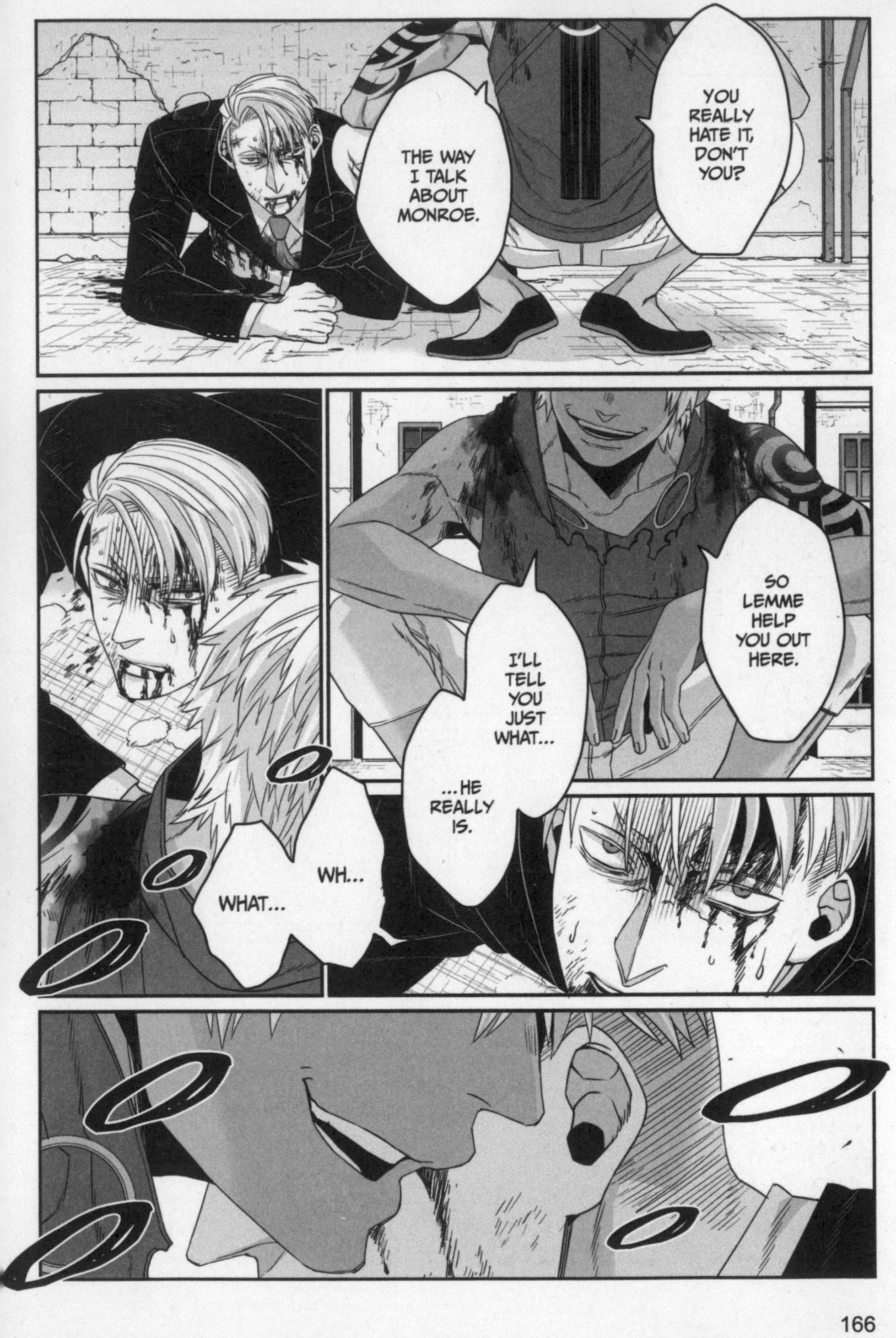
YOU REALLY HATE IT, DON'T YOU?
THE WAY I TALK ABOUT MONROE.
SO LEMME HELP YOU OUT HERE.
I'LL TELL YOU JUST WHAT...
...HE REALLY IS.
WH...
WHAT...

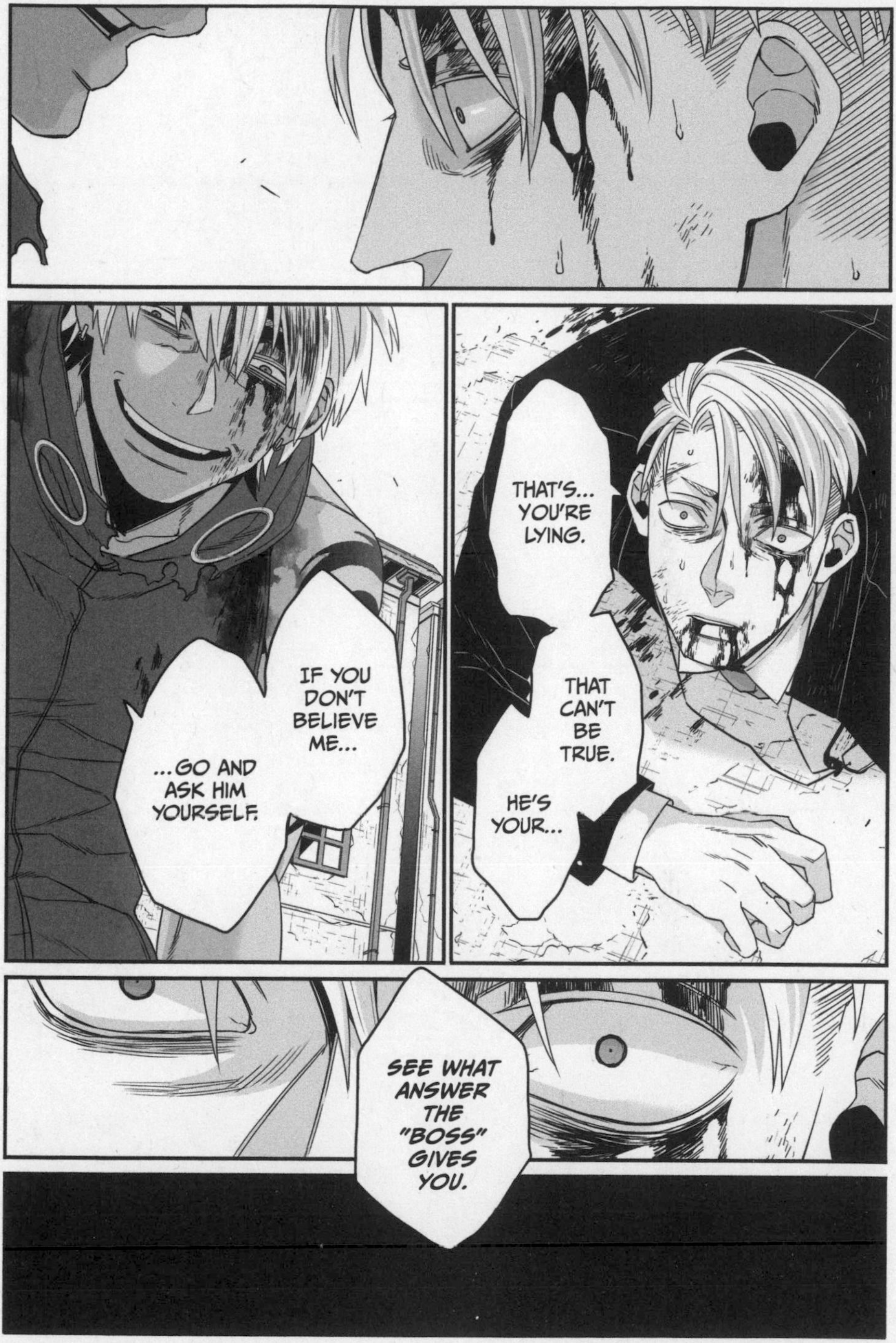
THAT'S... YOU'RE LYING.
THAT CAN'T BE TRUE.
HE'S YOUR...
IF YOU DON'T BELIEVE ME...
...GO AND ASK HIM YOURSELF.
SEE WHAT ANSWER THE "BOSS" GIVES YOU.

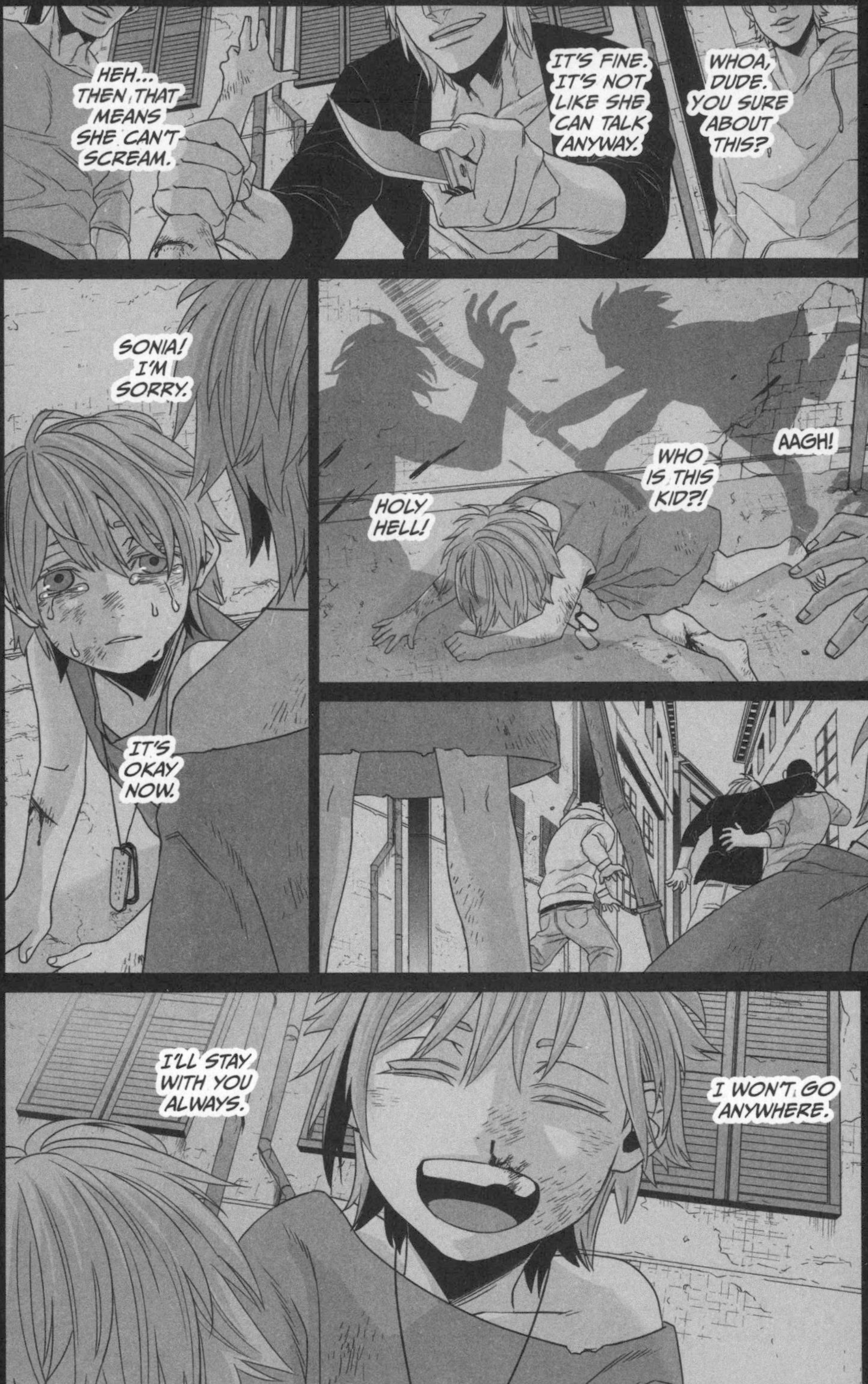
WHOA, DUDE. YOU SURE ABOUT THIS?
IT'S FINE. IT'S NOT LIKE SHE CAN TALK ANYWAY.
HEH... THEN THAT MEANS SHE CAN'T SCREAM.
AAGH!
WHO IS THIS KID?!
HOLY HELL!
SONIA! I'M SORRY.
IT'S OKAY NOW.
I WON'T GO ANYWHERE.
I'LL STAY WITH YOU ALWAYS.

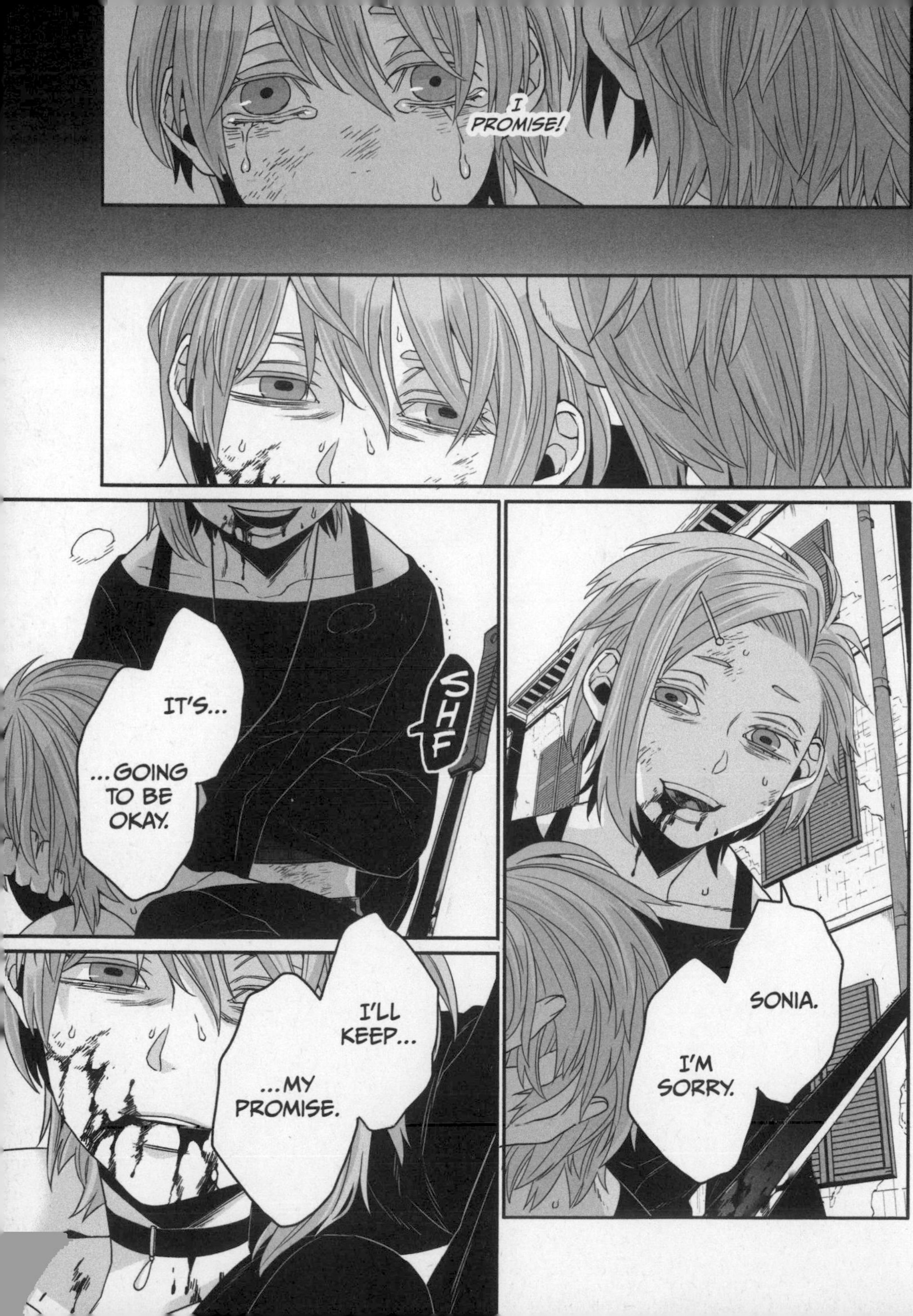
I PROMISE!
SONIA.
I'M SORRY.
IT'S...
...GOING TO BE OKAY.
SHF
I'LL KEEP...
...MY PROMISE.

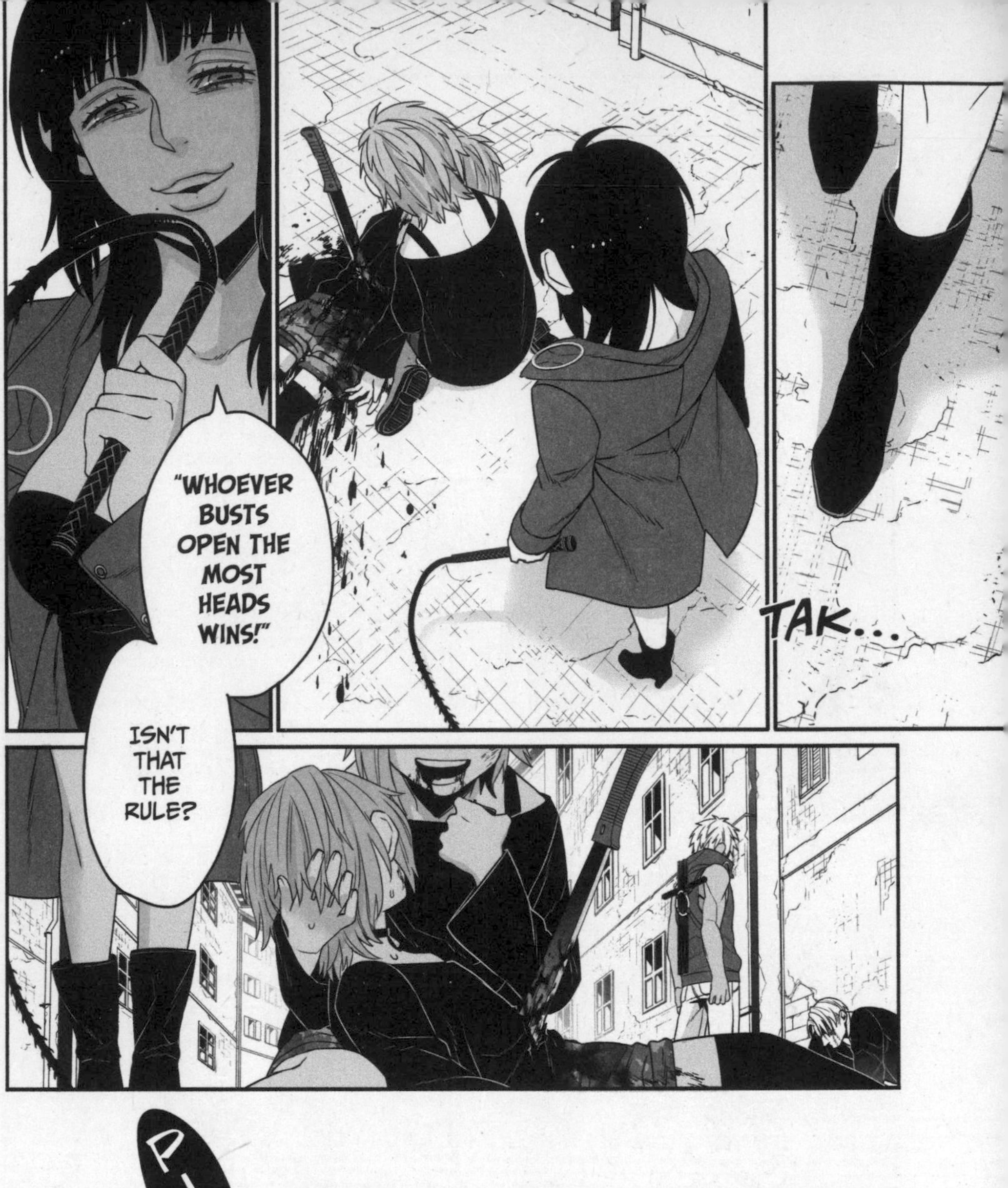
TAK...
"WHOEVER BUSTS OPEN THE MOST HEADS WINS!"
ISN'T THAT THE RULE?
PING

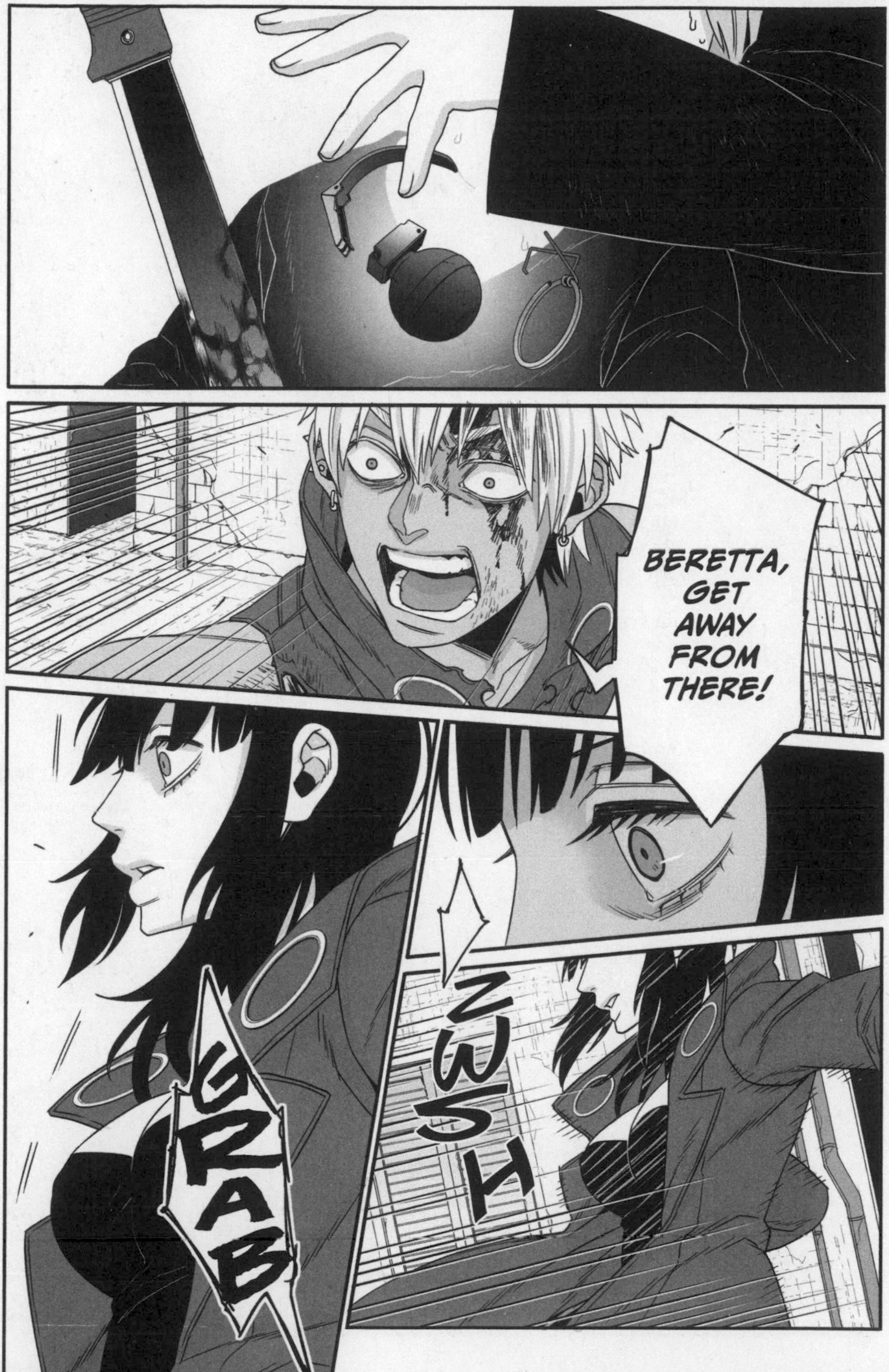
BERETTA, GET AWAY FROM THERE!
ZWSH
GRAB

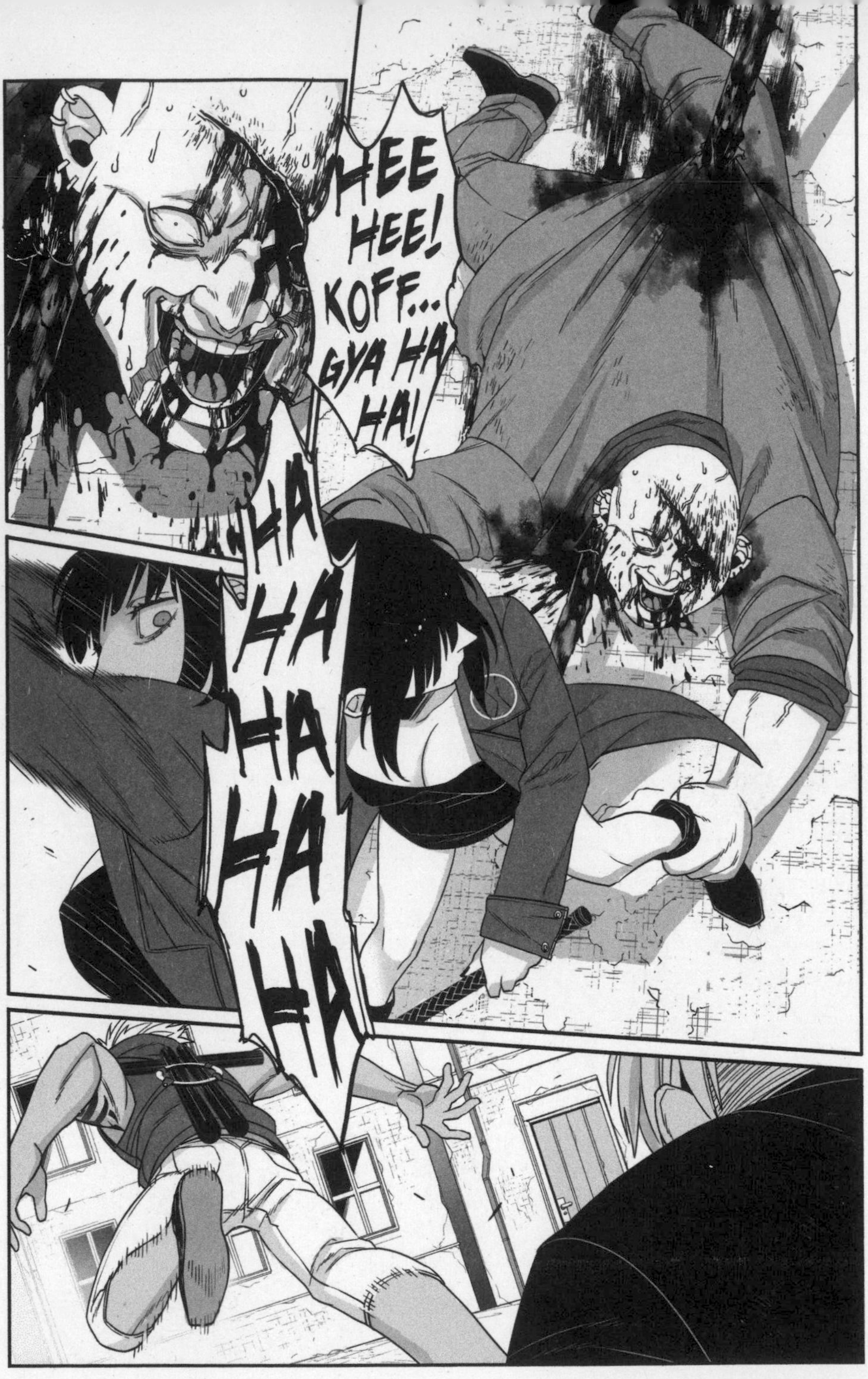
HEE HEE! KOFF... GYA HA HA HA!
HA HA HA HA HA HA HA

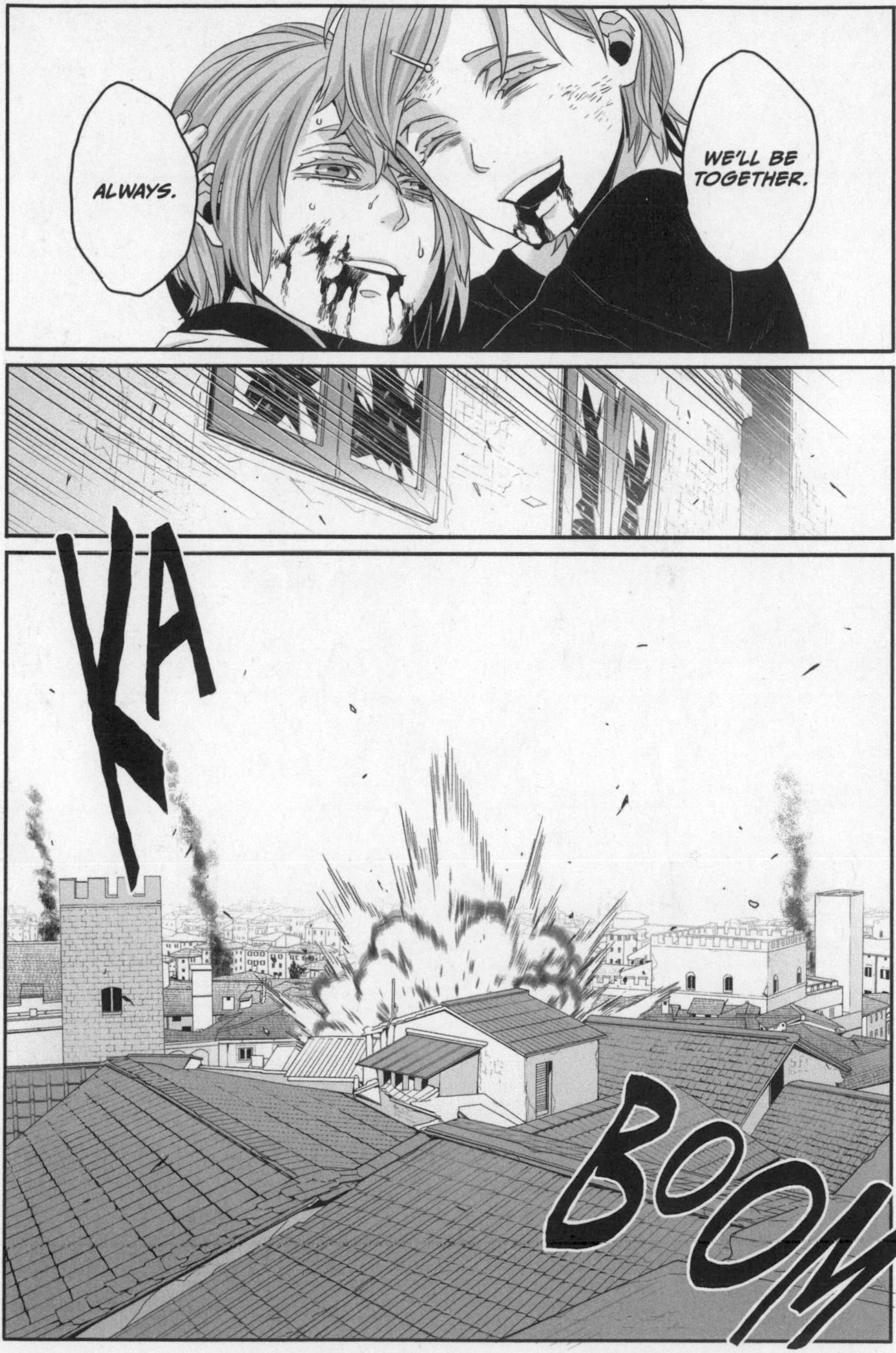
WE'LL BE TOGETHER.
ALWAYS.
KA
BOOM

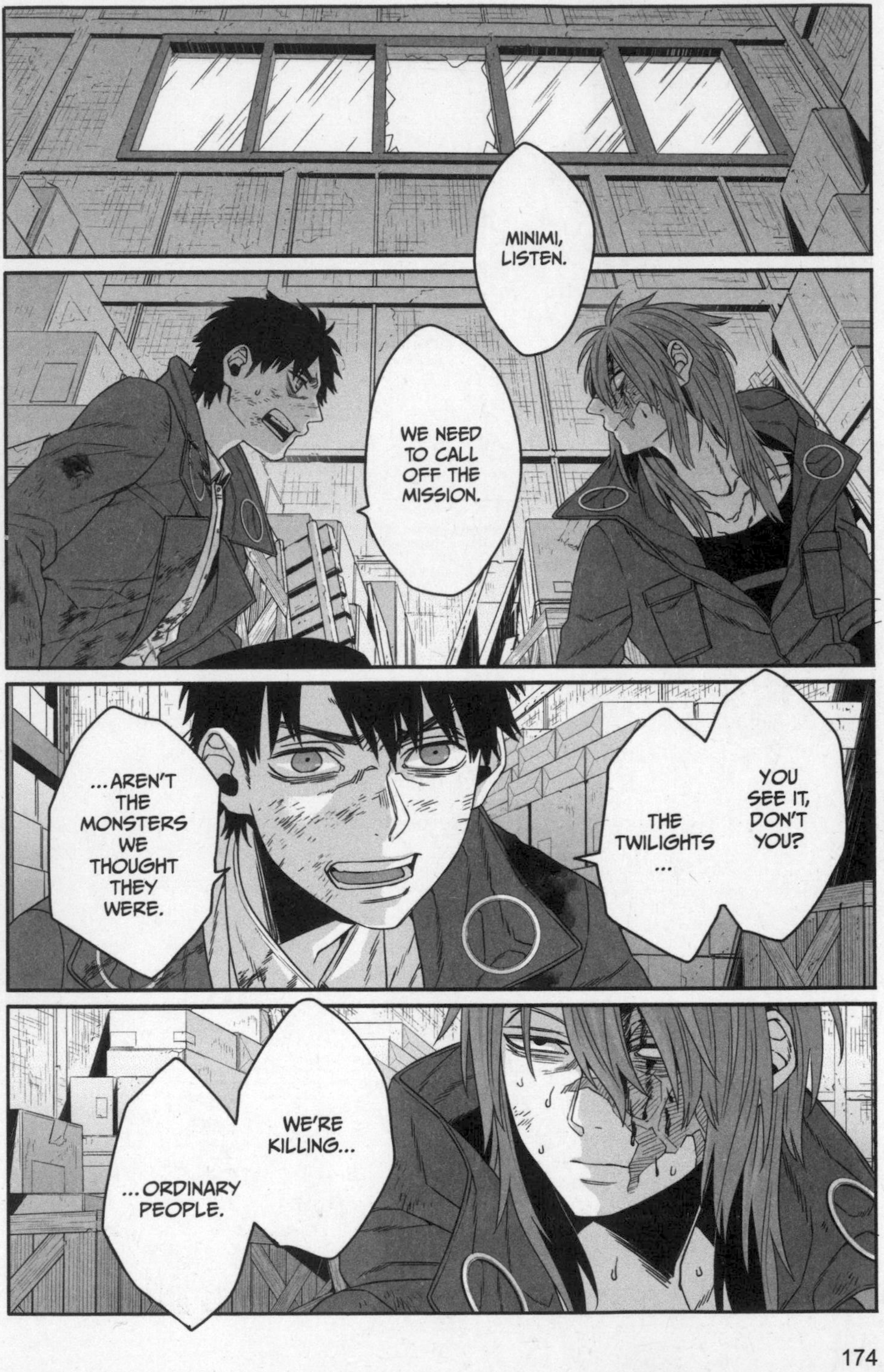
MINIMI, LISTEN.
WE NEED TO CALL OFF THE MISSION.
YOU SEE IT, DON'T YOU?
THE TWILIGHTS...
...AREN'T THE MONSTERS WE THOUGHT THEY WERE.
WE'RE KILLING...
...ORDINARY PEOPLE.

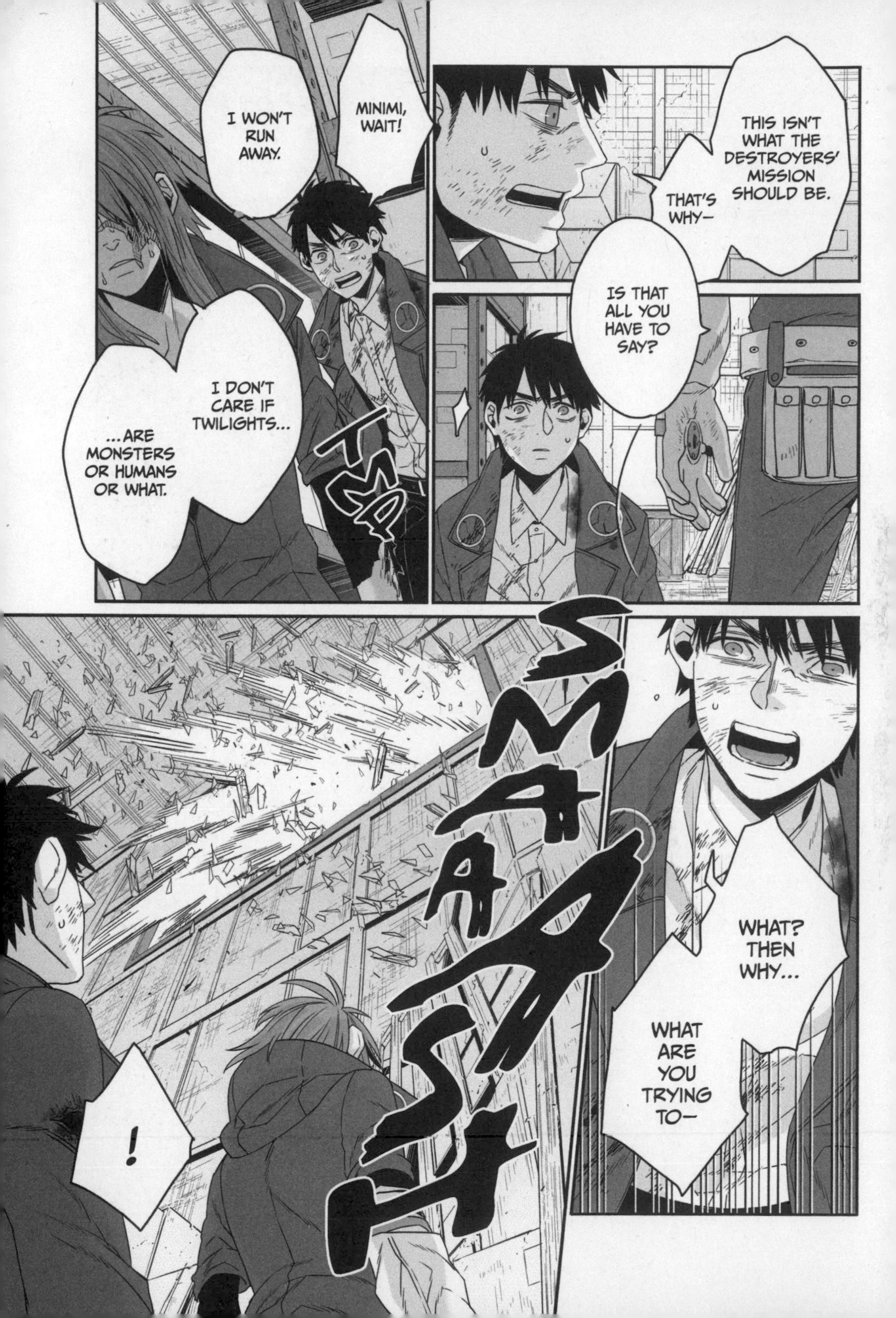
THIS ISN'T WHAT THE DESTROYERS' MISSION SHOULD BE.
THAT'S WHY—
IS THAT ALL YOU HAVE TO SAY?
MINIMI, WAIT!
I WON'T RUN AWAY.
I DON'T CARE IF TWILIGHTS...
...ARE MONSTERS OR HUMANS OR WHAT.
TMP
WHAT? THEN WHY...
WHAT ARE YOU TRYING TO—
SMAAASH
!

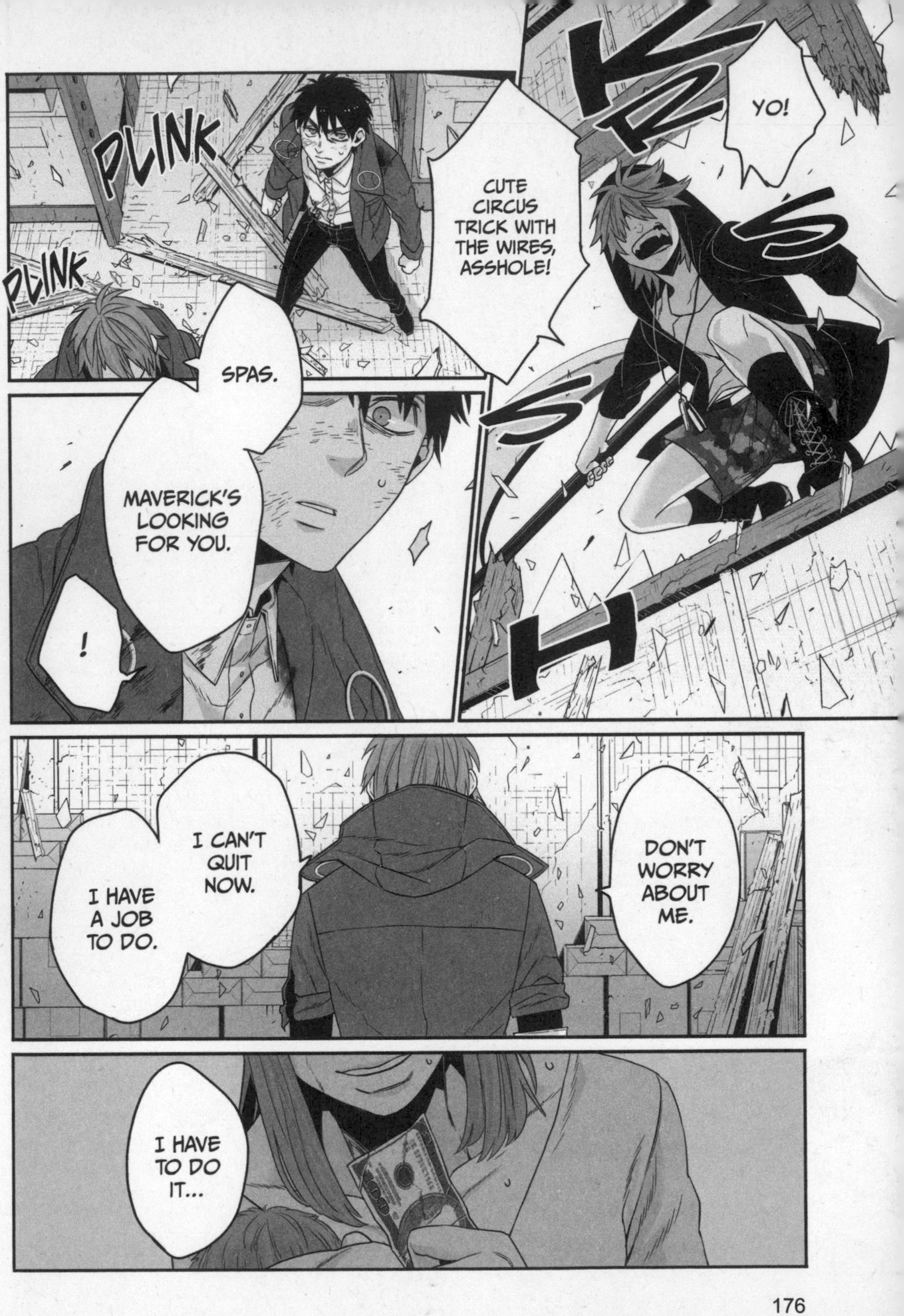
YO!
CUTE CIRCUS TRICK WITH THE WIRES, ASSHOLE!
PLINK
PLINK
SPAS.
MAVERICK'S LOOKING FOR YOU.
!
DON'T WORRY ABOUT ME.
I CAN'T QUIT NOW.
I HAVE A JOB TO DO.
I HAVE TO DO IT...

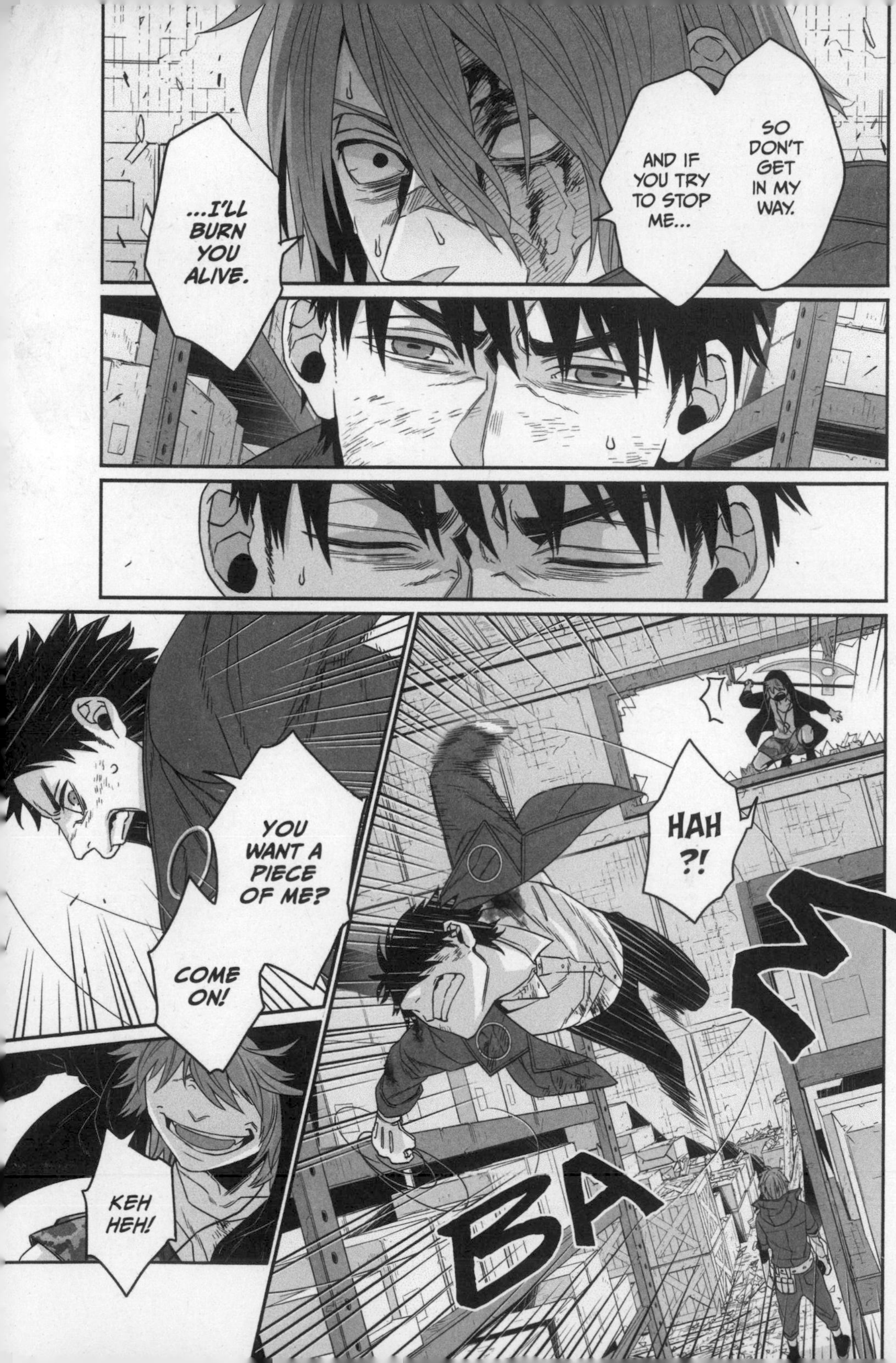
SO DON'T GET IN MY WAY.
AND IF YOU TRY TO STOP ME...
...I'LL BURN YOU ALIVE.
!
HAH ?!
BAM
YOU WANT A PIECE OF ME?
COME ON!
KEH HEH!

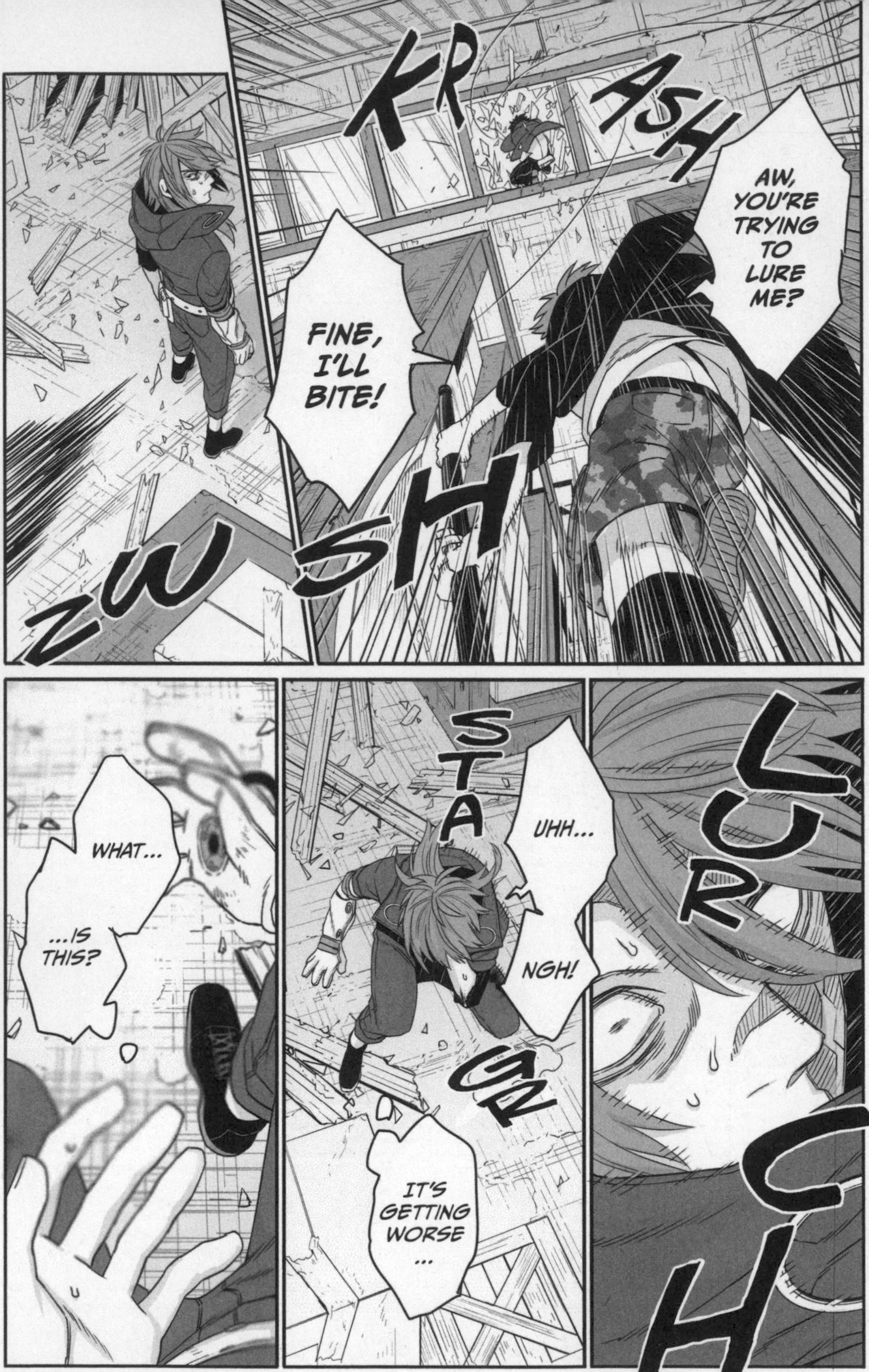
KRASH
AW, YOU'RE TRYING TO LURE ME?
FINE, I'LL BITE!
ZWUSH
LURCH
STAGGR
UHH...
NGH!
IT'S GETTING WORSE ...
WHAT...
...IS THIS?

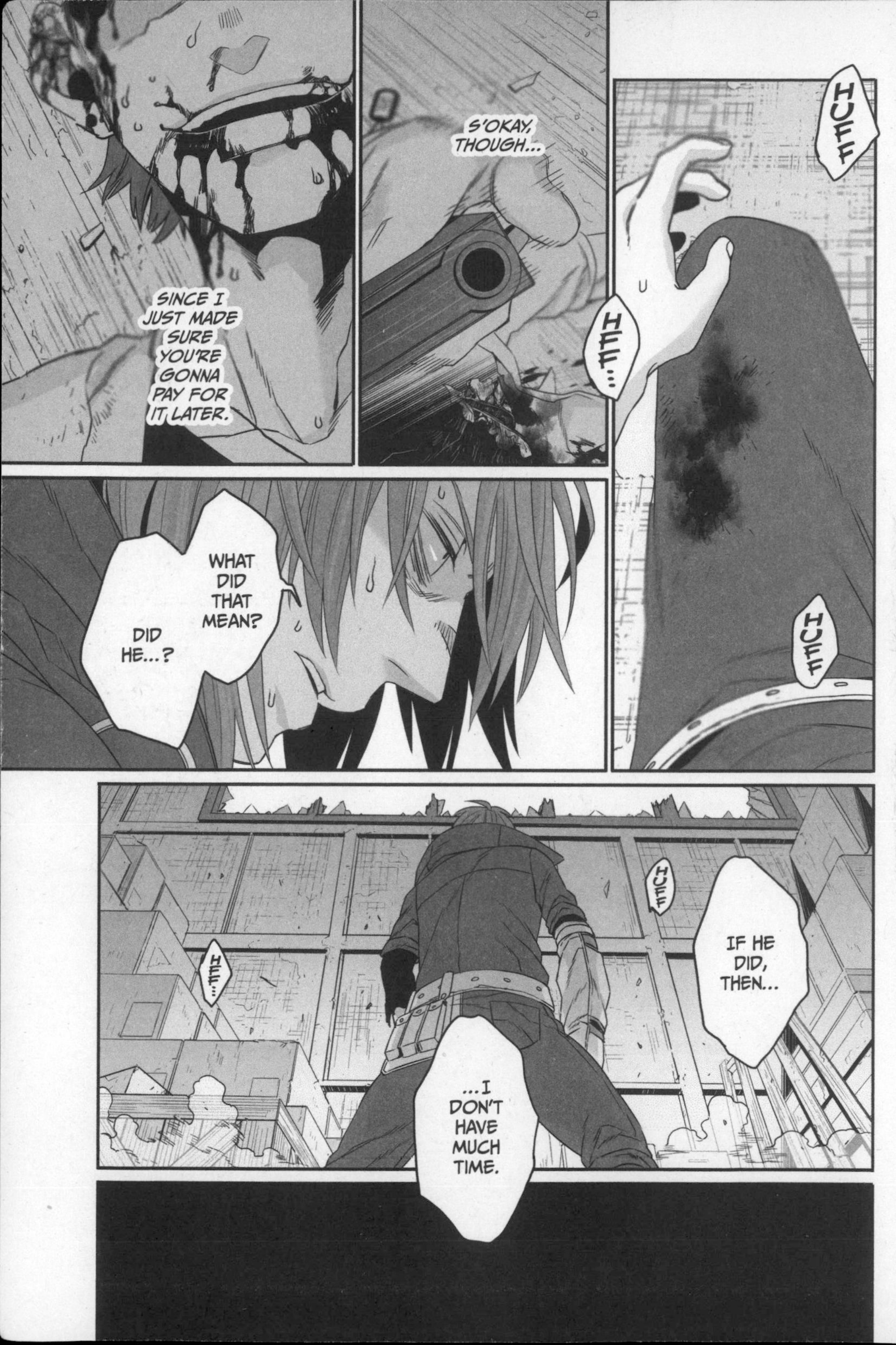
HUFF
HFF...
HUFF
S'OKAY, THOUGH...
SINCE I JUST MADE SURE YOU'RE GONNA PAY FOR IT LATER.
WHAT DID THAT MEAN?
DID HE...?
HUFF
IF HE DID, THEN...
HFF...
...I DON'T HAVE MUCH TIME.

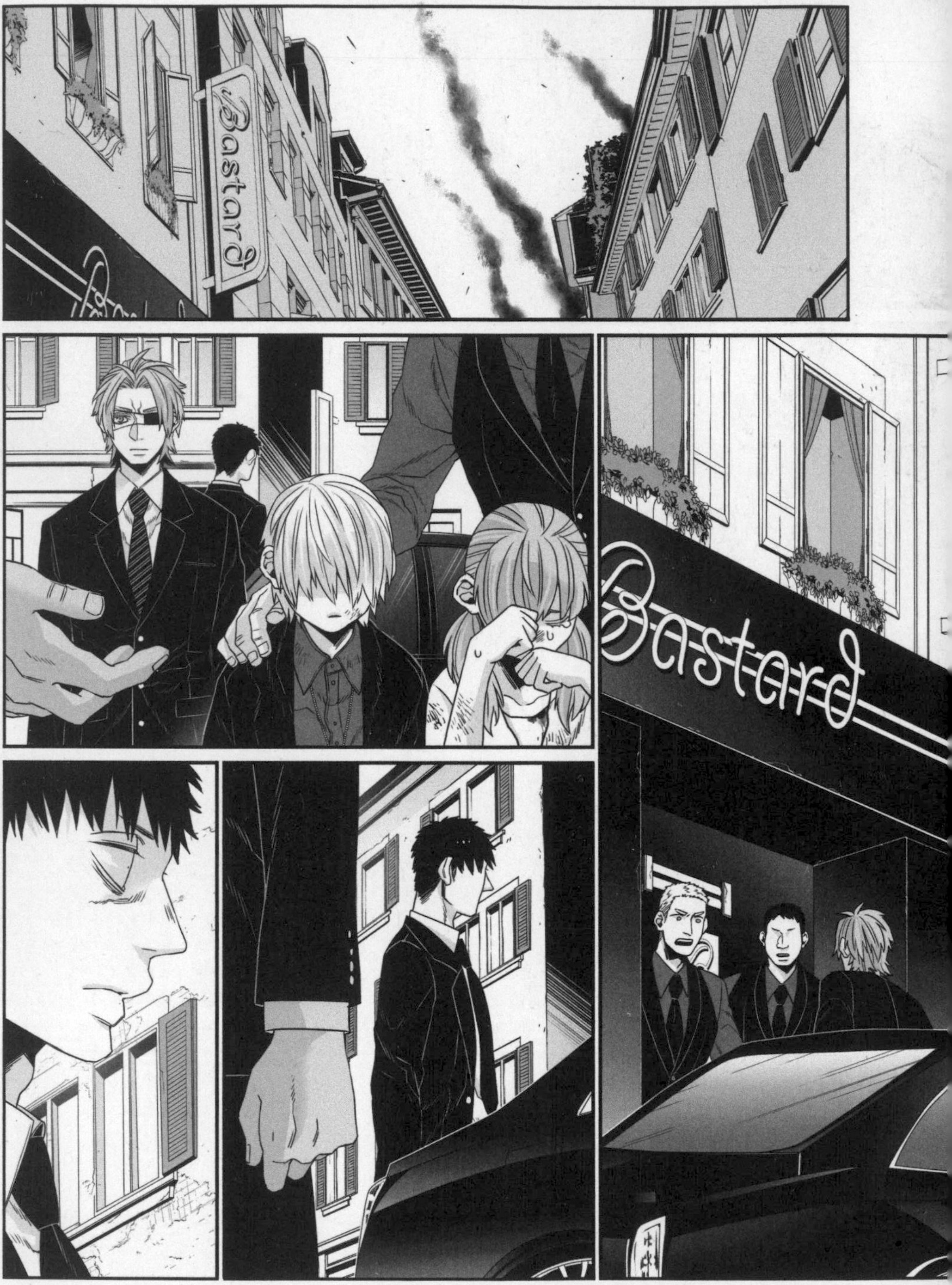
Bastard
Bastard

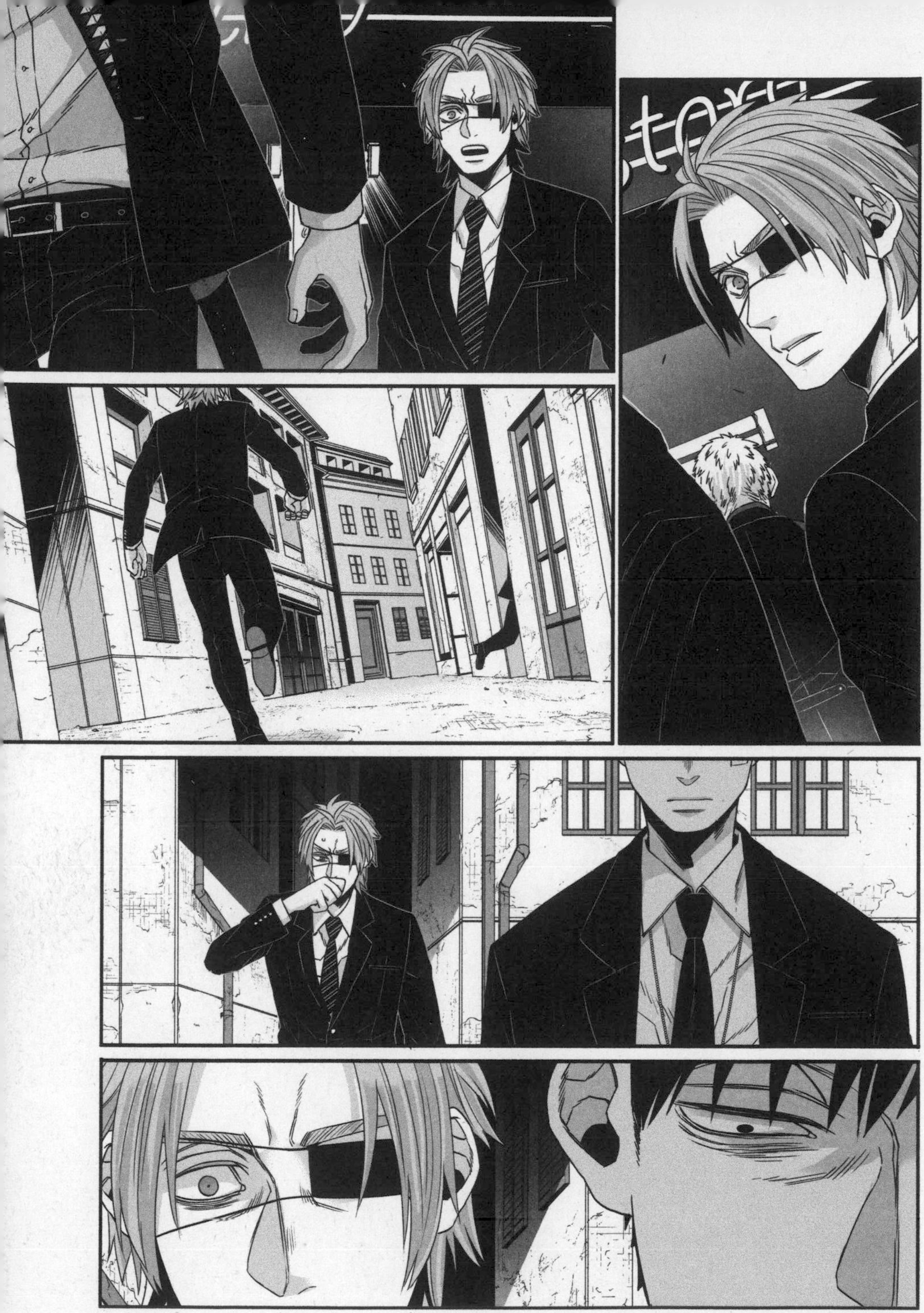

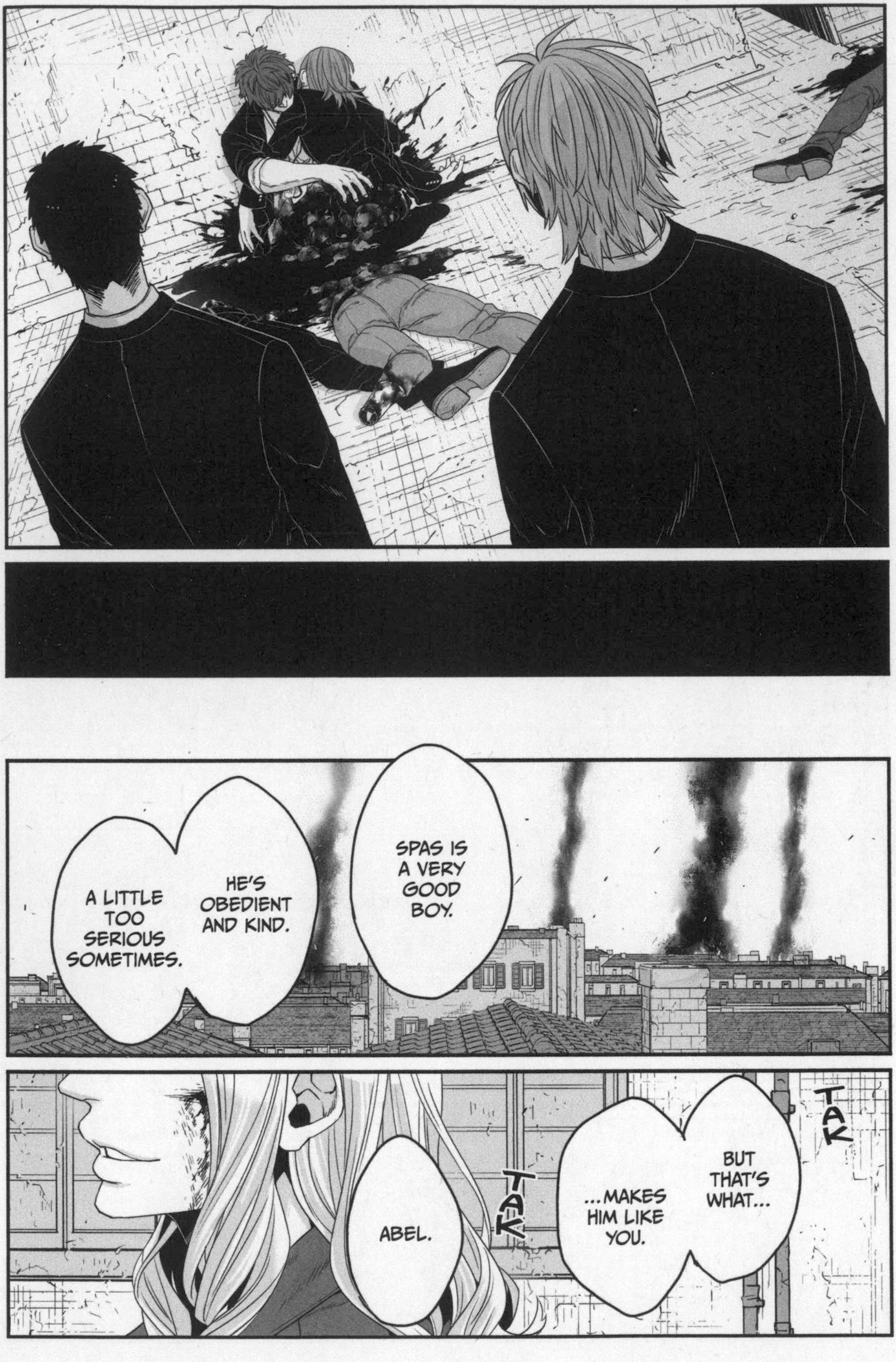
SPAS IS A VERY GOOD BOY.
HE'S OBEDIENT AND KIND.
A LITTLE TOO SERIOUS SOMETIMES.
TAK
BUT THAT'S WHAT...
...MAKES HIM LIKE YOU.
TAK
ABEL.

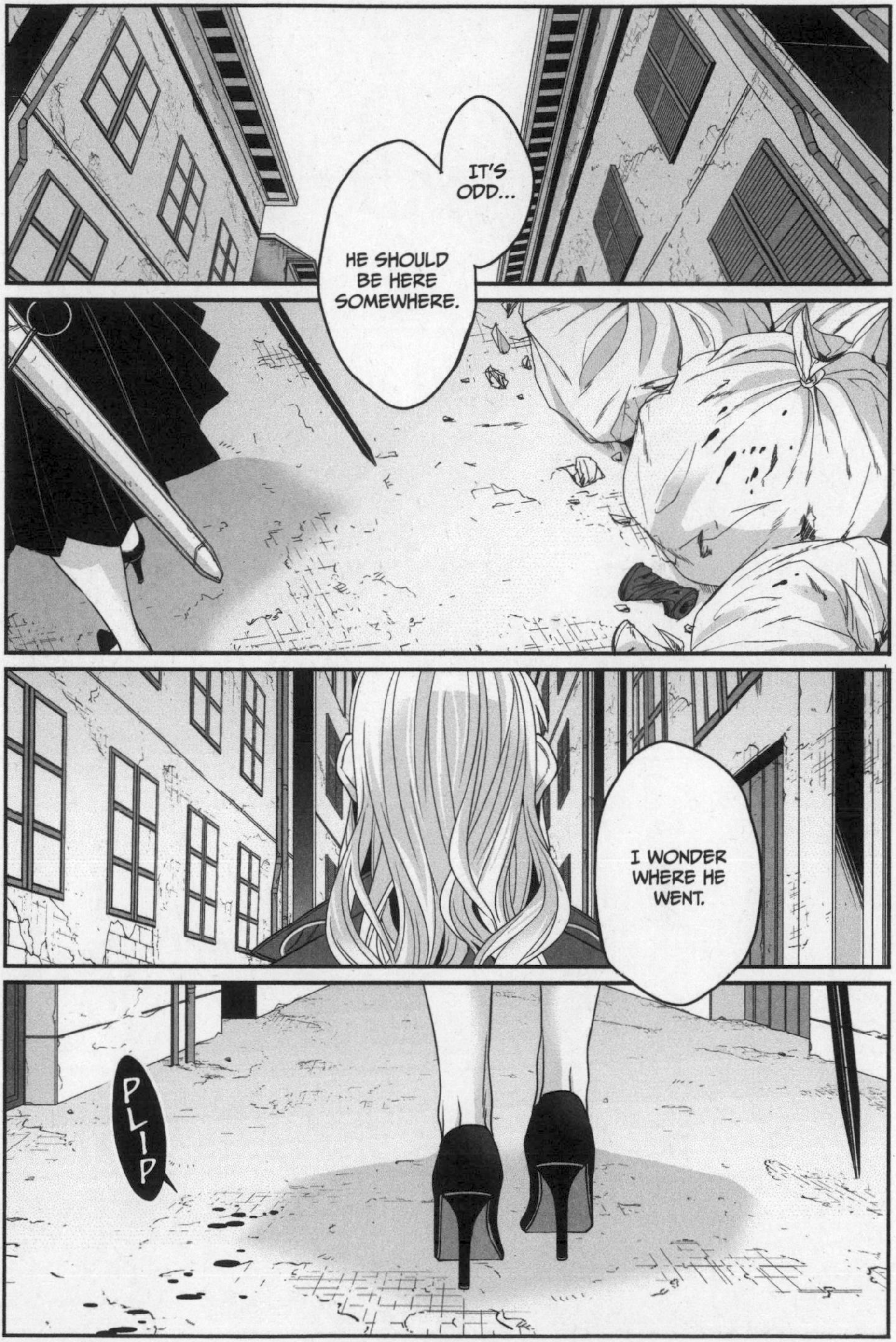
IT'S ODD...
HE SHOULD BE HERE SOMEWHERE.
I WONDER WHERE HE WENT.
PLIP

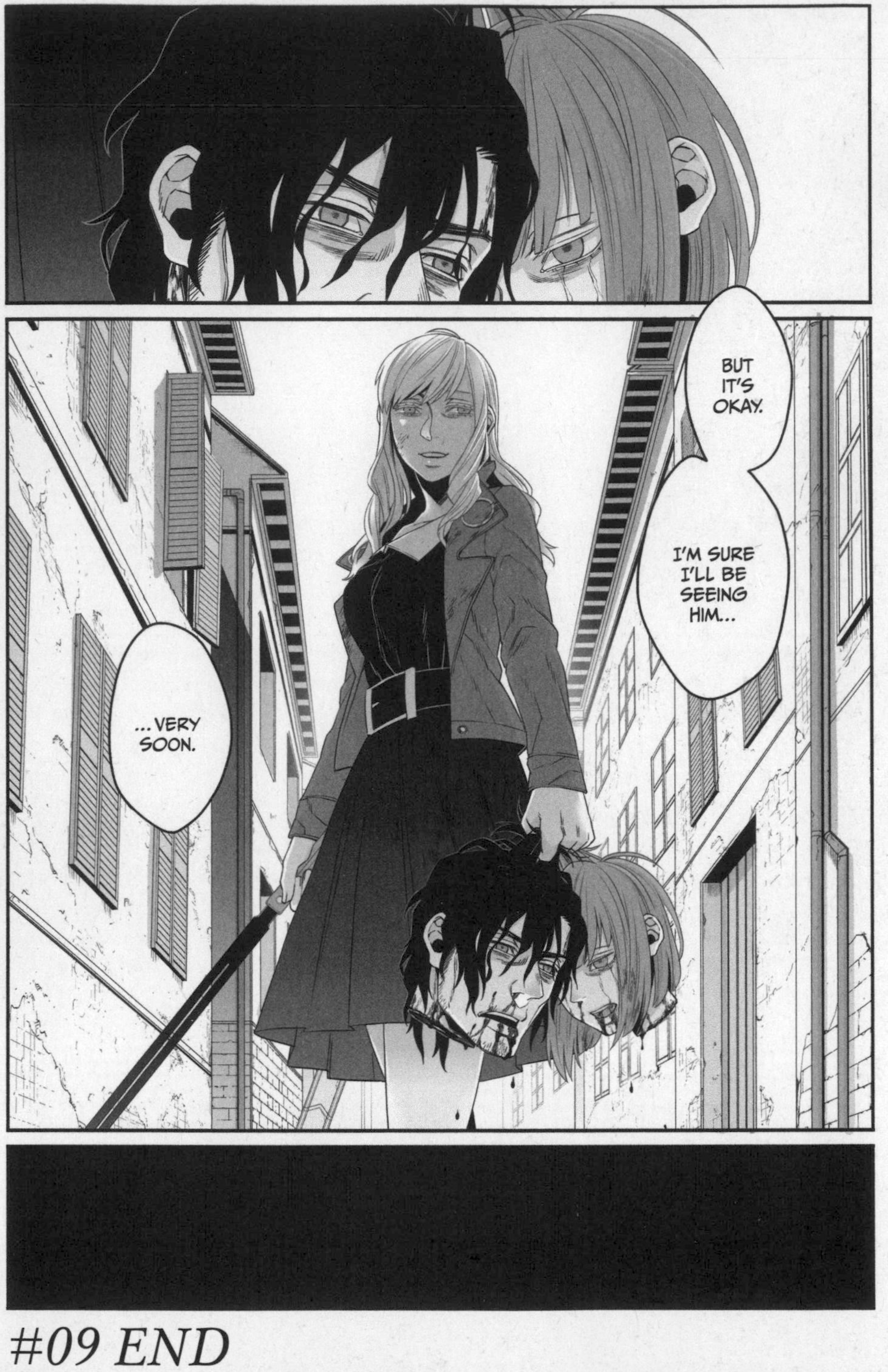
BUT IT'S OKAY.
I'M SURE I'LL BE SEEING HIM...
...VERY SOON.

#09 END

Destroyer Daily Life

Cut

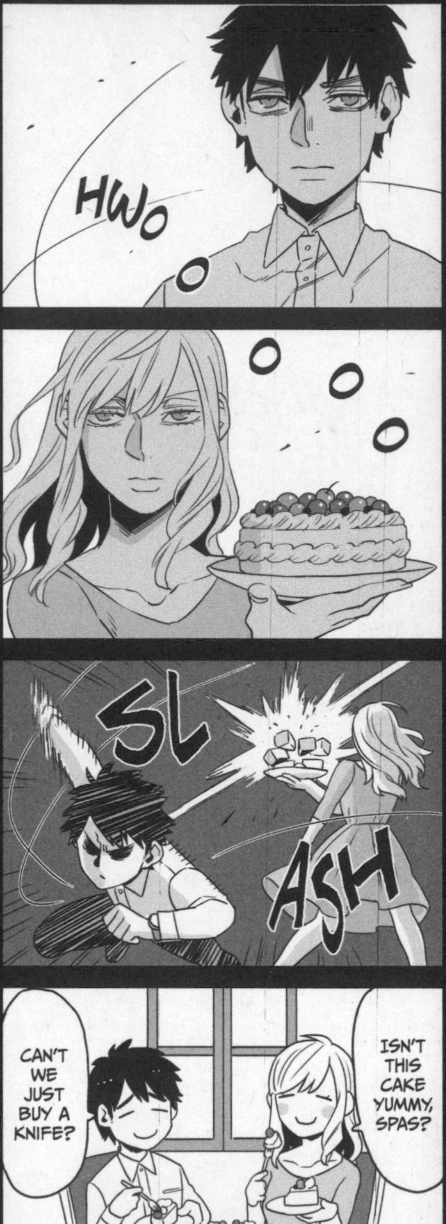
HWO
O
O
O
O
O
SL
ASH
ISN'T THIS CAKE YUMMY, SPAS?
CAN'T WE JUST BUY A KNIFE?

Emotion

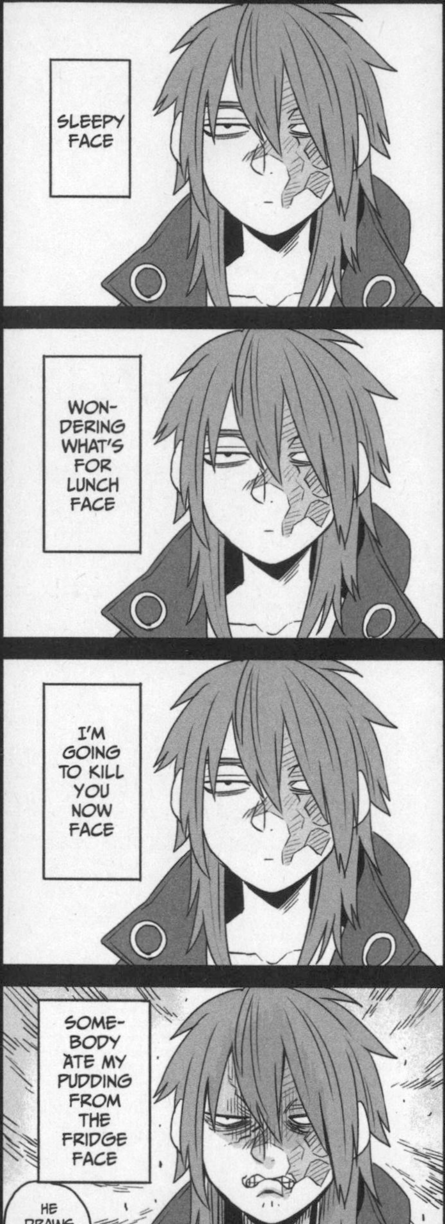
SLEEPY FACE
WON-DERING WHAT'S FOR LUNCH FACE
I'M GOING TO KILL YOU NOW FACE
SOME-BODY ATE MY PUDDING FROM THE FRIDGE FACE
HE DRAWS THE LINE AT PUDDING.

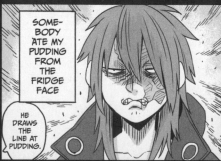

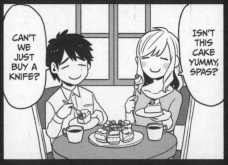

Destroyer Daily Life

Kabe-don

KYAA!
SLAM
SWOOON
KABE-DON!
SH
KRA
KOFF!
KABE-DON!

NOTE: "KABE-DON" IS A TROPE FROM ANIME WHERE A GUY HITS THE WALL NEXT TO A GIRL TO BOX HER IN.

Worry

YOU'RE SAYING YOU SAVED THAT LITTLE GIRL'S LIFE?
IT'S TRUE!
PLEASE, GO TO HER!
AND MAKE SURE SHE EATS A MORE NUTRITIOUS DIET!
?!
I COULD FEEL SHE HAS SOME BABY FAT LEFT NOW, BUT...
...SHE'S GOING TO BE SKINNY AS A RAIL WHEN SHE'S OLDER!
JUST KILL HIM ALREADY.
OKAY.
KLIK

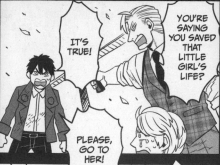

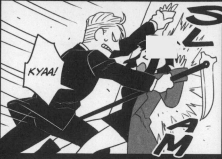

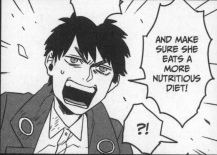

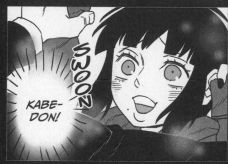

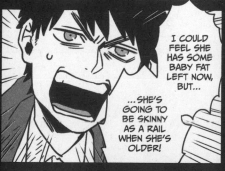

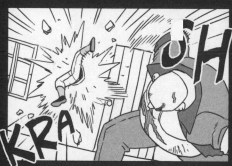

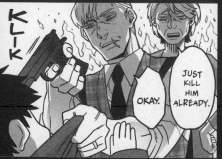

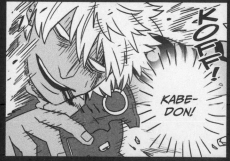

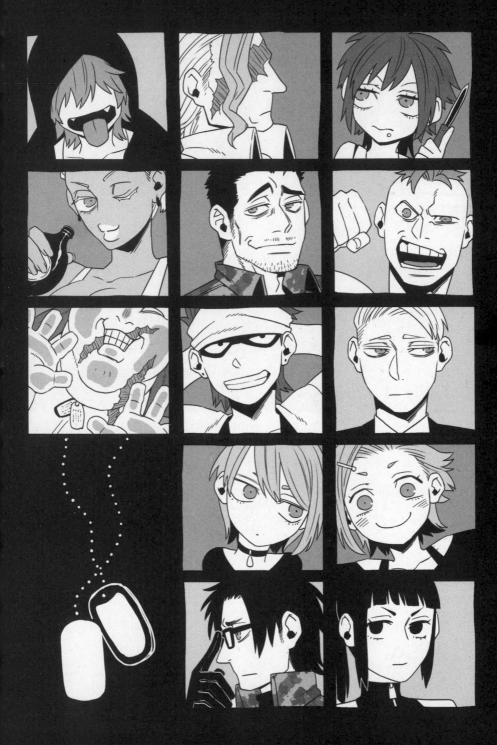

Afterword

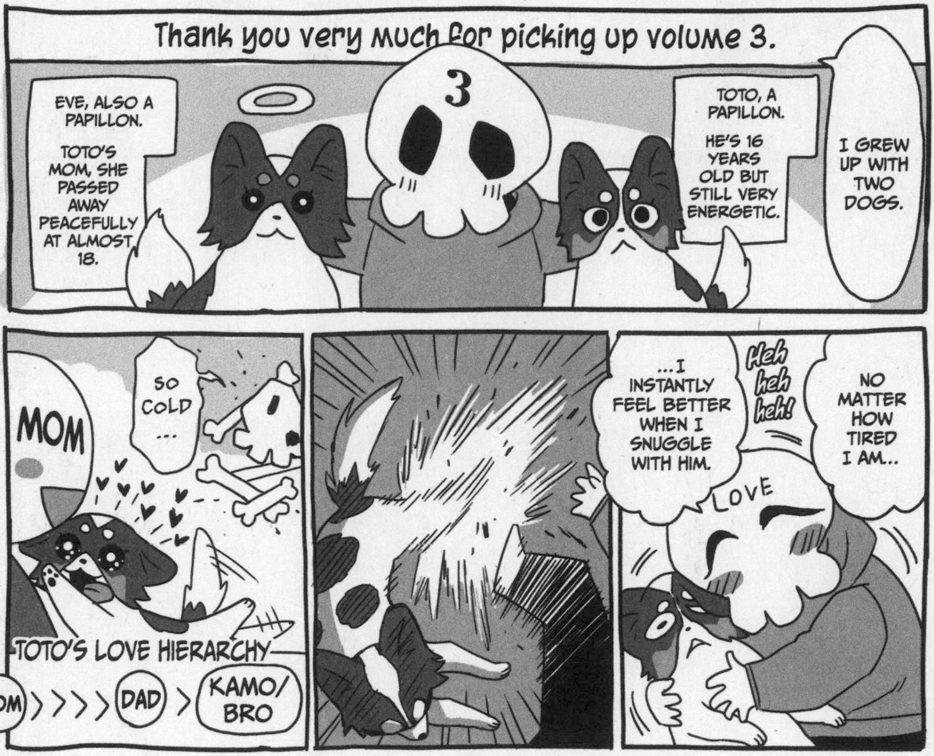
Thank you very much for picking up volume 3.
I GREW UP WITH TWO DOGS.
TOTO, A PAPILLON.
HE'S 16 YEARS OLD BUT STILL VERY ENERGETIC.
3
EVE, ALSO A PAPILLON.
TOTO'S MOM, SHE PASSED AWAY PEACEFULLY AT ALMOST 18.
NO MATTER HOW TIRED I AM...
Heh heh heh!
...I INSTANTLY FEEL BETTER WHEN I SNUGGLE WITH HIM.
LOVE
SO COLD ...
MOM
TOTO'S LOVE HIERARCHY
MOM > > > > DAD > KAMO/BRO

SEE YOU IN THE
NEXT VOLUME!

KOHSKE
ASSISTANT K / ASSISTANT M / ASSISTANT H
EDITOR H / DESIGNER ISHIKAWA
MOM / DAD / LITTLE BRO / MY DOG
AND TO EVERYONE WHO'S HELPED ME.

THANK YOU ALWAYS!

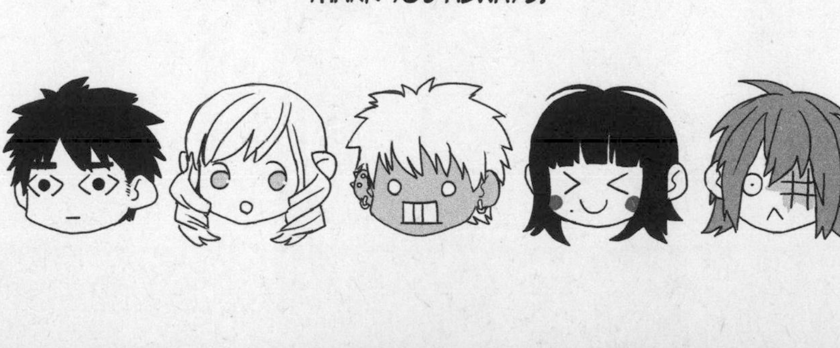

GANGSTA: CURSED. EP_MARCO ADRIANO

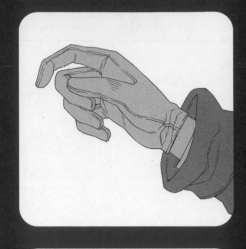

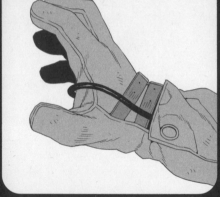

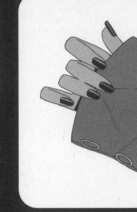

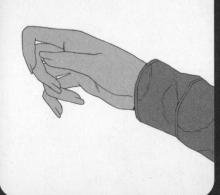

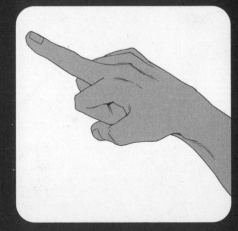

TO BE CONTINUED

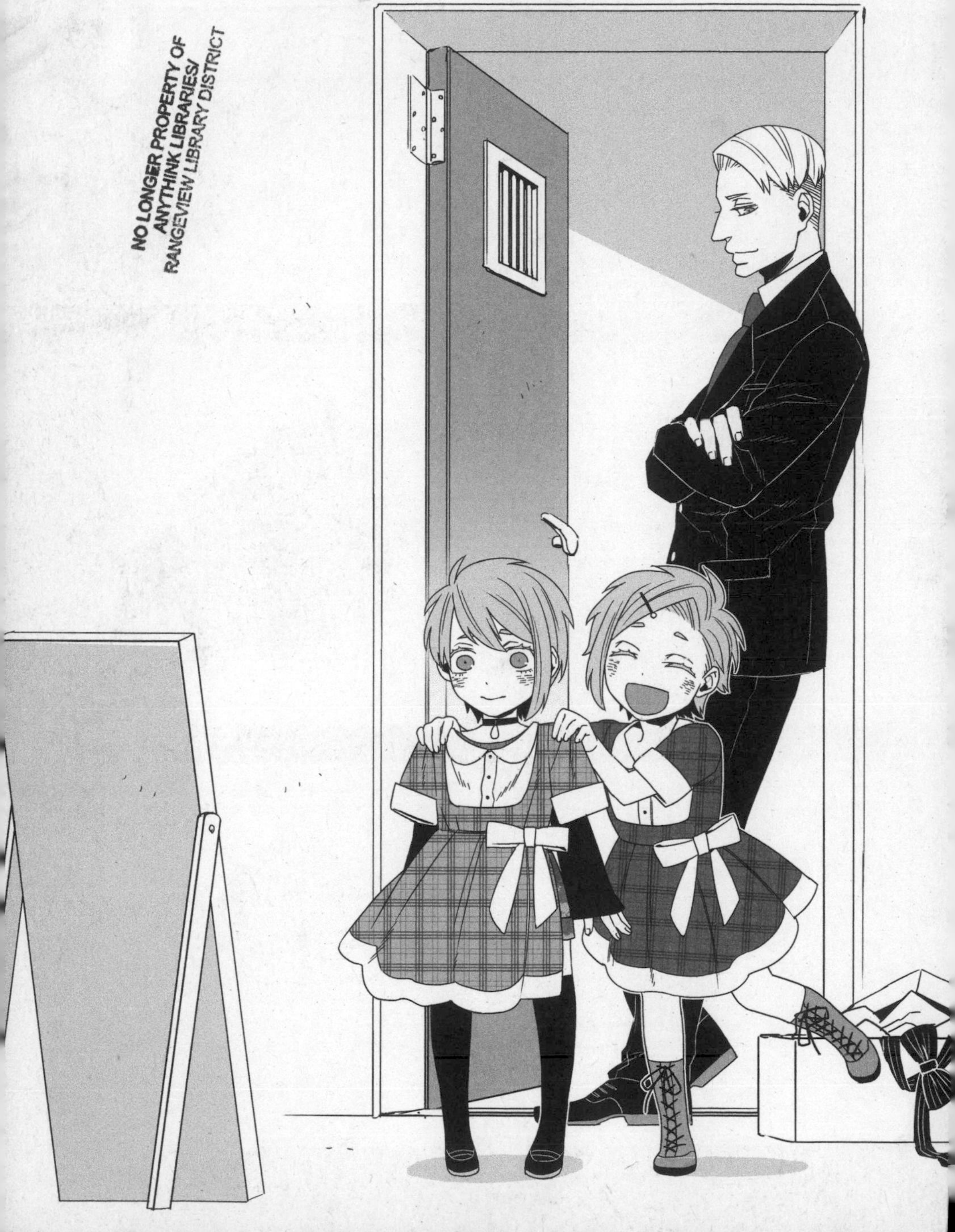

GANGSTA:CURSED.
EP_MARCO ADRIANO

Gangsta:Cursed. Ep_Marco Adriano
Volume 3

VIZ Signature Edition

Story by Kohske
Art by Syuhei Kamo

Translation & Adaptation/Christine Schilling
Touch-up Art & Lettering/Eric Erbes
Cover & Graphic Design/Sam Elzway
Editor/Leyla Aker

GANGSTA:CURSED.EP_MARCO ADRIANO
© Kohske 2015.
© Syuhei Kamo 2015. All rights reserved.
English translation rights arranged with SHINCHOSHA PUBLISHING CO.
through Tuttle-Mori Agency, Inc., Tokyo.

Printed in the U.S.A.

Published by VIZ Media, LLC
P.O. Box 77010
San Francisco, CA 94107

10 9 8 7 6 5 4 3 2 1
First printing, October 2017

viz.com

VIZ SIGNATURE
VIZSIGNATURE.COM